Trademark Acknowledgements

Wrox has endeavoured to provide trademark information about all the companies and products mentioned in this book by the appropriate use of capitals. However, Wrox cannot guarantee the accuracy of this information.

Credits

Author
Jesse Liberty

Managing Editor
John Franklin

Editors
Victoria Hudgson
Timothy Briggs

Technical Reviewers
Ian Clough
Anthony Kesterton

Cover/Design/Layout
Andrew Guillaume

Copy Edit/Index
Wrox Team

About the Author

Jesse Liberty is founder and president of Liberty Associates, Inc. where he provides training, consulting and mentoring in object-oriented analysis and design as well as contract programming and Internet and computer telephony development. He can be reached at **jliberty@libertyassociates.com**. His web site is: **http://www.libertyassociates.com**

Jesse is the author of seven books on object-oriented programming and C++ and was Distinguished Software Engineer and Architect for AT&T, Xerox and PBS, and Vice President of Technology for Citibank.

Author Acknowledgements

Beginning Object-Oriented Analysis and Design *with* C++ is the product of 18 months of work and literally hundreds of hours of conversation with many developers whose expertise far exceeds my own. This section can only fail to acknowledge everyone's help and contribution, all of which is greatly appreciated.

I must, again, start with my family. My wife Stacey supported me when, like a wild-eyed gambler at the dice table, I begged "just one more book, honey, I swear, just one more..." My daughters, Robin and Rachel are the only thing I've ever created of which I'm truly and unashamedly proud.

I also want to thank the extraordinary people at Wrox Press. I really pushed my luck with them this time; and they were incredibly helpful and supportive as I brought this book in for a safe landing. I've never met John Franklin, but I think of him as a true friend. The editors, Victoria Hudgson and Tim Briggs, not only helped me finish on time, but added tremendous value to the organization and content of the book as a whole. Never before, to coin a phrase, have so few done so much with so little, and I am deeply grateful. And the Maclean brothers continue to prove that one can make money and be a mensch at the same time.

Beginning
Object-Oriented
Analysis and Design

with C++

Jesse Liberty

Wrox Press Ltd.®

Beginning OO Analysis and Design *with C++*

© 1998 Wrox Press

Published by Wrox Press Ltd, 30 Lincoln Road, Olton, Birmingham B27 6PA , UK.
Printed in Canada
2 3 4 5 TRI 99 98

ISBN 1-861001-33-9

The OTUG email list (**majordomo@rational.com**) contributed enormously to my understanding of many issues. I want especially to thank and acknowledge the help of Robert Martin, John Goodsen and Barry Kaplan.

In addition, a group of nearly 100 students at Ziff Davis University (**http://www.zdu.com**) provided on-going feedback and help as I developed the book. While too many contributed to possibly acknowledge them all directly, I want particularly to thank Karena Andrusyshyn, Judith Calhoun, Michael Chomiczewski, Shane Herndon, Yitzchak Katz, Elliot Kearsley, Lari Kirby, Joe Korty, Lynne Malchiodi, Wallace Newkirk, Kevin Norris, Clifford Oginski, Gloria Reibin, Victor Romero, Lenny Stendig, Donald Xie, Tarek Zeineddine and especially Douglas Barringer.

The Phish program was in large measure designed and implemented by Rich Paul of Advanced Technology Consulting, Inc. I am greatly indebted to him for the many hours of unrewarded work that he put into this product, not only writing the first few versions of the code, but also walking me through his rich and fascinating design. Rich is a world-class C++ programmer who can be reached at **rich.paul@atcons.com**

Much of the material on persistence, concurrency and the architecture mechanisms was based on material provided by and private conversations with Ken Levine, president of Advanced Technology Consulting, Inc. His contribution to this book and to my understanding of object-oriented analysis and design cannot be overstated. Ken is a recognized expert in the analysis, design and delivery of large-scale distributed component-based business systems. His company provides consulting, mentoring and contract programming for object-oriented software development of mission-critical applications for Fortune 500 companies. Ken can be reached at **kenneth.levine@atcons.com** and you can learn more about his company at **http://www.atcons.com** or by calling 813-818-9152.

I must also thank Michael Jesse Chonolese, Chief of Methodology at Lockheed Martin, for once again helping me to understand many of these issues and finding my way through the thicket of competing methodologies. Michael is simply one of the smartest people I know, and his support and help is gratefully appreciated.

This book considers the entire process of software development, and so once again I must thank those who taught me to program: Skip Gilbrech, David McCune, Stephen Zagieboylo and Steve Rogers.

Finally, I want to thank David Twersky (Habonim 1973) for teaching me how to teach.

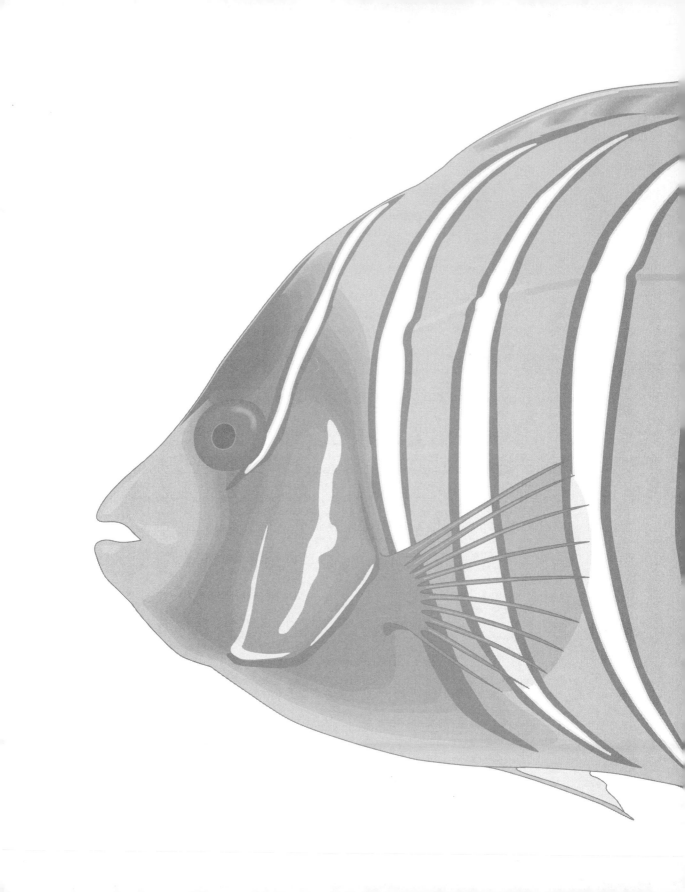

Beginning
**Object-Oriented
Analysis and Design**

Summary of Contents

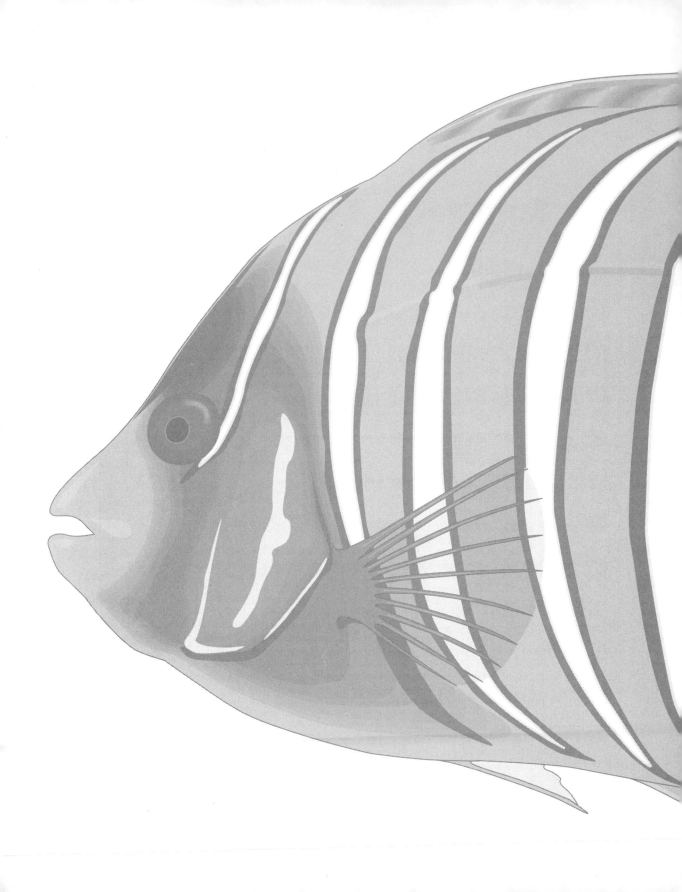

Beginning
Object-Oriented
Analysis and Design

Appendix B: Bibliography

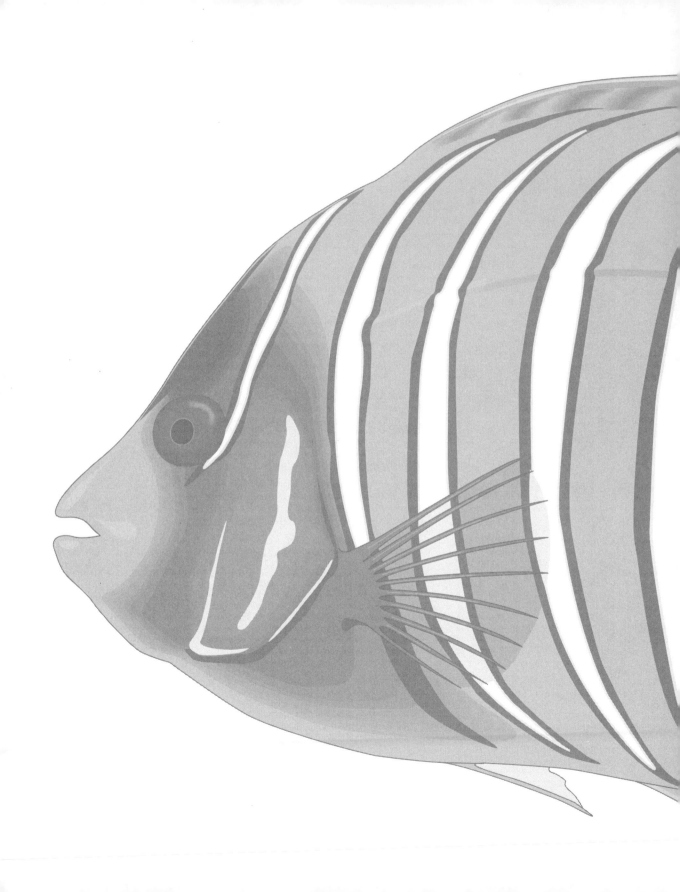

Introduction

How this Book is Different

Beginning Object-Oriented Analysis and Design with C++ takes a practical approach to object-oriented analysis and design (OOAD). Most books on this subject are written by methodologists — that is, by people who have developed a method or a process of object-oriented analysis and design.

When methodologists write their books, they must be exhaustive — they must show every aspect of their method, define every nook and cranny, every last detail and exception condition. This thoroughness is essential when creating or defending a method, but does not serve the developer trying to learn the process. Exhaustive review makes it all too easy for the reader to get lost in the details; the book becomes overly academic and impossible to read. As a working programmer I'm often tempted to shout, "Yes, but how do I *apply* this to my problem?"

To be perfectly honest, I sometimes fall asleep reading methodology books. This isn't because the authors write badly, nor is it because I'm uninterested. The problem is what futurologist Herman Kahn called MEGO — My Eyes Glaze Over. The overwhelming detail, in the absence of a real-world context, just does me in. This book aims to be an antidote to MEGO, and as such its tone will be a bit lighter and its stance a bit more aggressive; this is coding in the trenches, and there's little time to be polite.

In short, this book has no lofty aspirations. It does not define a method, nor does it attempt to explain one in precise and exhaustive detail. What this book *does* offer is a working-programmer's guide to building commercial software using state-of-the-art object-oriented analysis and design. I will discuss the entire process of professional software development. You will see how software is conceived, how you build a requirements document, how you make the "build/buy" decisions, and how to deliver high-quality software on time and on budget. Perhaps most importantly, you will learn how to translate an object-oriented design into solid and reliable C++ code.

Along the way, you will learn how to be effective in your use of inheritance, polymorphism and encapsulation — terms that will be defined and explained as we proceed. You will see how templates, exceptions and other advanced concepts can be harnessed in support of your project. You will also learn about the tools which you may wish to employ, both to facilitate your design and to create and test your software.

Who this Book is for

This book was written for programmers who want to build robust, high-quality commercial software that ships on time and on budget. While the examples are in C++, the book should be of value to those who program in any language which supports object-oriented programming, such as Java, Visual Basic and SmallTalk.

This book will also be of use to software managers, marketing managers and others who are responsible for the development of software and who must work with programmers and understand what they do. It describes a process which is rapidly becoming central to the development of world-class commercial software. *Beginning Object-Oriented Analysis and Design with C++* is written in a straightforward manner which should be readily accessible to anyone involved with the development of commercial software. If you are not a programmer, you can safely ignore the code examples and focus on the process and the notation.

What You Need in Order to Use this Book

You need an enthusiastic commitment to learning the subject matter and a fair amount of time. If you want to work through some of the examples, you need a working knowledge of C++, and a compiler. That's it. You don't need any additional tools.

That said, in explaining certain terms and concepts in this book, I've used Visual C++ 5 and the MFC, and Rational Rose. These, I hope, have helped demonstrate the practicality of the techniques we're discussing. We'll look at these and a number of other utility programs designed to assist with object-oriented analysis and design as we go, but there isn't anything taught in this book that you can't do on pencil and paper. When you are ready to build a ten thousand page set of documentation. you may need a few tools to make your life easier, but for now a stiff piece of papyrus, a sharp stick and a pool of ink will do.

How to Use this Book

Beginning Object-Oriented Analysis and Design with C++ can be used both as a tutorial and as a reference. Frankly, no book does both perfectly, and this book puts its emphasis on being a tutorial. I have worked hard to label each section clearly and to ensure the book is well indexed, but the focus is on teaching the material.*

---

*A quick word about first person singular. You will note that I say, "I have worked hard..." The reality, as shown in the acknowledgements, is that a number of people have worked very hard to make this book what it is. I write in the first person singular not to take credit, but to take responsibility — when I write software and when I write a book, I put my name on it and it is to me that you should send your complaints and suggestions. That is not meant in any way to diminish the amazing contribution of so many others to whom I am ineffably grateful.

A final word — you won't see many footnotes in this book as I find them distracting. Instead I have included a bibliography at the end, and I am indebted to each of these authors; I know that I stand on the shoulders of giants.

This book has a companion volume, *Clouds To Code*, which the material taught in this book to a particular software development effort — it is the case study of the development of computer telephony software. You do not have to read either book before reading the other, but here is the difference: this book teaches you how to do it, that book shows you how it was done.

I recommend reading through *Beginning Object-Oriented Analysis and Design with C++* in sequence. As Humpty Dumpty said, "Begin at the beginning, proceed to the end, and then stop." On the other hand, it is your money and more important, your time. Feel free to skip over sections that you see as either a review or as superfluous. I won't be insulted...

Conventions

I use a number of different styles of text and layout in the book to help differentiate between the various types of information. Here are examples of the styles I use along with explanations of what they mean.

Bulleted information is shown like this:

- **Important Words** are in a bold font.
- Words that appear on the screen, such as menu options, are a similar font to the one used on screen, e.g. the File menu.
- Keys that you press on the keyboard, like *Ctrl* and *Enter*, are in italics.
- All file, function names and other code snippets are in this style: **Video.mdb**.

> *Definitions for new terms are shown in boxes like this.*

Background information is shown like this.

And I've used this style to document use cases.

Code shown for the first time, or other relevant code, is in the following format,

```
#include <iostream.h>

int main()
{
}
```

while less important code, or code that has been seen before, looks like this:

```
intvariable1 = intvariable1 + 1
```

Feedback

I've tried to make this book accurate and enjoyable, and reading it worthwhile. But what really matters is whether or not *you* find it useful, and I would really appreciate your views and comments. You can return the reply card in the back of the book, or contact Wrox at:

feedback@wrox.com
http://www.wrox.com
or
http://www.wrox.co.uk

Getting Started

In this first chapter, I will provide an overview of object-oriented analysis and design. I will explain the problem that we are trying to solve and why this is the best way to get it done. I will lay out the phases of object-oriented analysis and design, and give you a quick sense of what happens in each phase. Subsequent chapters will fill in the details of who participates, what the goals are, how you get it done and what you have when you've finished.

This chapter will cover:

- The need for object-oriented design
- What object-oriented design promises
- How this is achieved
- Language considerations
- The development cycle
- The cost of object-oriented development

Object-oriented Development

It all starts with complexity. If software were simple, there would be little need for object-oriented analysis and design techniques. If the average program consisted of 60 lines of code, it wouldn't matter how convoluted the program was: a reasonably smart person would be able to figure it out in minutes.

> *Along the way, I will use and define a number of terms, including analysis, design, use cases, polymorphism, inheritance and so forth. Some of these terms can not be summarized in one sentence, and so I will devote quite a bit of space to explaining them.*
>
> *I will not try to be overly precise when explaining these terms. Academic precision can get in the way of initial understanding. I'll try to provide an intuitive definition within the context of object-oriented analysis and design. These new-term boxes are meant to be guides rather than dictionary definitions.*

> *The term **object-oriented** presents a special problem for a book like this, not unlike lifting yourself to a standing position by pulling on your bootstraps. The entire book is, in some ways, a definition of the terms object-oriented analysis, design and programming. For now, think of object-oriented programming as programming which thinks about **objects** (that is **things**) which have behavior and attributes or state.*

The problems we're now trying to solve are orders of magnitude more complex than the problems we were solving just ten years ago. The cost of hardware and memory continues to plummet and the cost of programmer time continues to soar.

As the problems we are solving become more complex and as the cost of fixing bugs rises, the frustration of large corporations increases. The software on which they are building their businesses is not solid. Development projects are typically late and over budget. The final product is often bug ridden, bloated and brittle.

The unreliability of so many programs is so well accepted, we've stopped noticing. No other industry puts up with this level of shoddy merchandise. If cars, televisions or kids' toys failed with the regularity that programs crash, there would be a great public outcry.

There is a line that never fails to get a laugh: "If cities were built like software, the first woodpecker to come along would level civilization."

It isn't funny.

There has been an explosion of new development. The World Wide Web has taken off and fueled the creation of literally thousands of start-up development companies. More and more traditional businesses now rely on software as a key element of their long-term strategy. The demand for quality product is soaring. Just as the demand is increasing, our ability to respond is decreasing.

Today's consumer is more demanding and has higher expectations, both of the quality of the user interface and of the reliability and performance of the system.

Periodically, the software industry announces a new technique touted as the silver bullet that will solve all these problems. Structured programming, component-based development, design by contract — none of these has fully solved the problem, but each has made its contribution.

In recent years, one approach has shown consistent advantage when programming complex systems. Developers have found that object-oriented software development helps them deliver high-quality commercial software, and it has become the most significant trend in software development in twenty years. It is being adopted because it works.

Products built with an understanding of object-oriented analysis and design techniques tend to be more reliable, extensible and robust. They are more likely to be delivered on time and on budget, and to meet the customer's expectations and requirements.

The Dirty Little Secret

The dirty little secret about object-oriented programming is that there is nothing magical about it. While it is often dressed up in fancy academic language and described in dry tomes with complex and esoteric diagrams, the simple truth is that object-oriented analysis and design is a straightforward process for understanding the customer's requirements and designing a software solution.

It isn't even all that difficult.

Some Definitions

To get started talking about object-oriented analysis and design, we need a common vocabulary. Here are some initial, working definitions of some common terms:

> **A model** *is a picture or a description of the problem we're trying to solve or represent, or a description of the solution itself.*

A child's globe is a model of the earth. Quantum mechanics describes how the physical world is observed to behave at the sub-atomic level. Models are workable representations of aspects of the world. They allow you to predict and to understand aspects of the thing you are studying.

> **An abstraction** *is an intellectual simplification.*

Abstractions allow us to generalize and idealize the thing we're considering. This strips away the abundance of detail and focuses on the essentials.

> **A methodology** *describes how you think about software and software development, and consists of a modeling language, a metamodel and a process.*

Many methodologists differentiate between a *method* and *methodology*. Their assertion is that methodology is the study of methods. Nonetheless, most folks in the industry use these terms interchangeably. The advantage of using *methodology* to refer to the overall process of object-oriented analysis and design is that we can then reserve the term *method* for member functions of a class.

> **A modeling language** *is a language for describing a system or business. The part of the Unified Modeling Language (UML) we will be looking at is its associated diagrams, which we will use to describe a software model.*
>
> **A metamodel** *describes and defines the modeling language itself.*
>
> **A process** *is the set of steps you take to develop software.*

It is worth noting that a model, either of the problem or of the solution, is an abstraction of reality. As such, it is one view among many possible views. A globe is a model of the earth. You can make other maps that model different aspects of the world. Models are, by their nature, incomplete, but a good model helps you to focus on the essentials, while eliminating distracting and trivial details.

A methodology is not arbitrary; it should map well to the work you must accomplish, and should be obvious and intuitive.

How We Got Here

In the 1950s and 60s programming was restricted to specialists in white lab coats who owned access to large, expensive mainframe computers. The cost of *computing time* was high and the tools available were primitive. The goal was to minimize the number of instructions in a program, to get the program to run as quickly as possible and to be as small as possible, because memory was a scarce resource. The problems they were solving, however, were relatively small and simple.

It didn't take long for even these small programs to become unmanageably complex. Programmers freely used **goto** statements to minimize the size and memory footprint of their programs, and spaghetti code was born. Spaghetti code is a great metaphor — it means that if you drew a line following the thread of execution of your program, from one line of code jumping to the next, you soon would have something that looked very much like a pile of spaghetti.

In the late 1950s, higher level languages such as COBOL and FORTRAN were developed in an attempt to provide a layer of abstraction for programmers. The goal was to take a step up from the machine language and focus more on the domain requirements.

> The **domain** *is whatever area you are trying to model.*

For COBOL the domain was business — banks, financial institutions and so forth, FORTRAN was (and still is) used in the scientific domain.

Along the way, programmers began experimenting with structured programming and functional decomposition. The idea was to break the program up into discrete functions. Any function that was very complex was broken down into sub-functions. You continued to break things down into sub-functions until it was obvious how to write each. When you then added together all these smaller sub-functions, you had a more manageable program, which still provided good performance.

Imagine teaching someone to make lunch. You might tell them all the steps one by one. "Open the bread, now get the peanut butter, now spread it. Pour some milk. Take out the vegetables for the salad. No, wait, first you have to make toast. Put the bread in the toaster. First take the bread out of the bag, now put it in the toaster..." Confusing, convoluted instructions, fraught with error. The more complicated the procedure, the more errors.

Now, break the procedure into sub-functions: make a sandwich, pour a glass of milk and make a salad. Each procedure stands on its own, and each may broken into sub-functions. Thus, *make a sandwich* might include, "Make toast, open the peanut butter and jelly, add them to the toast and cut the sandwich." *Making toast* might include, "Get the bread, put it in the toaster, cook it until it is burnt and then a little less." Each task is broken down until the steps are so obvious that there is no additional benefit in breaking it down any further.

Structured programming revolutionized the industry. Suddenly programmers could handle much greater complexity. You might have thought this would mean programs became more reliable. You would be wrong.

When urban planners look at a highway system this is what they see. Local roads become clogged as people begin moving out to the suburbs. To solve this, the state invests millions of dollars building a highway. This relieves the traffic congestion and everyone is happy; for about five minutes. Smart commuters say to themselves, "Hey, now that there is a highway, I can move further out where houses are cheaper and can still get to work in half an hour." Lots of folks make the same decision. Two things happen: those cheaper houses get more expensive and the highway gets crowded. A few years later there is enough clamor for relief that the state spends millions of dollars widening the highway. Once again it becomes possible for more people to move further out and still get to work reasonably quickly. So more people take to the roads. This cycle typically continues until the money runs out. In short, you can't win. If you widen the highway you don't get less crowded roads, you get more commuters.

When programmers created techniques which helped them manage more complex programs without confusion, they didn't end up with less confusing programs. Instead, the complexity of what they were expected to do increased. You see this all the time. Faster computers don't mean that you will do the same thing more quickly, it means you will do new things which require more speed. Bigger hard drives don't give you more room, you just get fatter software to run on them. Have you looked at Visual C++ lately? The fully installed version takes over 300 megabytes. When I was a boy, that was a lot of space.

Finding Bugs Early

It wasn't long before programmers were back in the soup. Even with structured programming techniques, programs were becoming unmanageably large. Bugs crept in, and finding and eradicating those bugs became a major cost of software development.

Here is a truism. The earlier you find a bug in your development cycle, the less expensive it is to fix. Bugs found in design are cheaper to fix than bugs found in code. Bugs found at compile time are easier and cheaper to fix than bugs found once the code goes to the Quality Assurance (QA) department, and cheaper there than once the code ships to your customers.

It has been estimated that 75% of errors in software aren't found before the code goes to QA, and about a third of those are found *after* the software ships. These bugs can be as much as 100 times more expensive to fix than bugs found earlier.

Software developers began looking for a solution to this and related problems. We wanted highly maintainable software, which meant that parts of it could be changed and revised without breaking all the rest. We wanted reusable program components, so we could stop perpetually reinventing the proverbial wheel. We wanted to handle more complex problems. We wanted it to be easy. The problem is, we wanted too much.

What Object-oriented Software Development Promises

The closer our methodology and programming language model the way we think about the world, the easier it will be to manage complexity.

In order to explain this statement, consider that, after twenty years of structured programming, most programmers tend to think about data and how we might manipulate that data, but this is not how anyone else thinks about the world. When most people look at a car they don't think about the information it has and how they might manipulate that information, they think about wheels, transmissions and gears. They think about the car going, stopping and accelerating. They think about roads and cops and speeding tickets. In short, most people think about *things* and what those things *do*.

In fact, this is how humans tend to think about *everything*. Ten million years of evolution has trained us to see the world as populated by things. Some things we eat. Some things eat us. But it is all things.

Think of this book as Beginning *Thing-oriented* Analysis and Design.

How Does it Achieve this?

Object-oriented software development deals in objects and their interaction. These objects are of certain user-defined types which consist of attributes and the ability to manipulate those attributes.

Objects

As programmers, we tend to think of objects as distinguished from the way we used to think about programming: with functions and data structures. We compare the new way of thinking to the old. A more powerful way to get a handle on objects is to set aside the comparison and to step back from the program altogether, and think about what we are trying to accomplish.

We want our software to model the real world closely. By doing so, we can write programs which are easier to understand. Objects in the real world have **characteristics**, and they have **behavior**; objects in programming must model this closely. To do this, in our design we must model the real world objects as abstractions.

By abstracting out the essentials of the object we simplify our task. The map you keep in your car loses some of the details of your town, but it provides the essential model you need when trying to navigate your way to the local market.

A model of the atom or of the solar system loses much of the detail, but provides an essential abstraction of the physical reality, which helps us understand what we are studying. More important, models are abstractions that can be manipulated (run in software and the like). They map back to the domain and are valued in so far as they help predict aspects of the real world. The model of the solar system is only valuable if it accurately reflects aspects of the world such as when the moon will be eclipsed. The aspects of the world that can be predicted by the model are driven by your purpose in creating the model in the first place. We model to simplify and to understand.

Classes

We draw a distinction between the idea of a car and that rust-bucket your brother-in-law sold to you when you graduated college. The *idea* of a car tells us all the things that all cars share in common, what attributes they will have and what behavior. The car is the type or the **class**. The individual car, that hot BMW you're driving now, or that old rust-bucket, are each instances of the class car; we say they are **objects**.

While the class car tells us what attribute every car will have (year, color, make, location), every object will have a particular *value* for each of these attributes. Thus, one car will be a 1997 blue Toyota parked on level 2 and another will be a 1995 yellow Ford on Third Street.

This distinction is mapped directly into C++:

```
class cat
{
    // class declaration
};

cat Boots;
```

cat is a class, while **Boots** is an object (**Boots** is the name of the **cat**). As a class, **cat** is a type, like **int** is in C++. An object is an instance of a class much like a variable is an instance of a type.

Attributes and Behavior

Each object has various attributes. An attribute is a name/value pair. For example, my age is 42. The attribute name is "age", the value is "42". Objects also have behavior. I can stand, walk, sleep etc. The attributes and behaviors we care about will be dictated by what we are trying to accomplish, and this will be decided in the analysis of the problem.

When we code we will typically implement characteristics or attributes in member variables, and we'll implement behavior in methods.

Relationships

Things don't get really interesting until we start to model how objects interact and relate to one another. There are a number of characteristic relationships we might model.

Dependency

The simplest is **dependency**.

> **Dependency** *is where one object must know about another.*

In a simple dependency relationship all we know is that one object has knowledge of another. For example, in C++, if one class requires the inclusions of the header for another, that establishes a dependency.

Association

One step up from dependency is **association**.

> *In an* **association**, *the* **state** *of the object depends on another object.*

In an association we say that, as part of understanding the state of one object, you must understand the relationship with the second object. There are many types of association which model real-world relationships such as owns (John *owns* this car), works for (Pete *works for* Bill) and so forth.

In an association the two objects have a strong connection but neither one is a part of the other. The relationship is stronger than dependency; there is an association affecting both sides of the relationship.

Aggregation

Objects are often made up of other objects. Cars are made up of steering wheels, engines, transmissions and so forth. Each of these components may be an object in its own right. The special association of a car to its component parts is known as **aggregation**.

> **Aggregation** *models the whole/part relation.*

Composition

Often, the component parts of an object spring into existence only with the entire object. For example, the whole of a person may consist of a number of parts including the heart, lungs, limbs and so forth. If you were modeling a person, the lifetime of the heart and lungs would be directly controlled by the lifetime of the aggregating person. We call this special relationship **composition**.

> **Composition** *models a relationship in which one object is an integral part of another.*

In aggregation, the parts may live independently. While my car consists of its wheels and tires and radio, each of those components may have existed before the car was created. In composition, the lifetime of the contained object is tied to the lifetime of the containing object.

Summary

Composition is said to be a stronger relationship than aggregation, which in turn is stronger than association. A relationship is stronger if it provides more information, is more specialized and more constrained.

Thus we see that we can strengthen the relationship from dependency to association to aggregation to composition:

- **Dependency** — **A** knows about **B**
- **Association** — **A** and **B** depend on one another
- **Aggregation** — **A** contains **B** in a whole/part relation
- **Composition** — **B** is part of **A** and its lifetime is tied to **A**'s

In C++ terms, you typically care about dependency only in implementation. In C++, you have a dependency when you `#include` **B**'s header file into **A**. You have an association when you have a reference to **B** within a method of **A**. You have aggregation when you have a reference to **B** as a member variable of **A**. You have composition when you have an *instance* of **B** as a member variable of **A**. You can also have composition using pointers or references, as long as **B** is created in **A**'s constructor and destroyed in **A**'s destructor.

Inheritance

> **Inheritance** *is a specialization/generalization relationship between two objects.*

It is our natural inclination to discover patterns and relationships. It serves us well, and in many cases it helps us predict behavior of otherwise dangerous animals. This helped our smarter ancestors avoid being eaten long enough to reproduce.

From these smarter ancestors we've inherited the ability to create categories based on the behavior and characteristics of the things in our environment. If something moves and breathes we say it is an animal. If one of those things that move and breathe also has live young and nurses them, we say it is a mammal. We know that mammals are *kinds* of animals, and so we can predict that if we see a mammal, it will in all likelihood breathe and move about.

If a mammal barks and wags its tail we say it is a dog. If it won't stop barking and runs about our feet demanding attention, we figure it's a terrier. Each of these classifications gives us additional information. When we are done, we have created a hierarchy of *types*. Some animals are mammals and some are reptiles. Some mammals are dogs and some are horses. Each type will share certain characteristics, and that helps us understand them and predict their behavior and attributes.

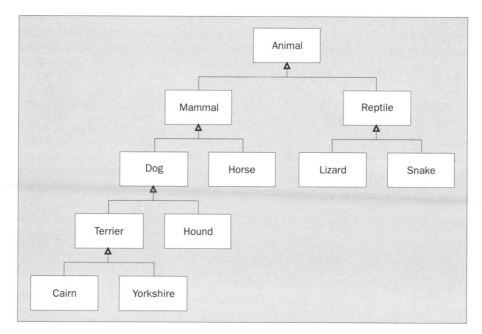

Once we have these categorizations, we can that see reading up the animal hierarchy reveals the **generalization** of shared characteristics. For example, all mammals bear live young (as opposed to laying eggs). The characteristic behavior *bear live young* need not be represented in every mammal sub-type. It can be generalized into the type mammal. We computer types say we *factor* the characteristic *bear live young* out of dog and horse. Mammal *generalizes* this characteristic.

The obverse side of the coin is that each sub-type represents a **specialization**. Dogs are a specialized type of mammal, as are horses. Mammals are a specialized type of animal, one which bears live young.

Object-oriented programmers refer to this set of relationships as an **inheritance hierarchy**. A dog is said to be *derived* from a mammal and to specialize the mammal class. A derived type *inherits* characteristics from its base type, thus dog *inherits* the ability to bear live young from mammal. Mammal is said to be the *base class* of dog and horse and thus generalizes their shared characteristics.

We see these inheritance relationships in many places. For example, buttons, list-boxes and edit boxes in a windowing system, can all be drawn. They all have a location. They all can be hidden or displayed. These characteristic behaviors can be factored out of these individual classes into a common base class. In the Microsoft Foundation Classes (MFC) that common base class is called **CWindow**. Understanding that list boxes and buttons are all derived from **CWindow** simplifies our understanding of each of these derived types, and tells us what we can expect from these classes.

Note that a few mammals actually don't bear their young live. They are mammals in all other respects except this. The duck-billed platypus actually **overrides** this behavior and has its young by laying eggs. One can quibble all day about whether they really are mammals; the point is that it is possible for the specialized object not only to inherit behavior, but to actually modify that behavior. Overriding also allows you to augment functionality that's in the base class. Thus, every window may inherit the ability to draw itself and to find its location on the screen, but the list box overrides this behavior to draw itself quite differently from a simple window.

You will often hear programmers say that generalization or inheritance represents an *is-a* relationship. The idea is that a dog *is-a* mammal and that a mammal *is-an* animal. This is usually distinguished from the *has-a* relationship of aggregation and composition. For example, a car *is-a* vehicle, and a car *has-a* steering wheel.

The "Three Pillars" of Object-oriented Programming

The inheritance relationship is one of the three pillars of object-oriented programming. The other two are **encapsulation** and **polymorphism**.

Encapsulation

Encapsulation *means that each object is self-contained.*

By being careful about encapsulation, we can make changes to small parts of our program without breaking any of the rest of the program. The essential goal in encapsulation is to build self-contained modules that can be plugged into and out of other modules cleanly and without "side effects".

A resistor is a well-encapsulated object. It provides a particular characteristic (so many Ohms of resistance) and you can plug it into a circuit and get the expected behavior. If you later decide to replace this resistor with one of another value, or by another manufacturer, you don't have to rewire the circuit—you just pop out the old resistor and plug in a new one. If you choose the right component, the light bulb lights, and the buzzer sounds. Of course, if you choose wrong, you burn your entire house to the ground and nullify your homeowners insurance.

A well-encapsulated object works the same way (without the house burning part). Let's say you have an object representing an employee. Other objects might ask the employee for his name, his age, his salary and so forth. We call any object that interacts with your object a *client* of your object.

> A **server** *is an object which provides any service.*
>
> A **client** *is an object which interacts with a server.*
>
> *An object can be a server to some objects and a client of others.*

For example, if your object represents an employee, it may be a server to the pension plan object, providing the pension plan with the employee's social security number, age and income. It may also be a client of that very same pension plan, asking the plan to provide benefits.

The employee may be responsible for a set of activities. Some time after the program is up and running, you decide to rewrite your employee object to change the way it interacts with the database. If your employee object is well encapsulated, you can modify its internal structure without breaking any of the clients with which it interacts.

I will extend the definition of encapsulation as we go along to emphasize that each object should have a single area of responsibility, and that you should draw a sharp distinction between **interface** and **implementation**. We'll return to this in some detail later in the book, but here is the essence:

> *An* **interface** *is a contract your object makes with all its clients. In coding terms, it's a list of global public functions specifying the parameters they take and their return values.*

Your object promises to provide certain services (create a report) and to provide certain information (the salary and employment date). You, as author of this object, publish an interface and say, in essence, "Here is how you interact with my object. If you make these function calls, I promise to provide valid information in this form or to take these actions."

Looking at interfaces from a programming point of view:

- In C++ an interface is a set of public members (and an associated description of their use). Interfaces can be modeled in code separately from any implementation by using abstract classes. Abstract classes allow you to specify a set of public members without supplying an implementation. (They also allow you to supply a 'name' to the interface in a way that can be used directly in code.) Typically, you will create a class that provides an implementation of an interface by deriving from an abstract class describing that interface. If you need to provide an implementation for more than one interface, you can use multiple inheritance.

- Java supports the notion of interfaces slightly more directly than C++ through the use of the **interface** keyword. Java classes can implement multiple interfaces.

- COM is built on the notion of components exposing functionality through multiple, uniquely-identifiable interfaces.

It is common for an object to offer interfaces based on the privileges of the client class. For example, one client might be allowed only a subset of the possible operations on your new object. In addition, an object might offer a second interface to accommodate updates and changes to the object without breaking old client code. That is, older clients use the old interface, but newer clients can use the newer and updated interface.

> **Implementation** *is how you perform these services.*

The implementation is entirely hidden from your clients. They do not know and ought not to care how you answer the salary question. You might cache the salary in a member variable, compute it based on a formula or look it up in the database. It is entirely invisible and irrelevant to the clients of your class.

This is the essence of **information hiding** — the principle that your class should not expose its data, but rather offer an interface allowing clients to access the data indirectly. Hence, you can modify how you represent that data in the class without breaking the interface, decoupling the implementation of your class from its clients. All this should help make your code reusable.

Polymorphism

> **Polymorphism** *is the ability to invoke a method on an object without knowing that object's type, and have the right thing happen.*

Poly means many, and *morph* means form. **Polymorphism** is the ability for one thing to take many forms. Once we have established an inheritance hierarchy, there is great power in being able to treat the various derived types polymorphically. Again, we'll see this in detail and in context later in the book, but the essential idea is this: you can interact with derived objects without knowing the specifics of their specialization.

An example will make this clearer. Let's say you have defined the relationship among list boxes, buttons, edit text and so forth as all deriving from the class **CWindow**. Next, you factor the ability to draw on the screen up into the **CWindow** object and you specialize this behavior in the derived objects. That is, while all windows can draw, the button draws itself differently from how a list box draws itself.

Given a window, you can tell it to draw itself, and each kind of window will "do the right thing". The *client* (the object telling the window to draw itself) doesn't know or care if the particular window is a list box or a button; by calling **Draw()** it can be assured that the window, whatever it really is (button or list box) will draw itself properly.

We say that the client can treat all the window objects polymorphically. In C++ polymorphism comes in two flavors: function polymorphism and object polymorphism. Object polymorphism is what we were just describing, and it is accomplished with virtual functions. Function polymorphism is accomplished through function overloading — the ability to give more than one function the same name. We'll come back to both forms of polymorphism later in the book.

While this description dipped down into the implementation details, the essential design point is that objects in certain relationships, most notably inheritance relationships, can be treated polymorphically.

The Goals of Object-oriented Software Development

What are we trying to accomplish? In essence, we want code that is correct, reliable, robust, extensible, maintainable, reusable, efficient, portable and delivered on time and on budget. Object-oriented techniques and methodologies serve these goals. To the extent they can make a measurable difference in our ability to accomplish these aims, they will be deemed successful, and the investment in up-front analysis and design will be paid back to the customer.

Whether your software ought to meet each of these goals will be determined by your understanding of the client's priorities. The client may well decide to make code that is less reusable, as a short-term economy. This is not necessarily a pernicious decision, as long as it is made consciously and not inadvertently.

Correct

When we say the code must be correct, we mean that it should conform to the requirements specification. This simple statement hides a great deal of complexity. The devil is in creating a specification that is sufficiently detailed, so we can build a design and implement a system that does what the customer envisaged. In some ways, creating the specification is the most demanding aspect of the entire project.

A specific technique of object-oriented development will be to articulate a set of requirements based on how the users of the system will interact with it, and how the system must respond. We will then implement the system in iterations. That is, we'll build it, and then we'll refine it and enhance it in progressive steps. Each iteration will target a particular set of requirements.

The components of this solution will be tested individually and in interaction with one another. Thus each "object" in the system will provide its own integrity and its own *correctness*, to ensure that the entire system, when fully functional, will also be correct.

Object-oriented analysis assists in building *correct* code, because the design maps closely to the problem. The requirements provide a specification, against which the code can be tested to ensure a correct implementation.

Reliable

The system must be reliable. There are two types of reliability. First, it must not crash unexpectedly. Second, it must perform as expected over a long period of time with little need for maintenance.

In each case, the exact level of reliability will be dictated by the requirements specification. The phone system strives for "seven nines of reliability", that is 99.99999% of the time the system runs without unplanned down time. When the phone company system crashes, you read about it on the first page of the Wall Street Journal.

Such a high level of reliability comes at a price, and for some projects reliability may be described somewhat more liberally.

The important issue is not how reliable the system must be *per se*, but whether the reliability requirement is well understood and articulated, and whether you've designed for and have an implementation that ensures such a requirement. Object-oriented techniques help build more reliable systems by helping us understand the complexity of the system and break the system down into individual components which can be tested independently of the entire system.

Robust

A system is robust when it can maintain its reliability under unexpected circumstances. Customers will not always act in predictable ways. They may enter unexpected data, hang up in the middle of phone calls, kill the power at the worst moment and so forth. Other systems can not be counted on to be any more reliable than human users — the network will time out, the operating system will crash, disks judder to a halt, memory fails; Murphy's law is no less effective in software than elsewhere in life.

It is harder to define what we mean by robust than what we mean by reliable and correct. Correctness can be measured against the specifications, reliability can be measured by down time. Robustness requires the evil antics of a professional quality assurance engineer. These half-demented denizens of malformed queries, wrongly entered data and inopportune power failures can uncover failures in robustness in a way that more polite and civilized engineers simply cannot. I am married to a QA engineer, who delights in uncovering unexpected failures in code I've tested dozens of times.

One definition of robust I like a lot comes from Fred Brooks' *Mythical Man Month* (Addison-Wesley, ISBN 0-201-00650-2). He suggests that the goal of building a robust program is not that there is some way in which your program will run successfully, but that there is *no* way in which it will fail.

Object-oriented development assists in building robust systems by encouraging localization of state through encapsulation. That is, each object is responsible for its own state, and thus the state of any individual object is not distributed over the entire system. A single object may fail but the entire system does not become corrupted.

Extensible and Maintainable

Software development is much like pinball. If you do well and get a high score, you get to play again. Unlike pinball, however, you don't start over, you build on what you have. The first version is, if you are lucky, not the last. Your customer's needs will evolve, often in response to seeing and using the first version of the software, and he will add new requirements and expectations. Your system must be able to be extended, naturally and cleanly, without breaking the existing systems.

Maintainability is closely related to extensibility. Extensibility talks about the system's ability to add new features. This is typically accomplished through careful encapsulation of the objects and data hiding, discussed below. Maintainability focuses on the developer's ability to understand the code, and is accomplished by careful documentation and commenting, which augments highly readable source code.

I'll have much more to say about writing readable code as we progress, but every programmer has an innate understanding of the mysterious transformation that code undergoes when you ignore it for a few months. I refer to it as code-rot. You write crystal clear code, comment it well, document your intention and then move on. Some months later you return to that same code but it has changed. Like a tomato sitting for too long in the refrigerator, it has begun to rot. The comments leak out first; what appeared just a few months ago as well commented code is now stark and naked. The source itself, which when you wrote it was practically poetic, is gibberish. The architecture is obscure, the design opaque and the objects, variables and methods ill chosen and bizarre.

Code that cannot be read cannot be maintained. Clever, cute hacks become traps and pitfalls to the poor sap who must maintain the code long after you've gone on to the next lucrative contract. The customer, of course, is left holding the bag.

Object-oriented programming encourages encapsulation, and this prevents changes in one section of the code from rippling through the entire design. This makes code much more maintainable. Polymorphism allows us to extend the behavior of the system, without breaking and rebuilding the existing, working and tested parts.

In a traditional C program, when you have behavior which you can apply to a set of data and you wish to extend that behavior, you must write a new function. You may want to capture some of the working code in the original function, and so you would cut and paste that code into your new function. If the old function is updated, you would have to find the various places you pasted it, and update them as well. This is unwieldy and error prone; it is a maintenance nightmare. In C++ you subclass the working class and add the variant behavior in the derived class and you are done. If you change the base class, the changes trickle down to the derived classes automatically.

Reusable

Reusability was the great promise of object-oriented programming. It was our collective intention to build plug-and-play components, which could be swapped in and out of new programs, like resistors and diodes are swapped in and out of circuits. Until recently, for many organizations this was something of a disappointment.

For some software development companies, code reuse is real and powerful. This is especially true in those organizations which are building foundation classes — the core classes that are, by their nature, designed to be reused in applications.

What *is* being captured and reused across the industry is the design patterns that are common to many software products. This ability to describe and to *name* design patterns has revolutionized the design process. We'll be looking at design patterns in detail later in this book.

In the Windows world we've seen VBXs, OCXs and, more recently, reusable ActiveX objects. These represent the first real, mass distribution reuse of application-level components, and may mark a turning point in the use of object-oriented techniques to build successful, reusable application components.

Efficient

The software must be efficient. That is, it must use as little memory, require as little disk space and run as fast as possible, all other things being equal. Not so long ago, this efficiency was a high priority, and we spent a lot of time profiling our product and tuning its efficiency.

> **Profiling** *is examining where a system spends the most time. Profiling software can report on how many milliseconds each method takes, how often you call that method, what percentage of your execution time is spent in each method and so forth.*

As the cost of memory and disk space plummets and the cost of developer time skyrockets, these priorities have become inverted. For many applications, it is well worth paying the price of slightly diminished efficiency in exchange for maintainability, clarity or even time to market.

This is typical of the kind of tradeoffs we are called upon to make in designing and implementing software. Efficiency is *a* factor, but often it is not the driving factor in the success of applications development.

It is worth noting that the definition of efficiency has evolved. Not so long ago a program was optimized to use as few machine cycles and as little memory as possible. However, these days machine cycles on a single machine are often not a significant performance issue. The cost in waiting for a few hundred extra cycles is swamped by the access time to the database, network latency issues, user input and other far longer delays. This, together with the dramatic fall in the cost of memory, means that this type of optimization is now rarely done.

Therefore, most of the time we don't worry very much about the size and performance of software in quite the ways we used to. Even if this leads to bloated and slower programs, it still may be the right trade off. After all, if you can make your program easier to implement, easier to maintain and faster to market, at the cost of making it a bit bigger and slower, that may well be a trade you'll be willing to accept. The key is to set your goals clearly and then make sure you've optimized for the right thing.

Portable

Portability is the ability to run, or at least rebuild, your software on a different hardware platform or operating system. For some applications, portability is crucial. For other applications, portability is a non-issue. These are business requirements that will be dictated by the customer.

Portability can be affected by the implementation language chosen (Visual Basic is highly non-portable, C++ offers compile time portability, Java offers run-time portability) as well as by the structure of the program. A program which carefully separates the user interface from the underlying engine is a more likely candidate for portability than one which does not.

Delivered on Time

The single greatest challenge, and the one which the industry fails most conspicuously and consistently, is getting the product delivered on time. This is a function of many factors, including poor management, inadequate analysis of the problem to be solved, faulty design, inept implementation and the unexpected but ultimately inevitable snags along the way.

Late software may never be delivered at all. The market window of opportunity may be lost, while competitors gain a toe-hold giving them an overwhelming competitive advantage.

A tremendous sea change has taken place in the past year or two, with which the industry has yet to come to terms. The time to market requirements for a substantial percentage of projects has shrunk from a few years, to two years, down to one year and in many cases can now be measured in months. This creates unprecedented stress on the analysis, design and implementation methods, and dramatically impacts our entire process.

Delivered on Budget

The counterpart of the timeliness issue is the budget. Software projects are notorious for running over budget. Since the greatest cost, by far, in the development of software is the payroll for the developers on the project, the budget is tied in large measure to the ability to deliver the product on time. If a product is late, not only will the market have shifted, but the brutal reality is that the budget may be broken and there simply may not be the funds to continue working. It is not uncommon for products to finally lumber out the door, only to have the project killed because the underwriting sponsors are no longer willing to spend the extra money to promote and market the product.

Object-oriented Languages

You can write object-oriented programs in any programming language. You can write object-oriented C, assembler, BASIC or even COBOL. But, to mangle George Orwell, while all programming languages are equal to the task, some are more equal than others.

Why C++?

You *can* create classes, enforce encapsulation and implement polymorphism in C or in COBOL, it just takes longer and it is a lot more painful. In this book, I will use C++ to demonstrate the implementation of object-oriented designs because C++ was designed to implement object-oriented programming.

C++ was invented, defined and originally implemented by Bjarne Stroustrup. It started out in 1980 as "C with Classes" and was renamed C++ in 1983. In C, the increment operator (++) adds one to a variable. Thus, C++ increments C; it adds the tools of object-oriented programming.

The genius of C++ was that it was a Trojan horse. It looked like a nice gift to the C community; a bit big, a bit wooden and rather harmless. Inside, however, was hidden object-oriented programming. Once the object-oriented perspective was let out, there was no stopping it.

I am often asked if one should learn C before learning C++, and I always answer "no". C++ is a syntactic superset of C. This means that you use the same *syntax* when writing your code, and any valid C program (with some minor exceptions) will be valid C++. However, the *semantics* are very different. That is, the way you think about and design programs is very different.

I would contend that the leap from C to C++ is substantially greater than the leap from Pascal or even Assembler to C. While Assembler and C have very different syntax, they share a common semantic understanding of how you should program. On the other hand, while C and C++ share a common syntax, they are worlds apart in how they solve problems.

Pretend you are an Italian scientist in 1600. You are presented with two science books. One was written in Russian in 1600. The other was written in Italian in 1997 and magically sent back to you. The first one has a funny alphabet and it takes a long time to understand the syntax, but once you learn the language, it doesn't say anything surprising. The second one looks a lot like the Italian you know, but what they are saying is outlandish, world-shattering and unheard of. C and C++ use the same syntax, but their meaning is worlds apart.

While learning the fundamentals of C++ is not particularly difficult, using it to write high quality object-oriented programs presents a significant challenge. Few books can possibly teach both the syntax and semantics of C++ and also provide a solid grounding in the complexity of object-oriented analysis and design. This book will endeavor to provide the latter.

Modeling Languages

As we saw earlier, modeling languages are used to describe a system or business prior to coding.

We will use the Unified Modeling Language (UML) to help model problems and their solutions. Using a standardized set of modeling symbols can save a great deal of time and confusion. Rather than having to say, "My boxes mean classes, and when I draw an arrow I mean that this box over here is a generalization of that box over there," and then having the next person say, "Well, I draw classes with circles, and my arrows mean some form of association," you can use the agreed upon symbols and just get on with it. Mathematicians, chemists, physicists and others have been doing this kind of thing for years, and it seems to work quite well.

> *The Unified Modeling Language has been released by a consortium of companies led by Rational Software Corporation, and was certified as an industry standard by the OMG (Object Management Group) in November 1997. The UML attempts to unify the diagrams and, to a degree, the methodologies of Booch, Object Modeling Technique (OMT) and Object-Oriented Software Engineering (OOSE). The author of the Booch Methodology is Grady Booch, the principal author of OMT is James Rumbaugh and the principal author of Object-Oriented Software Engineering is Ivar Jacobson. All three are the driving force behind the UML proposal, and they are affectionately known to the object-oriented design community as the Three Amigos.*

The Three Amigos are quick to point out that the UML is a "modeling language and not a methodology". What they are distinguishing is this: a methodology typically consists of a modeling language and a process. The modeling language helps you *describe* your design; the process is how you *create* it. Booch was recently quoted as saying, "The modeling wars are over, long live the process wars!"

While the UML will probably be modified slightly as it achieves its coveted status as an open industry-wide standard, overall it does not appear to be very controversial. Most object analysts are pretty comfortable that they can do their modeling with the UML about as well as with anything else, and there is increasing momentum behind the UML as books and tools are produced to support it.

There is however no consensus about process; in fact, the UML documentation specifically states the authors' belief that there can be no single correct process. On the other hand, the UML is driven by the idea of processes, which are iterative, incremental and use-case driven.

If a modeling language isn't a methodology, because it doesn't include a process, then what is it? The UML endeavors to define two vital tools: a notation and a metamodel. The notation is the set of diagramming syntax, which lets you think about and convey your analysis and design. The metamodel is the definition of the notation. It precisely defines how the pieces of the model work. To give you the flavor of the metamodel, here is the class diagram for collaborations. Do *not* try to understand this diagram. I've included it just to give you a quick sense of what the metamodel is like.

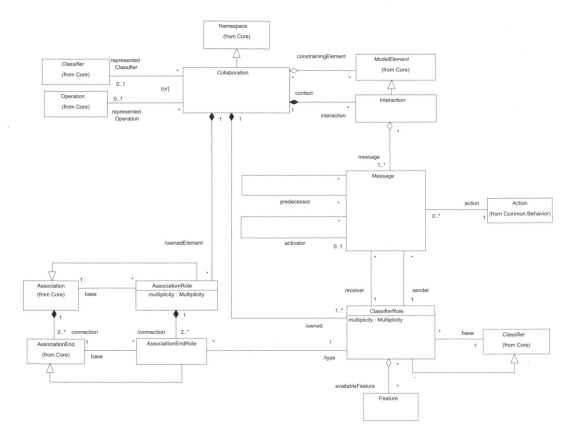

I won't try to walk you through this complex diagram, but I do want to point out that everything in this diagram is in UML notation. In fact, the notation is being used to describe the notation itself!

You must understand a bit about how a language, such as C++, works to program effectively, but you don't need to know all the details of the compiler's internals. In the same way, you need to understand the notation, and the purpose of the metamodel, but you can be a world-class software architect without fully analyzing the UML metamodel in every detail. So we won't. We will come to an informal understanding of the metamodel as we go along, through using it to document our analysis, design and implementation.

> *For those of you who want a detailed reference guide to the Unified Modeling Language, have a look at Instant UML (Wrox Press, ISBN 1-861000-87-1).*

What to do about Controversy

There are aspects of the UML, and especially of the metamodel, which are not settled and won't be for some time. The experts simply disagree about some of the fine distinctions. I will point out these areas of contention as we go forward, but I won't dwell on them. When the experts disagree, we won't bind ourselves to one camp or another; we'll find a middle ground which will survive either resolution, and we'll move forward. Most of the time, we just won't use the controversial aspects; after all they invariably are at the margin of utility. All the important stuff has been settled for some time.

The Full Development Cycle

This book describes the development of software through the entire development cycle.

Developing software starts with an idea. In the best of all worlds, it starts with a *need* — a requirement which only new software can fulfill. At times, rather than being *need-driven* the development of new software is *technology-driven*. That is, some new whiz-bang technology is invented, and someone in marketing goes looking for an application that uses the new technology.

> *Technology-driven software rarely succeeds. On the other hand, new technology* can *change customer expectations and thus requirements. Certainly radio, television, the telephone and VCR are proof of that. More recently CDs, laser disks, DVD disks and, for that matter, the World Wide Web, have demonstrated that a new technology can capture the imagination, and from that inspiration can come hundreds of successful products.*

Whether the idea for software arises out of a felt need on the part of consumers, or is a response to a nifty technology which expands the market, that idea must be nurtured and fully understood in detail. Too often in the past, we set out to write software before we fully understood even the fundamental requirements. When we finished, we had a product that no one much wanted.

An essential part of the development cycle is understanding the requirements, and a key aspect of that effort is to understand who will use the system, and what they want the system to do. Once we understand the requirements, we can create the design and implement it. Once implemented, the software must be tested and delivered.

It is the goal of the rest of this chapter to review these steps at a high level; the rest of the book will be devoted to exploring each issue in detail.

How much Formality?

The single biggest question in any object-oriented project is, "How much formality will you introduce into the process?" If you are overly casual, the process breaks down and you lose the benefits of having a process in the first place. If the process is *too* formal, you get caught up in the form, and lose sight of the substance.

When you first learn to drive you follow the rules quite strictly. After a while you find yourself easing up and trusting your judgement a bit more. The nice thing about driving, much like programming, is that if your judgement is poor you'll find out pretty quickly.

For most projects, the decision of how formal a process to use will be influenced by the size of the team. It is easier to be informal in a six-person development team than in a team of two hundred. Even when I'm working completely alone, however, I still follow the core methodology without cutting corners. This is not for the sake of form, but rather because it *works*. It helps manage complexity and ensures a better design and thus, in the end, produces a more robust program.

Iterative and Incremental Development

The entire development process is **iterative** and **incremental** — iterative in that we will continually go over the same phases and incremental in that we will make small but noticeable improvements in each iteration. We will not attempt to build a complete requirements document before beginning design, rather we will *iterate* over the requirements as we go forward. In the same way, we will not attempt to finish a complete design before beginning to code. In each iteration, we will incrementally improve the work we've completed to date.

Iterative development can be illustrated by a counter-example — waterfall development. In a waterfall environment, the process is one-way and discreet. An analyst determines the requirements and hands them to a designer. The designer describes the user interface, and hands his design and the analyst's requirements to an architect. The architect organizes the systems and modules and hands his architectural design to the coder. The coder writes the software and hands the result to QA. Finally, the Quality Assurance engineer tests the software and hands it to the customer.

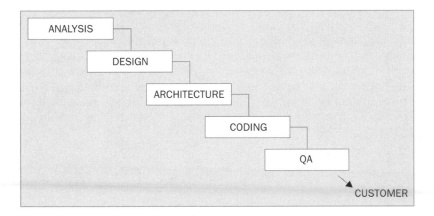

The waterfall methodology was created to prevent requirements from shifting. Because each phase is signed off and locked into place, the process introduces friction against shifting the requirements later. If requirements shift, they are noted and paid for in addition to the original budgeted amount.

> *From a developer's viewpoint, this limitation is a critical element in a fixed-cost contract, but often the customer ends up saddled with a product which isn't quite right. The customer must decide either to forgo the changes or he must pay for them, breaking through his budget of supposedly "fixed" costs.*

Requirements *do* shift. And for good reasons. For example, as we develop the system, the customer will better understand what he needs. Meanwhile, his market is changing, more rapidly than ever before. The requirements must evolve to meet those needs. At the same time that the customer's requirements are changing, the technology itself is evolving. This can make new opportunities available, and your customer is likely to want to take advantage of these new innovations.

What is needed is a system that can accommodate a rapidly evolving set of requirements. Iterative development is much better than waterfall methodologies at incorporating changing requirements. Because each iteration is small, we can successively refine our work as we progress. The danger, however, is that the requirements will never settle and you'll end up with a project which is late or never ships at all.

H.L. Mencken said that "for every complex problem, there is a solution that is simple, neat, and wrong." No solution is perfect, and most of us ultimately must compromise. We attempt to sign off as we go. While we understand that changes to the requirements are a natural part of the process, we will "set the bar higher" in each iteration. The image is this: as you cycle through the iterations, you must leap over a bar each time you want to change a requirement. Each round you raise the bar another notch. Once you find that nothing makes it over the bar, you're done.

The essential compromise is that you *can* iterate and change things in response to shifting market conditions, increased understanding of the problem and gain insight along the way. But these changes come at a cost, and that cost rises as the project progresses. Changes introduced early are less expensive, but requirements changes introduced late in development come at a much higher cost.

Phases of Development

Methodologies differ in their description and naming of the phases of development. This book focuses on **requirements analysis**, **design**, **implementation** and **testing**. While I take an eclectic approach, I will remain reasonably consistent with all the mainstream OOA&D methodologies.

The object-oriented development community spends a lot of time wrangling over what activities happen in which phases of the process, but the important global issues meet with general agreement among anyone who is working with one of these principal methodologies.

We will start by trying to understand the customer's requirements. We will go on to design a solution and then to implement that solution. Lastly, we will iterate over these phases, repeatedly refining and improving our understanding of the requirements, and evolving the design as our understanding improves.

As I said, there is nothing magical here. Judgement, experience and knowledge are required, but you've already learned the hard part. The rest is just detail.

The Vision

No great software has ever been created by committee; ultimately it is always one person with a clear and unwavering vision of a product who delivers the next killer application — VisiCalc, Lotus 1-2-3, Word, Notes — each was owned by a single visionary.

> *The **visionary** is the person with the clear vision of the essence of the product.*

This visionary must participate in every meeting in the early days of the project. It is his sole job to keep his eyes on the vision; to hold an unwavering grip on the essence of what he wants to build. The software analyst may help him flesh out the vision and understand its ramifications, but if the customer can't recognize the core of his vision in the final product, then the process has failed.

In very large projects, you may have a number of technical experts who will provide guidance when thinking through how the product will be used. Typically, these experts will work for the customer, but it is the designated customer who keeps the vision and who will own responsibility for the direction and overall quality of the product. The experts may provide testimony, but the visionary will provide leadership.

Articulating the vision doesn't take much time. It may involve nothing more than sketching an idea out on the back of an envelope or a short conversation in front of a white board. However long it takes, at the end of this phase one person will have a clear idea of what he wants the product to do.

The goal of this preliminary work is to decide if there is a good enough business case for the new product to move forward. Often, this is a tentative decision, depending on an understanding of the costs of development and marketing.

Requirements Analysis

Once the vision is understood, it is time to flesh out the detailed requirements. This is where the bulk of the work in object-oriented analysis and design takes place. During this phase, it is the architect's job to help the customer detail and understand how the system will be used.

> *The **architect** is the person responsible for the overall design and implementation of the software.*

A key tool in this phase is the development of use cases.

> *A **use case** is a description of an interaction between a person (or another system) and the system we are building.*

We will spend a lot of time discussing use cases in the next chapter: how they are created and how they are used to further our understanding of the system.

In order to build a robust and meaningful requirements document, we will need to analyze the **domain**. The domain is that area of business or human experience in which this software will be used. For example, if we are building software to support a video store, the domain is small business and entertainment. The outcome of domain analysis is the building of a domain model.

By joining the domain model, which tells us about the context of the software, with the use cases, which tell us how the software will be used, we can build a design model. The design model begins to flesh out what objects we care about and how they may interact.

While building the design model, we will focus on class diagrams, which tell us about the attributes and methods of the classes, and interaction diagrams, which describe how the objects interact. In addition, we will build **activity diagrams,** which give insight into the workflow — how tasks are accomplished in the interaction between the system and its users.

Domain Analysis

In **domain analysis** we examine the objects in the problem domain. That is, we look at what *things* are in the area of concern. These objects should be immediately recognizable to the visionary; they require no expertise in computers. In fact they don't relate to computers at all, they are entirely artifacts of the area being modeled.

If we were building software to manage a video store, the domain analysis would focus on customers, video tapes, rentals and so forth. If we were building software to manage a bank, the domain analysis would focus on accounts, customers, loans, foreclosures, widows and orphans.

In short, we are looking at the objects (or things) in the area of concern. We want to know what is there (videos and customers), how they relate to one another (one rents the other), what states they might have (rented, available), what behavior they might have (borrow, return) and so forth.

Architecture Design

Once we understand the requirements, it is time to focus on the **architecture**.

> *The* **architecture** *is an abstraction of the most important aspects of the system.*

The architecture provides the framework in which the design will be built. It states in broad strokes how the software will be organized and provides protocols for data access and communication among modules. It describes the scale and performance of the system, capturing the most important use cases and application requirements. The architecture will be refined throughout the design and implementation phase, but it lends direction and it constrains the rest of the design.

The architecture will include an abstraction of the most important aspects of the use cases and the domain analysis. It will also include design-level policies, such as how we'll handle error handling, memory management and so forth.

Class Design

With the architecture in place, we begin class design. During this phase we will endeavor to identify the principal classes and how they relate to one another. **Class diagrams** will be fleshed out to identify generalization (inheritance) relationships as well as various kinds of associations.

The focus in class design is on the responsibilities of each class, and how the classes interact and collaborate to fulfill these responsibilities. Each class should have a single, well defined and well understood area of responsibility; all of its methods and data will be created to fulfill that responsibility. Often, classes will delegate ancillary responsibility to other classes as we sort out how to implement the use cases discovered in the analysis phase.

We will use CRC (Class/Responsibility/Collaboration) cards to detail these areas of responsibility. CRC cards are nothing more than 3x5 index cards, on which we will write the name of each class and what its responsibilities are. We will also write the name of other classes, with which it must "collaborate" to get its work done. This is a simple and effective technique for teasing out the principal classes and what they are for. We will then translate this information into a series of diagrams that describe each of the classes, their relation to one another and their interactions.

Once we understand the objects and how they interact, it is time to begin thinking about how the objects will be implemented on a particular operating system, using a particular development language.

During this phase of the design we will typically begin prototyping the software, if we haven't done so earlier. This early work is not presumed to be part of the final software, it is more often a "proof of concept" in which we attempt to implement some of the riskier aspects of the technology in an effort to understand how these problems will be solved.

Implementation

During implementation phase, you translate the low-level design into code. Typically, the interfaces fall out of the design documentation, and the bulk of the work is spent on implementing the methods described in the interface.

Implementation is, by its nature, an iterative process. The goal is to get something working early, and to keep it working as you add new features.

Rational's Objectory product talks about *iterations* as a formal process. Each iteration will fulfill a set of use cases, and stands alone as a deliverable on your schedule. In Booch's original formulation, these were referred to as *micro-cycles*, that is, small cycles of analysis, design and implementation.

There are iterations within iterations. Each version or release of the software may represent a series of iterations of development, each sub-iteration adding new functionality or fulfilling additional use cases.

Testing and Delivery

When you are readying your code for final delivery, it is appropriate to begin considering **profiling** and **optimizing** the code to enhance performance. Profiling code is the process of determining where your program spends most of its time. Optimizing is the process of making segments of your code run more efficiently.

As you approach your ship date, you should offer tremendous resistance to adding functionality. This phase is often known as *code-freeze*. It isn't that you don't change the code, it is that all changes are to fix bugs.

The testing phase ought not be shortchanged; typically testing will represent 30–50% of the implementation. Thus, if you allow four months of implementation, allow at least two months of testing.

Is it Worth the Investment?

To understand why it is worth shifting to a model in which analysis and design represents upwards of 50% of the project time, you must look at the real costs in software development. It comes down to managing two risks: the risk that you will never complete the project and the risk that you will not be able to maintain and extend the software once it is written.

The industry is beset with failed software projects. I was at a conference recently where I heard this story. A lecturer at a programmer's seminar asked the group, "If you boarded a jet and there was a sign saying that the jet ran on software developed by your group, how many of you would be afraid of crashing?" After a moment's hesitation, hands began to go up. Soon everyone in the audience had raised his hands except for one person. "Why didn't you raise your hand?" the lecturer asked. The one hold out replied, "If the jet was running on my group's software there is no chance we'd ever get off the ground, let alone crash."

The frightening thing is that this story always gets a laugh. We are painfully aware that most software created today is bloated, unreliable, fragile and difficult to maintain. That, after all, is what drove the development of object-oriented methods in the first place.

There is little to offer to prove that object-oriented development works, except anecdotal evidence. More and more developers have found that when they invest in a solid analysis period, they understand better not only the requirements, but also the relative priorities of the requirements. This, in turn, increases the likelihood that they will build the most important aspects of the software first, and not waste their time on difficult and unimportant aspects of the project.

Experience dictates that a solid design reduces the risk of cost and schedule overruns, and increases the likelihood that the second version can be built cleanly on top of the first. Projects which skimp on the design phase invariably run late and end with software which is difficult to maintain and impossible to extend.

In short, it is the collective experience of companies worldwide that investment in up-front analysis and design more than pays for itself overall. There are risks in any process, but this process has proven itself remarkably successful, when done right.

Managing the Risks

While there is much evidence that object-oriented analysis and design can reduce the risks associated with software development, many teams fail at their first attempts. While the theory of object-oriented analysis and design is fairly straightforward, the skill of implementing this process in a real-world project team can be difficult to get right on the first try.

Once you're committed to an object-oriented approach, you can reduce your risk by getting help from an experienced mentor. Mentoring has become a popular way to transfer the experience of object-oriented architects to new teams. While training courses and tutorials can teach the fundamentals, it is only by living through a few projects that you will achieve a deep understanding of the process.

Obviously you must consider my advice as tainted by self-interest. Training and mentoring is a significant part of my business. That said, there is a growing consensus that adding a mentor to a development group can make the difference between success and disaster. Most mentors provide informal training while they contribute to the analysis and design; their goal is to make the team increasingly self-reliant and reduce the need for their services over time.

There are any number of risks in developing object-oriented software. The question that seems to generate the most concern, however, among novice analysts is this: how much is enough? When am I done with analysis and when am I done with design?

There is a tendency either to create a cursory analysis and design in the rush to get to programming, or on the other hand, to become so paralyzed by the need fully to understand the problem and to design the solution, that one never begins writing code at all.

Each of us has over-engineered a solution at one time or another; it is an occupational hazard. The trick in designing great software is to make it "good enough" but no better.

Good Enough Software Engineering

In the 1940s, British psychologist D.W. Winnicott wrote of the "Good Enough Mothering". It was his thesis that a mother must provide just enough support to give the child a sense of security without smothering the child and denying their independence.

The challenge in "Good Enough Engineering" is to build a product which meets the customer requirements and which is robust, reliable, extensible, maintainable and profitable, without smothering its development in so many features and refinements that it never ships.

This is not to deny the appeal of building "insanely great" software; but rather to introduce this reality: more software dies because it didn't ship in a reasonable time than because it did ship but didn't have enough features.

I have to be careful here. This is not offered as an excuse (let alone an inducement) to cut corners or produce shoddy work. A great scourge of the industry is that so much software is inadequate, poorly designed, fragile and unreliable. What I am suggesting is *not* that you build software of inferior quality, but rather that you consider producing smaller, less ambitious software that is well designed, that works and that *ships*.

Summary

To recap on what we've just discussed, we've seen how object-oriented development was borne out of necessity, that it aims to better represent, abstract and model the real world in software, in order to make software development more manageable and better able to deliver the required solution. This is achieved through the use of an iterative development process, a modeling language and an object-oriented programming language. Quite how is the subject of the rest of the book.

With that in mind, the next chapter will look at analysis, how to understand your problem and then case it in an object-oriented manner.

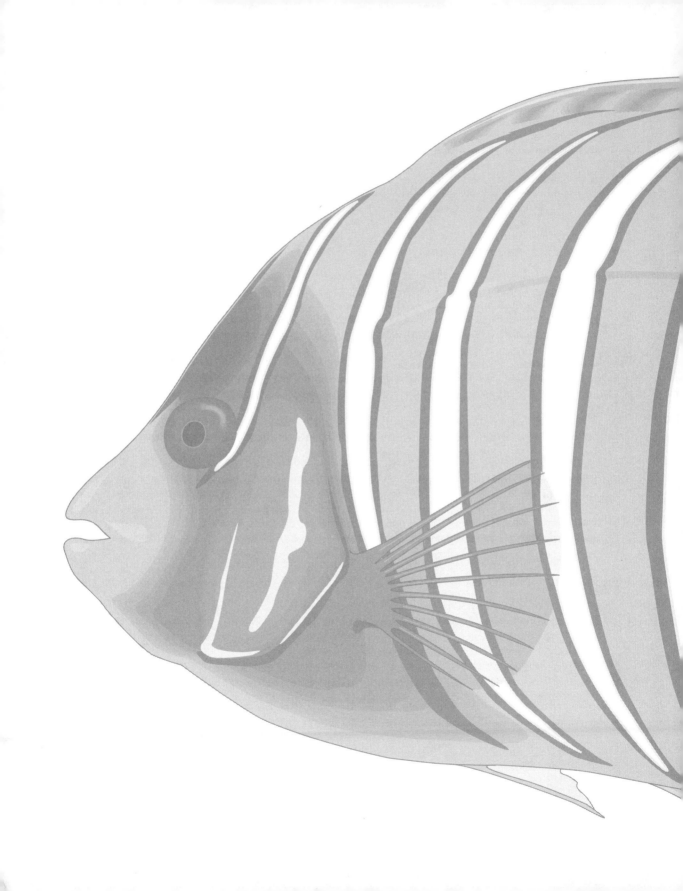

Analysis

Analysis is the process of coming to understand fully the problem you are trying to solve.

Requirements analysis, to give it its full name, is the stage in the development process where we state the problem and elucidate its subtleties. It encompasses:

- System analysis
- Application analysis
- Domain analysis

In this chapter, we'll look at the process of analyzing your problem, the way you should document this analysis, and the people you need to involve in the process. The use cases technique, which will be the focus of this chapter's discussion, is one of the most useful ways to break down the problem into its constituent parts. So, without further ado...

In the Beginning

Understanding the requirements begins with a great idea. Someone envisages a new product or a new version of an existing product. It is the software architect's job to nurture the fledgling idea, and to ensure that it is not asphyxiated by too many demands for details.

New ideas are fragile. They are easily destroyed, as often by over-enthusiasm as by skepticism. New ideas must be approached gently, with the lights dimmed at first, giving them time to form and to solidify. Push too hard on a new idea, and it will burst like a soap bubble.

As the person with the new idea articulates what he has in mind, the software architect must listen without judgment, working hard to share a common vision and gain understanding before applying critical reasoning. For just a moment, the task is not to evaluate the idea at all, but simply to understand it.

That non-judgmental period is short, just long enough to make sure the idea is reasonably well understood. Before sinking any significant time and money into development, however, we'll want to subject the new product idea to some simple reality checks to tell us quite quickly if it is worth pursuing.

- Is the idea coherent and cohesive?
- What is the value proposition?
- Is it viable?
- Is it valuable?
- It is ethical?

Is the Idea Coherent and Cohesive?

An idea is **coherent** and **cohesive** if it makes sense, if all the parts relate to one another. Here's a quick test — can you articulate the entire idea in a single sentence? If it takes much more than that to get your idea across, you probably don't have it clear in your own mind. The goal of asking if the idea is coherent and cohesive is to determine if this is a single, clear vision, or an ill-formed stew of half-thought-through concepts.

What is the Value Proposition?

While it is not necessary to have an entire business plan spring forth fully formed, like Athena from the head of Zeus, it is imperative that the new product offers something of value to its users and customers. Asking for the value proposition early on helps to focus everyone on the business imperative. If you are building software that no one will ever want to buy, simply because it is elegant or to exercise new technology, then either you've got the wrong product idea, or you're reading the wrong book.

Is it Viable?

There is a classic Dilbert cartoon in which marketing tells him they want a device with a 45" screen which fits in your wallet, acts as a communications satellite and a room freshener, cures deadly diseases while it whitens your teeth, is capable of time travel and has a telepathic user interface. He offers to write something that will make fish appear on your screen.

However valuable your idea may be, sooner or later, someone needs to take a hard look at it and figure out if it can be implemented in a reasonable amount of time for a reasonable amount of money.

It is the job of the visionary to keep his eye on the idea, and not to let go. It is the job of the business manager to figure out the value proposition and the business case. But it is *your* job, as the software architect, to help establish whether the idea proposed is technically viable.

Assuming the proposal clears these first hurdles, you are ready to begin the difficult process of turning an idea into a set of comprehensive requirements.

Is it Valuable?

If you've determined that you have a coherent idea which will be of value to your customers and which you can viably expect to build, it is time to figure out how you make money on it. If you are in the position of saying, "Well, we lose a dollar on every one, but we make it up in volume," then there is no point in going forward. It is amazing how many products are developed when no one has a clue how they will make a dime, even if the product is a success.

Look around at most of the web businesses. The vast majority are losing money. They have successful sites, they are selling ads, customers are showing up and they're hemorrhaging money. It is one thing to go broke because no one bought your product, it is quite another to go broke with a product everyone wants.

There are people who write software as an academic exercise, others write software because it is fun, still others because they can contribute to the betterment of society. All of these are fine motivations, but if you are writing *commercial* software, then you had better be pretty sure that your hot, new, viable, coherent, popular idea will turn a profit.

Is it Ethical?

Finally, you must make sure that what you are about to build is morally and legally OK. I can name a few 'coherent' ideas that have a high value proposition, will make you a bundle, and are certainly viable; their only problem is that they are unethical, illegal or both.

If your idea is legal, ethical, coherent, viable and will make you money in the commercial market, then congratulations! All you need do now is establish your product requirements, design your solution, implement it, test it, market it and sell it. Mere details.

The Goal

During the analysis phase, your goal is to achieve an understanding of the problem you are trying to solve. As part of this understanding, you'll want to explore how the system will be used, who will use it and which activities fall within the boundaries of the system (and which do not). You also want to identify the expectations and constraints imposed by your customer.

Investing Up Front

Most of us started our careers dividing up our time as follows:

- Think of a great idea: 1%
- Analysis (articulate the requirements): 4%
- Design (figure out how to build it): 5%
- Implementation: 90%
- Testing and bug fixes: the other 90%

We were building relatively small programs, we were eager to churn out code, and we were not rewarded for "wasting" a lot of time ruminating. The single greatest challenge in learning object-oriented analysis and design is *not* understanding the process, or memorizing the funny symbols used in the diagrams. It is accepting the necessary commitment to spend upwards of 50% of your time on analysis and design. In fact, on large projects, with a large team, working in a new domain, some architects devote fully 80% of the development schedule to analysis and design, with only 10% dedicated to implementation and another 10% to testing!

That is a lot of time. You had better be pretty sure it will be paid back before you make this commitment. And your customer will not be patient. What is worse, you will not see a concrete return on your investment until implementation, at the earliest. To make this even more of a challenge, the key benefits will be the absence of problems.

Most programs are never delivered. Those which are delivered are often plagued by bugs and those which are debugged are often impossible to maintain. A program which is robust and reliable, maintainable and extensible and which is delivered on time is therefore clearly a better program.

The problem is that the absence of problems is tough to sell. Imagine what you'd put on your shrink-wrapped box: "Not late, and with noticeably fewer bugs!"

If time to market is critical, and it always is, then spending four months of a nine-month project on analysis and design will make for a very jittery customer. We'll solve this in a number of ways: we'll involve the customer in the analysis, and we'll create a prototype early in the design so that we can prove our ideas and demonstrate tangible progress. More important, we'll *iterate* over the design and implementation so that there are frequent commercial releases. The bottom line, however, is that both you and the customer must believe in the process, because you'll be delaying gratification for a long time while you dig a sound foundation.

Getting Started

Let's assume that you are sold on the benefits of object-oriented analysis and design. You not only believe that you'll end up with code which is reliable, robust and extensible, you believe that you'll deliver the code on time and on budget, and that no other method will accomplish this for you. How do you get started?

It starts by setting aside objects and classes, inheritance, encapsulation and polymorphism. Set aside the compiler, the debugger and all the traditional tools of your craft. All of these will be used later, but for now we start with a clean piece of paper and a person with a vision. Someone came up with a great idea, and it is your job to help that person fully to articulate the details.

I'll call them the *visionary*, I'll call you the *architect*. How do you, the architect, help the visionary to get their idea down on paper, so that you can build it?

Do not underestimate how difficult and time consuming a process this can and will be. Getting the requirements straight is, in many ways, the most important aspect of your development work. Without clear requirements, you cannot possibly build the right thing. You will be in grave danger of your customer taking final delivery and saying, ruefully, "That is not what I asked for, and not at all what I wanted."

It will then be tempting to pull out the requirements and say, "But this *is* what you asked for. See, here's your signature." This is a losing proposition. Your customer may well agree that this is what he asked for, but if he isn't happy with the results, he isn't likely to call you again. What separates the great software developer from the merely competent is the ability to help the customer determine what it is he needs.

It is the goal of the **requirements analysis** phase to ensure that what you deliver is what the customer *really* has in mind. The good news is that he understands both his vision and his business. You, on the other hand, understand software. The goal of this phase is to build a common language. You need to become very smart about what he wants to do, and then you have to articulate your technological ideas into words which make sense in his business domain.

Who Participates?

Analysis is accomplished through a series of discussions. Each person in the discussion has a clearly understood role. These include:

- The visionary
- Domain experts
- UI designers
- Quality Assurance
- The architect

The Visionary

Again and again we return to the visionary. He is the single person who has a clear picture of what it is he wants to build. At least for the purposes of the analysis phase, this is the customer. He is the final arbiter of what the system should do and how it ought to behave.

The Domain Experts

While your customer may have a firm grip on what he wants to build, he may not know everything there is to know about every aspect of the way his business functions. He may want to bring in marketing expertise or representatives from other aspects of his business. These domain experts will participate in the analysis, providing "expert testimony" on how things currently work. When working with domain experts, it is important to distinguish between "how things work now" and "how they ought to work." You'll often find that many of your customers will have a very hard time imagining how different things might be. There is a tendency to describe the ideal system in terms of the existing system.

When the car was first invented, there was a clip under the dashboard for the buggy whip. The engineers and their customers must have realized that there was no longer a need for a buggy whip — there was no horse attached to the car — but old habits die hard. Throughout the analysis period it will be your job to challenge every assumption. Be particularly careful when the answer begins with, "Here's the way we've always done it."

The domain experts may prove rather cautious, even conservative in their estimates of what is possible and what is viable. They are the ones who must use and live with the new system, and they'll want to be very careful that long after you've been paid and sent on your merry way, they have a system which will work in every conceivable situation. If they've been in the industry for any length of time, they'll be wary of trying to do too much.

On the other hand, often they will surprise you with their creativity and inventiveness. They've been thinking about these problems for a long time, and their expertise will be invaluable in building the new product.

Many object-oriented mentors find that some domain experts become world-class analysts. Given a sufficient understanding of the process, and armed with the UML, they can bring their own understanding of the problem to fruition.

You have to be careful, though. Not everyone is as enthralled with the process as we are. After all, we believe in OO, we think it is cool. Sometimes we get carried away. We start by pushing diagrams at our customers, "Hey, look at this nifty model...." We are always surprised when their eyes roll and they start muttering about how they're late for an important meeting. If we're not careful, we soon find ourselves with shaved heads, wandering through strange airports thrusting object diagrams into the hands of unsuspecting strangers.

If your customer doesn't want to become an apprentice analyst, that's fine. Don't push him. He has plenty to think about focusing on his own business imperatives. And remember what Mark Twain said, "Don't try to teach a pig to sing. It probably can't be done, and it annoys the pig."

The UI Designers

User interface design is a special skill. Many developers fancy themselves UI experts, but you have only to see a site built by a gifted designer to see the difference. In a small team it may not be feasible to add a UI designer to the project — or at least not as a full-time participant. In this case, another participant, often the visionary himself, will fill this role.

Often it is tempting to try to add the UI at the end of the project, almost as an afterthought. While a solid architecture ought to be able to separate the UI from the internal "engine", slapping a user interface on at the end is a mistake. The user's interaction with the program is critical, and understanding that interaction from the very beginning forms the foundation of the requirements analysis we're performing in this chapter. Rather than waiting to bring in your UI expertise, you may want to involve them during the early requirements analysis phase, and then bring them back at the very end to tidy up the details.

Quality Assurance

It is imperative that someone is thinking about testing from the very first day of requirements analysis. Again, in a small team, this role may be fulfilled by another participant — often the architect. In a larger team, delegating this responsibility to a QA specialist, who participates in the project from the very first day, may well do more to ensure the overall quality of the product than any other decision you make.

The QA specialist is most active in the testing stage, of course, but QA plays a critical role in the requirements stage as well. After all, the requirements document will map directly to the testing plan — it is QA's job to ensure that what you require is what is delivered. Don't exclude the QA specialist from the design and implementation phases. While he may participate less in the discussions, having him in the room can ensure that he understands what he needs to know at testing time.

There is a school of thought that says that the QA specialist should be fully excluded. The reasoning is that they should know little about the internal design; instead, you hand them a requirements document and an executable and ask them to carry out testing, unencumbered by prior expectations. While this can be a very powerful form of testing, it is rarely sufficient for testing a large and complicated system. In the best of all worlds, you would do both kinds of testing: exhaustive testing designed from the outset, and user-acceptance testing by a second QA engineer.

The Architect

The architect is the person responsible for the overall structure and design of the system. In a smaller project, the architect may also serve the role of the analyst and the software designer; in larger projects, these roles may be filled by different people.

Organizations structure themselves differently, but I would argue that the architect should be the most senior and responsible person in the technical team. The architect becomes the owner of the technical vision, and his understanding of the overall system, coupled with his ability to design a model of the system, is critical to the success of the project.

As the architect, you have a number of responsibilities. During analysis, your primary job is to ensure that you fully understand the requirements and that the requirements are reasonably comprehensive. It is your job to keep an eye on the method, and to guide the process through the various stages. During analysis, it will be your job to help the domain experts articulate their needs, and, just as important, to help the developers stay focused on the requirements and not slip into premature design.

The architect will own the **architecture document**, which is a synthesis of the requirements analysis and design considerations of the project as a whole. To create this document, he must constantly distill the essence of every set of documents produced by the analysis and design teams.

In large teams, you may have a number of architects. The database architect may be responsible for the layout of tables, stored procedure calls and indexes, while the communications layer architect is responsible for the network topology, the transfer protocols and so on.

In a smaller team, the architect may not only be just one person, but may also be responsible for the totality of the analysis and design. That is, the very same person who is responsible for gathering all the requirements may also take on the responsibility of identifying and documenting the core requirements. In a *really* small team the architect, analyst, designer, implementer and tester may all be the same person — you.

The Architecture Document

The architecture document is designed to establish the overall structure of the entire project. It does this by describing various architectural *views*, including the use case view, the logical view, the process view, the deployment view and the implementation view.

> ◗ The **use case view** is a distillation of the package of use cases you develop during the initial requirements analysis — that's this chapter's work.

> ◗ The **logical view** describes the architecturally significant parts of the design, such as the sub-systems, components and modules. The logical view will also describe the principal classes once they are understood, along with their primary attributes and responsibilities. This is a topic for Chapter 3.

> ◗ The **process view** will describe the threads of execution expected in the implementation. This view will not be developed until late in the design phase. We'll look at this in Chapter 5.

▶ The **deployment view** describes the physical hardware configuration for the final system. Typically this is decided late in the process, but if the software is to run on a predetermined platform, much of this may be described very early in the requirements process as part of the systems analysis (see the second half of this chapter).

▶ The **implementation view** describes the architecturally significant portions of the code itself. It describes how the code is organized and the various layers of abstraction.

In addition to these various views, the architecture document also includes sections on:

▶ Systems analysis

▶ Applications analysis

▶ Operational constraints and restrictions

The architecture document evolves into a comprehensive overview of the technical requirements, assumptions, constraints, design and implementation of the system.

Don't fool yourself into believing that at the end of analysis you'll have a complete set of requirements. The reality is that the requirements will continue to evolve and to emerge as you progress through the entire process. This is why object-oriented analysis and design is called an iterative process: you will iterate over your requirements and improve your design as you learn more. The trick is to get a *good enough* set of requirements before moving on. Good enough to begin a meaningful design, but not so good that you get stuck in **analysis paralysis**.

> **Analysis Paralysis** *is persevering on the analysis to the exclusion of all else, in a vain attempt to get a perfect understanding of the requirements.*

About the Examples

Throughout the book we will look at two example projects and programs, and it will be helpful to focus on them in some detail. The first of these will be a large commercial hardware and software application, VideoMagix. I will use this project at various points in the book to demonstrate new concepts and ideas, although we'll not go into all the implementation details of this quite complex example.

VideoMagix will be a complete, integrated software suite for managing a video store. This will include both the traditional in-store software for managing client accounts and video inventory, as well as a web-based browsing system for reviewing movies in the store or on the Web. In addition, VideoMagix will connect to a central clearing house and distribution center for the stores, to purchase tapes at a discount. VideoMagix will also include a store-wide, a chain-wide or a system-wide database of movie reviews.

The second example, Phish, will be a far smaller 'toy' application, which we can use to get at the immediate implementation details. This example is shown as a case study at the end of the book. We'll use it to see how a project might play out from the initial vision, through the analysis and design stage and on to the delivery of working code. The source code for this project is available from the Wrox Press web site: **http://www.wrox.com**.

A Series of Models

Analysis and design consists of modeling the problem and the solution from different perspectives. Among the models we'll consider during the analysis phase will be:

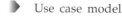

- Use case model
- Domain model
- User interface model

The **use case model** will describe how the system will be used. The **domain model** will extend the use case model to put the system into context, and will provide information about the business or activity in which the system will be used. Finally, the **user interface model** will describe how the users will interact with the system.

We will start with the use case model, as it will drive our understanding of the product and its requirements.

The Use Case Model

Use cases describe how the system will be used. In the last chapter, we said that a use case is a description of an interaction between the system we are building and a person or another system. Let's expand this definition to include the idea that the use case details a set of actions that the system performs to yield an observable result of value to the person. We call the person taking part in the interaction the **actor**.

An actor is a *role*. A given person can take on various roles when interacting with the system, but it is the role we are interested in, not the person who is playing that role. The use case focuses on the particular role of the moment. Just as people in a particular role may interact with the system, so may other systems. These other systems will fully expect the system under development to perform certain actions. We also call such external systems actors. For example, an automated teller machine may interact with customers and managers, but it may also interact with the Federal Reserve computer system. Customers, managers and the Federal Reserve computer system are all actors interacting with the ATM system.

Use cases are the cornerstone of your analysis. Creating a reasonably exhaustive set of use cases is the single best insurance you can buy to ensure that you are building the system the customer needs.

Use cases establish the set of capabilities of the system as a whole. Each use case is a set of actions. An action is something the system does, and each action should be **atomic** — either it is performed in its entirety or it is not performed at all.

What the Use Case does *not* Tell You

The use case says nothing about the internal working of the system. It is neither a design nor an implementation plan. To mangle Eldredge Cleaver, "It is not part of the solution, it is part of the problem." More accurately, it is the problem statement. The use case tells you how actors interact with the system and how the system responds.

Finding the Use Cases

You *cannot* build use cases without the active participation of your customer. Period. The customer understands how the system will be used. Trying to build a requirements analysis document without the active participation of the customer is like trying to take a picture with the lens cap on.

The role of the architect during use case analysis is information gathering. Your job is to interview the customer and guide him through the difficult process of articulating how his system will be used. The knowledge is in his head, your job is to help get it out and write it down.

The domain experts are another rich source of use cases. They have extensive experience in using and designing related products, and can help you understand in detail how their customers might interact with the system.

Developing the use cases is not particularly difficult; but ensuring that you have them all is murder. One immediate obstacle is that some aspects of how the system will be used are so "obvious" that it is easy to forget to articulate them. A second, more mundane problem is that, in the absence of a working prototype, it is hard to imagine every way in which you might interact with the system.

A number of years ago some of my colleagues at Citibank worked on the next generation of automated teller machines. While they probably didn't call them use cases, they did try to write down every way the system would be used. They discussed making deposits, transferring funds, getting cash and so forth. Among the domain experts who participated in the analysis were user interface and ergonomics experts, and so they paid a lot of attention to how the customer would interact with the system.

After a number of months work, they had a mock-up running on a desktop PC. The customer response was terrific. They went further into production and built a working prototype — a test ATM complete with an outer door, a waiting area and signage. They brought some customers into the lab, to watch them interact with the system. The first question from one of the customers was, "Where can I put my bag while I fill out this deposit slip?" Another customer transferred money from savings to checking but then couldn't figure out how to get back to the main menu to withdraw the money from checking.

It would have been hard to capture these interactions in the abstract, but once you see real people interact with the system, you can't miss them. The goal of the requirements analysis period is to try to think through all the ways in which the system will be used, but we allow for the fact that some of the requirements will emerge only once we have a working system with which to interact.

Use Case Issues

It isn't always easy to identify the customer when gathering use cases. For example, let's say you've been hired by a company to produce software to monitor the productivity of their office workers. The manager of the project is your customer, and he will give you your initial set of use cases. Understanding how the software will be used, however, requires that you also speak with the workers themselves. The problem, of course, is that they are not likely to be motivated to help you intrude upon their privacy and police their behavior.

Returning to the automated teller machine project, it was imperative that we understood in some detail what it is that tellers do, and what the interaction is like between the customer and the teller. The tellers, however, rightly understood that the ATM was a direct threat to their job security. They were not terribly motivated to help with our understanding of the problem.

The final end user of the ATM would not be the bank management, nor would it even be the teller. Our target audience was the bank's customer. However, early in the development of ATMs, few customers relished the idea of being shunted off to a machine when they were used to personal service.

How do you get the use case scenario when the potential customer doesn't see the benefit, and can't imagine the interaction?

Finding the Actors

The first step in finding use cases is to identify the actors who will interact with the system. These actors may be people or they may be other computer systems. In the video store, you may have the actors: customer, clerk, manager and owner. In a small shop, the clerk, manager and owner may all be the same person. In each role, this person will act differently, and will expect different responses from the system.

You often only have to think for a moment about how the system will be used, in order to find at least a few actors. To find more, ask your customer and the domain experts to identify who will perform the most obvious tasks. Who will perform the secondary tasks of maintenance and administration? Will the system interact with any other existing systems?

When you identify the actors, give them clear and easily differentiated names. Is there going to be confusion between the actor named manager and the actor named supervisor? Make sure you understand which set of responsibilities belong with each actor.

Capturing Domain Objects

You begin your domain model even as you start thinking through your use cases. The domain model consists of an entry for each actor and object in the problem domain. We'll return to the domain model in some detail later in this chapter, but for now, begin by making a simple entry in your domain model for each actor you identify. Shown here is the clerk class specification written into the Rational Rose CASE tool:

45

> *Note that an actor is a class with the **stereotype** of actor. A stereotype is an extension to the UML to provide additional information about an element. In this case, we are extending the idea of a class to include the idea of an actor.*

The collection of these classes (representing the actors and objects in the problem domain) together with their documentation will form the foundation of the domain analysis.

Recording the Use Cases

Once you have your first list of actors, you are ready to begin creating your preliminary list of use cases. All of the work is tentative at this point. As you progress, you will learn more about the domain, and this will feed back into your understanding both of the actors and the use cases. Be prepared to tinker with these lists as you progress.

Often, there are a number of "obvious" use cases, and the best way to get started is to let the customer name all he can think of. For each actor, determine what interactions or "results" they require of the system. Each of these constitutes a use case. Don't try to be overly precise about each use case just yet — simply write them down. There will be time for editing them later. Each use case should be written out as an English sentence or a short paragraph.

Let each actor describe a mental picture of those interactions and more use cases will fall out. There will probably be tremendous overlap in these use cases, and later we'll want to combine them and establish their interrelationships, but, for now, we just want to capture all the information. You can focus the customer by asking him to think about what *value* each actor will receive from the system. For each of these actors, you should consider:

> What tasks does the actor want the system to perform?
>
> What information must the actor provide to the system?
>
> Are there events the actor must tell the system about?
>
> Does the actor need to be informed when something happens?
>
> Does the actor help initialize or shut down the system?

To get a good feel for use cases, let's develop a few. Here are some use cases for VideoMagix:

> **Actor: The customer**
> *What tasks does the actor want the system to perform?*
> Find a movie to rent. Rent a tape, return a tape, reserve a tape
> *What information must the actor provide to the system?*
> Name, address, membership number, name of film
> *Are there events the actor must tell the system about?*
> Change of address
> *Does the actor need to be informed when something happens?*
> Reserved tape arrives ready to be rented
> *Does the actor help initialize or shut down the system?*
> No

Resulting use cases:

1. The customer joins and provides contact information including name, address, phone number, credit information, spouse and kids
2. The customer browses the system looking for a tape to rent
3. The customer comes to the store looking for a particular tape he hopes to rent
4. The customer rents a tape
5. The customer returns a tape
6. The customer reserves a tape for later viewing.
7. The customer is contacted when a reserved tape is ready

For now, these simple phrases are enough to capture the essence of the customer-system integration; we'll return shortly to provide more detail.

Actors and Interactions

At times, actors interact with one another. To the extent that this interaction is totally outside the system, there may be no reason to model these interactions. On the other hand, these interactions are often mediated by the system, or predicated on information retrieved by the system.

It is valuable to get a good idea of how the system is used, and what kinds of interactions occur in and around the system. Later, in design, you may find that some of the use cases are not relevant to implementing the system itself. That's fine, you'll have added to your overall understanding of how the system is used at very little cost, and you may, serendipitously, make a contribution to the customer's understanding of his business.

One Use Case or Two?

One of the first questions that novice analysts struggle with is when to divide one use case into two and when two should be aggregated together. For example, given the use cases "The customer browses the system looking for a tape to rent" and "The customer comes to the store looking for a particular tape he hopes to rent" — are these one use case or two?

The short answer is — *who cares?* These tools exist only to serve the team in understanding the problem, not to satisfy some academic requirement. If you think of these as two separate uses of the system, then model them separately; if you think of them as variants on a single use case, then fine, combine them.

I don't mean to suggest that getting it "wrong" won't have some price. If you build a system with ten thousand use cases, each differing in only a very small way, you'll have trouble keeping them straight. If you build a system with just one use case, and everything is a variant, you'll have lost some of the flexibility you might otherwise have obtained.

Relax. If you get it wrong, you'll fix it. It is more important to capture all the ways the system is used, than to tie yourself up in knots getting the method straight.

Here are some guidelines to help you differentiate between when to combine use cases, and when to split them apart. First, look for the value to the actor. Does the actor experience a significant difference in his goals and desires between these two use cases? To the customer, is there a difference between browsing the shelves looking for a tape to strike his fancy, and looking for a particular movie he already knows he wants? If so, then model these as two use cases.

47

A second reason to break one use case into two is mechanism. If the user must take different actions to follow one use case than the other, then it makes sense to split them up. Typically, if I know I want "Gone With The Wind" I will just go up to the clerk and ask for it. That is quite different from wandering the store looking for a film to rent. On the other hand, if we assume we'll have a kiosk, which will offer various ways to look at the entire store's collection, the mechanism may or may not be significantly different for these two use cases.

These are not rigid rules, and I'm sure you can find ambiguous cases that defy evaluation. That's okay, if they are too close to call then it probably doesn't matter. Flip a coin and move on. You can always come back to it later when you've learned more. The process is iterative; it is one of successive refinement.

> *I am on the Finance Committee in my town and we are spending a lot of time right now discussing the pending school budget. The school committee wants to build a new elementary school, and there is much discussion of what it will really cost, and what it will cost the town to maintain the old building if we don't build a new one. A member of the Board of Selectman, the governing body of our local town, told me he is uncomfortable estimating the costs until he has all the data neatly lined up. I respect that approach, it is one of purposeful and conservative deliberation. I offered him a different approach: successive approximation. Take a stab at the number and keep refining it until you run out of time. His way may be more exact, if he ever gets there. Mine provides a working model, which I can use even as I continue to improve it.*

Other Actors

We have found seven good use cases, but they only consider the customer. Now it is time to turn back to our list of actors. What about the manager of the store? He interacts with the system and his use cases are no doubt somewhat different from those of the customer. What about the clerk and the owner, do they use the system differently?

1   The clerk adds a new film to the system
2   It is time to order more films and the manager wants to know which films are popular so that he can get extra copies
3   The store orders ten new copies of a popular film and when they arrive, the clerk adds them to the system and then puts them on the shelf
4   The manager wants to know if he is making money

There is virtually no overlap between these use cases and those of the customer, but examining these may generate ideas which lead you to add to the customer's use case. For example, we have a use case *The clerk adds a new film to the system* This may cause you to add a use case *The customer wants to know what's new in the store.* Thinking about this may make you realize that as a manager you not only want to draw the customer to what is new, but also what is popular. Thus a new use case, *The manager updates the Top 10 list,* and of course, *The customer reviews the Top 10.*

Use Cases Based on Attributes

A good way to generate use cases is to look at the attributes of the things in your problem domain. Tapes have a name, a set of actors, a director, a release date, a rating, a review and so forth. Thinking about these briefly can generate a series of use cases. For example:

1 The customer wants to find every movie starring a particular actor
2 The customer wants to find a movie directed by the same director as the last film he rented
3 The manager wants to put together a list of all movies rated G

Each of these also implies additional use cases to manage these attributes. They must be added to the system, edited if they change and deleted when they become obsolete.

1 The clerk adds a new film to the system
2 The clerk removes an obsolete film from the system
3 The clerk updates information about a particular film

These use cases will in turn remind you of similar responsibilities for customers:

1 The clerk adds a customer to the system
2 The clerk removes a customer account from the system
3 The clerk updates a customer's account

You can readily imagine generating quite a few use cases based on manipulation of the attributes of various objects in the problem domain.

Adding to the Domain Model

This discussion of adding and removing films from the system may generate some discussion about the overloading of terms in the VideoMagix system. There are films — movies released by a studio. There are videos of these films (the video of *Gone with the Wind*, for example). Then there are tapes — the individual copies of the video. Each film or video has a title, as well. These terms are often used interchangeably and with some confusion.

As part of building the requirements, we'll want to define these terms and capture them in the domain model. The problem is that we must be careful to use these terms in a way which is unambiguous but which also is consistent with the way our domain experts use the term. Of course, different stores use them differently, and often ambiguously. Here are our working definitions:

We'll define:

▶ **Film** — The original film as released by the studio

▶ **TV Show** — The original TV version of a show

▶ **Video Title** — The collective name for all the tapes of a given film or TV show

▶ **Tape** — The individual copy that can be borrowed by a customer

We'll put these project-specific terms in the requirements analysis glossary.

Thus, the store may have many tapes of the same video title. If you have six copies of *Gone With the Wind* then the *title* the store carries is "Gone with the Wind", while there are six *tapes*, each with the same title. Title is in one sense an abstraction. You don't really have "Gone with the Wind", you have copies (or tapes) of the film of that name.

Is title the same as the name of the film? Clearly the terms are related, but in this context, the title is the abstract idea of the film, while the tapes are the individual copies. The *name* is yet another idea, the name of the tape is the name of the title, that is, it is the name of the film or TV show. Don't confuse the name (*Gone with the Wind*) with the title (the video tape version of the film) or confuse the title with the tape (the actual video of that title). You can't rent a title, but you can rent a tape. You can't rent a name, but every tape and every title has a name.

> *Clearly these ideas are closely intertwined, and they will make life very difficult. To make things even more confusing, object-oriented analysis talks about* actors — *people or systems that interact with the system you are building. Of course, videos have actors as well, and we'll have to be quite careful to keep these concepts distinct.*

Breaking Out the Detail

Once you have the fundamental use cases, it may be time to take a second look at each for hidden details. For example, we found:

1   The customer browses the system for a title to rent
2   The customer rents a tape
3   The customer returns a tape
4   The customer reserves a title for later viewing

The customer browses the system for a title to rent
We've already established that browsing the system for a tape to rent might mean looking for a particular title or just browsing. Are they checking particular areas of the store? How do they want to browse, by title (oops, by name) or are they looking for a particular genre? Or perhaps for a favorite actor or director?

The customer rents a tape
This particular use case hides a lot of detail. Is the customer already a member, and if so how did he become one? Is there a difference between paying cash or running an account? Can the customer get a discount based on a club or frequent renter program? Does he want to buy the tape rather than rent it?

The customer returns a tape
Is he on time or late? Is the tape broken?

These questions lead to a reordering of our use cases:

1   The customer browses the system to find a title he might like to rent
2   The customer searches for a particular title (based on name, actor etc.)
3   The customer reserves a title for check-out

```
4        The customer reviews his own borrowing history
5        The customer checks out a tape and pays for it
6        The customer checks out a tape using his club membership
7        The customer returns a tape on time
8        The customer returns a tape late
9        The customer returns a destroyed tape
10       The customer buys a tape
11       The customer wants to reserve a title which hasn't yet been released
12       The customer tries to reserve a title which isn't available
13       The customer loses a tape
14       The clerk adds a new customer to the system
15       The clerk modifies a customer's record
16       The customer joins a club
17       The customer quits a club
```

Aggregating Use Cases

Once you have a list of the use cases, it is time to aggregate the similar ones and break out various **versions**, **scenarios** and **variants**. For example, use cases 7, 8 and 9 can be consolidated into "Customer Returns A Tape" with variations depending on whether or not he is late, and the condition of the tape when returned. Most of the behavior in the use case is quite similar and it is easier to deal with half a dozen use cases, each of which has a number of variants, than to deal with dozens of individual use cases.

You could also argue that use case 13 ("customer loses a tape") is just a variant of "customer returns a tape", where the condition of the returned tape is "lost". The decision of whether these use cases belong together will best be decided by the domain experts. If they treat a damaged tape and a lost tape in very much the same way, then consolidating these use cases makes a lot of sense.

Name the Use Case

Once you settle on a preliminary list of use cases, give each use case a unique identifying name, and expand each use case enough to understand the preliminary details of what happens in that use case. For example, we have:

```
13       The customer loses a tape
```

We can name this *Loses a Tape* and expand it to say, "The customer comes to the store and reports he has lost a video tape he rented."

The use case description may need to be a few sentences to be clear, though some use cases amount to nothing more than their identifying names. Write enough so that when you return to it you will understand it without ambiguity.

Be sure to include information about the actor interacting with the system in each use case. In this case, we've identified the customer. Later, when we expand this use case, we may find it also involves the clerk and perhaps the manager. An expanded use case might read:

> **Loses a Tape**
> The **customer** reports to the **clerk** that he has lost a tape he rented. The clerk prints out the rental record and asks the customer to speak with the **manager,** who will arrange for the customer to pay a fee. The videotape will be updated to show it was lost, and the customer's records will be updated as well. The manager may also authorize purchase of a replacement tape.

Use Case Diagrams

While a textual description may be all you need to understand a single use case, drawing a diagram can help when you need to consider a body of use cases. Use cases can then be related to one another, and the set of use cases in which a particular actor participates can then readily be found.

We can represent the *Loses a Tape* use case in a diagram by drawing the actor (in this case the customer) as a stick figure and the use case itself as an oval:

Customer Loses A Tape

The line between them indicates that the actor communicates with, or is associated with, the use case. Use cases and actors communicate by sending messages to one another. Every actor that participates in a use case is connected by *one* line to that use case.

Diagram elements can have *adornments*.

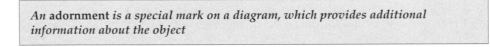

> *An **adornment** is a special mark on a diagram, which provides additional information about the object*

One type of adornment is called a **stereotype**. As discussed earlier, a stereotype extends the UML notation. The stereotype *actor* extends the UML class, and is marked with a different icon — the stick figure.

If you are using a Computer Aided Software Engineering (CASE) tool (such as Rational Rose) you can capture the text of the use case along with the diagram:

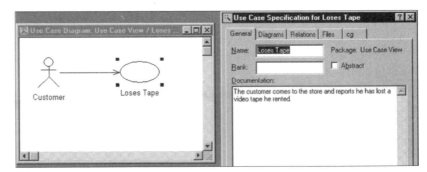

Use Case Relationships

As we build up our use cases we'll establish relationships *among the use cases*, which we can capture in our diagrams. For example, we may have a use case *Buy a Tape.*

The use case *Buy a Tape* may describe in some detail how the customer pays for the tape and how the tape is taken out of the database and delivered to the user. It may be that as part of the use case *Lose a Tape* the customer must pay for the tape. All of the steps in *Buy a Tape* are included in *Lose a Tape.* Rather than copying this use case in to be a part of *Lose A Tape* we can say that *Lose a Tape* «uses» *Buy a Tape.* When a use case «uses» an existing use case, the existing use case is fully incorporated into the «uses» use case. The symbols are guillemets («») although you can draw them by using two less than and two greater than symbols. We can represent the above situation like this:

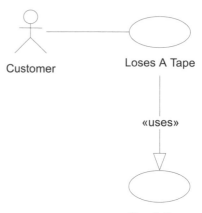

Uses and Extends

The «uses» stereotype built into the UML indicates that the *Loses a Tape* use case will always involve all the steps involved in *Buys a Tape.* The stereotype «uses» allows us to avoid retyping and redrawing the use case we are using. It is as if we copied *Buys a Tape* and pasted it into *Loses a Tape.*

Extends

There is a related stereotype, «extends», which can also be attached to a use case. The stereotype «extends» indicates a condition. Under certain conditions, you might follow a variant of how you manage *Loses a Tape.* For example, you might have *VIP Loses a Tape.* In the use case *VIP Loses a Tape*, the manager might decide that he doesn't have to pay for it after all, or that he gets a special discount. In this case, *VIP Loses a Tape* would 'extend' *Loses a Tape.* Not everyone gets this path, but if some special condition is met (very good customer), then you can use this extension of an existing use case.

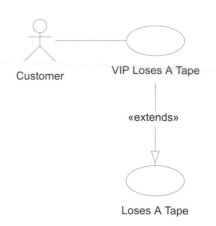

There is some controversy over the difference between «extends» and «uses», and you must be careful that you all mean the same thing. I was tempted to leave «extends» out of the book because of this confusion, but I find it offers an important and useful concept and so I've included it. Use it with caution.

Martin Fowler wrote one of the first popular books on the UML, *UML Distilled (Addison-Wesley, ISBN 0-201-32563-2)*, in which he suggests using «extends» when you are describing a variant of the normal behavior. That seems like a pretty good rule of thumb.

Abstract Use Cases

You can imagine that as you explore «uses» and «extends» relations, you will come across use cases which are never performed in their own right, but which encapsulate a set of steps useful to other use cases. For example, in VideoMagix it may often be useful to know where a tape is in the store, that is, on which shelf and in which section. It may not make sense for this ever to be a use case in itself, but many other use cases, such as *Rent a Particular Tape* or *Take a Tape out of Circulation* may want to «use» this use case.

In this situation we can create a use case, and fully document it, but mark it as *abstract*. This designation documents the fact that the abstract use case exists only in relation to others.

Scenarios

> *A use case scenario shows the flow of events in a particular instance of a use case*

A scenario should provide a specific series of events illustrating a "typical" instance of the use case. For example, we have the use case *Loses a Tape*. The scenario might read:

> The customer walks up to the central desk and tells the clerk he has lost the videotape he rented. The clerk looks up the record of the rental and prints out a document detailing which tape was lost. The clerk then asks the customer to speak with the manager. The clerk hands the manager the report on the tape and the manager asks the customer to pay a fee based on the age and original cost of the video. The customer pays the fee and his records are updated to show the resolution of the rental.

Notice that this scenario shows the most common case. Parenthetically, notice also that this scenario remains at the domain level. That is, it remains focused on the business problem rather than on the implementation of a solution. It does not detail how the clerk enters the customer information or how the tape is identified.

This detailed scenario uncovers a lot more information than the simple use case. You can delve into greater or lesser detail in your scenarios as required, to understand the flow of interactions. The goal is to understand this from the *domain* perspective. That is, again, the visionary should readily understand everything captured at this stage; we are documenting how the system will be *used*, not how it works.

This level of detail is not required for every use case, but understanding the flow of events in your key use cases can reveal relationships among the actors and objects in the system which might otherwise not be understood.

We differentiate between an instance of a use case, and the use case itself. An instance of a use case provides a scenario that may differ from other scenarios, based on particular choices and assumptions within the normal range of possibilities for that use case. For example, in one instance of the *Rent a Tape* use case the customer finds what he is looking for quickly. In another instance he does not. In one instance the tape is the last copy available; in another it is not. In one instance the title is new to the store, and available only for one day, in another instance he can keep it for three days. All of these are instances of the same use case. For each instance, a slightly different scenario can be drawn.

The architectural decision at this phase is to identify the most important use cases, those which are worth exploration in a set of scenarios. These scenarios may, if it is helpful, also consider exceptional circumstances. For example, once the flow of paying for a lost tape is understood, you may want to explore what happens if the customer has forgotten his wallet and isn't prepared to pay for the tape during this visit, or what happens if he disputes the manager's assessment of the value of the tape.

Formal Scenario Guidelines

If you will be capturing a lot of scenarios you may want to establish a set of guidelines for what each scenario ought to contain. Typically, every scenario would answer these questions:

> *How does the scenario begin?*
>> The customer enters the store and approaches the central desk.
> *What causes it to end?*
>> The customer and manager resolve payment.
> *What is the distinction between what the actors do and how the system responds?*
>> The clerk asks the system for rental information and the system prints out the rental history.
> *What feedback will the actor receive?*
>> The rental history prints.
> *Which activities may repeat, and what causes them to stop?*
>> The system works its way through the customer's entire rental history to evaluate the customer's value to the store.
> *Is there conditional branching in the flow of the scenario?*
>> If the customer is a very good patron of the store with a long history, and this is the first tape lost, and it is of little value, the manager may decide not to charge for the tape.

Note that answering these questions has added detail to the scenario. Consider noting exceptional conditions and behavior as *sub-flows* of the scenario. For example, if the manager asks the customer to pay for the tape, but the customer does not have money with him, it may be necessary to update the customer's records to indicate that he owes money on the lost tape.

Make Sure there is Always an Actor

A good rule to enforce is that every use case must have an identified actor. This enforces the guideline that the system should implement only functionality that users require, and nothing else. If no actor will receive value from a set of actions, then there is no reason to perform those actions.

The one *apparent* exception is a use case that runs forever (for example a use case detailing continuous background processing). Even here, while no actor may trigger the use case, except perhaps the sys-admin, certainly some actor must receive value from whatever work the use case provides, or there is no reason for the use case to exist. You can model the system as an actor, or you can add a "clock" object which models this behavior. You might even argue that the clock *is* an actor.

How many Use Cases might you expect

There are no hard and fast rules about exactly how many use cases are appropriate, but it is not surprising to find somewhere between ten and forty or even fifty use cases in the analysis stage. Much of this depends on how complex a system you are building. When we talk about actors interacting with the system, we mean system users in their various roles or other systems which interact with the system we're building. For example, the owner of a video store may interact with the system as a user, as a manager (setting prices) and as an owner (evaluating profit). These are three distinct roles. The more roles you can identify, the more use cases you'll find.

While you are working to find all the important use cases, it doesn't help to become obsessive about it. If the customer believes he has identified the principal interactions for the system from all of the significant actors, it is time to move on. The list is not written in stone, no doubt you'll revisit it, amending and extending it as the project matures.

Create Packages

As your use case model grows, you may find that you have an unmanageable number of use cases to keep straight. You can organize your use cases into **packages**.

> A package *is a set of related use cases, documentation and other packages*

You can package use cases together if they all interact with the same actor, or they establish «uses» relationships. You might package the essential use cases together and relegate the others to secondary or optional packages.

A package is like a folder of use cases and other packages. You can create a hierarchy of use case packages, with the topmost package designated as *top-level*. Each use case is like a document within these folders. In this case the document describes the actions, scenarios and actors involved in that use case.

Use case packages are shown in the diagram on the next page:

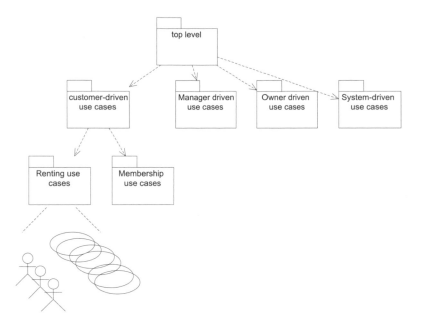

In a large project, the organizational structure of the use cases can help you keep track of the various requirements of the system. More important, these use cases will drive **iterations**, in which you will build versions of the software to satsify a subset of the use cases.

> *An* **iteration** *is a set of development activities leading to a release, either internal or to the customer.*

In order to decide which use cases will drive a particular iteration of the development, you must *prioritize* your use cases.

Prioritizing Use Cases

When the use cases are reasonably well understood and documented, it is time for the *customer* to prioritize them. This will help determine the development priorities of the system overall. Here again we see the need for a single visionary. Any two people will have different priorities; give this list of use cases to a committee and you'll end up with the United States Tax Code. Only a single individual can give you a coherent set of priorities.

Formal Description of the Use Case

You now have most of the tools to fully describe your use case. Each use case has a name and a brief description that documents the actors participating in the use case and the actions taking place therein. Many use cases provide a flow of events called a scenario. Some have multiple scenarios to explore various contingent activities.

Preconditions

A precondition describes constraints on the system before the use case can begin. For example, before the *Lost a Tape* use case can begin, the customer must already be a member of the system, and he must have rented a tape. The store must be open and the customer must be present. Which of these preconditions are actually modeled will be determined by the customer's understanding of the use case.

Typically the preconditions are observable states. These are not actions which initiate the use case, but are conditions which must exist prior to the onset of the use case scenario. A use case's preconditions should apply to all the scenarios, though each scenario may have its own detailed preconditions as well.

Postconditions

The postconditions describe the state of the system, and perhaps of the actors, after the use case is complete. These postconditions are true for *every* successful scenario, though individual scenarios can describe their own specialized postconditions as well.

> *The distinction of "successful scenario" lets me say that if the person changes his mind about renting the tape and thus cancels the rental, I consider that an unsuccessful rental, rather than a second use case. The postconditions are different within the same use case.*

Postconditions are powerful requirements tools, as they tell you the state of the system after the complete described use case. They can help in formulating a testing plan later in the development of the software.

Review the Use Case

Before you are done, take a look at the use case and make sure it is cleanly encapsulated. To achieve this, there are a number of checks you can make:

▶ Avoid mentioning any actors who don't participate in this particular use case

▶ Don't refer to other use cases. There are two exceptions:

    This use case «uses» or «extends» another

    Another use case is a precondition of this one

▶ If the order of events doesn't matter, write the use case carefully to avoid the appearance that order is important

▶ Be sure to indicate synchronization points if necessary

▶ Use simple vocabulary, and write short declarative sentences

▶ Ensure that you are using any special terms as defined in the requirements analysis glossary

Finalizing the Use Case

Interaction Diagrams

As part of exploring the use case, you may want to represent some of the interactions between the actors and the system in an **interaction diagram**. Interaction diagrams model how groups of objects interact with one another (hence the name).

Note that in use case interaction diagrams, the system is treated as a black box. We are not identifying or examining the objects within the system; rather we are looking at how actors interact with the system and how the system responds.

There are two flavors of interaction diagrams: **sequence diagrams** and **collaboration diagrams**. These are opposite sides of the same coin.

A sequence diagram can be drawn with a representation of each of the actors as a stick figure, and a single object representing the system (in this case VideoMagix). A vertical "life line" descends from each box, which represents the life of the actor or system over time. The arrows between lifelines indicate interactions among the actors and the system.

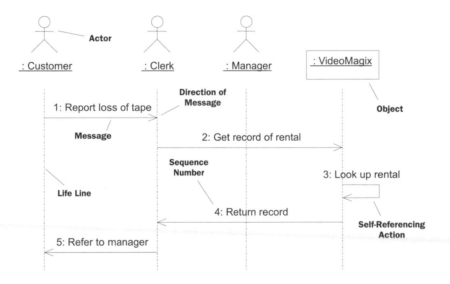

This diagram gives us a good picture of the interactions among the actors and between the actors and the system. Each action is tracked from its source to its target, with a very brief description. Internal activity, not broken out in the diagram is shown as self-referencing actions. The complete sequence diagram for the *Lost a Tape* scenario is overleaf.

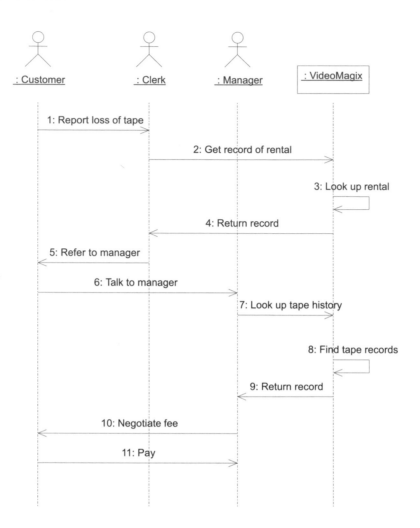

You can see that each event is ordered in time. If the interaction among the objects is of more interest than the sequence of events, you can generate a collaboration diagram. These diagrams are so intimately related that an automated tool should be able to generate one from the other. In fact, Rational Rose does exactly that.

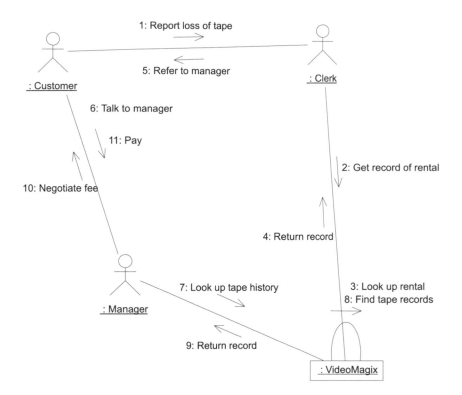

While the sequence of events is still marked, the emphasis is now on the relationship among the objects (in this case, the actors and the system). It isn't easy to follow the sequence, but it is easy to see that the manager and the clerk are getting information from the system and interacting directly with the customer. In more complex interactions, this can help identify which objects have associations with other objects.

Activity Diagrams

Interaction diagrams provide a dynamic view of the use case interactions, but they are limited in that they can only show one "thread" of activity at a time. Often, you will want to model how systems interact in parallel with one another. To do this, you turn to the activity diagram. Activity diagrams center on the activity symbol:

An activity is something that *happens*. Activities can occur in sequence or in parallel. The activity diagram is a powerful mechanism for showing activities in parallel and for demonstrating where synchronization must occur. The diagram typically has single start and end points, called **terminations**. There are any number of activity symbols connected by arrows. If progressing from one activity to another requires a condition, this is shown as a **guard** and is represented in the diagram by square brackets. Guards tell you what conditions must be met in order to continue down the path they mark.

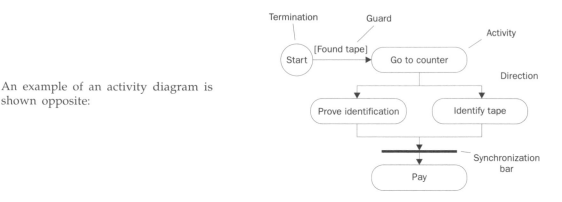

An example of an activity diagram is shown opposite:

The point of an activity diagram is to show parallel activities. When these activities must be synchronized, we draw a bold horizontal line called a **synchronization bar**. This activity begins with the condition that you've found a tape you want to rent. You walk up to the counter where you must provide identification and show the clerk which tape you want to rent, but it doesn't matter which you do first.

You must do both of these things before you pay for the tape, and the synchronization bar indicates that both activities must be completed before moving on.

To summarize, the strength of an activity diagram is showing parallel processes. Its weakness is that it can be hard to see a single line of interaction over time.

The Domain Model

We have been building a **domain model** from the very beginning of this chapter. We have carefully created objects which represent all the significant actors, objects and other entities in the problem domain. The domain model provides a context for the use cases. It documents the assumptions about the system that transcend the anticipated interactions with the system, and describes the underlying technologies, performance expectations and so forth.

It is time now to extend the domain model to include:

> Systems analysis
>
> Application analysis
>
> Domain analysis

Systems Analysis

Projects that include hardware and telecommunications will require that we extend the analysis to the systems as well as the software. In the case of VideoMagix, we'll need to understand what is required of the in-store kiosks. How do they connect to the central computer? Are they connected directly to the Internet? How will we manage communication with the distributors? Is there transaction processing to ensure data integrity?

This book will not endeavor to explore the **systems analysis** in all its detail, but in a commercial project this may well be a significant part of the effort. Automatic teller machines, point-of-sale terminals, pay at the pump stations, elevators, cars, planes and trains are all software delivery devices. Each of these has been standardized to some degree, but there is always an opportunity to revisit the underlying hardware and make improvements in efficiency, user interface or performance.

At Citibank, the team rejected the standard automatic teller machine models built by other companies and we set out to build our own. At the time, back in the late 1980s, there was significant resistance from the bank-going population; most teller machines were used regularly by fewer than 20% of the customers. It was our goal to increase Citibank's acceptance to over 80%.

They attacked this problem on two fronts — software and hardware. My involvement in this effort was at best peripheral, but I've talked at length with the principal designers and developers. They set out to analyze fully how the customer used automatic teller machines, where the inadequacies were and what was causing the resistance.

They discovered some interesting things. There was a lack of trust in the machinery. Most teller machines asked the customer to insert their card, which remained in the machine until the transaction was complete. Customers saw this as twice threatening. First, they were concerned that their card would never return, that it would be "eaten" or shredded by the machinery. They equated the card with money and did not want to give up control of the card. Second, they correctly saw this mechanism as an expression of a fundamental lack of trust — the system appeared to be saying, "I'll just hold this card as collateral until you are done." If the system didn't trust them, they certainly weren't going to trust the system. We made a simple change: rather than inserting your card (which was absorbed into the machine) we asked the customer to *dip* their card into a slot. For many people, this changed the entire interaction.

Customers found it difficult to align the buttons with the text. The screen was upright, and pressing the buttons caused their hands to obscure the text, especially if they were left handed. We moved the screen down and gave greater cues to alignment. In time, we eliminated the buttons and introduced touch screens.

Customers were concerned about privacy. Moving the screens down helped, but they were still worried. We polarized the glass to make it appear black as you walked up to it, flickering into view when you were within 12 inches. This led some customers to think that the system was broken, so we changed the design and polarized only that part of the screen which displayed account information.

Customers were unsure where to put down their bags, where to throw out the garbage, how to fill in deposit envelopes. System design extended beyond the screen and immediate hardware to the entire environment.

A huge problem with ATMs is system reliability. If the ATM is down even briefly, customers revert to using tellers, and it is hard to get them to try the ATM again. More important, a broken ATM undermines the customers' faith in the system, and if you have five ATMs that are all down, you send a powerful message of unreliability. Of course, if the problem is that you've lost your connection to the host, all the systems go down at once. This isn't a problem if you insist, as we did, that *every* ATM location, no matter how small, have at least two machines and at least two independent connections (separate dedicated lines) to the host. Thus, at worst, we lost only half our machines. Our reliability score, measured as at least one working ATM machine at a location, soared well above the industry average.

63

Paying attention to performance, security, user interface and reliability paid off. Citibank's acceptance rose to over 85%, and continues, as far as I know, well above industry average.

Application Analysis

Application analysis captures the customers' specific requirements, for his specific business. This may include hardware and software requirements, or idiosyncratic business needs. For example, the customer dictates that his system will run on Windows NT, or that it must be highly reliable, or that it must produce sixteen reports, then these are captured in the application analysis. If this particular customer has a unique requirement — for example, all video tapes must be eight digit numbers because that is what fits on the labels he bought — then that would also fall under application (rather than domain) analysis.

By comparison, domain analysis is the process of building the domain model, and understanding the actors and objects in the problem domain. The distinction between domain analysis and application analysis is this: one is general to the problem, the other is specific to this system built for this customer. Any software supporting a video store will need to model tapes and customers and rentals. Thus, these are in the domain analysis. A particular store may require a unique set of management reports — these would be captured in the application analysis.

Items captured in the application analysis are those which would have been decided in your design phase, had the customer not dictated a particular requirement. For example, how we identify the customer to the system is typically a design decision. If the customer pre-empts that decision by dictating a requirement, such as identifying the customer by his home phone number, that is recorded during the application analysis.

Implicit Requirements

There are certain system requirements which are never made explicit by the customer, but which are implicit in the requirements you do receive. For example, our analysis of the VideoMagix system may tell us that we need to keep track of the customer's tape rental history. This does not explicitly state that these records must be persistent, or that we need some mechanism for managing these records, but the requirement is implicit.

We *could* just ask him what he has borrowed, but that solution is sub-optimal in most towns. Similarly, we could keep the information in the computer's memory, and insist that the store never shut off the computer, but that solution has been demonstrated to be error-prone.

While the *mechanism* for persistence is a design-time decision, it is important to capture this and other implicit systems requirements during analysis.

Operational Constraints and Requirements

As part of the application analysis we will capture the operational constraints under which the system must operate. For example, if the customer has already invested in a particular operating system, the new project must run on that operating system, and this becomes an operational constraint. Designing a solution which is perfect in every way, except that it can't run on his computers, is considered less than optimal.

Among the issues which might be considered in your operational constraints document are:

- Who the target audience is
- Hardware, operating systems and portability
- Reliability and robustness
- Integrity, accuracy and precision
- Extensibility and maintainability

Who the Target Audience is

This is the single most important operational constraint. Understanding the target audience is critical to the analysis and design of a successful project. Watch out for hidden assumptions — these can be murderously difficult to change.

For example, if the customer for VideoMagix were to tell us that all of the clerks will be computer literate, we might design the system to be a bit more powerful, even if this might make it a bit harder to use for total novices. On the other hand, if the target audience is the general population, we must spend a lot of time and money making the system as easy to use as possible.

While a video store may well want to assume a low common denominator of expertise, the designer of a head's up display for an F14 fighter can make a different set of assumptions ("Hey! What does this button do? … Uh oh...").

Hardware, Operating Systems and Portability

Has the customer predetermined the hardware and operating systems for the new software? What assumptions can you make about the end user's environment? This can be very tricky. Today's high-speed technology will almost certainly be obsolete before you can complete even a reasonably trivial application. The pace of change is itself increasing.

> When we were designing the Interchange Online Network for Ziff Davis, most power users were operating with 2400 bps modems. We wanted to make the assumption that our users would have 9600 bps modems. At the time this was an audacious assumption (unless you assumed we'd slip a few years, in which case it was perfectly reasonable). Getting this right made a great deal of difference in how we'd design the user interface.

In the face of this uncertainty, it is tempting to avoid making any assumptions at all. The problem is that as you decrease your hardware and operating system assumptions, you *increase* the complexity and difficulty of implementing your system. An infinitely portable system is harder to write than one which is targeted at a particular platform.

The answer is to make reasonable guesses, but write your code with sufficient encapsulation, so that if you have to change some assumptions you don't break everything. It should be possible to plug in the new platform-dependent components as your assumptions change.

Reliability and Robustness

We defined two forms of reliability in the first chapter: not crashing unexpectedly, and needing little or no maintenance. Robustness is a related issue: it speaks about the ability of the program to tolerate unexpected events such as bizarre customer inputs, power outages, network failures and so forth.

Your customer will define his expectations of reliability and robustness, but you must help him understand the tradeoffs. Typically, the cost of reliability is not linear. It would be a simple decision if the graph looked something like this:

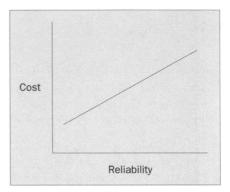

The more reliability you want, the greater the cost. Normally, however, the graph looks more like this:

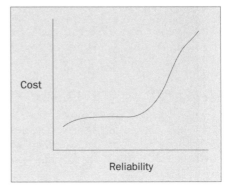

Your customer hopes you can help him find the *knee* — the point at which cost begins to rise dramatically for little additional reliability. Often the customer will choose to forgo the extra benefit in light of the additional cost.

This is all great in theory, but putting an accurate measure on reliability can be terribly difficult. It is especially difficult to do at analysis time. Often, you will fudge it, you'll identify the goal within broad parameters, and decide on the final numbers later in the development.

Accuracy, Integrity and Precision

Integrity measures how correct the data remains over time. A system with great integrity can be trusted to provide accurate and meaningful information. Accuracy is a measure of how correct the information is, whilst precision is related to the granularity of the information. Can you count on the information to be not only correct, but exactly so? If the actual time is 12:01:30 and the system says it is just after noon, then your program is accurate. If the system says it is 12:01:30:00 (and this is the actual time) then your system is also precise.

Your customer expects 100% data integrity. If the system fails in this measure, it must not do so silently. It is one thing to report that the data may be corrupted and that you must now go to your back up tapes, but, bad as this is, it is better than to sit fat, silent and happy in the corner while you mangle the customer's data. A system which appears to be working, but which gives broken data, is a lawsuit waiting to happen.

Accuracy and precision are decided by the requirements of the particular customer, his clients and his business proposition. If you are firing missiles, a circular error probability of a few feet may be considered excellent. If you are controlling lasers for ocular surgery, you may need to be a bit more accurate and precise.

Extensibility and Maintainability

Extensibility and maintainability are the American flag and mom's apple pie of programming — everyone is for them, but not everyone is willing to die for them. How extensible the program must be depends on what you're doing. If you are building a framework for applications development, then extensibility may be the raison d'être for your program, and thus you'll be willing to spend a lot of time ensuring that every module you build is highly reusable, extensible and well encapsulated. If you are writing a quick and dirty utility, you may well decide to forgo these considerations in exchange for faster time to market.

Even maintainability, that golden icon of all programming books, may be exchanged for immediate gratification, if the program you are writing is expected to have a very short shelf life.

Each of these issues must be considered in some detail and then the decisions must be documented in an Operational Constraints and Requirements document. This will become a critical part of the overall requirements documentation.

Cost and Planning Document

You're almost done with requirements analysis, but there is one more pesky issue you must attend to — the plan. Your customer will probably ask, "What's it going to cost, and how long is it going to take?"

Schedule

Building a schedule is terribly difficult, and enormously important. Perhaps the hardest part of managing a software project is projecting how long it will all take. This is especially difficult as you are often called on to make this estimate before you fully understand the requirements, let alone the design. Unfortunately, the only way to be 100% accurate is to wait until you are done.

Most of us have built up enough experience writing software to have a good sense of the magnitude of a project, but the larger the project, the less reliable our estimates tend to be. Back in the early 1980s, it was Philippe Kahn, president of Borland Software, who said, "Kahn's law: everything takes longer than you expect, even when you take into account Kahn's law."

I don't have a good answer for this problem except to suggest that you be brutally honest with your customer. Tell him what you do know and tell him what you don't yet know. Help him understand when you'll know more, and then update your estimates as you go.

Unfortunately, as you progress in your schedule two things will happen:

- Your early soft estimates will harden: since they've not been challenged, your customer will start to believe in them
- Your customer will become increasingly impatient — the last thing he wants to hear, three months in, is that you just slipped two months

Keep your customer involved. Let him experience the progress of each design and implementation iteration, and make sure he understands how your understanding of the problem is evolving. If the system is more complex than you originally estimated, make sure your customer's understanding is evolving in synch with your own.

Cost

Estimating costs should be a direct extension of estimating the schedule. You need x workers, for y days, making z dollars per day. Multiply it out and get the answer. And then quickly erase it, because the customer will have a coronary if you show him *that* number.

Estimates for the schedule and staff costs should be included in the Cost and Planning Document. This particular part of the document should probably be written in pencil. As you make progress you will learn more and continuously update the schedule and cost estimates. Do this as early as possible in the process; no one likes a nasty shock at the end.

Once you have an estimated schedule and a set of prioritized use cases, you are ready to think through your iterations. An iteration is a delivered set of code which satisfies a set of use cases. There are typically many iterations between the first twinkling of an idea and the final sign off of a completed project.

Milestones

Along the way towards each of your iterations you will want to identify milestones which mark the end of each phase of work.

I believe in hitting milestones. It is a simple notion: we'll do what we promise. To do this, you must be quite clear with your client; you can't possibly identify the *location* of any milestone beyond the one you're approaching, at least not with any precision. After I understand the problem, I can probably tell you what the milestones *are* for design and implementation, but I can't with any reliability tell you when we'll hit them. What I can make a good stab at is when I'll hit my *next* milestone.

Many companies now offer fixed-cost, fixed-duration contracts. This is terrific for the customer, as he can "box" his risk — he can know in advance how much money and time he is risking and can therefore budget for it and stop worrying about it. It is, however, enormously risky for the systems development organization: if they guess too high they may lose the contract, and if they guess too low they will be required to "eat" the difference.

The solution to this dilemma is not simple, but there is tremendous motivation to get it right. When you are bidding a fixed-cost fixed-duration contract you want to be exquisitely accurate, yet you have insufficient information. The way most organizations manage this dilemma is this: they promise a fixed cost and fixed duration only on the very first phase.

During the conceptualization, they come to an understanding of the project and are ready to quote a fixed price on the analysis. After analysis is complete they have a sufficient understanding to quote a price on design. In this way they manage their risk but at the cost of locking in requirements which are difficult (or at least expensive) to change later.

To make this work, you must ensure that the phases are short and that the entire cycle for a full product iteration (from a set of requirements through testing) is measured in months. Otherwise, you lock in a contract on a product that may be obsolete by the time you release it.

Domain Analysis

As we've seen, domain analysis is the process of building the domain model, and understanding the actors and objects in the problem domain. Domain analysis is not specific to the particular customer's hardware or software expectations; in fact it may not be specific to a particular customer. It is focused on the business imperatives and real-world interactions within a particular field of interest (for example, video stores in general).

Once you understand how the system will be used, it is important to understand and to model the system within the context of its domain. For the purposes of this book, we'll assume the domain is a business venture; though certainly software might be written for other domains, such as government, education, research and so forth.

The more you understand the software within the context of the domain, the more likely you are to get the priorities right. Therefore, your first object diagrams are created in terms of the real world, without regard to computer systems. These models should be understandable to the customer, and require little or no understanding of how computers or programming works. Sound familiar? These diagrams are driven by the same imperatives as your use cases.

Objects in the Domain

Each use case identifies, at the domain level, actors and the objects with which they interact. In the previous diagrams we treated the system monolithically, now it is time to break out the objects in the system itself.

In the case of VideoMagix, the objects in the domain include the customer, the tape, the store, the receipt we give the customer, the kiosks and the rental club.

At this stage, we want to model the significant aspects of these objects. What are their most important attributes and capabilities? We model these objects in an object diagram, but we stay at a high level of abstraction, again and again reminding ourselves that our concern is the object as perceived by the customer as an entity in the world.

First, let's take a look at some of the most important diagram elements:

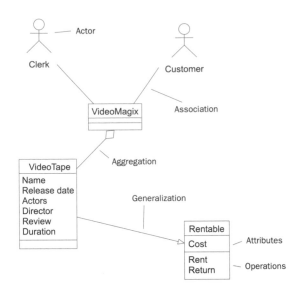

The boxes represent classes (the **VideoTape** class and the system itself). Note that in the analysis phase, the system itself is modeled as an entity. We are beginning to crack the surface of the VideoMagix class, but only later, in design, will we explode out all the component classes which make up this system.

To understand the diagram:

▶ The lines between the boxes represent relationships. Relationships *may* be named, though that is not required. In addition, the relationship may capture multiplicity — how many objects are in this relationship. Typically, this shows one to one, one to many; but it may show that zero or one objects can be in this relationship, or exactly one, etc.

▶ Plain lines indicate association.

▶ A line with a diamond indicates aggregation.

▶ Generalization is shown using an arrow head (a **VideoTape** is one type of thing which can be rented). The specialized class points to the more general class.

▶ The name of the class is in the top section of the object box, the attributes are shown in the middle section and the capabilities are shown in the bottom section.

▶ One special type of class is an actor, drawn as a stick-figure, just as it was in a use case diagram.

> *Appendix A contains a summary of the main features of the Unified Modeling Language.*

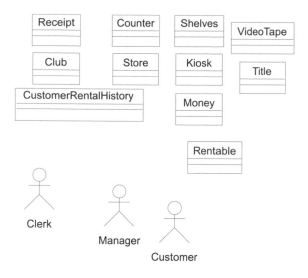

The preliminary domain model diagram shown above quickly captures some aspects we've determined about the system based on the use cases. We see that there are three actors — the Customer, the Manager and the Clerk. We know that we have video tapes and that they are some kind of **Rentable** item. We model the **VideoTape** separately from the **Rentable** concept as we expect there to be other rentable things. There is a difference between an individual video tape and a title — a movie or other recording of which the store might have many copies. I've captured this very preliminary understanding in the **Title** object.

A quick understanding of the domain indicates that there are other obvious objects which *may* be modeled in our design, including the rental club, the receipt, counter, shelves and kiosks, not to mention the store itself. I model money as an object for now as well, as every significant transaction will include money.

At this very preliminary stage, I've not tried to establish the relationships between these objects, though some relationships are so obvious it is almost painful to try to ignore them. To reduce this tension, I take another cut at the diagram, filling in only the most obvious relationships. While I'm at it, I'll take a stab at the most obvious characteristics and operations. Again, all of this is just to get started, this is not a final diagram by any stretch.

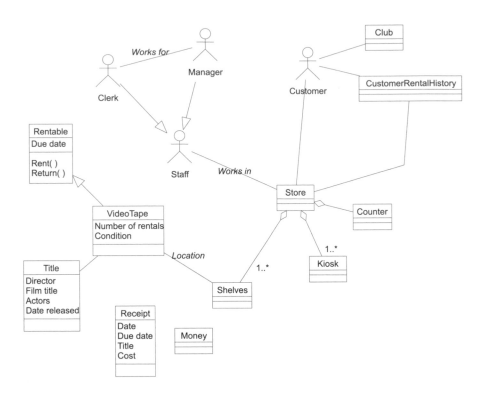

Even as a preliminary cut at the relationships, we've already established a lot of information. We show that the clerk and manager are staff and that the clerk works for the manager and works in the store. The customer belongs to a club and has a rental history (these exact relationships are not yet fully documented). The store has kiosks and it has shelves. There is a relationship between **Shelves** and **VideoTapes**, and **VideoTapes** have a relationship to the **Title** they represent. They are a kind of **Rentable**.

We've certainly not worked through all the details, but we've made a start. The relationships that we actually model in detail will depend a lot on our understanding of the domain, and on the part of the problem on which we want to focus. There is not much consistency in this diagram yet; we need to examine the types of relationships all around and the multiplicity of these relationships. We'll iterate over this diagram numerous times. Each attempt at filling in the details forces issues to be discussed that may have escaped close examination had we just written out the use cases and described the principal domain classes in text.

It is possible to overdo it — to try to model all the relationships. You don't have to show very much for the diagram to become uncomfortably crowded and complex:

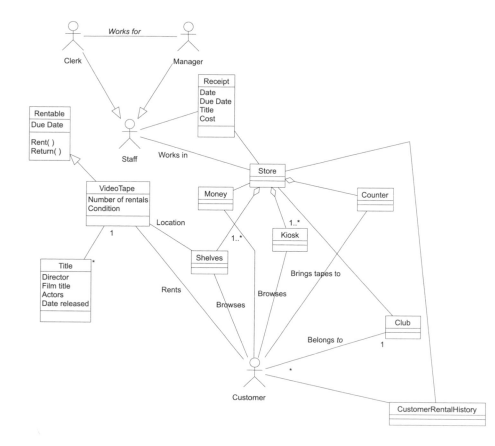

This diagram endeavors to show so many relationships and at such different levels of abstraction that it borders on being unreadable. The goal is not to show every possible relationship; it is to model meaningful relationships in a way that helps you understand the problem you're trying to solve. It is far more useful to break the diagram into smaller pieces and let each piece fully explore one aspect of the system. The totality of the pieces will then provide a model with manageable complexity.

The best way to manage this complexity is to take a step back and think about what you want to model. Do you want to model how the store is organized? This will let you look at store, counter, shelves, kiosk, video tapes and so forth. This would be a valuable model and will force you to think through some of the attributes of these items. Later, when we get to design, they may or may not appear in the design of your software, but that decision will be better informed once you understand the problem domain.

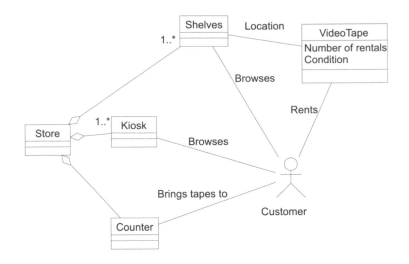

This simple diagram illustrates a number of relationships within the store. It highlights that there are two ways for the customer to browse: either using the kiosk or directly browsing the shelves. It suggests, perhaps incorrectly, that every video tape is on a shelf. The location of a video tape may prove to be a very powerful concept in this system, and we may want to model the location as an abstraction. Further analysis suggests that the important relation between customer and counter is not that he brings the tape to the counter, but rather that he checks the tape out *from* the counter. So we can alter the diagram:

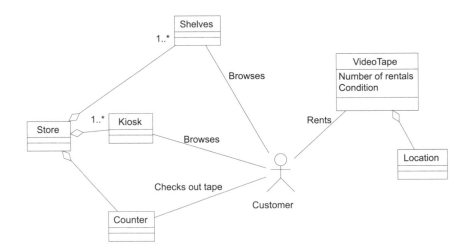

Examining the diagram helps force many issues to the fore. There is a feedback and reinforcement between our diagrams and our analysis of the problem. As we examine the diagram, new questions emerge, and, as we increase our understanding, we modify the diagram.

The User Interface Model

Most often, the customer will dictate, as part of his requirements, some guidelines on user interface. On large projects, the user interface (UI) will be designed by a team of UI specialists. On other projects, the UI will be created as you go. In either case, it is important to understand these requirements as soon as they are available. There are two fatal mistakes you might make with regard to the UI:

 Add the UI after the system is implemented

 Let developers design the UI

Software developers believe to their core that they can design great user interfaces. They can't. The design of a compelling user interface is the domain of graphic artists and experts in human factors, and few of us are able to keep up that level of expertise while staying afloat of the technical requirements of our craft. Leave the creation of the UI to the specialists. Your product will be better for it, and you'll keep their union happy.

If the UI team has provided a specification as part of the requirements, it is appropriate to fold that into your requirements documentation. Often, the user interface specification will be augmented by a visualization. This can take the form of story-boards, pictures, or if you are lucky, a working (if very limited) user interface prototype.

Visualization

A visualization is an example of the UI. Typically, this will be a set of screen shots, a collection of sketches, or other diagrams to help visualize what the project will look like when it is done. On larger projects, it can be very valuable to create a working model of the system in a prototyping language. This might be built in HTML, Visual Basic or another powerful scripting alternative. The prototype does not have to work, of course, it just has to look and perhaps behave like the real product.

Artifacts

When I provide mentoring to companies in this process, I'm often asked, "Okay, but what do we produce? Are there documents? How many, and in what format?" These documents, which are the product of the analysis and design, are referred to as **artifacts**.

> *An **artifact** is a product of the formal analysis and design of your product*

Artifacts can also be reports, diagrams, prototypes, web pages — the medium is less important than the message. The message is a concrete realization of your analysis work and then, later, of your design. Of course, the ultimate realization of your design is your code — artifacts are the things you produce along the way.

Every project should have a set of guidelines for producing artifacts. If your project is very small, these can be fairly informal, but each such set of guidelines should tell you:

▶ What will be produced (content, style and format)

▶ When to expect them

▶ Who will create them

▶ Who the intended audience is

In this book, I will build the artifacts guideline as we go along, indicating what must be contributed, how it will be used, who will create it and who will use it. The information outlined in the table below provides one reasonable set of guidelines, but you will need to tailor these expectations to your own project.

Artifact	Description	When produced	Created by	Audience	Attributes
Use case Report	A document detailing, in text, all of the use cases, with appropriate diagrams, pre- and post-conditions	At end of initial analysis	Use case Analyst	Customers - to validate your understanding of how the product will be used End users as part of focus groups and feedback Documentation writers Quality Assurance Testers The architects, designers and implementers to know what it is they must build	Use case name What package it belongs to (default == top) Description Scenario(s) if any Stereotypes, including abstract Preconditions Postconditions Related visualizations Related constraints
Use case Packages	A diagram indicating the relationship among the packages of use cases	At end of initial analysis	Use case Analyst	The architect - understand the organization of the use cases Quality Assurance	Package Name Description Set of use cases, including the actors, objects and relationships described Set of contained packages Relationships, including «uses», «extends» and generalization
Architecture Document	A document detailing a high level abstraction of the overall structure of the problem	As analysis progresses	Architect	Other architects Analysts and Designers Customer	Use case model Systems model Domain model Operational Constraints
Domain Analysis	Document and set of diagrams detailing the domain objects and their relationships	During analysis	Analysts	Architect Analysts Designers Customer	
Analysis Collaboration Diagrams	Collaboration diagrams describing interactions among entities in the problem domain	During analysis	Analyst	Architect Analysts Designers Customer	
Analysis Activity Diagrams	Activity diagrams describing synchronization of activities among objects in the problem domain	During analysis	Analyst	Architect Analysts Designers Customer	

Artifact	Description	When produced	Created by	Audience	Attributes
Systems Analysis	Report and diagrams describing low level and hardware systems on which the project will be built	During analysis	Architect	Architect Analysts Designers Customer	
Application Analysis Document	Report and diagrams describing customer's requirements specific to this particular project	During analysis	Architect	Architect	Analysts Designers Customer
Operational Constraints Report	Report describing performance characteristics and constraints imposed by this client	During analysis	Architect	Architect Analysts Designers Customer	
Cost and Planning Document	Report and Gantt and Pert charts indicating projected scheduling, milestones and costs	During analysis	Architect	Architect Analysts Designers Customer	Milestones Preliminary phases First guesses about costs Team structure and planning

Summary

We have examined the task of gathering requirements and analyzing the problem domain, the systems and the particular requirements and constraints for your new system. The result of this work is the creation both of the requirements documentation and the beginnings of an architecture document.

The next step is to realize the use cases in a design which details how we will build a system that provides the behavior described in the use cases. Design itself will be divided into two phases: class design and architectural design.

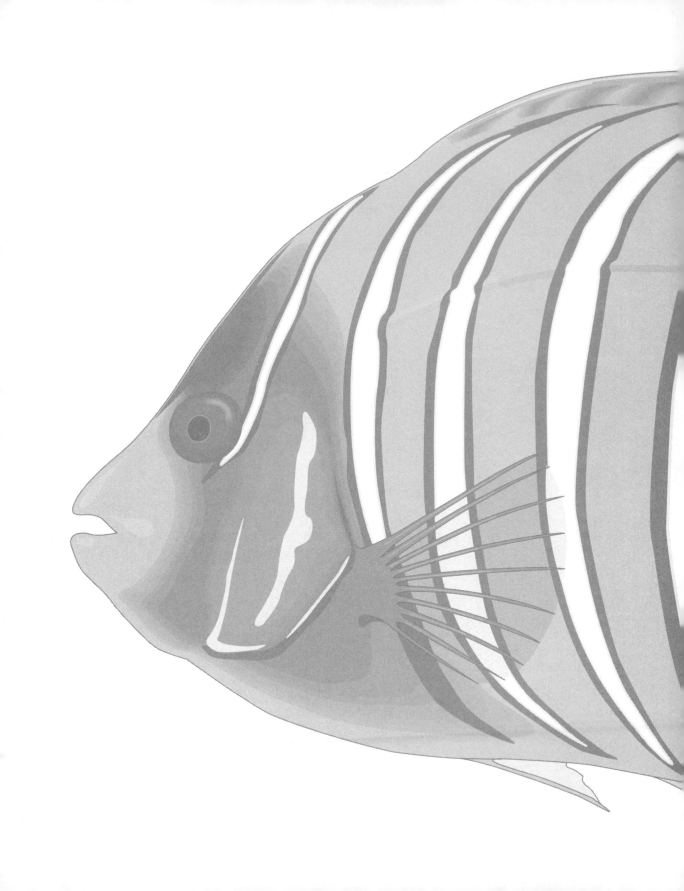

Class Design

We begin the class design by drawing on the analysis of the problem domain, which we covered in the last chapter. Throughout this chapter, we will undergo a steady evolution from an understanding of objects in the problem domain to building the **object model**; that is the design of the objects in the solution.

We'll use a number of techniques concurrently in out design, including:

- Class diagrams
- CRC cards
- Collaboration diagrams
- Sequence diagrams
- State transition diagrams

The Design Process

For each use case, we'll identify those objects which are needed, and we'll flesh out the functionality of the objects, based on the behavior dictated by the use case. We'll build at least one sequence diagram for every identified use case.

As we progress, we'll flesh out the design of the classes, filling in the operations, attributes and relationships, based on the information implicit in the use case. We'll model the changes in state of objects in state transition diagrams. In addition to considering the objects individually, we'll examine how they interact, and we'll model these interactions in collaboration diagrams. For interactions which have a specific order or which must be synchronized, we'll model the interactions in sequence diagrams. The sequence diagrams will contribute to our understanding of the functions each class requires, and as these member functions are identified, we'll update the sequence diagrams to reflect the method names.

The architecture document will track these changes, incorporating decisions about the implementation environment, including the language we'll use to program these classes, how we'll manage persistence, and so forth. The constraints and requirements identified in the analysis phase will be folded into the architectural design and documented in the logical, process and deployment views (which are described in the next chapter).

Once the classes have been identified and their attributes and methods detailed, we'll be ready to assemble the classes back into packages. These packages may be organized in a number of ways, depending on our design goals. For example, we may aggregate classes by visibility — higher level classes in one package and lower level classes, on which the higher level classes depend, in a second. Alternatively, we may want to aggregate classes based on how often they are likely to change, or which system (client or server) they run on, or even their level of abstraction.

The entire architecture rests on the **design patterns** we'll identify as we progress. The design patterns will provide an overarching architectural context for the classes and will help with structuring and ordering the packages and layers of the architecture.

What are Design Patterns?

One of the essential goals of object-oriented programming is to promote code reuse. When you reuse code you gain the benefits of building on the hard work of others. You know you are using well designed, highly robust and well tested code.

Along the way, a number of programmers and designers have noticed that many problems yield to similar designs. Wouldn't it be great if we could reuse these well-tested designs, just as we reuse well tested code? The design patterns movement is an attempt to name, codify and explore reusable design concepts.

Naming a design is critical. If I meet with another designer and say, "I think we'll make the application a *singleton* and use the *façade* pattern for the interface to the database," we have established a short hand that can save a lot of complicated explanation. Further, by naming the design, we can exchange information about our experiences with that design, and perhaps even improve it or derive modifications to it as we learn more.

Design patterns were first introduced to many of us in the book *Design Patterns — Elements of Reusable Object-Oriented Software* by Gamma, Helm, Johnson, Vlissides (Addison-Wesley, ISBN 0-201-63361-2). Because there were four authors, this became affectionately known as the *Gang Of Four* book, or GOF. You will often hear novice programmers saying "Who is Gof and what is this book he wrote?"

Rather than attempting to teach design patterns (which is done quite well in the *Design Patterns* book and its sequels), I will weave both design and analysis patterns into my discussion of class design. You can learn more about design patterns in the *Design Patterns* book, as well as in the *Patterns* column in *C++ Report*.

What is Design?

When we go through the process of requirements analysis, we focus on creating the use cases which identify how the product will be used. Along the way we identify the interactions and associations of objects in the problem domain.

In design, you turn your attention to the solution. You must ask yourself the following questions:

▶ What are the objects in the design?

▶ What are their attributes and capabilities?

▶ How will they interact?

Analysis objects are things in the real world (employees, companies, offices). Design objects, on the other hand, are logical constructs which may *map* to the objects in the real world, but which will find their existence only in code.

By the time design concludes, you will have made a number of technical decisions which were deferred during analysis. This will include decisions about which container classes you'll need to implement your collections, what the properties and methods of your objects are, what their parameters and return values of these methods will be, and so forth. You will have sketched out the public interface for all of your classes, and for some, you'll have uncovered many of the implementation details, such as which helper functions are needed, and which data variables will be used to capture state information.

Along the way, you will have built your inheritance hierarchy and have mapped use cases to object interactions. Every responsibility of the system will have been delegated to a specific object and the collaboration among objects will be fully understood. In short, you will have created the object model that that serves as the blueprint for your implementation.

Find the Classes

One of the stumbling blocks in object-oriented design, and not just for novices, is finding the principal classes. On the one hand, you would think that this would be easy. After all, you were thinking about the *things* in the domain from your first analysis of the problem. Yet many designers are plagued by a nagging insecurity that they have somehow found the "wrong" classes.

Many design books suggest examining your use cases and extracting the nouns as objects and the verbs as methods. This is a fine starting point, but not surprisingly, it is a bit too simplistic. I prefer to think in terms of **transformations**. There are any number of concepts and constraints in your analysis, which will be transformed into objects in your design. The first step is to transform the objects from the domain analysis into objects in the class design.

> **Transformation** *is the process of turning a real world domain abstraction into an object in the model.*

Transform Objects from the Domain Analysis

Just about every significant object in the domain analysis is a candidate for being transformed into one or more design objects. Some objects in the design could be surrogates for actors or abstract concepts in the domain. For example, the VideoMagix design might include objects for the video tapes, the title, the customer and the member club. You may recall the discussion from the last chapter about the separation of the concepts of the video title and the video tape itself. The title is an abstract idea with no corresponding concrete real-world entity. You could talk about all the video tapes of the title "Gone With the Wind", but you can't go down to your local video store and rent a video title — you always rent a tape — yet the title can well be an object in the design.

It is important to distinguish between the objects in the design and the entities in the real world that they represent. There is little likelihood of confusing Joe, your customer, with the instance of your customer object in your code, but we need a vocabulary which makes clear the distinction between the real world person and the software representation of that person. We therefore talk about the software object as being a **surrogate** or a **proxy** for the real world entity.

> **A surrogate (or proxy)** *is an object in the design which represents key aspects of a real world entity.*

A good starting point on finding the objects is to create surrogates for all the actors in the system. You also want surrogates for many of the real world objects in your domain, such as video tapes, the shelves, and so forth. Some of these classes from VideoMagix are shown below:

Note that the customer, manager and clerk are shown as rectangles rather than stickmen. This is because they are proxies — classes in the VideoMagix design representing the actors. The actors themselves exist only outside the system.

Views

If your requirements analysis has detailed a series of reports, you could consider representing each report or view of the data as a class. If you find that this will produce dozens or even hundreds of classes, you might want to aggregate similar views into a single class, and use member variables to manage the various aspects of the representation. Some example view classes from VideoMagix are shown below:

Interfaces

Another set of classes will represent the interfaces between various components of the system, especially the interfaces between classes you create and other systems with which you must interoperate.

An interface is the point at which one object (for example one of your classes) interacts with some other object (for example, a printer driver or a class from a library). It makes sense to delegate responsibility for managing these interactions to a dedicated class — an interface class. The interface classes will provide a layer of abstraction, which will protect your design from changes on either side of the interface.

For example, let's say you have an **Employee** class which must be able to print information about the employee. You don't want to have your **Employee** class knowing about how to print, so your first thought might be to have the **Employee** class interact directly with the printer driver. We can introduce an additional abstraction, however, by creating the **PrinterInterface** class. In this model, the **Employee** class talks to the **PrinterInterface** class, and the **PrinterInterface** class, in turn, talks to the printer driver. If you later change the printer driver, you simply need to change the interface, and the **Employee** class is not broken.

You will also want to create classes which manage the interface between any two objects representing data differently. For example, if your **Employee** objects will be stored in a database, and that database uses a different internal representation of dates and money than your **Employee** class, then you'll want to create an interface class. This interface class serves the same function as described above, to create a layer of indirection between the two classes (**Employee** and **Database**) and thus protects the **Employee** class from changes in the **Database** (and vice versa).

You'll want to pay special attention to interfaces that represent data transformations. If your data is modified as it moves into and out of another system, you should encapsulate these transformations in a class. For example, if you need to interact with a third-party inventory system, you'll want a class which represents the interface to that system. You may, however, want additional classes which represent the data transformations necessary to get your data into and out of that accounting system.

Once again, this protects your system from changes in the representation. If the other system changes its data representation schema, only the interface class will change; the rest of your classes will remain blissfully unaware.

Devices

Another rich set of classes that exist are those that are required to represent the various hardware devices with which your system must interact. VideoMagix will interact with a kiosk as well as with a bar code reader. Each of these devices should be represented in the design as a class. Other devices to consider are printers, cash registers and so forth.

Representing devices and interfaces as classes allows you to encapsulate their particular requirements. If you substitute other devices later you will not break all of your existing code.

Identify Operations

Once you have found the fundamental classes based on transforming your requirements, it is time to start looking at how the objects interact. Each interaction will imply an operation on a specific class. To understand these interactions, we will need to return to the use cases that we examined in the last chapter. For example, the VideoMagix system has the following use case:

> The customer walks up to the central desk and tells the clerk he has lost the video tape he rented. The clerk looks up the record of the rental and prints out a document detailing which tape was lost. The clerk then asks the customer to speak with the manager. The clerk hands the manager the report on the tape, and the manager asks the customer to pay a fee based on the age and original cost of the video. The customer pays the fee and his records are updated to show the resolution of the rental.

No doubt you've created classes for the customer, the clerk, the manager and the video tape. One of the first operations to fall out of this use case will be `PrintARentalDetail()`. This operation may be transformed into a method on your clerk class, or alternatively it may be a method on the video tape class. Or perhaps it should be a method of the manager class, as it is the manager who wants the information? How do you decide?

This question plagues all new object-oriented developers. There is no exact science, no cookbook with a set of rules to follow. The object-oriented design community has developed a set of guidelines which may help to guide you and to distinguish good designs from bad, but these are nothing more than "best practices". There are no absolute answers.

In Arthur J Riel's seminal work *Object-Oriented Design Heuristics*, a number of heuristics (or rules of thumb) are described for identifying a good design. These have been augmented by other collections of heuristics by other authors, all offering essentially the same overarching set of guidelines. The rules are not terribly complex, but there is no reason to keep reinventing them.

For example, when deciding where the `PrintARentalDetail()` method goes, we rely on a number of guidelines:

- Put the responsibility in the class with the most knowledge
- Spread knowledge horizontally throughout your design
- Ensure that your classes are cohesive
- Minimize coupling — reduce dependencies among classes
- Delegate wherever possible

Cohesive Classes

Each class should be responsible for one body of knowledge and behavior. A class in which all the attributes and operations relate to the same area of concern is said to be **cohesive**. Thus, the `VideoTape` class should know all about video tapes, but nothing about customers.

Spreading knowledge horizontally means that knowledge (information, behavior and so forth) is not centralized in one or two *manager* classes that know what has to be done; instead, knowledge is spread among all the participating classes, with each class specializing in one area of concern.

Taking the opposite of this approach would mean you had a very small number of smart classes and a large number of small dumb data-only classes. This latter perspective is the natural inclination of C++ programmers who have graduated from a procedural language like C. They are inclined to create small dumb data-only classes, which are similar to C style data structures, and a few global smart manager classes, which are essentially global functions in class clothing.

This design of a limited number of omniscient classes interacting with a rabble of worker classes undermines the delegation of responsibility essential to clean and robust object-oriented design. The rabble classes become deeply coupled to the manager classes, eroding encapsulation. When a manager class is redesigned, the effects ripple uncontrollably and destructively throughout your design. The manager classes tend to become large and unwieldy and it is difficult to reuse them or even to derive from them as they bring so much baggage and overhead.

If, instead, you distribute the knowledge among a number of equal classes, each of which is cohesive within its limited area of responsibility, then you can assign new operations to the class which has principal responsibility for that area of concern. Any other class that must accomplish a related task will then *delegate* to the class most responsible.

You see this all the time in human interactions. A company might have a Chief Financial Officer, a lawyer, a developer, a graphic artist and a marketing specialist. Each one has a narrow, cohesive set of responsibilities and expertise. The company as a whole encompasses a lot of expertise, but it is spread more or less evenly across the people involved. When you add a new responsibility, you assign it to the person with the most knowledge. If you were adding the responsibility of ensuring that we have not violated a copyright, you might assign it to the lawyer, who is most knowledgeable about the law. If the lawyer needs to determine which algorithm we used in a particular part of the project, he might delegate that responsibility to the developer, who, again, has the most knowledge in that particular area.

Now, let's take another look at the question of where to put the `PrintARentalDetail()` method. Following these rules, we do not want it in either the clerk or the manager class, as neither should know anything about the details of a tape rental. They ought both to delegate this responsibility to the class with the most knowledge of what has happened to the tape and which has, as its central responsibility, managing and tracking tapes. At first glance there are two viable candidates:

▶ The `VideoTape` class
▶ The `Customer` class

The `VideoTape` class is responsible for knowing what happens to this video tape and so will want to know who rented it. The `Customer` class is responsible for knowing what each customer has done in the past, and so will want to know what tapes he has rented.

An alternative is to create a `RentalHistory` class. The advantage of having a `RentalHistory` class is that it neatly separates concern for the rental history from other aspects of the video tape or the customer. Delegating responsibility to a neatly encapsulated `RentalHistory` class offers the advantage of decoupling it from the other two classes.

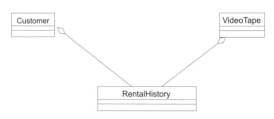

Notice that this diagram captures the aggregation relationship between **Customer** and **RentalHistory**. The **Customer** *has a* **RentalHistory**. In C++, a *has-a* relationship is created by making the **RentalHistory** object a member variable of **Customer**. The UML allows you to represent two different variants on *has-a* relationship: **composition** and **aggregation**. In aggregation the connection is a white diamond placed next to the aggregated class. An aggregation relationship between **Customer** and **RentalHistory** means that these classes may have different life-times. The **RentalHistory** may preceed or outlive the **Customer** object. As such, in C++ it is usually implemented as a reference or a pointer.

A black diamond represents composition, and is usually implemented using a member variable, although this is not strictly required. Composition implies that **RentalHistory**'s lifetime is controlled by **Customer**. You could solve this by having **Customer** create the **RentalHistory** — often by having **Customer**'s constructor create the **RentalHistory** and its destructor destroy the **RentalHistory**. This composition relationship is shown in the diagram below:

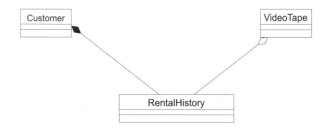

This begs the question of whether the **RentalHistory** of the **Customer** and the **RentalHistory** of the **VideoTape** are really the same class. There are three choices:

- They are totally independent classes
- They are the same class
- They are related classes

One would expect at least some relationship, as they have very similar responsibilities — keeping track of who rented what and when. They might have the same operations: adding, editing and updating events, such as video tape rentals, renewals and returns, but they may go about these things differently, given their different areas of responsibility. One approach is to imagine a generic operation of adding a rental history record, and specializing it for the two requirements. This is shown in the UML by an arrow with an open arrowhead, pointing toward the more general class, illustrated in the diagram opposite:

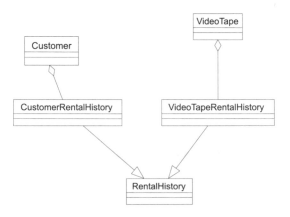

Model the Association

We hit a problem in the design stage of VideoMagix when we asked the question of who owns the **RentalHistory** and who will drive its creation. An alternative approach to this problem is to return to the domain model. We know that **Customer** and **VideoTape** have an association. The **Customer** rents the **VideoTape**, and this fact is indicated on the association:

```
              Rents
┌──────────┐         ┌──────────┐
│ Customer │─────────│ VideoTape│
├──────────┤         ├──────────┤
└──────────┘         └──────────┘
```

We can capture that association in a class **RentalAgreement**. The **RentalAgreement** is known as an **association class**, and it should know when the rental began and when the tape was returned.

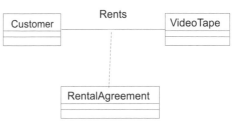

In this redesign, the **RentalAgreement** is part of the association. It is owned neither by the **VideoTape** nor by the **Customer**. What's more, this object is "active". It is the **RentalAgreement** that acts as a controlling class in this use case. The **RentalAgreement** brings together the **Customer** and the **VideoTape** to implement the rental association. When it is time to rent a tape, the **RentalAgreement** is created, and, in turn, it queries the **VideoTape** for its cost and the customer for his rental status. The **RentalAgreement** collaborates with the **VideoTape** and the **Customer** to generate a price and the other terms of the agreement, such as when the tape is due back.

The **RentalAgreement** is a persistent class, and we will implement the **RentalHistory** class just as a collection of **RentalAgreement**s. This allows the **Customer** and the **VideoTape** to be in a many to many relationship; it is possible for the same customer to rent a given tape more than one time, with a new rental agreement generated for each rental.

The **RentalAgreement** is a controller class, but it is not a *God* class. It does not treat the **VideoTape** as an entirely passive object; rather it relieves the **VideoTape** of responsibilities which are not in the **VideoTape**'s natural domain. The **RentalAgreement** encapsulates knowledge of what it takes for a **Customer** to rent a **VideoTape**.

CRC Cards

One way to get started with determining the responsibility and the fundamental associations of a class is by using a technique called **CRC cards**. CRC cards are simply index cards on which you write the name of each of your significant classes. CRC stands for Class-Responsibility-Collaboration, and these cards will track the responsibilities of each of your classes. You will also note the collaborators — the other classes to which each class delegates responsibility.

What are They?

CRC cards are about as low-tech as you can get. They are just 4x6" index cards that you can buy in any stationary store. They ought to be lined on one side, and blank on the other. Note that these are 4x6" — not 3x5". The smaller cards are often used for analysis, but experience dictates you need the extra room in design. But no more room than this. If you can't fit it onto a 4x6 inch card, it is time to question whether your class is doing too much.

Across the top you write the class name. You may want to indicate its derived classes and, perhaps more important, you should write its superclass — the class from which this class derives.

Divide the rest of the card in two. I divide the card unevenly, dedicating the left two thirds to responsibilities and the right third to collaborations.

Class: VideoTape Superclass: Rentable	
Responsibilities	*Collaborations*

On the back of the card you may write a short definition of the class. This should be a succinct and reasonably precise definition of the abstraction represented by the class.

CRC cards are not automated, and they should not be. The idea is to have a card you can pass around the room, hold up or tack on a board.

How are they used?

CRC cards represent classes, and they facilitate anthropomorphizing the class. That is, you can take on the role of the class, hold up the CRC card and say "I'm the **VideoTape** and I know how to check myself out." This is a powerful technique because it allows a group of designers to work together around a table quickly to explore any number of interactions among the classes.

It is easy to understand delegation. For example, the **VideoTape** class might say, "In order to check myself out, I need you," pointing to the **Receipt** class, "to print a receipt." This give and take among the classes becomes real, concrete and understandable, when humans interact in the appropriate roles.

CRC cards are an informal technique, to say the least. It is tempting to adapt the method to your own style and needs, but this can create problems. CRC cards are simple and straightforward — usually when you set out to improve the technique, you make it more complicated and less useful. I recommend using CRC cards as designed for a while, and resisting changes until you are fully comfortable with the techniques.

CRC Card Sessions

CRC cards are not used by a lone designer sitting at a computer. They are used by a design group, typically sitting around a large conference table. I've used them in virtual sessions conducted over the phone, but that is significantly less gratifying.

The hardest part about using CRC cards is picking the right folks to work with. The quality of a CRC card session will be determined not by the care with which you fill out the cards, but rather by the experience, intelligence and attentiveness of the group of folks with whom you interact. The ideal group is three to five participants. Below three, it is harder to get a lively conversation, and the number of classes becomes too large for the group to manage. Above five or six, the number of interactions between people becomes too complex, and there is a tendency to decompose into smaller groups. Side conversations begin and the group splinters.

Who Participates?

The ideal session consists of the chief architect, one or two other experienced object-oriented designers, and one or two domain experts. If you use CRC cards during the earlier phase of analysis, you may want a few more domain experts. If you are restricting your use of CRC cards to the design phase, you'll want fewer domain experts, but make sure at least one is in the room — preferably the visionary.

One person to keep out of the room is the manager. In an ideal environment, where a manager has the total trust of his staff and is more of a development lead, it may be appropriate for the manager to participate. In most companies, however, having a manager in the room immediately transforms the session into a dangerous and competitive arena, significantly undermining the work before it even begins.

Your role as architect is to facilitate the session. In some companies, they bring in an outside facilitator, so that the designers can concentrate on the problem at hand and not worry about the process. The job of the facilitator is, first and foremost, to stimulate conversation and thought. The facilitator wants to challenge assumptions, encourage ideas and to ask provocative questions about the design.

Successful Sessions

Running a good CRC session is pretty straightforward. Before the seesion begins, make sure everyone is familiar with the work done so far. Also, be sure that everyone who will participate is pretty clear about the process. A terrific resource is the book *Using CRC Cards* by Nancy M Wilkinson (Sigs, ISBN 1-884842-07-0).

In order to run a successful session you should:

- Set the agenda for which part of the design you want to talk about
- Don't try to tackle too much in one session — it is better to go deep than broad
- Structure your sessions around the use cases — begin with a single package of use cases, or even just one or two individual use cases
- Identify the principal actors and objects and create CRC cards
- Distribute the CRC cards among the participants — each person is responsible for a small group of cards, and it is his job to keep the cards up to date and to act in that class's persona

In a great CRC session, there is a rapid exchange of ideas among the participants. Cards are being created, debated, exchanged, edited and tossed about. Be careful about tearing up the cards — if you think a class is "dead", then set it aside. It helps to have a shoebox, into which you can toss dead classes. You'll be surprised how often they come back to life, as your requirements and understanding evolve.

Getting Started

If you have not fleshed out your use case scenario (or flow of events), then now is the time to do so. The scenario will drive the CRC session, and should be as specific as possible. To get started, let's track a CRC session for VideoMagix.

We gather the visionary, a domain expert who knows all about video store operations, the chief architect and two object-oriented programmers in a room, around a large conference table. The participants are:

▶ Vincent — the visionary

▶ Dominic — the domain expert

▶ Jesse — the chief architect

▶ Patti — a programmer

▶ Paul — another programmer

In front of us is a stack of blank, lined 4x6" index cards. Each person has a box of pens. There is a shoebox marked "Morgue" and a large bulletin board with dozens of push-pins.

I begin by choosing a use case for us to consider: *Rent A Tape*:

> The customer indicates he wishes to rent a tape and brings the tape to the desk. The clerk enters the video tape number into the system. He may do so by hand or by using an optical device, such as light pen. For each tape, the system finds the record and displays the title, so that the clerk can confirm he has entered the right information.
>
> The clerk asks the customer for his membership number (or phone number or membership card) and enters it into the system. The customer's record is brought up and the clerk can check to see if there are tapes outstanding or other credit problems.
>
> The clerk clicks on "total" and the system displays the appropriate information, such as the cost and the date the tape is due back in the store. If the customer belongs to a club and is eligible for a free rental, then the system indicates this information and the customer may choose to take this as a free rental or not. If money is due, the customer pays and the clerk enters the payment into the system.

How does the scenario begin?	The customer brings a tape to the desk.
What causes it to end?	The tape is rented, the customer leaves the store.
What feedback will the actor receive?	Either the record is displayed or a receipt is printed.
Repeated activities?	If the customer rents more than one tape, the entry of the tape information into the system is repeated for each tape. This ends when the last tape has been entered and the clerk indicates that the rental is complete.
Conditional branching?	The customer may be eligible for free rentals, may have outstanding rentals which need to be resolved or may decide not to rent a tape after all (due to cost or other constraints).

We examine the set of classes discovered so far and decide to start by creating CRC cards for **VideoTape**, **Customer**, **Club**, **Store**, **Money**, **Receipt**, **LightPen**, **CashRegister**. Some examples of these CRC cards are shown below:

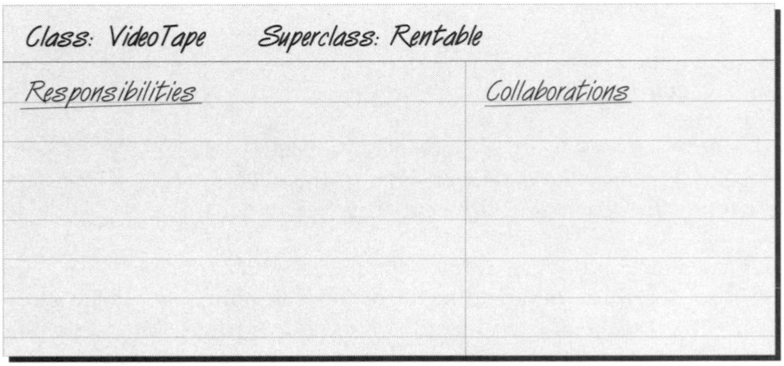

Class: VideoTape	*Superclass: Rentable*
Responsibilities	*Collaborations*

Class: Customer	
Responsibilities	*Collaborations*

```
Class: Club

Responsibilities                    Collaborations

```

Once we have the cards, we assign them to various participants. There is no particular logic to these assignments; in fact, is should be pretty much at random. Some CRC experts say you should distribute the classes to the domain expert who knows the most about how they will work, but I resist this suggestion, as it often ends up that one or two people get 90% of the cards. It is better to have an even distribution, even at the cost of some card "owners" not knowing very much about what is expected of their classes. The domain experts will still be in the room and they can help to sort out these issues.

While we did note the generalization (superclass/subclass) relationship on some of the cards, it is not important to establish these relationships in the CRC session. If they are obvious, you may want to capture these relationships, but it is fine to set this issue aside for now.

The CRC cards are not good at capturing complex relationships; we'll use the UML diagrams for that. We'll use the CRC cards for focusing in on responsibilities — which class owns what set of operations. To get us started, we return to the *Customer Rents A Tape* use case, which begins when the customer hands a tape to the clerk. There is no card needed for this, as it will be done outside the system, by the human actors. You do not need to model responsibilities that are outside the system.

The use case continues:

> The clerk enters the video tape number into the system. He may do so by hand or by using an optical device, such as light pen.

Patti holds up the **LightPen** card and says, "I provide data entry, entering the tape number."

Paul holds up the **CashRegister** card and says, "I bring up the video tape and display it on the screen. I'll need the video tape's help to give me information about things like the title, actors and release date."

At this point we run into a common design issue. If the **CashRegister** is responsible for displaying the information about the **VideoTape**, it will use the **VideoTape** as a dumb object which contains nothing but data. In such a design, we might see classes like this:

SmartCashRegister		DumbVideoTape
		GetTitle
DisplayTapeInfo ( )		GetActorsList
		GetDirectors
		GetProducer
		GetReleaseDate

The argument in favor of this design is that it separates the data from its display, making the data reusable. The argument against it is that it violates encapsulation and produces a controlling class (which has all the intelligence) with a dumb repository class.

The relationship here is between an all-knowing class filled with methods and a dumb-class filled with data, and while this is not necessarily wrong, it should be seen as a warning flag. You see this approach quite often from programmers who haven't quite made the leap from C to C++ — they are still thinking in terms of global controlling functions and data structures to be manipulated. Be careful that this isn't just a thin object layer wrapped around a procedural approach.

If we modify this design to allow the **VideoTape** object to display itself, then we get a cleaner encapsulation, but at the cost of losing the separation of the view from the data. It becomes harder to provide multiple views on the same object.

CashRegister	Displays	VideoTape
DisplayVideoTape ( )		DisplayAttributes( )

Also, we are asking the **VideoTape** to do something which is beyond its responsibility in the real world. Further, if **VideoTape**s know how to display themselves, will they also know how to be rented? To be bought? We are in danger of asking this class to know entirely too much.

Paul argues that the **VideoTape** should be responsible for its own display as it knows what information is required. Patti counters that only the cash register can know what information to display and where to put it. I point out that each class has a specific set of knowledge and shouldn't be overly dependent on the other class's expertise.

One choice is to couple these classes tightly. The **CashRegister** can ask for the specific information it needs and then display it, but this coupling breaks encapsulation and makes the system harder to manage. On the other hand, the **VideoTape** can display itself, but this suffers from the same problem: the **VideoTape** knows too much about the display device.

As an alternative, the **CashRegister** can negotiate with the **VideoTape**, saying, "Here's a rectangle, display yourself here." While this has a lot of appeal, it isn't clear that the **VideoTape** will know what information to supply. Is there a standard way for a **VideoTape** to display itself? Isn't it the **CashRegister** that knows what information it needs and can display it in neat columns?

The answer to dilemmas like this is, to focus on what each object should know and how that object will be used, that is, what its responsibilities are. If the **CashRegister** is never going to display anything but **VideoTapes** then fine, it can have that knowledge. If, as is the case, it is going to display a lot of things — **VideoTapes**, **RentalRecords**, **CustomerRecords** and so forth — then it should know *what* it wants to display, but none of the details of *how* to display it. If **VideoTape** will do nothing but be displayed in a **CashRegister**, then it can know how to display itself. However, its *primary* responsibilty is to know all the details of that particular tape, for example its rental history, and it must work with another class to handle display details.

The **CashRegister** can be expected to know what it wants to display, but not how to display it. For that, we need a class which specializes in display issues. Each object should have a narrow set of responsibilities, and the **CashRegister** should delegate to the **CashRegisterDisplay** class all the responsibility for *how* to display the information about the **VideoTape**.

The **CashRegisterDisplay** (CRD) is one of many types of display devices. Each display device will need to know what information to ask for from the item. In this case, the CRD must know what to ask for from the **VideoTape**. We'll encapsulate that information in a description class — **VideoTapeDescription**. This decouples the knowledge of how to *describe* an object from the object itself, thus maintaining encapsulation.

Thus, at a minimum you have four classes:

- **CashRegister**
- **CashRegisterDisplay**
- **VideoTape**
- **VideoTapeDescription**

What is the relationship between **VideoTape** and **VideoTapeDescription**? While it is premature to decide at this point, there are two good alternatives: association and specialization.

In C++, we implement specialization using inheritance. In this case, we would probably use a **mix-in**. **VideoTape** would derive from (for example) **Rentable** and multiply-inherit from **Description**. **Description** would be a mix-in — an abstract data type, which provides only methods, no data. Mix-ins are also called **capability classes**, because they are typically used to add a capability to a class (in this case, the ability to be described).

The problem with using a mix-in is that we anticipate wanting the **VideoTape** to also mix in the ability to be rented, to be bought and to be put on a shelf. If we use multiple inheritance, we will end up creating a very large class with many base classes.

So, how about using association for the relationship between **VideoTape** and **VideoTapeDescription**? Implementing association can be accomplished by using a pointer. For example, the **VideoTape** object might have a pointer to a **VideoTapeDescritption** object:

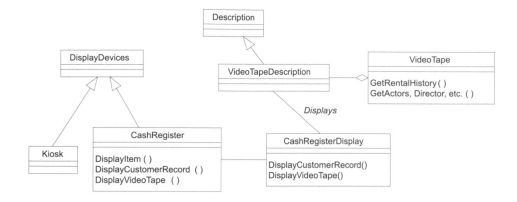

If the information about a **VideoTape** must be displayed by an HTML browser and also by a Window's application (and perhaps also on a Mac or Unix system) then the **CashRegisterDisplay** becomes somewhat more complicated. In this case you must separate display considerations from internal data representation, and the CRD will need a bit of help to be platform independent. You'll want to consider using the Abstract Factory design pattern (*Design Patterns*, Gamma et al) to solve this problem.

Separating Data from View

It is, in general, a good design rule to separate data from views of that data. This allows you to create multiple views of the same information, and to change the internal representation of that data without having to change the view. This decoupling of data from its representation is part of a larger goal of minimizing the dependencies among all the principal classes.

In the design we've evolved, the **VideoTape** is the *model* of the data (what Microsoft calls the document) and the **CashRegisterDisplay** is the *view* of the data. In the Model/View/ Controller (MVC) design pattern (*Design Patterns* again), you would want to separate the object which views the model from that which controls it. In this case, the **CashRegister** object might serve as the controller.

The MVC pattern provides a mechanism for you to separate your data (model) from views of that model as well as from those objects that interact with the data (controllers). The motivation is that you may want to provide multiple views of the same data. For example, given data about the local school budget, you may want to view that information in a spreadsheet or in a graph. Further, the objects responsible for manipulating that data (entering it and updating it) may be quite different from either the spreadsheet or the graph, or may be common to both.

Microsoft's variant on the MVC design pattern is the somewhat simpler Document/View pattern. In Microsoft's approach, the data (document) is still separated from the view, but the view and the controller are merged. Document/View is so intrinsic to the Microsoft Foundation Classes (MFC) that it is sometimes a challenge to write programs which ignore this pattern.

It is important to note that in both of these patterns, the *Model* or *Document* is any data your program uses. Documents need not be word processing documents — they can be collections of records, tables or amorphous data structures.

Class: *VideoTape*   Superclass: *Rentable*

Responsibilities	Collaborations
Know Title, Actors, Producers etc.	
Provide rental history information	RentalRecords
Know ShelfLocation and Categories	

Class: *CashRegister*   Superclass:

Responsibilities	Collaborations
Display VideoTape	CashRegisterDisplay
Display SalesRecord	SalesRecord

Class: *CashRegisterDisplay*   SuperClass:

Responsibilities	Collaborations
Manage display details for the	CashRegister,
cash register	VideoTape

Agents

At the OOPSLA '87 conference, Meiler Page-Jones posted this question:

> On an object-oriented farm there is an object-oriented cow with some object-oriented milk. Should the object-oriented cow send the object-oriented milk the un-cow yourself message, or should the object-oriented milk send the object-oriented cow the un-milk yourself message?

The answer to this puzzle is to create a **Farmer** class, who milks the cow. This corresponds to reality and simplifies the design. The farmer is an example of an **agent class**.

> *An* **agent** *is a class that mediates between two existing classes to accomplish particular goals, which are not the responsibility of either class, but which requires the participation of both.*

Properly used, agent classes can *decouple* classes which might otherwise know more than they should about each other's details. In the design we're evolving, the **CashRegisterDisplay** functions as an agent, mediating between the **VideoTape** and the **CashRegister**.

Agent classes can solve many design problems, but there is a tendency among novice designers to overdo it. An agent class which does nothing but pass messages between two other classes, adding nothing to the interaction, is redundant and should be eliminated. These "middle management" classes add overhead, without contributing any extra value.

Continuing the CRC Session

Once the display issue is settled, we continue the CRC cards, returning again to the *Rent A Tape* use case:

> The clerk asks the customer for his membership number (or phone number or membership card) and enters it into the system. The customer's record is brought up and the clerk can check to see if there are tapes outstanding or other credit problems.

Patti holds up the **CashRegister** card and says, "I display the customer record object, with help from the **CashRegisterDisplay**." Paul holds up the CRD card and says, "I get the information I need from the **Customer** object." Paul then holds up the customer card and says, "I know all about this customer's credit and rental history."

We immediately note that this is very similar to the previous interaction around the **VideoTape**. No new responsibilities are added to **CashRegisterDisplay**, but we do add the responsibility for displaying the customer record to the **CashRegister**, and we also add **CashRegisterDisplay** to the collaborations column:

Class: CashRegister	Superclass:
Responsibilities	*Collaborations*
Display VideoTape	CashRegisterDisplay
Display SalesRecord	SalesRecord
Display Customer	CashRegisterDisplay

We also need a card for the **RentalAgreement** class.

Class: RentalAgreement	SuperClass:
Responsibilities	*Collaborations*
Keep record of history of rentals	Customer,
	VideoTape

We will generate exactly one **RentalAgreement** for each specific tape rented. What happens if a customer rents two tapes? We decide that the system should generate two **RentalAgreement**s, but will print them on a unified rental report. Now, we are still left with the question of which class will control the generation of the report and the aggregation of the rentals into a single transaction. We decide to create a **RentalTransaction** object that manages the customer's interaction with the store for a single transaction, and which may in turn consist of multiple **RentalAgreement**s:

Class: RentalTransaction	SuperClass:
Responsibilities	*Collaborations*
Aggregates rental agreements	RentalAgreement
Acts as controller for rental activity -	
creates rental agreements	

Each **RentalAgreement** knows how to persist. When an object knows how to persist, this just means that it knows how to write itself back to the database. (We'll take a look at persistence and persistence mechanisms in greater detail in Chapter 6.) The collection of **RentalAgreement**s of a particular customer constitutes that customer's **RentalHistory** — a collection class that will be of some interest in its own right. Similarly, we may want a collection of all of the rentals for a particular **VideoTape**, or set of **VideoTape**s. We need a **RentalHistory** collection that can be generated with various filtering criteria.

Class: RentalHistory	SuperClass: Collection
Responsibilities	Collaborations
Find a particular rental history based on various criteria (filter)	RentalAgreement
List events in a particular order based on various criteria (sort)	

How Many Responsibilities per Card?

CRC cards force you to think about a critical question in class design: how much responsibility do you assign to each class? As a rule of thumb, I say that each class should be responsible for a single clearly defined set of responsibilities. This set should be cohesive — all the sub-parts should fit together. It should be discrete — there should be little question what belongs in and out of the set.

As a general guideline, you should become suspicious when a CRC card indicates more than half a dozen responsibilities. Many classes will have just one or two. You may find that each of these responsibilities requires three or four public methods and possibly a large number of private methods as well.

Be particularly wary of responsibilities such as "knows the value of..." or even, "supplies the value of...". While it is perfectly reasonable to think of classes in this way (e.g. the **VideoTape** knows its actors, producers and directors), if this is *all* the class does, then you have created a dumb data structure, which as we said earlier, is not a good idea.

If you have a second class which does nothing but manipulate the dumb data structure class, then you probably should combine them into a single class, which would have both the responsibility for the data and for its manipulation.

Translating CRC Cards to Diagrams

Once you have completed your CRC card session, it is time to fold the classes you've discovered back into your UML diagrams. You should expect to create or update each of the classes to reflect the responsibilities you've uncovered. Many of these responsibilities will translate into new methods of the class, modifying its public interface.

This translation from the CRC cards back into the UML is a great starting point, but there is much more detail that the UML can capture which won't fall out of the CRC cards directly. Thus, this becomes an opportunity to fill in the multiplicity and to name and detail the relationships among the classes.

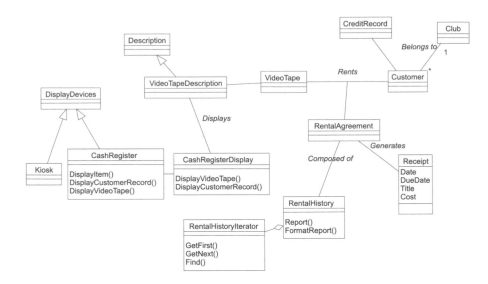

Problems with CRC Cards

CRC cards are a powerful, if informal, technique for getting a handle on the primary responsibilities of the principal classes. They have not been embraced by the object-oriented development community with quite the same enthusiasm as some other tools and techniques. This is because of their limitations — you can only accomplish so much. I use them because they are good at helping a team go from a set of requirements to a preliminary design.

On the other hand, once you translate a section of the design from the CRC cards into your UML diagrams, it is too difficult to keep the CRC cards up to date. Usually, I don't return to those classes in subsequent CRC sessions. I do a one time one-way port from the CRC cards into UML and then I tear up the cards. I sometimes return for short CRC sessions to sketch out areas we've not yet examined.

CRC cards don't scale terribly well. While you can sketch out a small design entirely on CRC cards, they become unwieldy in larger projects. The interaction between dozens of classes can be very hard to understand using nothing but CRC cards.

Finally, CRC cards are by their nature, low-tech. It is tempting to automate them, so that updates become easier and translating from CRC cards to, for example, UML diagrams can be automated. The problem is that while this solves many of the ancillary problems, it does so at the expense of destroying their principal reason to exist. The big advantage of CRC cards is their simplicity. You can pick them up, pass them around and generally manipulate the physical card. This is *much* harder to do with electronic cards.

Sequence Diagrams

Once the responsibilities are understood, it is time to turn your attention to how these responsibilities will be played out in object interactions. The path from CRC cards to sequence diagrams is often quite straightforward. You have assigned a responsibility to a particular class, and that class will then interact with other classes to fulfill that responsibility. The sequence captures these interactions. Look at the diagram below:

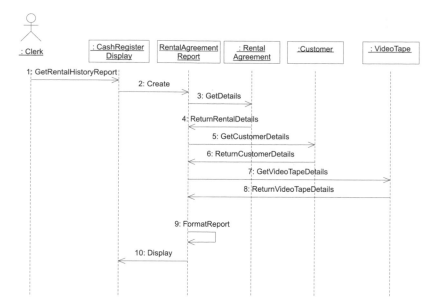

This sequence diagram captures the interactions between the various design time objects, over time. Note that in the UML, objects are distinguished from classes by underlining the name of objects. The notation **:Customer** means an object of the **Customer** class. A second thing to notice about the sequence diagram is that there is an implicit and repeated delegation of responsibility. This can best be understood by transforming the sequence diagram into its closely-related collaboration diagram:

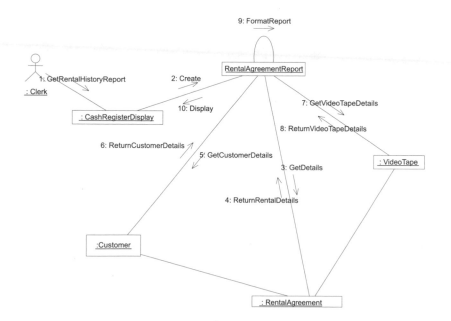

This shows explicitly that the **CashRegister** delegates the responsibility for creating the rental record to the **RentalAgreementReport** object, which in turn delegates responsibility for display back to where it belongs — the **CashRegisterDisplay**. The **RentalAgreementReport** asks the **VideoTape** for details about the tape, and the **Customer** for details about the customer, but it turns to the **RentalAgreement** object for details about the rental itself. Note that the **Customer**, the **VideoTape** and the **RentalAgreement** need not interact for this use case (at least so far).

These object interactions can be examined in far greater detail. The previous diagram handled both the UI and the database in a rather hand-waving fashion. A better understanding of the relationships and interactions among these objects can be obtained by dropping another level of detail into the sequence diagram:

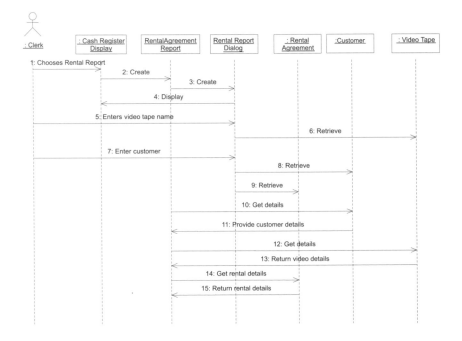

We've now begun to model the UI interactions. As we refine the sequence diagrams, we can add more detail and flesh out these interactions in progressively greater detail. We may want to add interactions which describe the internal actions of the various objects, and the interactions with the database as well.

You may find it useful to integrate the various sequence diagrams to provide a full sequence of events, from the beginning of a use case through the end; or you may find that one interaction diagram provides details for another — not unlike zooming in on a map.

State Transition Diagrams

As we come to understand the interactions among the objects, we'll need to understand the various possible **states** of each individual object.

> *The **state** of an object is the current set of values for each of its member variables.*

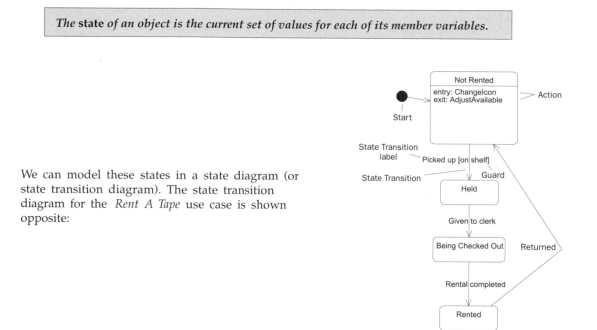

We can model these states in a state diagram (or state transition diagram). The state transition diagram for the *Rent A Tape* use case is shown opposite:

Every state diagram begins with a single **start** state, and ends with zero or more **end** states. The individual states are named, and the transitions may be labeled. The **guard** indicates a condition that must be satisfied for an object to move from one state to the other — it is a logical condition returning either true or false — and the **actions** indicate what the object does on entry to or exit from the state.

VideoTapes may change their state as well (such as **NotRented** to **Reserved**). A more ambitious state diagram may capture these alternative states. For example, you might model the **Reserved** state as shown:

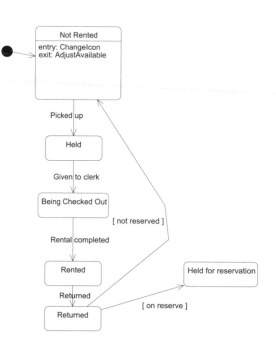

105

Super-states

At various stages along the way, the customer may change his mind and decide not to rent the tape. He may do this while the box is in his hand, or while it is being checked out, or even immediately after renting the tape. We can reflect this by calling out to a **Cancelled** state:

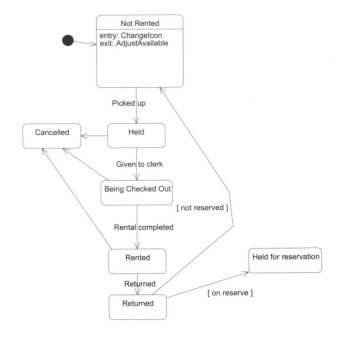

However, the **Cancelled** state quickly becomes a distraction. This is especially troubling, as cancellation is more of an exception than a natural path. We solve this by using a **super-state**. All three states of **Held**, **BeingCheckedOut** and **Rented** can be described as being in the **Cancellable** super-state and can be modeled as follows:

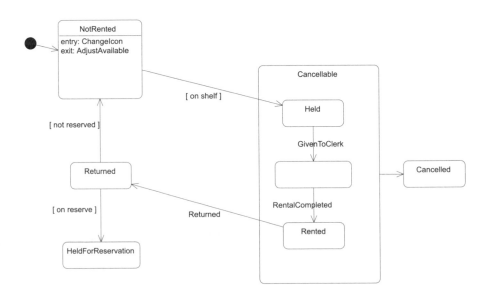

This diagram provides the same information, but is much cleaner and easier to read. The **VideoTape** can go from the **NotRented** to the **Cancellable** states as long as it is on the shelf. The first **Cancellable** state is **Held**. It goes from **Held** to **BeingCheckedOut** when it is given to the clerk, and when the clerk completes the check-out process the tape goes to **Rented**. When the tape is returned it is no longer possible to cancel the order, so the tape goes to the **Returned** state. In this model, **Returned** is different from **NotRented**. Only tapes which are **NotRented** can be rented. The tape can go from returned to **NotRented** if it is not reserved. The tape can go from **Returned** to **HeldForReservation** if it *is* reserved.

What happens if your design requirements change, and you decide that the customer cannot cancel a tape rental once it is rented? You simply drag the **Rented** state out of the **Cancellable** state to reflect this change:

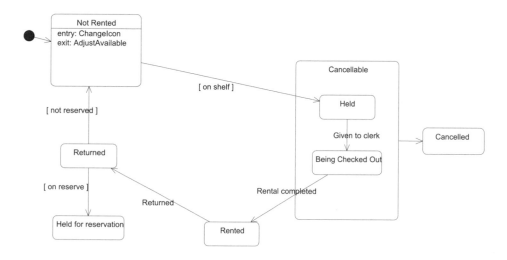

As you move these states around, you may decide to add additional states. For example, you might determine that the actual domain rule is that a tape rental can be cancelled within one hour of rental. (The customer goes home and his wife says, "We've seen that twice already. Take it back and get *Holiday Inn* instead".)

Once again, modifying the model is a relatively easy task and allows you to gain feedback between your use cases and your understanding of the various states of the system.

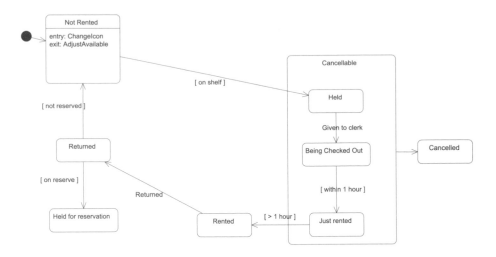

Identify Properties

As you learn more about the responsibilities of your classes, together with the various states through which they may transition, the attributes and priorities will become clearer. Responsibilities map cleanly to methods and the state maps cleanly to data members.

While most of member variables will be simple primitive data types, such as integers, some will need to be classes in their own right. For example, while the number of rentals to date may be captured as an **int**, the release date is a candidate for a **Date** class, and the cast of the film will almost certainly be modeled as a collection of **Thespian** objects. (We'll call them **Thespian** to distinguish them from the object-oriented reserved word, *actor*.)

Each **Thespian** object will capture the name of the actor it represents, a list of the films in which this person has acted, as well as other important information, such as their birth and death dates. At this early stage of development, I'm less interested in building a complete set of attributes for each class than I am in exploring what additional classes I need to capture complex attributes, such as the cast of a film, or, as I should say, **VideoTitle**.

The examination of the **VideoTitle** class will quickly generate the **Thespian**, **Director**, and **Producer** classes, and perhaps even classes for **Studio** (e.g. MGM vs. Paramount), **AcademyAwards** and **Distributor**:

Thespian
Name
Films : List
Birth Date : Date

Producer
Films : List

Director
Films : List

Distributor

Studio

AcadamyAwards

Identify Events

In the same way that operations and attributes may create either class members or classes in their own right, events can also be captured as classes. An event is anything that signals your program to take an action. Key presses, mouse movements, messages from the Internet may all be events. Encapsulating events in classes can help with managing the complexity of information which each event represents. Some examples of events in VideoMagix that may be encapsulated as classes are shown below:

Rental	Return	Customer Joins

Examine Design Goals

Let's review what we've done so far to find classes:

- We started by transforming objects from the domain, creating surrogate classes for all the actors and all the abstract concepts in the problem area

- We continued by creating classes for the principal views, including reports and user interface objects

- We then added classes for interfaces between the various systems and for the devices the system will use

- Finally, we looked at operations, attributes and events to find those which were sufficiently complex to warrant treating them as classes

By this time, we have a rich set of classes, but we're still not quite done. It is time to review the design goals, and to consider classes which represent performance, robustness and reliability. While these abstractions will rarely be made into classes themselves, related objects, such as optimizers and test modules, may well be sources of new classes.

Finally, we need to identify those areas of the design which will evolve and change over time, either because the requirements will change, or because we might want to take advantage of emerging technology. Each of these aspects of the system must be encapsulated, so that when change does arrive, it won't break your entire design.

Look for the Right Level of Abstraction

Once all of this is done, we should have iterated over these issues enough times, so that few new classes are being created. Now, it's time to look at whether we've found the right level of abstraction for our classes. We need to remove low-level classes that have no interesting instances.

For example, if we are modeling a supermarket, we may have a class which represents a product line, such as ketchup. The problem is that we can end up with thousands of classes, each of which is distinguished only by a very small difference. In a supermarket, the 7oz can of salted Delmonte peas is considered a different product line from the 6oz can of unsalted, but to the design of the supermarket software, this is a distinction with little difference. Further, the individual instances of the 7oz salted Delmonte peas class are not significant — we don't much care to track the state and life-span of each can of peas.

The solution to this is to move up a level of abstraction. Create a class called **CannedPeas**, and make the specific product lines the individual instances of this class. We lose the detail of the individual cans, but that is probably all to the good; we could create a set of member variables to keep track of the inventory, if that is required.

Relationships

Once you have sketched out your preliminary set of classes, it is time to turn your attention to detailing their relationships. This is the time to show **association**, **aggregation**, **composition** and **inheritance**.

Earlier, we modeled our understanding of the relationships between the objects in the problem domain. Now it is time to model the relationships in the solution — to create our object model from which we can implement the classes in code.

In the first chapter, we looked at these terms and I gave you a working definition for them. We'll now describe these relationships in more concrete terms — they are best understood in terms of the code that will manifest these relationships.

> *If class A #includes class B's header file, then A depends on B.*
>
> *If object A sends a message to object C then A associates with C (A uses C). This relationship is stronger than depends on, and includes it. That is,* association *is a superset of* dependency.
>
> *If class A has a pointer or reference to an object of class D then class A aggregates class D.* Aggregation *is a superset of* association.
>
> *If class A has a member variable of type E then A is composed of E.* Composition *is a superset of* aggregation.

In composition you are modeling the fact that **E**'s lifetime depends on **A**. Usually, this means that when **A** is created, **E** is created, and when **A** is destroyed, **E** is destroyed. Thus, if **A** has a member variable of type **E** then **A** is composed of **E**, aggregates **E**, associates with **E** and depends on **E**. The way these different relationships are displayed in the UML is shown in the diagram opposite:

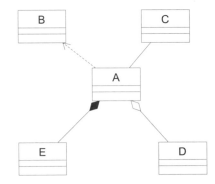

The implementation of these relationships is language dependent. The following code illustrates one possible implementation, in C++:

```
#include B.h                                      // dependency
Class A
{
//...

SomeFunction(C theC) {theC->SomeMethod(); }       // association

//...
C * pC;                                           // association
D * pD;                                            // aggregation

E m_E;                                            // composition
};
```

This code declares a new class, **A**. It begins by including **B**'s header (for whatever reason) which creates a dependency. If **B** were to change its header, **A** would need to recompile.

The member function **SomeFunction()** takes as a parameter an object of type **C** by value and invokes a method on that object. This is an example of association. **C** is not a member of **A**, but **A** must know about type **C** to call the function. This is a simple association. As an alternative, **A** can have a pointer to a **C** and can implement the association through that pointer. While **pC** is a data member of **A**, what is modeled is association, not aggregation.

C has two data members. **pD** is a pointer to an object of type **D**. Here **A** does aggregate **D**, implemented through this pointer. What is the difference? In C++, the implementation of **pC** and **pD** is indistinguishable; but they represent different *logical* relationships. In the case of **C** the relationship is association, in the case of **D** the relationship is aggregation.

Note that it is possible for **pD** to be null when **A** is created. The **D** object will be created independently of the **A** object. While **A** aggregates **D**, it does not control its lifetime.

The member **m_E** however is not by reference. It is an aggregate held by value. When an instance of A is created, **m_E** is crated, and when that instance of **A** is destroyed, **m_E** is destroyed. This relationship is composition: **A** aggregates **m_E** and controls its lifetime.

Which Relationship Should You Use?

The issue of when to use association, aggregation or composition is troubling to novice designers, but in practice it turns out to be much ado about nothing. Typically, the problem domain will dictate the relationships. For example, a **VideoTape** has a **Producer**, a **Director** and one or two **Thespians**. Should these relationships be modeled as aggregation or composition? Ask yourself this: is the producer created when the video tape is created and destroyed when the video tape is destroyed? Obviously not — the same **Producer** object may be aggregated inside any number of **VideoTape** objects. Thus, **VideoTape** would aggregate **Producer**, and the **VideoTape** object would hold a pointer to a **Producer** object as a data member.

111

Grounding your design in the domain helps resolve the great majority of these questions. What do you do if it doesn't appear to make any difference whether the member is held by reference or by value? Fortunately, if it doesn't make any difference in the problem domain or in the model, then it won't make any difference in the implementation! In reality, however, this is rarely the case. Again, follow the imperative of the domain whenever possible.

Inheritance

What is a car? What makes a car different from a truck, from a person, from a rock? One of the delights of object-oriented programming is that these questions become relevant to us; understanding how we perceive and think about the objects in the real world directly relates to how we design these objects in our model.

From one perspective, a car is the sum of its parts: steering wheel, brakes, seats, headlights. Here, we are thinking in terms of aggregation. From a second perspective, one that is equally true, a car is a type of vehicle. By saying that a car is a type of vehicle we are using a short hand rich in meaning.

Because a car is a vehicle, it moves and it carries things. That is the essence of being a vehicle. Cars *inherit* the characteristics *moves* and *carries things* from their "parent" type, that is, vehicle. We also know that cars *specialize* vehicles. They are a special *kind* of vehicle, one which meets the federal specifications for automobiles.

We can model this relationship with inheritance. We say that the car type inherits publicly from the vehicle type; that is a car *is-a* vehicle.

Public inheritance establishes an *is-a* relationship. It creates a parent class (vehicle) and a derived class (car) and implies that the car is a specializaiton of the type vehicle. Everything true about a vehicle should be true about a car, but the converse is not true. The car may specialize *how* it moves, but it ought to move.

What is a *motor-vehicle*? This is a different specialization, at a different level of abstraction. A motor vehicle is any vehicle which is propelled by a motor. A car is one such type, a truck is another. We can model these more complex relationships with inheritance as well:

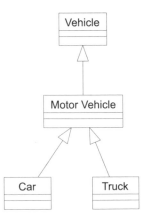

Which model is better? The answer to this question will depend on what you are modeling. There is nothing intrinsic in object-oriented analysis and design that dictates which of these models makes more sense. They model a different subset of reality. Here's how you decide — is there something about motor vehicle you want to model? Are you going to model other, non-motorized vehicles?

Standing on its own as shown, one might argue that there is no reason not to collapse motor vehicle into vehicle. On the other hand, perhaps motor vehicle has a lot of functionality and states that are specific to its being motorized, and if you are designing for reuse, the you should allow for the possibility that, at some future time, you *may* want to create other non-motorized vehicles.

As a rule of thumb, I would not separate motor vehicle from vehicle, unless I were going to also derive other vehicles which are not motorized. I might want to use an inheritance hierarchy like the one shown in the diagram opposite:

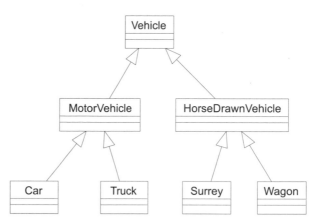

Public Inheritance

A critical aspect of **public inheritance** is that it should model specialization/generalization, *and nothing else*. If you want to inherit implementation, but are not establishing an *is-a* relationship, then you would use **private inheritance**.

Private inheritance establishes an *implemented-in-terms-of* rather than an *is-a* relationship. You might, for example, implement your new **PartsCatalog** class in terms of your linked list. You would do this if your parts catalog was not a kind of linked list (there were fundamental differences in the interfaces they made available to the client), but there was code in the linked list that you'd like to reuse. A more common solution, however, would be to give your parts catalog a linked list as a private member variable and delegate responsibility to that linked list as required.

Public inheritance is used to *factor out* common attributes and behavior among a number of classes. If a solution is found in a couple of classes, and you can make that a generalized solution of a public base class from which you can then derive various other classes. Later in the design, you reverse the flow, creating new classes which are specializations of existing classes.

Inheritance trees tend to get very large and tangled if you are not careful, and the connections between classes and higher base classes can become increasingly tenuous. While in theory it is possible for inheritance hierarchies to be infinitely deep, in my experience it is difficult to maintain such a hierarchy of more than half a dozen layers. It is simply too difficult to keep the topology of the inheritance map clear in your own mind.

Inheritance (single inheritance as well as multiple inheritance) can create a number of design issues. The most common design issue in inheritance is the *fragile base class* problem. As more and more of the functionality gets pushed up into the base class, that class becomes increasingly brittle. Every change in the base class forces changes to be rippled down through the derived classes.

A second problem with inheritance is that it is tempting to push interfaces higher and higher into the hierarchy, thus allowing more classes to respond polymorphically to a given message. The issue, however, is that as these interfaces percolate upwards in the hierarchy, there is greater likelihood that at least some of the derived classes will not support that interface.

For example, suppose you create a **Car** class. You then create derived classes **StationWagon**, **SportUtilityVehicle**, **Coupe**, **Roadster** and **FamilySedan**. You'd like to treat these cars polymorphically, so you assign the following virtual methods to **Car**:

```
class Car : public MotorVehicle
{
public:
Car();
~Car();
virtual Heat() = 0;
virtual AdjustRadio(bool turnOn = true) = 0;
virtual Accelerate(int howMuch = JUST_A_LITTLE) = 0;
virtual Decelerate(int howMuch = JUST_A_LITTLE) = 0;
//...
};
```

Now, suppose you want to model a VW Beetle. You derive this car from **FamilySedan**.

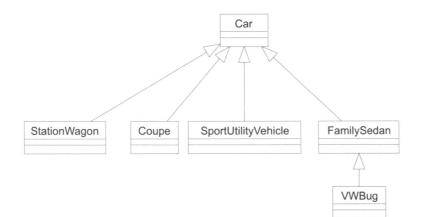

You can now happily create instances of **VWBug** and they will inherit all the characteristics and performance of **FamilySedan** and **Car** (as well as **MotorVehicle** and **Vehicle**). Oh, there's just one problem — the '64 VW Bug didn't come with a heater. How will you override the pure virtual function **Heat()**?

There are a number of possible answers, but they all have their difficulties:

▶ You can make this method non-abstract and give it a do-nothing operation — but this is a cheap trick and a poor model of the world

▶ You can override **Heat()** in **VWBug** to do nothing (or return an exception), but again, you fail to model the world — it isn't that the Beetle's heater does nothing, it is that there is no heater

▶ You might decide to move **Heat()** out of the base class and distribute it to the derived classes, but that is a big price to pay for the fact that just one particular derived type doesn't have a heater

▶ Finally, you might decide that a **VWBug** isn't a car after all, but that is absurd — while all cars (with this exception) have heaters, it certainly is not *essential* that they do — no one ever wrote a review in *Car & Driver* saying, "This vehicle is not a car, it has no heater."

Multiple Inheritance

One of the capabilities available in C++, which is not available in Java, is **multiple inheritance** (though Java has a similar if limited ability with multiple interfaces). Multiple inheritance allows a class to inherit from more than one base class, bringing in the members and methods of two or more classes.

Experience has shown that multiple inheritance should be used judiciously. From the design perspective, it is important to understand how we model these relationships. In simple multiple inheritance, the two base classes are unrelated. An example of multiple inheritance is shown in the diagram below:

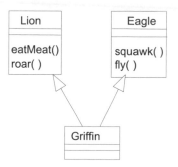

In this simple illustration, the **Griffin** class inherits from both **Lion** and **Eagle**. Thus, a **Griffin** can **eatMeat()**, **roar()**, **squark()** and **fly()**. A problem arises when both **Lion** and **Eagle** share a common base class, for example **Animal**:

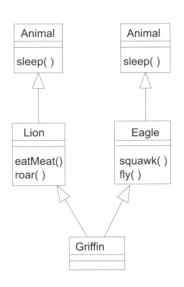

This common base class, **Animal**, may have methods or member variables which **Griffin** will now inherit twice. When you call **Griffin**'s **Sleep()** method, the compiler will not know which **sleep()** you wish to invoke. As the designer of the **Griffin** class, you must remain aware of these relationships and be prepared to solve the ambiguities they create. C++ facilitates this by providing **virtual inheritance**:

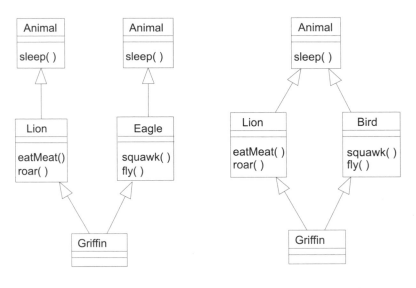

Without Virtual Inheritance   **With Virtual Inheritance**

With virtual inheritance, **Griffin** inherits just one copy of the members of **Animal**, and the ambiguity is resolved. The problem is that both **Lion** and **Eagle** classes must know that they may be involved in a multiple inheritance relationship; the **virtual** keyword must be on *their* declaration of inheritance, not that of **Griffin**.

Is Multiple Inheritance Worth the Effort?

Some design patterns, such as the Observer design pattern (*Design Patterns*, Gamma et al), are much easier to implement with multiple inheritance and are difficult to implement properly in languages that don't support it. Robert Martin explores this exact issue in his paper *Java vs. C++ — A Critical Comparison**. In this paper, he shows that implementation of the Observer pattern is very much more difficult in a language such as Java that does not support multiple inheritance.

In addition, the use of mix-in's can simplify your design, though if they are misused, they can in fact complicate it. The question is not an easy one, and many C++ programmers find they can work quite productively without ever needing multiple inheritance.

Using Multiple Inheritance When You Need Aggregation

How do you know when to use multiple inheritance and when to avoid it? Should a car inherit from steering wheel, tire and doors? Should a police car inherit from municipal property and vehicle?

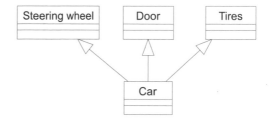

The first guideline is that public inheritance should always model specialization. The common expression for this is that inheritance should model *is-a* relationships and aggregation should model *has-a* relationships.

Is a car a steering wheel? Clearly not. You might argue that a car is a combination of a steering wheel, a tire and a set of doors, but this is *not* modeled in inheritance. A car is not a specialization of these things — it is an aggregation of these things. A car has a steering wheel, it has doors and it has tires. Another good reason why you should not inherit car from door is the fact that a car usually has *more than one* door — this is not a relationship which can be modeled with inheritance.

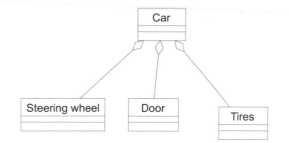

*"Java vs C++ — A Critical Comparison" by Robert Martin, first published in C++ Report in January 1997, and available on his web site at http://www.oma.com/Publications/publications.html.

Is a police car both a vehicle and a municipal property? Yes, clearly it is both; in fact clearly it is a specialized form of both. As such, multiple inheritance makes a lot of sense here:

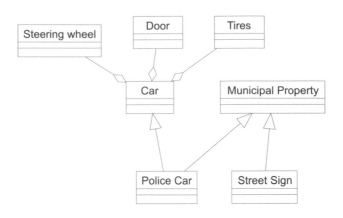

Why does Multiple Inheritance have a Bad Reputation?

In many development shops, multiple inheritance is looked on as an aberration, to be shunned whenever possible. This has two historical roots. First, for a long time the commercial compilers, debuggers and other tools did not support multiple inheritance properly, and so introducing it into your program only increased the difficulty of writing, testing and debugging the program.

Second, there was a great deal of confusion about what multiple inheritance modeled, and so a lot of the programs which utilized it did so in a way that created code which was harder to maintain. Once multiple inheritance was better understood, designers discovered that there were many situations where it closely modeled the real world and made for cleaner interfaces and better delegation of responsibility.

Base Classes and Derived Classes

Derived classes must know who their base class is, and they depend on their base classes. Base classes, on the other hand, should know nothing about their derived classes. Do not put the header for derived classes into your base class files, and be wary of dependencies down the inheritance hierarchy.

You want to be very suspicious of any design that calls for *casting down* the inheritance hierarchy. You cast down when you ask a pointer for its "real" (run-time) class and then cast that pointer to the derived type. This often reveals a fundamental flaw in the design of your system. In theory, base pointers should be polymorphic, and figuring out the "real" type of the pointer and calling the "right" method should be left to the compiler.

The most common use of casting down is to invoke a method that doesn't exist in the base class. The question you should be asking yourself is why are you in a situation where you need to do this. If the semantics of the program demand this knowledge, then you must ask yourself why you have a base pointer in the first place. If knowledge of the run-time type is supposed to be hidden, then why are you casting down?

Interestingly, Stroustrup resisted putting casting down into the language, and the initial definition didn't support it. Down-casting has become sufficiently common, however, that it was added as part of the ANSI standard, along with the **dynamic_cast<>()** operator. This operator is designed to ensure the safety of down-casts, and more important, it is designed to ensure you can quickly find (and eradicate!) such casts from your code. That is, while its use is *safer* than using an old-fashioned big sledge-hammer C-style cast, it is not desirable. Nonetheless, there are times, especially when using a vendor's library, when casting down is required.

Single Instance Classes

You also want to be very wary of derived classes for which there is only ever one instance. Don't confuse this with the Singleton Pattern (*Design Patterns*, Gamma et al), in which the application needs only a single instance of a type (e.g. only one document or one database per application). What I'm discussing here is the case where you have, for example:

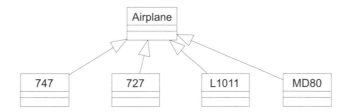

If you plan to instantiate objects of each of these subtypes (e.g. you are modeling an airport), then this design is fine. On the other hand, if you don't have individual instances of each of these types, but simply use each one as a protoype, then you don't need classes, you need objects. Consider the case where each of these airplane types is used to describe the seating pattern, so that a reservation clerk can help you decide where to sit. You will never need an instance of a 727, you only need the single concept of all 727s. In this case, what you need is an instance of an airplane seating pattern, whose name attribute is 727.

No-op Methods

Assembler programmers used a no-op method when they wanted nothing to happen at that point in the code. The modern equivalent of this is to "no-op" a method in a class. For example, suppose you have a **Car** class and within that class you have a **TurnOnTheRadio()** method. Nearly every car that your are modeling has a radio, but one inexpensive car does not. You may be tempted to just override the **TurnOnTheRadio()** method to do nothing. This is almost always a design mistake.

The problem is that the semantics of turning on a radio don't apply to your miserly car, and the experience of the driver is not that he turns on the radio and nothing happens, it is that there is no radio to turn on! Your model has diverged from reality, and if this is significant to your design, you must change your design.

One solution to this problem is to derive **CarsWithRadios** from **Car**.

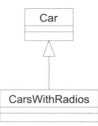

One problem with this solution is that radios may not be the only optional equipment on the car — perhaps the heater is optional, as are power windows, power breaks and automatic transmission. Trying to model all this with inheritance is difficult, the combinitorial explosion that results from mixing and matching these options quickly shows this to be impractical.

When you have two or more optional values, you can model the object by using containment — each of the optional features will be modeled as an object member of the class. The semantics of your problem may allow you to use a pointer to the object that models the optional feature, with a null pointer indicating that the feature is not included.

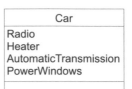

Inheritance vs Attributes

Perhaps one of the most perplexing design dilemmas is the question of which differences should be reflected in inheritance, and which should be managed by attributes. For example, which of the following two designs is better? Should different types of houses be modeled as a set of derived classes, like this?

Or, should the type of house be modeled as an atttribute of the house itself, like this?

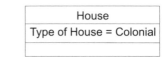

And which type of design should we use if we're modeling color?

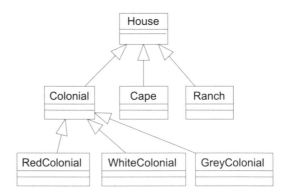

Clearly, the color of the house is not sufficiently significant to warrant subclassing the various types of houses — doing so would cause an enormous proliferation of types, with little additional advantage. Is the house type, on the other hand, sufficiently significant to warrant subtyping?

The general rule is to use subtypes when there is a *significant* and *meaningful* difference in the domain you are modeling. A second useful rule to remember is to avoid specialization that doesn't change behavior. White and red houses behave identically, except in response to queries for their color.

The change in behavior must be significant within the domain you are modeling. If you are building a game, for example, where the only difference between a colonial and a ranch is which icon you are going to display, then you may argue that an attribute of house will be more than sufficient. If, on the other hand, you are building an architectural planning product, in which the house type will drive a series of operations and functionality (e.g. what types of windows are needed and whether or not there is an upstairs), then you almost certainly would use derived classes.

Changing State vs Inheritance

You have been asked to design an elevator control system. Your requirements state that an empty elevator should return to the ground floor between the hours of 6am and 10am. This is a significant difference in behavior from how an elevator with passengers operates. Does the diagram below represent a sensible design?

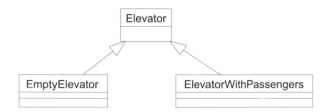

The problem here is that any given instance will move into and out of being empty many times during its lifetime. Rather than migrating between two *types*, it will be easier (and more sensible) to change the *state* of a single type. In this particular case, you may want a Boolean value: **Elevator::IsEmpty**.

If the behavior of the class changes significantly depending on the state of the object, you may want to consider implementing the State Pattern (*Design Patterns*, Gamma et al). In this pattern, you encapsulate the state and the appropriate behavior in an inheritance hierarchy of state objects. The original class then delegates state-dependent behavior to the state class, in this case, the **ElevatorState** class:

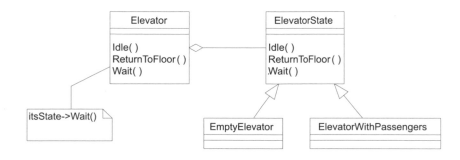

121

The note in the bottom left hand corner is shown in the UML as a rectangle with the top right hand corner folded over. This notation is used to add descriptive information, attached to the relevant part of the diagram by a dashed line.

Discriminators

In each of the previous examples, we looked at specializing to subclasses based on various simple discriminators. We first considered subclassing **Car** based on optional equipment, but this quickly broke down because of the combinatorial explosion. We looked at an example of a **House** class, which we considered subclassing based on color, but found it didn't make a significant difference to the behavior of the house.

The normal solution is to fold all of these classes together (into a single **House** or **Car** class) and to put the **discriminator** into the class as an attribute.

> **Discriminator:** *the distinction that makes the difference between two instances or two types.*

Thus, a single **House** class can have a **Color** attribute, a single **Car** class can have a set of attributes or a collection of attributes representing the options for that car. This reduces the inheritance hierarchy, and makes sense if the various discriminators are fairly simple and have no impact on the behavior of the original class. Since houses behave the same regardless of their color, then encapsulating this concern in an attribute (**Color**) makes sense.

At times, the discriminator is best modeled as a class. It may turn out that a simple value (**red**, **blue**, **green**) is insufficient to model the discriminator. In this case, the discriminator can be modeled as a class, rather than as an enumerated type, and the discrimination can be encapsulated in an instance of that type. Thus, the car might model the various options in an **Options** type, which would include a collection and some intelligence about which options might be mixed and matched (e.g. you can't get the sunroof unless you buy the powerpack, in which case you can no longer get the five speed transmission). These classes become policy objects, which reflect domain-driven business considerations.

If the discriminator class is sufficiently powerful, then you can model an infinite variety of types, without specializing the discriminated object. That is, you can model many different types of cars without subclassing **Car**, but rather by varying the attributes of the instances of the discriminating type.

For example, suppose you were modeling a car company that offered a variety of car types. These are not individual cars — they are whole families of models based on their performance characteristics:

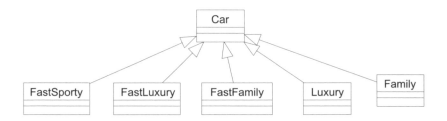

The car company in this example measures these performance distinctions based on a combination of the size of the engine, the acceleration characteristics and the transmission policy about when to shift gears. The luxury feel is dictated by shifting earlier in the gear (at lower RPM) and the speed is dictated by a combination of the size of the engine and the shift point. These factors are complicated, yet deterministic — given the right data, you can determine which size engine and which shift point will provide a given performance characteristic.

There are two problems with modeling this using specialization (inheritance). The first is that you may well run into a combinatorial explosion. If the car company provides a new engine with higher performance and a new policy on when to shift, and then later decides to factor in tire size, you may end up with dozens of subclasses. More important, you cannot create new types of performance cars on the fly, which limits the system's ability to model proposed new car lines. That is, if an engineer decides to try building a superfast family car, he needs a developer to recompile a new derived type!

The answer to this problem is to factor out the discriminator into its own class. The **Performance** class will encapsulate *all* the performance characteristics of any given type. Once you have the **Performance** class, you no longer need various car types — you can collapse all the car types into a single class:

The UML stereotype for a class which encapsulates a discriminator, and which can be used to create *instances* of a class (**Car**) that are logically of different types (**LuxuryCar**) is a «powertype». In this case, the performance class is a **powertype** for car.

> **Powertype**: *a class which encapsulates the discriminator for another class. You indicate a powertype in a UML document with the «powertype» stereotype.*

In the previous model you did not instantiate a car, you instantiated a **FastSportyCar** or a **LuxuryCar**. In this new model, when you instantiate **Car**, you also instantiate a performance object, and you associate a given performance object with a given car.

Each instance of the **Performance** class corresponds to a particular type of car. If there are six types of cars you are modeling, you'll have six instances of the **Performance** class. On the other hand, every car of the same performance type shares a single performance object. If you instantiate six **Car**s, each of which is of logical type **FastSportyCar**, then you simply associate all six **Car** objects with the single instance of the **Performance** class which describes the characteristics of a **FastSportyCar**. This one performance instance is shared, and its job is to lend each of these cars the right characteristics.

Creating Types on the Fly

This model of powertypes lets you logically create new types on the fly. Each type is differentiated by the parameters to the constructor a powertype. This means that you can, at run time, create new types of cars on the fly. That is, by passing different engine sizes and shift points to the powertype, you can effectively create new performance characteristics, and by assigning those characteristics to various cars, you can effectively enlarge the set of types of cars.

Changing Types Dynamically

You can extend this model and allow your cars, at run time, to drop their performance objects and pick up new ones, thereby creating **Car** objects that can change their types at run time. You might use this technique to model the performance change that a car undergoes when it shifts in and out of all-wheel-drive. In most cases, you would prohibit this by modeling the relationship between the car and its performance object as constant, but that is a domain-driven decision.

Extending Powertype Flexibility

In the use of powertypes described so far, the attributes and methods of a given powertype instance are fixed at compile time. That is, you can create new cars by varying the engine size and the shift-points, but those are the only characteristics you can vary. You can imagine extending this model to say that the characteristics your performance class encapsulates are themselves determined at run time:

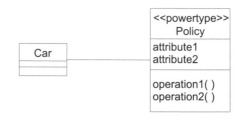

Here the **Car** is associated with a **Policy** object, which provides two attributes and two operations, and the meaning of these attributes and the effect of these operations is determined at run time. This provides far greater flexibility, although someone has to impose meaning on those attributes and operations. One option is for the **Car** itself to do so. A second option is for there to be another object partipating in the relationship, which provides context and meaning to the attributes and operations. This *interpreter* may be quite complex and may amount to building an interpreted language, such as a script, which would, at run time, generate arbitrarily complex types.

Building the Model

By this point in the design, you should have found and sketched out a number of classes. In VideoMagix, we have identified a number of important relationships in our model. We know the kind of relationships we are modeling (aggregation, specialization etc.), and often the multiplicity of these relationships (for example, one-to-one or one-to-many). In some cases, we've designated the role each class plays in the relationship, and for many objects, we've sketched out the most important methods. Our design for VideoMagix is shown in the following diagram.

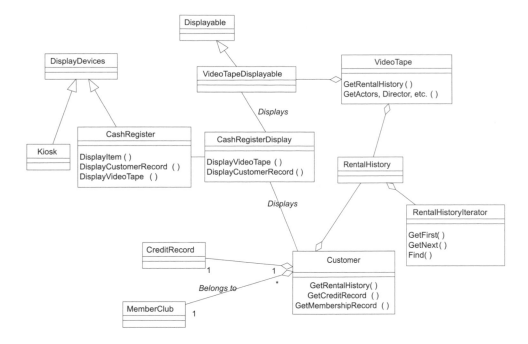

With the sequence diagrams and collaboration diagrams, we've modeled the interactions among the objects, and with the state transition diagrams, we've modeled the various states through which the objects may pass. Now it is time to begin prototyping the design in code, even as we proceed to flesh out the public interfaces of the various classes.

Beginning the prototypes will force issues to the surface. Not only will we discover holes in the public interfaces of the various classes, but we'll return our attention to the architecture and the architectural mechanisms we'll call on to build the application: operating systems, persistence mechanisms, concurrency and component mechanisms and so forth. This enhanced understanding will then feed right back into the class design.

Prototyping

Prototyping lowers risk in a software development project by bringing implementation issues and concerns to the surface early in the process.

Prototyping is a process of developing software quickly to explore the requirements (problem space prototyping) or the design (solution space prototyping). When prototyping, the developer intentionally departs from the goals of the final product to ensure that the prototype is developed quickly. During prototyping, the developer may not comment the code, may leave out error handling, may hard code values and generally produce code that is designed to provide fast answers, rather than being designed to be easily maintained, to enhance performance or to scale well.

In short, during prototyping we aren't interested in a fully functional, robust, reliable, scalable and maintainable system. We are interested in being able to examine quickly the risky areas, thus allowing us to determine if we have a strategy in place to reduce or eliminate that risk.

The usefulness of prototyping is based on the idea that it is quicker and cheaper to find errors early in the development process. In the book *Succeeding With Objects,* Goldberg and Rubin reference an article in IEEE's *Computer* magazine, which asserts that two thirds of software errors are due to incorrectly stated requirements and poor design.

Prototyping is also used during the requirements gathering stage to explore the UI. A series of screens is presented to the user and interactions are simulated. The display process is user driven — the user's inputs are used to determine the next screen to be shown. These prototypes can be used to discover user acceptance or rejection of the look and feel of the software. The interactions revealed during early prototypes inspire a dialog between the user and the programmer that can lead to a more elegant and useful UI.

Prototyping is used during the design phase to try out ideas that are not well understood. For example, an implementation of an inter-process communication (IPC) mechanism can be tried on a small test program. First, the client and the server can be put in the same machine. When this works, they can be moved to separate machines, and ultimately to separate locations.

Another use of prototyping during the design phase is to test the performance of the infrastructure. This can be used as an early test of whether or not the system can meet the performance requirements.

Build it to Throw it Away

The question that most vexes software developers is whether or not they should be expected to reuse the prototype code. Managers say yes, as their schedule and budget would look better if they could reuse the code. Programmers say no, as they know all about the shortcuts they took in developing the prototype code. After all, they were told to develop the prototype quickly: the lessons to be learned were more important then the quality of the code.

Code written to test the UI tends to be less usable in the final product than code written to test out a design idea. Often the UI prototype will be developed in a RAD language such as Visual Basic.

> *RAD - Rapid Application Development. RAD languages provide fast development at the cost of larger and perhaps slower code.*

Use of a RAD for prototyping the UI can greatly accelerate the process of producing the prototype and getting it in front of real users, while at the same time it *forces* you to rewrite when it is time to develop the commercial release.

Design prototypes, on the other hand, often include code that can be reused in the next prototype or the final system. An example of this would be a prototype developed to test whether a new shrink-wrapped component can fit into the architecture. Perhaps the component does not provide a class-based interface — code would have to be written for the prototype to test that component, to wrap it in a class interface, to report the test results, etc. If the decision is made to use the component in the final system, then the code written to wrap the new component may be reusable.

Ultimately, the danger is that we have two requirements that work against each other:

 Building it fast

 Making it reusable

Either you are going to write it quick and dirty, in which case you do *not* want it in the final product, or you are going to write it carefully, in which case it will take too long to be useful as a prototype.

Summary

Throughout this chapter, we have been concentrating on building the object model for an application, and we employed a number of interesting techniques in the process. We began by transforming objects from the problem domain (identified in the analysis stage) into objects in the model, and we added to these by including those objects that represented more abstract concepts.

We discussed CRC cards, which present a powerful technique for examining the interactions between the classes we have identified, and pinpointing the functionality for which each class is responsible.

There are a number of UML diagrams that can be used to document our design and to flesh out particular parts of it. The different diagrams can show different perspectives of the model. The UML diagrams we looked at in this chapter included sequence and collaboration diagrams, class diagrams and state transition diagrams.

We investigated the different types of relationship between the classes, from the simple association to aggregation and composition, and saw how we would implement these in C++ code. Inheritance hierarchies play a crucial role in the way your classes are structured, so we examined when and how you should use these, and also the many issues related to multiple inheritance.

Another powerful technique we examined was the use of discriminators, and particularly the UML stereotype, «powertype», which can encapsulate the discriminator as a class, and be used to create new user defined types at run time.

The issues we have been looking at in this chapter are all related to designing the classes that we will eventually implement in C++ code. There are, however, many other design issues that we need to consider relating to the architecture of the whole design. We need to consider how the application is actually going to work in the real world, what operating system will it run on, how many users will there be, whether it will be distributed across a network and so forth. Such issues impact on the design of the architecture of the system, which is the subject of the next chapter.

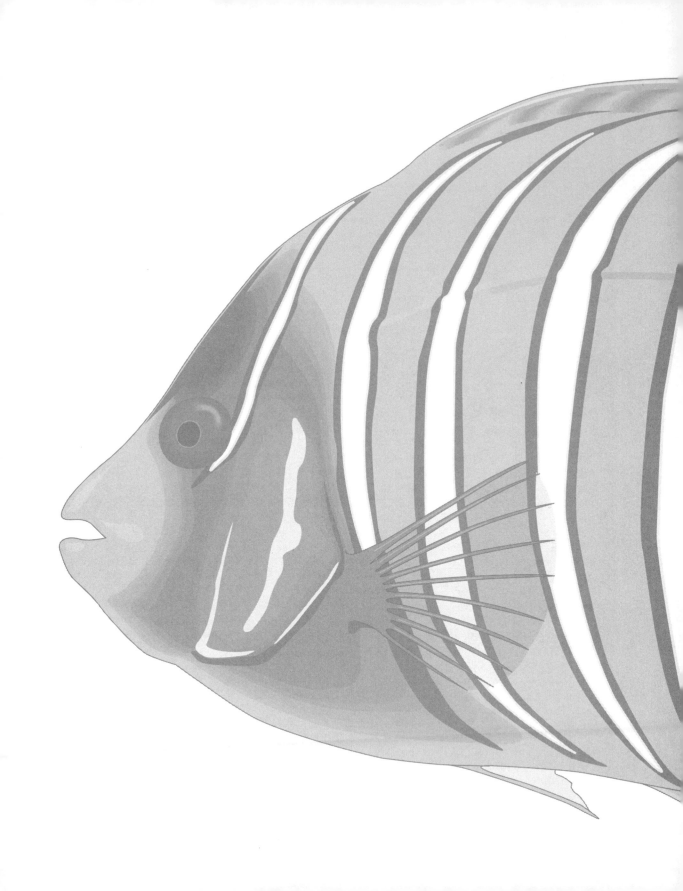

4

Architecture Design

In Chapter 2, we looked at how to analyze the problem domain. We looked at the actors in the system and examined various use cases to uncover the requirements. Once the problem is fully understood, it is time to go on and design the solution — a process that we began in Chapter 3 by creating the object model that will eventually be transformed into C++ code as part of the implementation. We will continue looking at the design in this chapter, but now we shall focus on the architecture of the design. The issues we have yet to consider include:

> The resources we can call on to help us realize the use cases and classes

> How the application will make use of the classes

> How the user will interact with the application

> The actual implementation of the classes

This chapter and the following two will examine the first three issues listed above. Implementation issues will be the focus of Chapter 7.

Specifically, in this chapter, we will look at:

> Architectural views

> Client-server architectures

> Partitioning code

> Web-based architectures

> Distributed objects

Where Now?

During architecture design, we focus on the overall structure of the system. An architecture design is divided into sections or **views**.

*A **view** is a specific perspective or focus. Typically an architectural view is a subset of the entire architecture.*

We will contribute a number of views to the **architecture document**, something we introduced in Chapter 2. These will be the following:

▶ Logical view

▶ Process view

▶ Deployment view

▶ Use case view

▶ Implementation view

These views will be described in sequence, but they are actually built in parallel, and, in fact, in some ways they overlap, as they each provide a different perspective on the same body of information. Typically, you will switch between developing the various views even as you create the class design. To keep things manageable, we focused on the class design before looking at architecture design, but in a real project these influence one another and will be developed iteratively; working back and forth among the various areas of concern.

In addition, we will begin to write the **design guidelines**. The design guidelines will capture critical strategic design decisions as we progress through the design phase. It is in these guidelines that we will consider the following type of questions:

▶ What programming language will we use?

▶ What operating system will we write for?

▶ Are we going to write for multiple user-interface libraries?

▶ How will the system's workload be distributed?

▶ How will updates be distributed?

▶ Will there be a database system? If so, will it be relational, object-oriented or something else?

▶ How will we fulfill the performance requirements?

▶ Is there a memory management strategy?

▶ How will we handle exceptions and errors?

▶ Is networking necessary?

▶ What is our transaction strategy?

Much of this will be discussed in this chapter, although the questions concerning the transaction strategy are discussed in the next chapter, database issues will be examined in Chapter 6, and implementation issues are covered in Chapter 7.

Architectural Views

We've talked about architectural views in earlier chapters. Let's summarize them using the following diagram, developed by Philippe Krutchen:

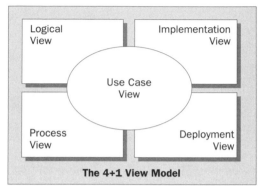

The 4+1 View Model

The **logical view** represents the *organization* of the most significant classes and how they relate to one another. It is here that we focus on components and "layers" within the design — differentiating among various levels of abstraction and working to understand the larger picture of the entire software architecture. When we looked at class design, we focused on the trees; here, at the architecture design stage, we step back to take a look at the whole forest. Ultimately, we'll feed the class design into the logical view, creating an integrated perspective of the entire system.

The logical view is the most comprehensive architectural view. It incorporates the most significant aspects of all the other views and provides an overarching picture of the system as a whole. It is to the logical view that other developers will turn to learn about the system and how it fits in with their work. The logical view provides an overview of the entire architecture, and, in conjunction with the code itself, provides a guide to the software.

In the diagram, the **use case view** has precedence over the other views, because the use case view — the collected use cases from the requirements analysis — drives and motivates the rest of the design.

Each of the other views, the **process view**, **deployment view** and **implementation view** will provide the specific details for their area of concern, but the logical view provides the overall road map.

In a system with multithreading or with multiple processes, as we'll see in the next chapter, the **process view** focuses on how these concurrent tasks interact. It is here that we document the design of the thread-safe architecture, and the outcome of considering issues relating to network latency and object location transparency. The next chapter will look at these issues.

In a distributed system, the **deployment view** focuses on the physical allocation of resources and the allocation of tasks among those resources. The deployment view describes the physical architecture of the system. This is the subject of this and the next two chapters.

The **use case view** has been created during requirements analysis. It is the end result, the artifact, produced as a result of developing the use cases. This view will be used as a driving force in the development of an architecture; it is the job of the architecture and ultimately of the implementation to *realize* the use case requirements. This again returns our focus to the interactions of the classes, and how these interactions serve to implement the use cases we analyzed earlier.

The **implementation view** is embodied in the code with its supporting documentation. We will devote Chapter 7 to implementation issues, before the final chapter on Phish.

The Logical View

The hardest part of building a design model is getting started. There is tremendous inertia that must be overcome; like starting a large parked truck. Once we are rolling it will be much easier to keep going, building up speed as we proceed.

We begin building the logical view by organizing our intuitive understanding of the problem, the domain analysis, the systems requirements and our own experience as software developers. This initial logical outline is created to bootstrap us into a working model, which we can then modify and extend. A common starting point is to **layer** the architecture.

You may have an intuitive, if preliminary, understanding of the layers that can be captured at the outset. For example, there may be an underlying systems layer, which supports networking protocols and so forth. On top of that systems layer, there may be a middle layer, which supports distributed objects and platform independence. On top of the middle layer, you may place your business-specific or industry-specific knowledge, and on top of that, you will build the application components.

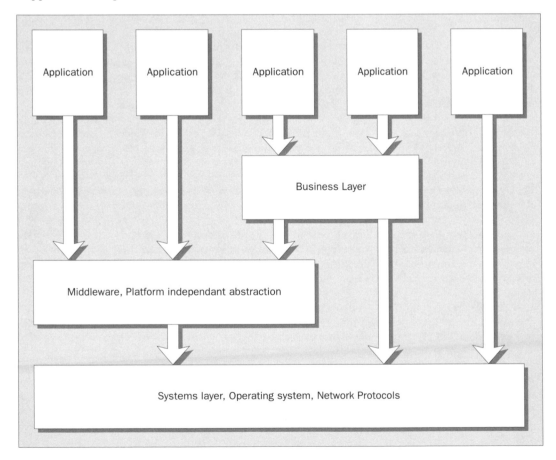

This approach should allow us to divide the project along obvious fault lines, which may help with allowing smaller teams to work in parallel. If your system is larger and more complex, you may want to do this initial cut at the major sub-systems, so that you can work out the high-level interfaces among the subsystems before going on to decompose those subsystems into interrelated classes.

The danger, of course, is that as you understand more about your design you may come to realize that some of the initial assumptions were wrong, and you've created false interfaces between components which really ought to be integrated.

At one project I worked on, we started with the assumption that the server and the client constituted two separate components that could be designed and developed independently. After all, the server would run on a different operating system at a different location, using a different organization of the "data". This initial assumption created terrible difficulties down the road, as we discovered that some of the "natural" divisions were not so natural after all, and that the transformations back and forth from one realization of the data to another introduced inefficiencies at both ends.

Significant Classes in the Logical View

In addition to describing the layers and the packages in the system, the logical view includes the *architecturally significant* classes. Each time you add a class to your class design, you must ask yourself if it also belongs in the logical view — is it an architecturally significant entity?

You'll certainly want to include each class that encapsulates a meaningful abstraction from the problem domain. In the VideoMagix example, we include tapes, video titles, customers and so forth. You'll also want to include classes that provide services to other classes, as well as classes that provide significant interface mechanisms with, for example, other products or the operating system.

The logical view should also include classes that have a significant effect on the performance or reliability of the system. Finally, you'll want to include any classes that require special attention or comments: those classes that are especially unusual.

The essential idea is to capture the most important and significant classes into the logical view part of the architecture document. This allows you to ensure the consistency and integrity of the overall design.

Packages

We are organizers. Even the least organized of us can't help making piles of related things. Walk through your house, chances are all the dishes are in one place, all the clothing in another. It is hardwired into our brain to see the world in terms of classifications, hierarchies, groups, aggregations and collections.

As developers, we organize classes into hierarchies based on behavior, performance, generalization, how the classes fit together in the development environment, what objects will be compiled and linked together, which objects will run on various platforms, and so on and so on. We need our development methodology to provide for these groupings.

As we saw in Chapter 2, the UML offers **packages**. A package is a set of classes organized by the designer in any way he sees fit. It is an arbitrary collection of classes provided as a convenience to the designer. This organization into packages is not restricted to classes; you can also package use cases and other artifacts in your design.

> *Many CASE tools allow you only one set of packages. This is unfortunate as you may want a given class to belong to one package based on its performance, and a second package based on its deployment. It would be good to have overlapping packages, organizing your objects as you see fit. Rational Rose allows visual grouping; provided that the class is owned by just one package, it may be displayed in others.*

In any case, packages are simply a convenience. You can certainly create a complete and robust design without worrying about them. This "utility drawer" approach, in which you throw everything in one box works fine for small programs, but can get rather messy and hard to work with in larger projects.

The Deployment View

The deployment view will describe which objects are on what machines and how the objects will fulfill the various processes required by the use cases. While the server may be "location transparent" to the client, it is the responsibility of the architecture document to describe the actual distribution of objects and the impact this distribution will have on performance and other system considerations.

Client-server Design

A key part of the deployment view is the **partitioning** of the application. This is different from layering, which looks at the software layers on one machine. Partitioning groups together classes of related functionality.

Many commercial business problems are solved by building **client-server applications**. Let's look at the reasons why client-server is the order of the day.

When many of us started programming, we did so on PCs: personal computers sitting on desktops which were not networked to anything except, perhaps, a printer. These actually represent a very brief moment in history, sandwiched between the age of centralized computers with dumb terminals on the one hand, and smart inter-networked computers on the other.

Centralized computing, with a server controlling common data, is a sound idea — you have one integrated source of information, you can build in extra failover measures in that server and put it under more stringent security. All in all it makes managers feel safer.

The traditional implementation of centralized computing, with mainframes and dumb terminals, seems too restrictive in the days of PCs and GUIs. On the other hand, the PC in its current incarnation (rather disparagingly known as a 'fat client' in some quarters) has proven to be too difficult to maintain and upgrade. And heterogeneous systems (that is, those supporting multiple platforms) with their different operating systems and binary standards have made interfacing computers difficult. We'll look at ideas on this later in the chapter.

What's the solution? Well various solutions are advanced, including:

▶ Client-server computing — this makes the client thinner, but does little else to reduce the maintenance needed on client machines.

▶ Web-based/intranet computing — the use of HTML as a language that is reconstituted by a web browser has opened the possibility of very thin clients which work literally everywhere. Of course the rapid and often mutually incompatible development of HTML makes this slightly tricky, but does improve the user-interface.

▶ Applet-based/Java computing — this gives us the thinnest clients, using computers that download all the applications they need to work on the fly. The server controls everything, and the client has the ability to support GUIs.

Your decision as to which solution to follow is not helped by the intermixing between the three, nor by larger questions of providers and politics.

Client-server Computing

Client-server computing comes in a number of flavors, or **tiers**.

Two-tier Architecture

The simplest variant, two-tier computing is useful for small-scale applications. Basically, the data management is moved to a dedicated server, where it's accessible to multiple clients over a network.

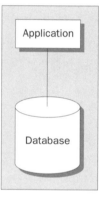

Three-tier Architecture

Two-tier client-server computing helps, but doesn't necessarily make the most of the server's processing power. If you have objects that work just with data, that perform business-related functions or that can perform background work (for example indexing), then you can put them on an **application server** and call them from clients as and when you want. This reduces some of the network traffic, and allows closer integration between the application server and the database server, so the system doesn't become overloaded.

Of course the 'client' and 'servers' can all be on the same machine — that certainly helps with debugging. What really matters here is the partitioning of the user interface, the application business objects and the data management layer.

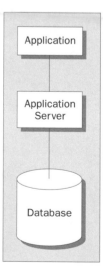

N-tier Architecture — Web-based Client-server

Taking the above discussion to its logical conclusion, we could have as many partitions as we want or need. Theoretically, you could have:

> A user interface

> A set of business objects that check and organize the client's request

> A mirror image of those business objects that provides persistence code

> A database

You could add a web-based interface too, for maximum flexibility, and make your client code work on multiple platforms — you can see how such complexity can develop. But the strict division in functionality makes each partition easier to maintain, upgrade and extend.

Distributing Servers

If your system is large enough to have multiple servers, you will need to decide how to distribute them within your network and, more importantly, how to balance the "load" on these servers. Your deployment view will document these decisions, including your design for ensuring that the servers remain in "synch" with one another, so that you avoid the possibility of data corruption among the servers.

A significant issue with multiple servers is managing the number of individual threads running on each processor. Parallel processing offers a tremendous opportunity to tune performance, but requires careful planning. In addition to managing the distribution of processes and threads, you'll also want to examine which machines write to which hard drives and how your overall load on the machines, network and the system as a whole is distributed.

The deployment view is also the place to discuss use of RAIDs (Redundant Arrays of Inexpensive Disks), data backup strategies, fail-over and fault-tolerant hardware and so forth. This is also a good place to document your design decisions about network infrastructure, including such matters as network topology and routers.

The Design Guidelines

The design guidelines are an overarching aspect of the architecture document — they cut across the views and describe issues, such as performance, size and reliability, which are not specific to the logical, process or deployment views. The design guidelines will answer questions relating to:

> Partitioning

> Operating system

> Development language

> Performance issues

> Storage issues

> Frameworks

One might argue that these decisions as to the operating system and language ought not to influence the design, but in the real world, they often dictate many significant aspects of how we'll actually build the software. We have two choices: we can design an idealized system, and once that system is fully designed, we can then modify the design for the constraints imposed by the operating system and the development language of choice, or we can cook these assumptions right into the design.

Make no mistake; we pay a price either way. In the first case, we end up with a much more flexible and portable design, but we take longer to get to market. After all, you are designing twice, once for the ideal and then again for the reality. In the second case, we build the product a bit more quickly, but we cook the operating system and language assumptions right into the design and it will be terribly difficult, if not impossible, to remove them later. As a general rule, it is better to get the design right with as few operating system constraints as possible. The reality, however, is that most of the time we know the operating system and perhaps even the development environment before we begin. It is nearly impossible to ignore these considerations during the design, so we're better off acknowledging them and documenting our assumptions.

Most of us accept the price of a constrained design, and build a system that is operating-system dependent. Building platform-independent applications is very difficult, and if you don't know at the outset that it is absolutely required, you may pay a very heavy price for a level of flexibility you don't really need. Moreover, if you then decide to switch platforms a few years later, you may find that the portability which you bought at so high a price is a chimera; the operating systems change so rapidly that what was portable yesterday is an encumbrance today.

However, if you are going to allow your platform to constrain your design, you must be on your guard not to allow any implementation details to slip into your architecture design. It is appropriate to record the platform dependencies, but not the details which should be encapsulated in the objects themselves.

Partitioning

As we've seen, there is a strong argument for separating your user interface (UI) from the "engine" of your design, so that you can change user interfaces as systems evolve. This gives you the flexibility to modify the UI independently from modifications to the underlying design. Once again, this is hard to do, although there are design patterns, such as the Abstract Factory, the Builder and the Factory Method (*Design Patterns*, Gamma et al), which can assist in this effort.

A principal goal of decoupling the UI from the engine is that UI requirements tend to change independently of, and often more quickly than, engine requirements. As the UI team tinkers with the user experience it is important to shield the underlying engine from the impact of these changes. Decoupling can also help you build platform-neutral designs which increase application portability.

In this way, you can build a series of user interfaces for different purposes, but keep the underlying business logic identical.

Note that we can also push the UI into the system itself. This is the approach taken by both Java and HTML. In these languages, the UI is described rather generally, and the engine, supplied by the client side machine, interprets the language in the "idiom" of the native environment. Thus, when a Java application runs on Windows, it looks like a Windows program, but when the same application runs on Unix it looks like a Unix application.

The partitioning argument is nearly academic, however, if you decide to implement the client with industry-standard web browsers. In this case the de-coupling of the interface from the application engine is automatic. In this design, the engine is your server code and any client-side scripting you write, and the UI is being written by your friends at Netscape and Microsoft. You have accomplished nearly 100% separation of engine from front end. Congratulations! Wasn't that easy?

The Operating System

The decisions about which operating system you use may be one of the most controversial decisions you'll make in the history of your product. Here's my opinion — the right answer is 32-bit Windows. Prove that I lie.

Now that is a bold and outrageous assertion. I know nothing about your system, and it may well be that you have special needs and issues that I can't address here. Further, there are many other candidate operating systems, most notably Unix and MacOS. Well, Unix anyway.

The bottom line, however, is that the desktop wars are over. If your product is a mass market product, or a business product, then the default answer is and must be 32-bit Windows (whatever they happen to be calling it this year: NT, Win98, Win2001...). There certainly are exceptions (for example, you're writing software to be embedded in a jet engine) but in these cases the choice of operating system won't be open to much question, and my advice won't be worth a tinker's cuss.

So here is my suggestion: unless you know that you absolutely *must* write to something else, the right answer is Windows. From a technical point of view, and certainly from a business point of view, for the overwhelming majority of *commercial* software there is only one viable operating system to consider.

Development vs Deployment

At times it is advantageous to do the bulk of your development in a more robust environment than that in which your application will run. A classic example is this: you are developing for Windows 95 but decide to develop on Windows NT. The reasons to do so are quite strong — Windows NT is much more robust and much less likely to crash if you do something wrong. Early in your development, when you may have memory leaks, stray pointers and so forth, Windows NT will be much more tolerant of your errors.

If you are going to release on Windows 95, however, be sure to test your code on Windows 95 itself, before you release it to your customers. While the two operating systems are very similar, they are *not* the same, and some things, which work on one environment, may very well fail on the other. *Always* do your final testing on the same operating system, and if possible the same hardware on which your customer will run your product.

The Development Language

If you are building commercial software for Windows (and we have already established that, in all likelihood, that is just what you are doing) then there are three viable development languages for medium-to-large projects:

- Java
- C++
- Visual Basic

Many professional software developers have yet to come to terms with Visual Basic, because, for many, it looks and feels like a toy. Visual Basic products still tend to be too big and too slow to be used for large commercial software. However, applications are getting faster and smaller, and memory is getting cheaper while programmer time is getting more expensive. Keep your eye on this product — soon it will be eating your lunch.

For now, however, for serious commercial software projects there are only two viable languages: Java and C++. They each have their advantages. In a nutshell, the big advantages of Java are that it has garbage collection and is highly portable. The big advantage of C++ remains the quality of the tools and the overall performance of the code. C++ is simply a more mature language, and as such, the compilers, editors and class libraries are superior.

This book will describe implementation issues in terms of C++, but the two languages are so similar that nearly everything discussed (except memory management and garbage collection) will apply to Java as well.

Performance Issues

The design guidelines should reflect the design decisions that you made to respond to the performance requirements found in analysis. This might include discussion of optimizing compilers, network topology, caching and memory requirements etc.

Storage Issues

The requirements analysis articulates the persistence and storage requirements; the design guidelines should detail the design decisions you make to implement these requirements. For example, if you decide to use a database, the design guidelines should detail which particular database you'll use and what impact this decision will have on the overall architecture of the system.

This is *not* the place to detail the logical design of the database, nor the physical design of how you will deploy the database technology; those go in the logical and deployment views, respectively. The design guidelines, however, should discuss issues such as whether you will use SQL or another access language, whether you will use a relational database management system (RDBMS) or an object database. These issues are the subject of Chapter 6.

Frameworks

As window-based operating systems like Windows NT become more complex, there is increasing market demand from developers for better tools to build applications. Application frameworks have been created in response to this demand.

A framework consists of a set of cooperating classes. These classes provide the skeleton of a design for a particular application; they define the overall structure of the application, including the definition of the class's responsibilities and collaborators. The framework includes all of the

139

high-level classes that define the application's basic interactions. The application developer is expected to subclass his domain-specific classes from the application framework's hierarchy and thus quickly builds working applications.

The framework therefore defines the architecture for the application. All applications built from the framework will have the same "spirit" — the same basic behavior — but different specific components.

The idea behind frameworks is that one basic design will suffice for a number of related applications. Whether a framework will be successful depends on finding the right balance — enough support to ease the work of the developer without overly constraining the final design of the application.

Frameworks vs Design Patterns

Design patterns are typically recorded as text, a written culture of "best practices". Frameworks are usually provided as working code, a library of predesigned solutions. These differences are significant, but both design patterns and frameworks provide general solutions to sets of application problems and, as such, they are related.

Frameworks tend to be larger in scope than design patterns; they are often composed of several design patterns. Frameworks also tend to be more application-family specific than design patterns — either horizontally, like a GUI framework, or vertically, that is, a domain-specific framework. Design patterns are general patterns that are typically coded from scratch each time they are needed; frameworks typically consist of ready-to-use concrete classes and a larger set of abstract classes from which you can subclass your application-specific objects.

Frameworks vs Class Libraries

Frameworks are essentially large, integrated class libraries, but there are some subtle differences.

Typically, class libraries package functionality into modular components. Applications instantiate objects from the libraries and call their member functions. This treats an individual class as the unit of reuse. The application designer then has to combine these classes into the fundamental mechanisms that underlie the architecture. When you build an application with a class library, you write the control logic yourself. The library gives you pre-defined objects, but the connections between them — the flow — is designed for the specific application.

A framework goes further than this and treats the core of the application as the unit of reuse. A framework typically defines the responsibilities and collaborations of each class *as it is used in the framework*. The application designer works within the flow of control defined by the framework. The assumption is that any application in that domain, or at least any that would be based on the framework, would follow the flow that the framework defines.

MFC

There are a number of commercial application frameworks available for various operating systems and serving a number of vertical markets. Probably the most successful application framework at the moment is the Microsoft Foundation Classes, the MFC. The MFC is a set of classes representing a relatively thin wrapper around the Win32 API for Windows.

Many object-oriented purists deride the MFC as being a cheap imitation of an object-oriented framework. They complain that the class library is not well designed and that it does not fully encapsulate the API. All of this is true, but in my opinion, it misses the point. The MFC was intended to be a bridge from C style API programming to C++ style object-oriented design. As such, it was enormously successful. The MFC provided sufficient mapping between the API and the object viewpoint that tens of thousands of Windows programmers could make the adjustment.

> *The MFC is also attacked for not being sufficiently polymorphic. Briefly, the MFC handles message mapping through a series of macros rather than through the inheritance hierarchy and virtual function tables. The problem Microsoft was working to solve, however, was that there are thousands of messages a window might receive, and subclasses of windows would have huge virtual function tables to lug around in memory. The MFC was created back in the days of Win 3.1 when memory was scarce, they could not afford to be profligate about the size of objects in the application framework.*

You can also argue that MFC is a class library and a framework. The framework is based on the **document/view architecture**. The document/view architecture allows the data stored in a document to be accessed in various ways by different views. Word is a good example of such an architecture. If you want document/view apps, then MFC is useful as a framework. However, the increasing acceptance of partitioning of GUI, logic and data, multilanguage programming and distributed apps are leaving MFC behind. It remains useful for its GUI classes, but I think its framework days are numbered.

Its commercial success speaks for itself, however, and Microsoft has committed to moving, not only to a more sophisticated, component-based application framework (of which we'll learn more in a minute), but eventually to an entirely object-oriented operating system.

Distributed Objects

One of the principal considerations in your Design Guidelines document will be how you distribute your objects. Will you build a monolithic executable, or can you break the application into smaller, self-contained units of binary code — components — which inter-operate and are easier to maintain?

Today, applications are not just distributed across local area networks, but over the entire Internet. It has become increasingly important that client software should not know or worry where the server code is physically located.

History of Inter-process Communication (IPC)

Several inter-process communication (IPC) mechanisms are now in common use. Each of these brings with it an architectural style, a set of terminology, development and run-time environments, and so on.

IPC is a good illustration of software layering. The underlying protocol is TCP/IP — the de-facto Internet standard. Atop this are built a variety of APIs — socket and, remote procedure calls (RPC). Remote Procedure Call (RPC) was developed in order to make function/procedure calls transparent across processes. For the internet, HTTP operates on top of the sockets layer. And, finally, for complete object-object interactions across processes, there exist distributed object frameworks like COM and CORBA.

Network Layers

SSL	HTTP		COM	CORBA
Sockets			RPC	

Transport Layer, TCP/IP
Internet Layer, IP
Physical Layer (e.g. Ethernet)

When comparing these architectures there are a number of characteristics to consider. You can use these characteristics to compare and contrast each of these architectures and to choose the one that is right for your project.

▶ The overall system architecture and the environment provided for distributed processing

▶ The inter-process communication mechanism supported and its characteristics

▶ How the system deals with errors

▶ How objects are uniquely identified

▶ Common services offered by the architecture

▶ How does one find services? How are these services described?

▶ How does the system deal with security?

▶ How does the system provide object persistence?

▶ What facilities are available to support transaction processing?

▶ What is the system's performance?

Distributed objects may be as small as a business object, like a customer, or as large as a whole application. Different architectures provide different levels of support for distributed objects.

Distributed Object Architecture

The architectural framework supporting distributed processing both smoothes the way and constrains the application programmer in his design. Among the issues to consider when deciding upon a distributed processing framework are:

▶ How do the individual objects relate to the rest of the system — how much of their behavior and structure is encapsulated? How finely do they define their interface? Do they announce their exception handling?

▶ How are the system services structured — Are they horizontal (available to all objects) or vertical (application specific)? How are these services announced?

▶ What restrictions, constraints, guidelines and skeletons are provided to the developer?

▶ What development tools and environments are available for this architectural pattern?

Inter-process Communication (IPC)

Inter-process communication may be supported by the operating system, or by a set of design and programming conventions. IPC may be lightweight and simple, or heavy-duty and complicated, depending on what you need to accomplish and the degree of security, integrity, reliability and robustness your application requires.

In the following few sections, we'll look at some of the issues that IPC mechanisms may address. Much of this detail will be most relevant to the cutting edge of the industry — namely CORBA and COM. And because of our Windows bias, COM will be the focus of our discussion.

Location Transparency

Remote objects ought to be **location transparent** — that is to say the calling software need not know where they are located.

> **Location transparency** *is where the client code need not know the location of the server code*

Objects can have one of three locations with respect to the process using their services:

▶ in-process

▶ local

▶ remote

In-process servers (often abbreviated *in-proc*) run in the same process and memory space as the application (typically from within a DLL) and have very high performance, at the cost of representing some risk to the application. Since the control is in the same process space, if the control crashes, it will bring down the application.

Objects running locally (rather than in-process) run in their own process space but can communicate with the application. These controls are safer, if they crash they can not bring down the calling application, but they run slower. The principal performance cost is in **marshaling** data across the process boundary.

> **Marshaling** *is streaming data so that it can be copied or mapped into a different memory location.*

143

When you marshal an object across a process boundary (or across a network) you recreate its image in a different memory space. The effect of this is that the calling application thinks it is talking directly to the object, though in reality it is talking to a **proxy**.

> *A proxy is an object which represents the intended object, but in a different memory space.*

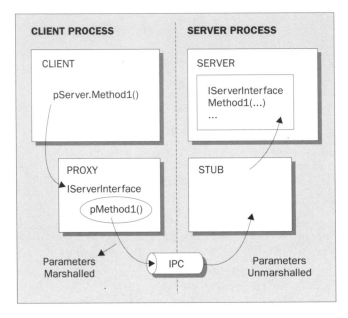

The client in its process wishes to talk with the server in its process. The data sent as parameters or returned as return values must be marshaled across the process boundary. To accomplish this, a typical architecture is to create a proxy for the server in the client's memory space and to put a proxy for the client (called a **stub**) in the server's memory space.

The client talks with the proxy and cannot tell that it isn't talking directly to the server. The proxy and stub work together to marshal the data across the boundary. The stub then forwards the request directly to the server.

> *The mechanism for this cross-process communication is a general pattern for your projects, if it isn't provided as part of the environment. Marshaling and unmarshaling the parameters for your request should be done by mirror objects that then communicate to the respective client and server objects.*

Finally, *remote* objects can be located anywhere on the network. Once again they operate by proxy and stub, but this time the proxy and stub must talk across a network, which can be orders of magnitude slower.

In theory, the client ought to be unaware of these differences. It should call a method on the server and not know or care if that server is running in-process, locally or remotely. And this is how you should program your server objects. The reality, however, is that network performance is significantly slower than in-process performance, and this will affect the design and necessitate deployment optimizations.

Data Format Transparency and Security Issues

In addition to concerns about finding the object and how quickly it will respond, you must cope with differences in data format between your client code and your server code, which may, in fact, be running on a completely different operating system. COM, CORBA, and other frameworks for handling remote objects, manage the necessary data transformations as part of the data-marshaling process.

In addition, they provide the data security required to ensure that those clients which access data on the server have been authenticated and have the necessary level of permission.

Synchronous vs Asynchronous Messaging

As part of the architecture of your application you must decide which requests for objects and services will be **synchronous** and which will be **asynchronous**.

> *In* **synchronous** messaging, *also known as "request/reply", the client and server maintain a link, and wait for a reply to their previous call, and hang up once they're through, barring "technical difficulties".*
>
> **Asynchronous** messaging *is closer to mail- or fax-based communication, you "fire and forget" your message and it will get delivered and answered in due course.*

In essence, synchronous calls block the execution of the caller (that is, the client) until the call and reply are completed. Synchronous communication across networks can suffer from "long" delays, compared to intra-machine calls. If the client needs to continue working while waiting, it should make the call in a separate thread.

Asynchronous calls allow the caller to continue with other work as soon as the call has been made, and have the advantage that the client and server don't need to establish and maintain a link. Programming with them is rather like working with events. Such messaging is ideal for:

▶ Mobile clients

▶ Servers with dial-up connections to networks

▶ Internet-based exchanges between businesses, rather like an extended email

▶ Queuing of jobs, allowing server load-balancing

Application integrity may be put at risk by the use of remote objects and asynchronous communication, as there is more opportunity for the client and the server to get out of synch with respect to one another. The application must be designed so that the asynchronous request allows the client and server to work independently.

You'll address these issues throughout your architecture document, but to the extent that your multi-process approach has an impact on these issues, you'll document these concerns in the process view.

Connection-based vs Connectionless

Note that there is another deeper IPC division, at the level of the network protocol — connection-based and connectionless communication — which differs subtly from the above discussion. It relates to the way the transport layers on the client and server talk to each other.

Synchronous and asynchronous calls can be either connection-based or connectionless. Connection-based communication, like TCP, guarantees that **data packages** arrive and do so in the order they were sent. It is very like a telephone conversation. This incurs greater overhead at the transport layer. Connectionless communication, like UDP, means you have to manage the low-level connection yourself. It is still possible to build a connection-based protocol on top of a connectionless protocol — for example, UDP is COM's preferred protocol.

Exception Processing

Whatever method you choose for inter-process communication, you'll need a way to signal failure. If the serving object can't be found, or if the transmission times out, or for whatever reason your request can't be handled, the IPC mechanism must at least report back the failure.

Some applications can manage with fairly unreliable and slow communication among processes. An application that distributes, for example, a time update to a PC clock every 20 ms can handle dropping the occasional message now and again. An application which is responsible for sending the launch command to an automated nuclear weapons facility may need a higher degree of security, integrity and reliability.

A particular architecture needs some method of reporting errors to calling objects, which transcends machine boundaries, the programming language in which the object was written and even the C++ compiler used to compile C++ classes. We'll see how COM does this later.

Security

Open distributed systems have special security concerns. Once you put your application on the Internet you expose yourself to hackers of every description. It may not be possible to make a system 100% secure, but, once again, market imperatives are driving the need for quick and reliable solutions. The revenue expected from on-line transactions over the Internet is projected to rise to billions of dollars over the next five years, and this is enough money to fund significant development in the area of security.

Over the last few years a consensus has been reached at least on what issues must be solved:

▶ Authentication: knowing who is the "author" of a message

▶ Authorization: knowing the author is allowed to use the resource

▶ Integrity: knowing the message has been received without being changed

▶ Non-repudiation: proving who the author of the message is

▶ Confidentiality: knowing no one other than the recipient has read the message

Making a decision as to which IPC mechanism to use for your application requires a good understanding of what you need to accomplish mapped to the capabilities of the various distributed services architectures. The rest of this chapter will briefly review the leading candidate architectural alternatives.

Sockets

Sockets were one of the first mechanisms that offered any form of inter-process communication implementation transparency. Their purpose was to make network I/O like file I/O on Unix, which they do through a C API.

Architecture

Sockets can be connectionless (e.g. datagram sockets built on top of UDP) or they can be connection-based (e.g. stream sockets built on top of TCP). Sockets help to insulate the application code from the underlying transport and inter-networking protocols, as well as the underlying wire-level protocols. Sockets have proven to be enormously popular. They are now incorporated directly into most serious operating systems, and they are the primary peer-to-peer API for TCP/IP.

The socket architecture is based on the ideas of communication endpoints: a named entity with a given address. An example endpoint might be an FTP listener. The address is a host ID and a port number.

Connectionless, or datagram, sockets provide for delivery of independent packets. As with all connectionless protocols, however, delivery is not guaranteed, and managing the order of the packets is left to the application.

Connection-based, or stream, sockets do guarantee that packets will be received in the same order in which they are sent, and they protect against errors being introduced into the stream of data.

Inter-process Communication (IPC)

There are two ends to any socket. One end is the "client" that is making the request. The other end is called the peer or server. Object location is not transparent with sockets. The addressing information required includes a host address (for example, an IP address) and a port number. There is some level of standardization, in that all port numbers less than 1024 are pre-allocated for common services. For example, port 21 is reserved for FTP.

Data Format Issues and Errors

Data formatting is not transparent with sockets. The application is responsible for interpreting the data, including mapping byte ordering or other information into the appropriate format. Sockets do not support the concept of objects or data typing; they deal only with a stream of bytes. Sockets do not support exceptions, though they can return error codes just like any other information: as a series of bytes in the stream.

Object Identification and Security

An object is identified to a socket by its address: host address and port number. Sockets were originally used by C programs and deal with memory at the level of a **struct**. Sockets provide no services beyond their basic read and write functionality. The client must know the address and port number of a server to establish a connection. They provide no directory assistance, no repository, and no information at all about where to send the message. This must be provided by the application.

Furthermore, sockets provide no built-in security, though a Secure Socket Library (SSL) is now available. SSL is used on the Internet, though it will probably be modified significantly (and perhaps unrecognizably) before it is integrated into the ultimate electronic commerce protocol for the Internet.

Persistence

Sockets come with no notion of persistence and do not support transaction processing. They are, however, employed in many transaction processing systems. They are an infrastructure technology for these systems, as they are for COM, CORBA, and other distributed architectures.

Performance

Sockets add some overhead to raw TCP/IP, but they are a lot "closer to the metal" than more full-featured distributed object frameworks, for example, COM or CORBA.

Web-based Architecture — HTTP/CGI

The Hypertext Transfer Protocol (HTTP) is a protocol built on top of sockets. It is used to access resources on the World Wide Web.

Architectural Pattern

HTTP was built to support the retrieval of Web (HTML) pages, images, files etc. In the traditional Web environment, browsers communicate with the web server using HTTP, and get back HTML pages and perhaps CGI scripts.

CGI is the Common Gateway Interface protocol and was a first attempt at providing dynamic services over the web. These days CGI is fading, as JavaScript, VBScript and Active Server Pages provide much "smarter" web pages, which distribute processing among clients and server machines.

Inter-process Communication (IPC)

HTTP is a stateless connection-based protocol.

> **A stateless protocol** *does not maintain* **state** *(e.g., the current value of variables). Each transmission must supply all necessary state information.*

A connection lasts long enough to service one request/response pair; a new connection is needed for every interaction. This is a synchronous protocol; the web client waits for a response from the web server before proceeding. Thus one TCP connection is needed for each request — which is a large overhead for the server.

Because HTTP is stateless, it is not possible to maintain an ongoing session using pure HTTP. Vendors are overcoming this limitation through the use of "cookies" — binary data stored on the client machine as temporary (or sustained) identifiers. This allows for the creation of "virtual sessions".

Data is encoded in an internet-specified self-describing format known as MIME (Multipurpose Internet Mail Extensions). Web clients use parameters in the request to tell the web servers what kinds of data format they can understand. As this is a stateless protocol, this has to be done for every exchange.

An HTTP request is stylized. Each request consists of a request line, a variable number of request header fields and the request entity body (an unformatted "blob" from the system's viewpoint). The request line consists of the method (for example, **GET** and **PUT**), the resource identifier (for example, a URL), and the HTTP version number. Each request header field consists of a name and a value separated by a colon. These can be used to specify the languages and encodings understood, authorization information and other such data.

An HTTP response consists of a response header line, a variable number of response header fields, and the entity body. The response header line contains the HTTP version, a result (error) code and an explanation of the result code. The response header fields designate, for example, the type and length of the entity body. The entity body contains the actual response to the request. This could be, for example, the HTML document that was originally requested.

Object Location and Data Format Issues

All identification is by way of URLs. Any object, such as an audio clip or HTML page, is identified by a URL. An object may have more than one URL, but a URL uniquely identifies one object. Data is sent in self-describing formats under the rules for MIME encoding. MIME supports several data types, including text, audio, video and still images. It also includes the capability for multi-part messages.

Exception Processing

The results of running an HTTP request are encoded in the response header. The result code is an integer code and the explanation field is a textual description of that field. No other error or exception processing is provided.

CORBA

The Common Object Request Broker Architecture (CORBA) offers a general client/server specification based on peer-to-peer communications. CORBA is built around the concept of an Object Request Broker (ORB) mediating between the client and the server. The ORB functions as a universal backbone for inter-process communication across the network. The ORB provides location transparency, as well as source language and operating system transparency.

> *It should be emphasized that CORBA is a specification. There are many ORB vendors, who each implement a selection of the various standardized services. In addition the specification is still evolving. Have a look at http://www.omg.org for more information.*

In the following sections, the bare bones of the specification are outlined. This should give you an idea of what services a full-fledged distributed object environment should be able to provide. Anything which isn't yet implemented is up for grabs in your own projects!

Architecture

The following figure shows the overall CORBA architecture, known as the Object Management Architecture (OMA). There are four types of objects that communicate over the ORB:

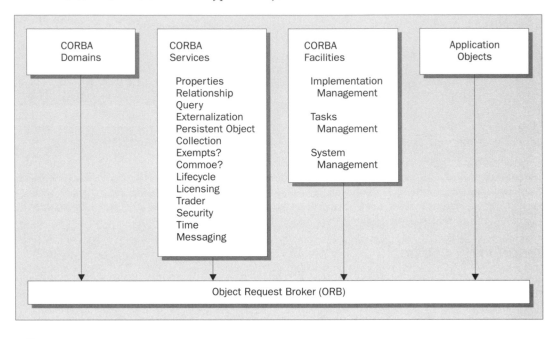

▶ **CORBA Services**, providing services to all application and system objects. These include, for example, white pages (naming service) which allow you to find objects on the network. These services are divided into information management, task management, system management and infrastructure services.

▶ **CORBA Facilities** are higher-level functions such as user-interface management or information management. They are divided up into information management, task management, system management and user-interface management facilities.

▶ **CORBA Domains** are used to create vertical application domains, such as manufacturing.

▶ **Application objects**

Each CORBA object describes its interface using CORBA's Interface Definition Language (IDL). IDL looks like a restricted portion of C++, emphasizing the static class structure. All that is captured are a class's publicly available members and hierarchy information. There is a class-like construct, called an **interface**. An interface defines functionality, not implementation. It includes a definition of each member function supported, including its signature (type and order of input parameters) and the type of return value.

CORBA has an IPC mechanism that provides location, host operating system and language independence. CORBA ORBs come with a standard set of services, which are described below. The CORBA services provide, by today's standards, a full environment for developing applications based on cooperating, distributed objects.

Inter-process Communication (IPC)

The IDL statements are run through an IDL compiler, which produces stubs for the clients and skeletons for the servers. Stubs marshal parameters for the outbound call and unmarshal and deliver replies. The skeleton unmarshals the request and makes the call to the server's member function. It also marshals the reply and sends it back to the stub on the client. Thus the ORB's stubs correspond to an RPC's proxy and the ORB's skeleton corresponds to an RPC's stub.

Objects may call each other's member functions using the ORB as the communications backbone. The stub and the skeleton work together to make the call appear like a local member function call to the client. In addition to this (call-and-return style) synchronous interface, a limited asynchronous capability is also provided.

This is the normal way that an object makes use of services advertised by other objects. It fits well with the normal C++ paradigm: an object knows which other objects it wants to communicate with and knows the signatures and return values, as well as the semantics (uses, pre-conditions and post-conditions) of each member function.

CORBA provides a second style, available when the client cannot know in advance what services will be available on the server. In this case, the IDL statements for a server are compiled into a run-time format and kept in an "interface repository". The client can obtain information from this repository that describes each available interface, including the calling parameters and return value types for the member functions that comprise it.

Object Location and Data Format Issues

CORBA makes object location completely transparent. CORBA's IPC mechanism and IDL definitions provide data *format* transparency. A client written in one language can call a server's method written in another language, running on another machine, under another operating system. The client and the server can pass data back and forth; the ORB takes care of the rest.

Exception Processing

CORBA's protocol guarantees that any invocation returns a result or throws an exception. The IDL definition of each member function includes a specification of what exceptions it can throw. Exceptions at the IDL level map to C++ exception classes and objects in the code.

Object Identification

Object references in CORBA are opaque. However, objects also have string names. The naming service (white pages) can be used to obtain an object reference from its name. There is an additional service, the trader service, which is often called the yellow pages. With this service, clients can obtain a reference to an object that has certain capabilities without knowing the name of the server.

Services Offered

CORBA offers a number of services which are domain independent. They are intended to be used as-is or specialized by applications. Since each service is specified by IDL definitions, it is possible to implement a primitive version of a service and then replace it when a more robust, commercial version is available.

151

The Information Management Services include the following services:

Properties Service. Properties are dynamic typed attributes, whose value is not known at compile time. The properties service defines two interfaces. The first is called `PropertySet`. This interface lets you define properties and read their types and values. The second is `PropertySetDef`, which lets you modify the property *modes*. These include normal (read, write and delete), read-only (read and delete), fixed-read-only (read only) and fixed normal (read and write).

Relationship Service. The Relationship Service allows the user to define associations between objects and have these associations captured in a publicly-known place and scheme. Note that the use of relationship objects adds to the number of objects in the system. It is presumed that they will be used on ORBs that support large numbers of fine-grained objects.

Query Service. The Query Service provides an integrated set of mechanisms for querying relational and object databases. The queries are based on the SQL2 standard, the SQL3 standard, and the object query language, OQL. The Query Service should be layered over various existing query languages for different types of databases. Only dynamic queries are supported. The queries can respond synchronously or asynchronously. The standard also defines recommended ways of representing query results as collections — the query collections interface. This interface includes an iterator, and the ability to create, modify and destroy elements of the collection.

Externalization Service. This service serializes a data stream. This can be used, for example, to marshal parameters, or to prepare a stream of data to be transported to a persistence service.

Persistent Object Service. The CORBA Persistent Object Service provides persistence to CORBA objects. Persistence is discussed in Chapter 5.

Collection Service: This service provides a set of language-independent collection classes. These classes are based on the C++ STL containers, and are defined by IDL. These collections could be used, for example, in support of the CORBA Query Service (subclasses of the query collections interface).

The Tasks Management Services include the Events Service and the Concurrency Service,

Events Service. This service provides general capabilities to pass event information between objects. It can be used, for example, to implement a publish-and-subscribe service. The service defines event channels, which can contain objects. The channel is instantiated by an Event Factory. Once it is defined, the channel is the communications port between the event source and the event sink, known as the event supplier and the event consumer.

Concurrency Service: This service implements the locking functions required to make an application thread-safe. It includes the concepts of a lock set, a lock set factory and a lock coordinator. Locking modes include read, write and upgrade (read with intention to modify — used to avoid deadlocks). The locks can be applied at multiple granularities. The lock service includes deadlock avoidance algorithms that work with mixed lock granularities. We'll discuss concurrency further in the next chapter.

The System Management Services include the Naming Service, the Lifecycle Service, the Licensing Service and the Trader Service.

The **Naming Service** is a white-pages service. It provides a hierarchical, system-wide map of object names to object references. The bind operation is used to add a name to the directory. The **resolve** operation is to find a name in the directory and return its object reference.

The **Lifecycle Service** is a suite of services used to copy, create, move and delete objects, including any aggregated components and constraints on their relationships. Objects can be created with a factory. The factory registers the new object with the object adapter on the ORB. Objects can be copied with a clone operation, using the factory on whatever machine the copy will reside.

Licensing Service. This service is used in support of electronic commerce, and allows a developer to assign limited usage licenses to software.

Trader Service: This is a yellow pages service. It maps from object capabilities to object references. The trading service advertises all objects that have been registered with it. Queries are supported that find objects based on their capabilities and their "quality of service".

Finally, the infrastructure services include the Time Service, the Security Service and the Messaging Service.

The **Time Service** provides a secure service for synchronizing clocks in a distributed environment. This is used by the **Security Service**, which is in fact the only service that works directly with the ORB. Between them they provide confidentiality, integrity, availability, non-repudiation and accountability. Security information is propagated through all ORBs that are involved in a request.

Finally, the **Messaging Service** allows you to call methods asynchronously.

Performance

CORBA ORBs do not add a large amount of overhead. The performance penalty is comparable to a traditional RPC call. A remote function call in a CORBA environment is roughly comparable to the same function call exercised in a DCOM environment.

COM and DCOM

The Component Object Model (COM) is Microsoft's distributed object architecture. In COM, functions defined by a COM interface may be called by objects on other machines, written in different languages and running on different operating systems.

> *In some ways COM competes directly with CORBA, but when you consider the platforms on which the two architectures run, you see that they're complimentary. For this reason, software bridges have now been created between the two architectures.*

> *In the last section, we've saw how CORBA maps out the distributed object universe. COM does much the same thing, though fewer parts are standardized.*

COM is tightly integrated in Microsoft's operating systems, Windows 95/98 and Windows NT, and it underpins Microsoft's view of current and future application development.

Component-based Development

Microsoft is heavily committed to the use and reuse of binary software components across their systems. As a demonstration of this commitment, they've split much of their own software into COM components — for example the Office suite and Internet Explorer.

Let's review the reason why component-based development is such a good idea — namely, code reuse.

Code reuse can be as simple as copying and pasting source code. But whenever you change the original source code, to add features or to fix a bug, you need to paste the revised code into every application.

To improve source code sharing, object-oriented programming recognizes object relationships and object-oriented languages automate reuse of parent class code, and allow polymorphic method calling.

But this too has its limitations – any changes in the parent classes necessitate recompilation of any applications that reference child classes.

The next stage along is use of precompiled libraries; in Windows these are Dynamic Link Libraries (DLLs). This solves an additional problem — how to protect the code on which you've worked so hard from being stolen. But the problems of keeping DLL versions up-to-date while providing for legacy applications are well documented.

> *Along the way, the idea of code that worked cross-platform without recompilation has lead to a variety of languages, the most famous being Java. But this is subject to the same problems as mentioned above.*

The industry solution to this is to define a unique interface to an object, which has the following attributes:

- Unique identification
- Interface set in perpetuity
- Exposes public methods, and acts as a level of indirection between the caller and the object. Thus, it supports strong encapsulation

This is implemented through a binary-level compatibility specification. This specification is based on the use of what COM calls a virtual table, or **vtable**.

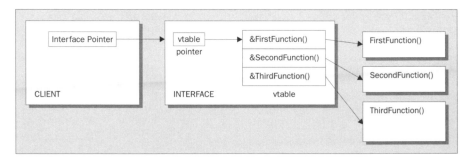

When it comes to that bug fix, you can recompile the new, improved COM object to support the same interface, and no-one will ever know, except by the error disappearing — as it supports the same interface.

Anytime you want to expand the functionality of an object, you can create a new interface. This will have a new name and a new identifier. And because COM objects support multiple interfaces (as a means of supporting different sets of functionality), your COM object can still support the old interface.

COM Architecture

As we've seen, COM separates interface from implementation. Your COM client never obtains a direct reference to the COM server object; it only obtains a pointer to an interface object appropriate to the COM server. COM servers are executables or DLLs that contain the code that implements one or more COM classes.

Interface Chic

The interface is defined in an Interface Definition Language (IDL), not very different from CORBA's IDL.

Every interface has a name to make it easy to reference, but it is uniquely identified by a **G**lobally **U**nique **ID**entifier, or GUID.

Each COM interface derives from **IUnknown**, which provides three methods essential to all COM objects. Two, **AddRef()** and **Release()**, deal with reference counting, something to which we'll return in Chapter 7. This allows COM to ensure that the object remains in memory when any client has a pointer to an interface on that object. The other method, **QueryInterface()**, allows a potential client to acquire a reference to an interface it wants, if that's one the COM server supports.

As we've implied here, COM interfaces can inherit from one another. In practice, COM interfaces look very like a virtual function table (vtable) in C++, and **interface inheritance** just carries over the inherited interface as the first entries in the new vtable.

> *That the COM interface layout is so similar to the vtable used in C++ to support virtual functions, means that most C++ compilers can build COM-compatible interfaces automatically. If you want to do the same thing in C you have to do it manually.*

To get the interface on an object of a particular class, you create an instance of a special component called a **class factory**. The class factory has only one responsibility: creating the class you need. Because class factories have a predefined COM interface (**IClassFactory**), they provide a standard mechanism for creating objects of a class.

COM provides clients with both static invocations using proxies and stubs, and dynamic invocation using a registry of meta-information.

▶ Static invocation follows the common RPC paradigm: the proxies marshal the parameters and pass them with the call through COM to the stubs, which unmarshal them and deliver them with the actual method call to the server.

▶ Dynamic invocation in COM uses a type library, generated from the IDL description of an object's interfaces. Then, at runtime, clients can use the COM object without knowing what services it provides. Common clients include VBA and the ActiveX scripting languages (VBScript and JScript etc.)

Servers that support dynamic invocation implement an interface called **IDispatch**.

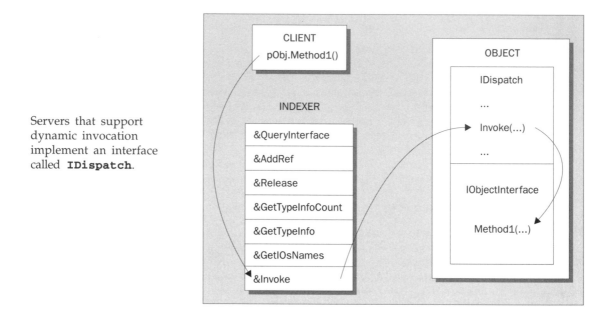

IDispatch supports a function **Invoke()** which, in its implementation, is essentially a large case statement that forwards the method request to the appropriate method implementation. The point here is that the calling application need only know to call the seventh method, **Invoke()**, in the vtable, simplifying its work considerably.

Exception Handling

COM provides a standardized set of status codes for handling error conditions. The convention is that COM method calls should return their results through **[out]** parameters (buffers passed in by reference) and the actual return value should be reserved for success or failure.

The status code can be taken apart to determine where the error was reported (e.g. RPC, Win32 or structured storage) and what it was. If you want to translate COM errors into C++ exceptions, there are various tools (notably the compiler COM support in Visual C++ 5) that will generate a wrapper class for an interface defined in a type library and automatically translate COM errors to C++ exceptions.

Conclusion

The two leading candidate frameworks for robust, reliable, secure, location-transparent inter-process communication are COM and CORBA. A full description of these two technologies, and their comparative strengths and weaknesses is a big topic, enough for at least one other book.

A comprehensive description of how COM works and how to use it runs over 500 pages in Dr. Richard Grime's masterful book *Professional DCOM Programming* (Wrox Press, ISBN 1-861000-60-X). COM has a reputation for being difficult to use, but that is changing as Microsoft provides better tool support for COM.

If you are embarking on a large project that will rely heavily on this technology, you'll want to invest the necessary time in investigating these technologies. My personal short answer is this: if I'm building a Windows-only application, COM is the obvious answer. If I'm building a system which is either multi-platform or especially one which doesn't include Windows, then CORBA is a stronger candidate. The decision is complex, however, so don't assume this quick rule of thumb is sufficient for your needs.

Summary

In this chapter we've looked at the general architectural questions you will need to ask your team, and then document. We've looked at:

▶ Architectural views

▶ Client-server design

▶ Design guidelines

▶ Distributed objects

> *It is important to emphasize, once again, that the activities of designing the architecture and designing the classes actually occur in tandem. There are tiny micro-cycles of development in which you focus first on one and then the other, each design influencing the other. We've split the discussion of them in this book in order to group the issues coherently.*

In the next couple of chapters we'll focus on two important architecture mechanisms: concurrency and persistence, and then, in Chapter 7 we'll look at implementation issues when programming with C++. You may find parts of these architecture chapters tougher going; if so feel free to skip over the details in your first reading.

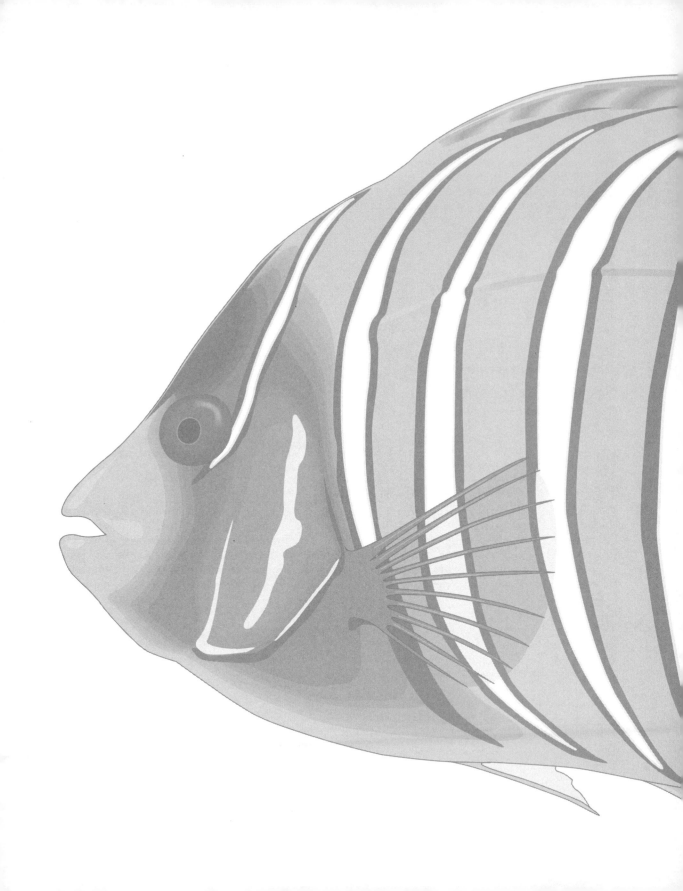

Concurrency

In a simple program, one user interacts with the system, which does one thing at a time. You push a button and the system reacts. You wait for that reaction to end and then you take another action.

In a modern system, running on Windows 95, NT or another multi-tasking operating system, you no longer have the luxury of assuming that only one thing will happen at a time. Windows is quite content to manage multiple tasks "simultaneously". Simultaneously is in quotes because the operating system provides the *illusion* of simultaneity, rather than the reality. It does so by **time-slicing**.

> **Time slicing** *is where the operating system divides a second into many parts and works on each task for a fraction of a second; switching between them in sequence. Since these tasks switch quite quickly, it appears to the user that they are happening at the same time.*

Some computers have more than one CPU, and Windows NT is capable of using each CPU for a different task. In this case, the illusion gives way to reality. With more than one CPU it *is* possible to achieve true simultaneity.

The interesting thing, though, is that nothing should change except performance. In a well-designed system it doesn't matter to your code at all whether it is running in a multi-CPU environment, or just in a time-sliced single-CPU environment.

This chapter introduces threads and processes, the elements essential in creating applications that support multi-tasking. It also explains the benefits you will derive from creating a multi-threaded application. We will also look at the difficulties threads create, and the techniques you can employ to overcome these problems.

Processes and Threads

A **multi-process system** is one which allows two or more programs to run at the same time. A **multi-threaded system** is one which allows a single program to do more than one thing at a time.

A **process** is an artifact of the operating system. In a robust OS, like Windows NT, a process consists of an allocation of memory, protected from all other memory and processes running at the same time. Each time you start an application under Windows you launch a new process.

> *A process is roughly equivalent to an executable running on a single CPU.*

A given process may have one or more **threads** of execution. Typically these threads share some resources, perhaps memory or access to files.

> **Threads** *are lightweight processes, with little overhead but less protection from one another.*

Threads are the mechanism by which your application can appear to do more than one thing at a time. A typical multithreaded application may be writing to the disk while it is reading from the database, at the same time that it is updating its display. Another very important use of threads is in server applications that support multiple users. Each new user is given a separate thread of execution for their data.

Threading, done well, can greatly increase the performance of your application. If the system would otherwise be waiting to print or to read data from the disk, the ability to continue working can be a great benefit.

On the other hand, many applications are actually slowed down by the addition of threads. If two tasks are going to proceed in parallel, in memory and without human intervention, multi-threading can make them both go slower than they otherwise would, as the system must switch back and forth between the two activities. Each switch brings a bit of overhead in setting up and dismantling the necessary structures in memory.

If there is a user interface, even a display, having the two tasks appear to occur simultaneously may be worth the overhead. On the other hand, if the two tasks are independent and invisible, it is almost always more efficient to run them in series with one another, rather than in parallel.

Multi-threading has a significant impact on your application, and you must design for it from the very start. The presence of threads has a dramatic affect on the overall design of the classes and how they interact. The guiding idea proves to be that:

> *The best way to build large systems successfully is to provide an environment in which each user (human or thread) feels that all of the system resources are available to him.*

In this chapter, we will see that the operating system, database, other system components and the persistence framework must all be carefully coordinated to give the programmer this illusion. Programming with this metaphor has proven to be much more reliable than programming with a metaphor of shared resources and contention.

Issues Arising from Multi-threading

Multi-threaded applications create significant issues for applications developers. When more than one thread may access resources, such as the disk or areas of memory, there is a risk of data corruption.

Also, in a modern operating system, a programmer cannot assume that their program will run in the order in which the code was written. It is possible for more than one function to run at the same time, or for one function to be stopped and restarted before it completes its first complete cycle.

Shared Resources

Let's say you have a precious resource, such as a restroom on a 747. You want only one person to have access to that room at a time. Having someone interrupted in the middle of his process by a second passenger would be inconvenient. You solve this problem by providing access to the restroom to the first passenger, and then *locking* the resource. Other passengers who want access will have to "wait". They may wait patiently, or they may "time out" after a while and return to their seats to resume what they were doing, without having had their turn. The question of how long they wait, and whether they can return to what they were doing or must wait indefinitely, is up to them.

Once the first passenger has finished using the resource, he unlocks it and provides access to the next passenger. He was guaranteed that once he began using the resource, he would have uninterrupted access until he was finished. Because this produces an enormous inefficiency (all those other passengers are blocked from getting any useful work done, until they either get access to the resource or give up waiting and return to their seats), you want to be careful that you only lock folks out when absolutely necessary, and for as short a time as possible.

Failure to lock a resource can lead to **data corruption**. Because you can't predict when the activity will be interrupted, you must guard all data access by some form of **synchronization**.

> **Data corruption** *is when various aspects of your data are inconsistent with one another.*
>
> **Synchronization** *means the coordination of various parts of the program to ensure orderly access to shared resources.*

Consider the following example — your program is walking through a list of employees giving each one a raise. One thread accesses Employee 1, increases Employee 1's salary by 10% and then writes it back to the database. Meanwhile, another thread is busy updating everyone's zip code with the new plus four designations. It accesses an employee, looks up his address, updates his zip code and then writes it back. The problem is this — what if they both access Employee 1 at the same time?

Thread 1 accesses Employee 1, whose record looks like this:

Name: John Q. Employee
ID: 12453
Salary: 50000

Address: 1 Maple Lane
City: Anytown
State: XZ
Zip: 00010

It then changes the salary to 55000, but while it has the record out, thread 2 accesses it and changes the zip to 00010-0010. Thread 1 writes the record back to the database, so that it looks like this:

Name: John Q. Employee
ID: 12453
Salary: **55000**
Address: 1 Maple Lane
City: Anytown
State: XZ
Zip: 00010

Subsequently, thread 2 writes it back to the database, and it looks like this:

Name: John Q. Employee
ID: 12453
Salary: 50000
Address: 1 Maple Lane
City: Anytown
State: XZ
Zip: **00010-0010**

Oops, the update to the salary has been overwritten. Not good. Both threads completed successfully but the result is corrupted data. There are any numbers of variants on this theme, which leave data in a bad state.

In a sophisticated database, you would be able to update a single field at a time, but there are conditions where two or more threads might need to update the same field, and the same set of problems arises. In short, you need to be able to *synchronize* access to your data to ensure that one thread does not overwrite the work of another thread in a way which might corrupt the data.

Most commercial database systems will manage thread safety for you, but other aspects of your code will need to be managed by your own synchronization objects. There are two great dangers: the first is that you won't protect your data, leading to data corruption. The second is that you'll overprotect your data, adding enormous inefficiencies to your project and slowing your system to the point where it is unusable.

In the above example, thread 1 *could* lock Employee 1 the moment it gets the record. It could then read the salary, compute the new salary, update it and then unlock it. All this time, thread 2 might be waiting for access. Suppose computing the new salary involved looking up survey information on what similar managers earn nationwide. Such a computation could take many minutes. Certainly, we don't want thread 2 to be waiting all that time.

A more efficient algorithm might be to read Employee 1's record, compute the new salary and *then* lock the record and update it and unlock it. This may drive down the lock time from many minutes to a few milliseconds, greatly enhancing the performance of the system overall. On the other hand, this kind of locking may not sufficiently protect your data from corruption by other threads, as the data may have been changed after you have read the record, but before you locked it and updated it. In this case, the solution may be to track whether the data has been changed from the time you accessed it until the time you locked it. If so, you may need to flush your data, that is remove it from memory, and then get it again, this time with the record locked. Each solution creates new problems, and finding the right balance to ensure high performance and absolute data integrity is what makes writing multi-threaded applications so interesting.

The process view concentrates on the question of how you solve these problems, trading off performance considerations with data integrity.

Interrupting an Operation

Multi-threaded servers are tricky to program, because multiple threads can access the process's memory simultaneously. A task that requires several steps may fail if the set of steps is interrupted before completion.

Nearly all modern operating systems, such as Windows95, NT and Unix support pre-emptive multi-tasking. Older systems, such as Windows 3.1 and the Mac, support cooperative multi-tasking, as do many of the shells that programmers put around DOS to run more than one DOS program at a time.

> *In* **pre-emptive multi-tasking,** *the CPU and the operating system work together to support multi-threaded applications by interrupting one task in order to begin another. This interruption is outside the control of the programmer and may come between any two machine instructions.*
>
> *In* **cooperative multi-tasking** *the programmer must yield control to the system, and methods are never "pre-empted". Cooperative multi-threading is easier to program, but more prone to poor performance. All modern operating systems are pre-emptive.*

If your operating system supports pre-emptive multi-tasking, the thread cannot know when it might be interrupted. A given thread may be interrupted between any two machine instructions, and if your code is not **thread-safe**, this can be disastrous.

> **Thread-safe** *means the application designed so that no harm can come from being interrupted in mid-operation*

A task that tests and sets a flag in two sequential instructions is not guaranteed to succeed. A second thread may set the flag in between the two instructions. In this case, the update from the second thread is lost. (For example, thread A makes a test and gets the value 1. Thread B sets the value to 5. Thread A writes back 2. The value is at 2 and Thread B's change is lost.)

To create a thread-safe application, you must be able to synchronize access to critical objects, so that one thread cannot corrupt the work of another. Synchronization mechanisms were created to solve this problem, and we will come to these later in this chapter.

Reliability

Because an operation may be interrupted by another thread or by a second user, there is no guarantee that any particular set of commands will complete before some other set begins. This can create significant challenges for the application programmer.

When I go to my bank and deposit that check you gave me at the poker game last night, I expect that the amount of the check (say, $100) will be deposited in my account. That is my contract with the bank — I make a deposit and the money winds up in my account. Your contract with the bank is such that your account winds up being debited the same $100. For checks to "work", both of these effects have to happen. If my account is credited and yours is not debited, the bank suffers. If your account is debited and mine is not credited, the bank is in danger of losing a customer.

In a well-designed system, there are only two possible outcomes: either both accounts are adjusted or nothing changes. The latter would be the case, for example, if your checking account had less than $100 and you had no overdraft protection.

The idea here, that either all of the changes (to the banking database) take place or none take place at all, is the essence of a **transaction**. After all of the changes are made, the transaction is **committed**. If the transaction cannot commit, all of its changes to the database are **rolled-back**. The transaction is said to be **aborted**.

> **A transaction** *is a set of related operations, of which either all or none must be completed.*
>
> **Committing** *is writing all the changes to the database at once.*
>
> **Rollback,** *or* **abort,** *is undoing all the changes.*

The following processing mechanisms are required to support multi-tasking and multi-user programs:

- Start a transaction, update the database and commit the transaction
- Start a transaction, update the database and abort (or roll back) the transaction
- Recover from a system software or hardware failure
- Recover from the loss of a disk drive
- Archive the database
- Checkpoint the database

> **Checkpoint:** *a copy of the state of the database at a particular moment in time, which can be restored in case of failure*

Deadlock

We looked at an example earlier detailing the way data can become corrupted if two threads are trying to access it at the same time. One of the principal concerns in a multi-threaded application is to ensure that such a data corruption scenario does not occur. We also need to be very careful to avoid **race conditions** and **deadlock**.

> A **race condition** *exists when the success of your operation depends on which of two threads finishes its task first, and the two threads operate independently of one another.*

Assume one thread is responsible for initializing your printer, and another is responsible for adding a print job. The one that adds the print job must first make sure the printer is ready, or throw an exception if it is not. If the two threads are uncoordinated, sometimes the initialization will happen first and the job will print. Other times, however, the attempt to print will precede the initialization and thus will fail.

Overall, the system will fail about half the time, and this will be terribly difficult to debug as it will be hard to reproduce reliably. Programmers hate flaky problems; we like systems which either work, or fail reliably. Race conditions breed unreliability.

> **Deadlock** *exists when thread A is blocked, waiting for thread B to take an action, but thread B is blocked waiting for thread A to take another action.*

Assume you have a function to record a customer's deposit in the bank, which works as follows:

1   Lock the customer record

2   Lock the bank account record

3   Update the bank account

4   Update the customer

5   Unlock the bank account

6   Unlock the customer

You have a second function to compute the month end statement which works as follows:

1   Lock the bank account record

2   Lock the customer record

3   Update the customer

4   Update the bank account

5   Unlock the customer

6   Unlock the bank account

Both of these are well behaved, that is, they unlock in the reverse order in which they lock. Now imagine this scenario: thread A is running the first algorithm and thread B is running the second.

Thread A: lock the customer record
Thread B: lock the bank account record
Thread A: try to lock the bank account — block waiting for thread B to release
Thread B: try to lock the customer record — block waiting for thread A to release

You are stuck. This is a deadlock (often called a **deadly embrace**). There is nothing either thread can do to get free except, if you are lucky, to time out.

Synchronization Mechanisms

There are a series of strategies that may be employed to solve these problems, depending on what you want to accomplish and what tools you'll be using (e.g. application framework libraries). The most common solution to all of these problems is **thread synchronization**.

> **Thread synchronization** *is the art of forcing one thread to wait until another thread finishes a specific task.*

It is common to utilize synchronization objects to ensure that methods are thread-safe. Synchronization objects allow threads to coordinate with one another.

Whenever an object's state information is accessed, you must ensure that the state will not be corrupted if the thread is interrupted and another object then accesses the object's state. Without synchronization, you cannot predict or control when a thread will be interrupted. To recap, an object is thread-safe if it cannot be corrupted when being accessed by multiple threads (or processes).

Synchronization objects provide mutually exclusive access to objects, so that only one thread at a time may access that object. The details of their implementation are operating system and development framework specific, but they all accomplish the same thing; they say, "One at a time, boys," to each of your threads.

Classic Semaphores

"Semaphore: An apparatus for conveying information...any of various devices for signaling by changing the position of a light, flag, etc."
The Random House Compact Unabridged Dictionary, Second edition (ISBN 0-679-4499-8)

The dictionary includes a picture of a railroad semaphore, which communicates by moving its arms to different positions: horizontal for stop, at an angle for go. If two trains approach a switch, only one will be allowed to pass. The second will wait. When the first train passes the semaphore, it will be reset so that the second train may go.

A **semaphore** in a computer system serves an analogous purpose. It is used as a gatekeeper to allow only one process or thread to enter a critical region at a time. A critical region is a section of code that only one process or thread may execute at a time. Languages with built-in multi-threading, such as Java, provide mutual exclusion semaphores as a synchronization mechanism. The operating system typically uses semaphores to protect its critical regions, such as process control blocks. Database servers use them to protect shared structures.

Definition

The classic semaphore was invented by Dijkstra. He described the semaphore as an object that provides two operations, known as **P** and **V**. **P** stands for the Dutch word *Proberen*, to test and **V** stands for *Verhogen*, to increment.

P is used to get access to the protected resource. **V** is used to give up access. The specific uses for **P** and **V** depend on the type of semaphore.

Uses of Semaphores

There are two basic uses of semaphores in systems. The first is to protect a critical region, and the second is to share resources.

Exclusive Use

A semaphore provides exclusive use when it prevents two or more processes or threads from accessing the same data simultaneously. An activity uses the **P** operation when it wants to access the resource and the **V** operation when it is done accessing the resource.

Such a critical region of code might be one that supports table access and update, whenever there is more than one process or thread that can access the table at a time. This would be true, for example, for an operating system and its list of process control blocks (PCBs). Various threads in the operating system kernel may have access to the PCBs, but only one of them may update the list pointers at a time, or the semantics of the list will be violated.

Producer-Consumer

A producer-consumer semaphore can be used to regulate the flow of data between n producers and m consumers. Many systems or sub-systems have the architecture of a data-flow system: the output from one stage becomes the input to another stage. Each stage waits until data is available, gets the data, and processes it. The result is the output data for the next stage. Database systems are often organized using such a data flow architecture. Semaphores can be used to regulate the flow of data: consumers issue **P** operations when they want to receive data, and producers issue **V** operations when they make data available.

Implementing Semaphores

Classically, semaphores were implemented with a global data structure and an API for the **P** and **V** operations. These days, semaphores are encapsulated within objects. Typically, an abstract semaphore class defines the basic **P** and **V** operations. Exclusive and shared semaphores are derived from this base semaphore class. An exclusive or shared semaphore can be named or can be created as an anonymous semaphore. Named semaphores can be shared across processes — so that a client and a server can both access the same semaphore. Anonymous semaphores are named as variables within your application, but that name is not visible to any other process.

Implementing Exclusive Semaphores

The pseudo-code shown below sketches an **ExclusiveSemaphore** class. The semaphore is not aware of the region that it is protecting. It is passed a reference to the entity that wants to use the region, and either grants access or suspends the entity until access can be granted.

167

Ignoring inheritance from the base semaphore class, the **ExclusiveSemaphore** class may be defined as:

```
class ExclusiveSemaphore
{
Public:
ExclusiveSemaphore();
~ExclusiveSemaphore();

// get access to semaphore or add caller to list of waiting entities
P(Entity e);

// give up access to semaphore
V(Entity e);

private:
// if in use, who has access
Entity* owner;

// list of waiting entities (list used for illustrative purposes)
Entity* entityListHead;
};
```

The **P** operation examines the semaphore. If the semaphore is free, access is granted to the entity. If not, the operation suspends the entity and adds it to the list of entities waiting for the semaphore.

```
void ExclusiveSemaphore::P(Entity e)
{
// examine the list of waiting entities;
// if semaphore is free, set owner to this entity and return;
// otherwise add entity to end of list and put entity to sleep;
}

void ExclusiveSemaphore::V(Entity e)
{
// in one atomic step: clear owner data member;
// if no entity waiting, return;
// remove first waiting entity, set owner to this entity;
// wakeup entity;
}
```

The **P** and **V** operations are passed a reference to the calling entity. The **P** operation suspends the entity until it is granted access to the region. An atomic procedure, or machine instruction, is used to set the list of waiting entities and the owner.

> *An atomic instruction is indivisible, that is it cannot be interrupted. Such operations are normally supported through hardware — the CPU instruction set.*

Implementing Shared Semaphores

This next example of pseudo-code demonstrates a class, **SharedSemaphore**, which can be used to grant access to one writer or many readers of the resource. This is similar, for example, to the semaphores that are used for locking database pages.

Shared semaphores keep a list of waiting entities and a count of the number of entities that have been granted the semaphore (for an exclusive semaphore, this is always one). They also have a mode, which can take the values **free**, **shared** or **exclusive**.

```
class SharedSemaphore
{
public:
enum SemaphoreMode {free, shared, exclusive};

SharedSemaphore();
~SharedSemaphore();

// get access to semaphore or add caller to list of waiting entities
P(Entity e, Semaphore Mode m);

// give up access to semaphore
V(Entity e);

private:
SemaphoreMode mode;

// if in use, how many entities are using it
unsigned int numberOfOwners;

// list of waiting entities (list used for illustrative purposes)
Entity* entityListHead;
};
```

The pointer to the **entityListHead** is used to wake up those entities waiting on the semaphore. In the **ExclusiveSemaphore** there is a member pointer **owner**, which is used as a flag to indicate whether or not the semaphore is free (e.g. if the pointer is **NULL**, the semaphore is free). The **SharedSemaphore** may have more than one owner, so we keep a count of the **numberOfOwners**, but there is no need for the **owner** pointer.

The **P** and **V** operations are passed a reference to the calling entity. The **P** operation is also passed the mode that is requested. The semaphore is granted if it is either unused, or in use in share mode with no waiters and the request is for share mode. Otherwise, it suspends the entity, until that entity is granted access to the region. An atomic procedure or machine instruction is used to set the list of waiting entities and the owner.

```
void SharedSemaphore::P(Entity e, SemaphoreMode requestMode)
{
//  if numberOfOwners = 0 increment numberOfOwners and return;
//  if entityListHead = NULL AND mode = Shared AND
//  requestMode = shared increment numberOfOwners and return;
//  add entity to end of  list and put entity to sleep;
}
```

169

```
void SharedSemaphore::V(Entity e)
{
//  if numberOfOwners = 1 and mode = shared
//  and entityListHead = NULL
    //  then decrement number of owners and return;
//  if numberOfOwners > 1 decrement numberOfOwners and return;
    //  Wake up all the waiters that want shared access
}
```

Locks

Locks are semaphores that are customized to participate in the commit and abort protocols. They are used to serialize access to critical regions, such as the objects in the model or their images in a database.

Phantom Locks

In a database, locking is usually performed on a range of items. Locking an individual item is a bit more difficult. Consider a typical query:

```
Select * from Customer where city = "Acton" and state = "MA";
```

One way to protect the data retrieved by this select statement is to lock a set of rows. What happens if we just lock the individual items that meet the search criteria? This is dangerous, because it can create a **phantom**. If another thread is updating the database, and in that thread an entry meets these same criteria (e.g. a new customer is added from Acton, MA), then that customer will be a phantom. He will be added to the database even though you intended to lock him out. Locks that don't keep out phantoms are called **phantom locks**.

Predicate, Precision and Granular Locks

To prevent the creation of phantoms, you must avoid locking individual rows. The alternative, however, locking the whole table, will have an unacceptable impact on performance.

Another alternative is **predicate locking**. Predicate locking specifies a predicate (a function that returns true or false) that is used as a filter on rows. A predicate lock will lock every record that satisfies the predicate; that is, for which the predicate returns true. Thus, in the above example, when you tried to add another customer from Acton MA, that customer would meet the predicate `City == Acton and State == MA` and thus would find the database locked; the addition of the record would be blocked until the lock is released. Predicate locks are expensive, however; and their performance is poor, so they do not tend to be used in real systems.

Yet another alternative is **precision locking**. Precision locking grants locks without computing predicates. Instead, they find conflicts when transactions attempt to read or write records. Precision locks are less expensive than predicate locks, but they tend to have more deadlocks than other locking schemes. They also are not generally used.

Up until now, we have been talking about locks that are set at a uniform granularity. The **granularity**, or size of a lock, is the size of the locked item: a database table, a row, a field of a row. While queries tend to access a whole table, updates often touch a single row or just one field of a row. There would be advantages in a locking scheme that allows transactions to lock at multiple granularities.

Granular locking restricts transactions to a small set of predefined predicates. These predicates form a tree of granularity (table, row, record). At the top of the tree is a predicate that returns the whole database. The next level of a distributed database might be an individual site. The level below that might be a table, below that would be records and finally an individual field.

This type of structure has some useful mathematical properties. For example, if a predicate subsumes another predicate (that is, if all records that satisfy the second predicate also satisfy the first predicate) then it is above the other predicate in the tree. A lock at a higher level of the tree locks all of the records that all of the locks at lower levels of the tree do. A problem would occur if one transaction locked the database at the record level and then another transaction locked the database at a higher level that included that locked record. This would lead to the second transaction being blocked, thus lowering performance. Because of this, when locking is allowed at multiple granularity, a more complicated set of lock modes is used. In addition to shared and exclusive locks, a new type of lock called an **intention lock** is defined. The idea is that you can set an intention lock at one level, to declare that you intend to set locks at a lower level. Thus, you can set an intention lock at the *table* level in order to declare that you intend to lock *records*.

The protocol is to declare an intention lock at every level higher than the one you will use. Thus, to obtain a **SHARE** lock at a record table, the transaction would first declare an intention lock at the database, site, and table levels. Only if all of these are granted is the **SHARE** lock requested.

Locking Granularity, Lock Escalation and Hotspots

Locking often starts out at a high level, such as a table level lock. Some systems make page locking available instead. A popular combination is to make both page and record locking available. Coarse-grained locking, such as page locking, is easy to use, but may be plagued by specific items that many transactions try to access (known as **hot spots**).

An example of a hot spot is a directory listing in a repository. The directory listings are small and many fit on one page; this page could become a hot spot if the directory is frequently searched. When hot spots are a serious problem, a lower-level protocol, such as record-level locking, is required.

Dealing with Deadlocks

As we saw earlier, two threads may be unable to make progress because each is waiting for a lock that the other holds. This is known as deadlock or a deadly embrace. The only way out of a deadlock is for one of the threads to give up a lock. More generally, deadlocks are broken by aborting one or more transactions.

Deadlocks can either be prevented, or allowed to occur and subsequently dealt with. It turns out that the standard locking protocols lead to a small percentage of deadlocks. Also, it is hard to prevent deadlocks in transactional systems, without overly constraining the concurrency allowed. Therefore, deadlocks are usually allowed to occur, but a deadlock detection mechanism is required.

Deadlocks are especially problematic in distributed systems, as the locks are held at individual nodes. There is no easy way for one node on the network to know which locks are held by another node.

There are two techniques in use for deadlock detection. The first is simply to set a timer for the transaction. Any deadlock will cause the transaction to time out and be aborted. This may free up other transactions that were waiting on the locks the aborted transaction was holding. This method is easy to implement, but has the drawback that it may abort transactions that were merely slow, not deadlocked.

The other method is based on creating a data structure called a **waits-for graph**. The nodes of the graph represent transactions. An edge (straight line between nodes) from transaction 1 to transaction 2 means that transaction 1 is waiting on a lock held by transaction 2, or that transaction 1 is behind transaction 2 in the list of transactions waiting on a data item. Deadlocks are represented by cycles in this graph. Because deadlocks are sparse and most paths in the graph are short, an incremental algorithm is used to search for deadlocks. This algorithm also uses a data structure that lists all of the locks that each transaction is waiting on.

The list of locks is itself protected by semaphores. This kind of deadlock detector is usually run on a periodic basis, which is cheaper than running it each time a lock is added, removed or changed. The algorithm works by visiting each transaction and making a list of all the transactions that it waits on. This process will eventually find a deadlock when the list of transactions that transaction 1 is waiting on includes a transaction whose own such list includes transaction 1.

The MFC Perspective

The Microsoft Foundation Classes (MFC) supports four synchronization objects: **critical sections**, **mutexes**, **semaphores** and **events**. The MFC also supports two types of locks: single locks and multi-locks.

The details of the implementation of the locks and even of the synchronization objects are encapsulated in the objects and opaque to the application developer. You can build your application without worrying about how the locks are implemented; as long as you follow the correct protocol, MFC will ensure synchronization.

Critical Sections

Critical sections are the simplest form of MFC synchronization objects. They are easy to use and they are "lightweight" in that they don't have a lot of overhead and hence they are very fast. You can provide synchronized access to a section of code by marking it as a critical section. Once the **CCriticalSection** object is initialized, you simply bracket your code with calls to **EnterCriticalSection** and **LeaveCriticalSection**, passing in the **CriticalSection** object by reference.

```
EnterCriticalSection (&myCriticalSection);
{
        // do the work which requires synchronization
}
LeaveCriticalSection (&myCriticalSection);
```

Mutexes

Critical sections are fast and easy to use, but they have no features. You cannot set your code to "time out" waiting for a critical section, the code will just block and wait forever. You also cannot have two processes wait on the same critical section, as there is no way to "name" a critical section so that it appears in both processes. For either of these features, you need to step up to a mutex.

Mutex stands for *Mutually Exclusive*, and provides exclusive access to a section of code, much like a critical section does. The typical use of a mutex is somewhat different, however.

```
CSingleLock theLock ( &myMutex );
if ( theLock.Lock(WAIT_TIME) )
{
        // do the work which requires synchronization

        theLock.Unlock();
}
else
{
        // handle the failure to lock
}
```

You start by declaring a **CMutex** object, often as a member variable of your client object. At the point where you need to protect your code, you create a **CSingleLock** object and pass in the mutex by reference. You then attempt to shut the lock, by calling the function **Lock()** and passing in as a parameter the amount of time you are willing to wait (in milliseconds). Either you will acquire the lock or you will time out. If you time out, you must handle that situation yourself. If you get the lock, you do the work and then release the lock by calling **Unlock()**.

If you specify **0** (zero) as the wait time, it will not wait at all. Alternatively, you can specify **INFINITE**, in which case it will wait until the Red Sox win the World Series.

If you need to acquire access to multiple objects before you are ready to do the work, you will want to use the **CMultiLock**. A **CMultiLock** takes an array of **CSyncObjects** and waits on them all. **CMultiLock** takes three parameters:

▶ The length of time to wait on the lock
▶ Whether you are waiting for all of the objects or just any one of them
▶ The **dwWakeMask** parameter

This latter parameter controls whether the multilock should return on events other than those for which you are waiting. For example, you can set it to return if it receives a point message, a timer message, a hot key message and so forth. Typically it is set to zero, which means, "Just wait for the objects I told you about."

Semaphores

MFC uses the term semaphore in an unusual way. In the MFC, semaphore refers to a specific variety of synchronization objects — one that is used to manage access to a limited set of resources. For example, if you have five ports available for output and multiple threads which

173

may want access to these ports, you may want to design a **PortController** object, which would be responsible for allocation of ports to waiting threads. This allocation must be made thread-safe, but you don't want to block out any thread until you've allocated all the ports. Furthermore, as ports become available, you want to be able to allocate them to waiting threads.

The **CSemaphore** object will keep count of how many ports you have, and how many are in use. It will release waiting threads when there is a port available, and otherwise allow them to wait.

Events

In some circumstances, you may want your thread to wait until other threads have accomplished a certain task, or some other UI event is registered. You may want to initialize a number of resources, and when they are all fully registered, go forward and interact with these resources. As an example, imagine you have a number of outgoing telephone ports connected to your machine. Each port will be controlled by a single thread, so that if you have 72 such ports there are 72 threads. You also have a port manger thread, which is responsible for spinning up the 72 threads and keeping track of their status. This port manager may want to initialize all the threads before any calls are made on any port.

```
// For the total count of outbound ports…
for (i = 0; i<m_nTotalCallers; i++)
{
        // ... (preliminary set up)

        // create the threads
        CCaller * pCaller = new CCaller(// parameters);
        BOOL bRc = pCaller->CreateThread();

        // ... (other book keeping work)
}

CSingleLock theLock ( &m_CallersReadyEvent );

if (theLock.Lock(WAIT_VERY_LONG_TIME))
{
        for (int j = 0; j < m_nTotalCallers; j++)
        {
            // set them calling
        }

        theLock.Unlock();
}
else                    // never got event!
{
        // handle error
}
```

In this pseudo-code, I create a **CCaller** thread object for each port (**m_nTotalCallers** holds the number of ports). This calls the initialization routine within the thread. That initialization routine signals back to the port manager that it is complete. When all the ports have said they are complete, the **CallersReadyEvent** event is *set*, allowing **theLock** to be acquired. Once **theLock** is acquired, I iterate through the callers, telling them to begin calling.

Since the callers are initialized, each in their own threads, the port manager must be sure to wait on the **CallersReadyEvent** to make sure it doesn't begin instructing some threads to begin calling before they are all initialized.

Transactions

Earlier, we defined a transaction as a set of related operations, whose completion is an all-or-nothing affair. In a simple case, a transaction begins, issues requests, commits the changes and completes. This is called a **flat transaction**. If an error occurs, the transaction is aborted, and all evidence of its existence is erased from the permanent stores, including databases and other resources, such as persistent message queues. Either all of the changes are made, or none at all.

Let's look at an example of a transaction from the VideoMagix application, introduced in Chapter 2. In his book, *Analysis Patterns: Reusable Object Models (Addison-Wesley, ISBN 0-201-89542-0)*, Martin Fowler examines the Inventory and Accounting Patterns, and discusses the essential abstraction of an account. There is a striking similarity between a book-keeping account and the customer records in the VideoMagix application. Fowler says that an accounting system must not only report on the current state of an account, but also on all of the transactions which have affected that state. He creates a class, **Entry**. An **Entry** is a record of a change to the account. In UML, the relationship might look like this:

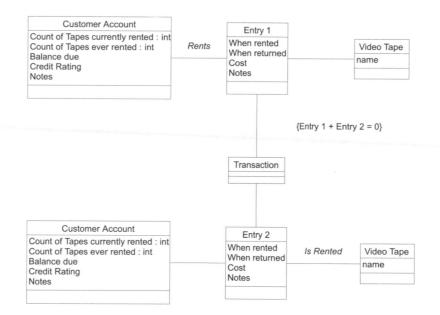

In this diagram we see that a **CustomerAccount** and a **VideoTape** enter into an association which is documented by two **Entry** objects:

▶ One entry updates the **CustomerAccount** to show that a tape was rented

▶ The other entry updates the **VideoTape** account to show that a particular customer rented the tape

A transaction links two or more entries into a single entity, so that for one to happen, the other must be successful. This approximates the key idea in double entry accounting, in which each credit must be offset by a balancing debit. It enforces the idea that value is never created or destroyed, it is just reallocated from one account to another.

This diagram attempts to capture the transactional relationship. Each transaction has two entries, and each entry is a member of a single transaction. Note that I've added a **constraint**: **{Entry1 + Entry2 = 0}**. The two entries must offset one another. You mark a constraint by placing it in curly braces **{}**.

> **A constraint** *is an adornment which restricts the relationship*

This diagram illustrates the essence of double-entry accounting. Each time the customer account is updated to indicate that the customer has rented a video tape, an offsetting, or balancing entry is made in the video tape account indicating that the tape has been rented.

If, in the middle of this transaction, you found that you could *not* update the videotape, you would then roll back the update to the customer account. Again, either both entries succeed or neither can.

Compensating Transactions

Once a transaction is "committed", it cannot be undone. Of course, in some circumstances, another transaction (called a **compensating transaction**) may be used to negate the effects of this transaction. An example would be a transaction that recorded a sale and updated an inventory table. A second transaction could be used to change or remove the record of the sale and reset the inventory figures.

A compensating transaction is not the same as a balancing or offsetting entry, though this can cause some confusion. A compensating transaction is a second, discrete transaction (also with two entries in this case) which undoes the effect of the first transaction.

Notice also that running a compensating transaction is not the same thing as aborting a transaction. Let's imagine that a database has a table, **priceVolatility**, which keeps track of the number of times the price of each item has changed. In this case, running a transaction and a compensating transaction would change the **priceVolatility** table, adding two entries and making the price look more volatile. An aborted transaction would not create any additions to the **priceVolatility** table. The significant difference is that an aborted transaction removes all record of the transaction, while a compensating transaction undoes the net effect, but the records for both the original and compensating transaction exist.

The ACID Test

The ACID test for transaction processing is that the system be Atomic, Consistent, Isolated and Durable.

Atomic

> *Atomic — indivisible — an effect is* **atomic** *if it cannot be partially implemented*

Every transaction must be indivisible. The system must either complete the transaction or return to a state that is indistinguishable from the state it was in before the transaction began. We say that the transaction is **atomic**. Of course, a transaction takes system resources even if it aborts. It clearly has an effect on the database, if only on its performance. When we say it has no effect on the database, we mean that none of the tables in the database are changed, none of the ID's are used or retired etc. It is as if you went to sleep for a few milliseconds and nothing happened — the transaction had no permanent effects on the system (usually meaning the database). Other transactions might have been processed during the same time, and these might have affected the database, but the point is that the effects that these other transactions have on the database are the same as if the aborted transaction had never existed.

Atomic transactions are designed to leave the database in a consistent state — the information in each of the tables is consistent with the information in all of the other tables. Transaction-based systems become complicated in multi-tasking environments; so the developer must take steps to protect the integrity or consistency of the database tables.

Consistent

It is assumed that a database is initially **consistent** and that all transactions leave it consistent. This assumption is realized in the database world through the use of **integrity constraints**. In the object world, we assume that the objects represented in the database satisfy all of the constraints that are defined in the static object model (as described in Chapter 3).

Isolated

We have been speaking about transactions as if they were processed one at a time. No system processing transactions could afford to do this: it would make the cost-per-transaction of the software and hardware an order of magnitude higher. Instead, transactions are interleaved like any other activity in a modern multi-user multi-tasking computer system.

That said, the effects of a transaction must be the same whether it is run alone or at the same time as other transactions. A set of transactions which *could* run one after the other, that is in series, is said to be **serializable**. A system is **isolated** if each transaction is serializable. That is, to the system, it appears as if this transaction occurred in isolation of all the other transactions. Nothing in this transaction requires any activity in another transaction. If no other transaction occurred, this transaction would remain consistent and valid.

Business rules define which actions in a domain have to happen together (for example, payment is a combination of debiting my account and crediting your account). Together, these activities make a single transaction.

Implementing Isolation

The mechanism that is usually used in database systems to implement isolation is **locking**. Isolation theory is based on the idea of constraints, consistency and concurrency.

Constraints are the invariants of the domain; that is, they dictate what must be true within this domain for the object to be valid.

An example of a constraint is, "The relationship between the customer and his membership ID is one-to-one." This constraint would prevent a single customer from having more than one membership ID, or one ID being shared among two or more members.

An object model is consistent if all of the constraints of the model are satisfied. All object models should be consistent before they are written to the database. This is reinforced to some extent by the data integrity mechanisms that the object or relational database supports.

Every transaction must end with the system in a consistent state. This is fundamental to the idea of transaction processing. Transactions are assumed to have a **pre-condition** which states that the object model is in a consistent state. They supply the **post-condition** that the object model is in a consistent state. In the middle of a transaction, anything goes.

If each transaction is consistent, then any serial ordering of them must be consistent. That is, if the object model is consistent before the set of transactions start, and each transaction is consistent, then the object model will be consistent at the end of the stream of transactions. This is not necessarily true, however if the transactions are interleaved, as they may update shared data.

To support multi-tasking, systems that process transactions must meet two requirements: concurrent execution must not cause inconsistency, and must not lower throughput or raise response time significantly compared to serial execution.

Violating Isolation

There are three ways concurrent transactions can violate isolation:

 Lost Update: this can result from one thread reading, a second thread writing and then the first thread overwriting that work with its own write.

 Dirty read: this can result from one thread writing, a second thread reading what the first thread wrote and then the first thread overwriting what it originally wrote. The second thread has now read incorrect data.

 Unrepeatable read: this happens when the first thread reads data, the second thread overwrites that data and then the first thread re-reads the data. The data is not the same as the first read.

If the algorithm used can be shown to avoid lost updates, dirty reads and unrepeatable reads, then concurrent execution of transactions is guaranteed to be consistent.

The following set of rules is sufficient to ensure that these three types of anomalies are avoided:

 Other transactions do not write any data read by any transaction before that transaction completes

178

▶ Other transactions do not read or write any data written by any transaction before that transaction completes

▶ A transaction does not read dirty data from any other transaction, nor overwrite dirty data of any other transaction

> **Dirty data** *is data that has been altered in any way*

If these rules are followed then transactions will be isolated, the database will be consistent, committed transactions will be durable, and aborted transactions will be ephemeral.

Implications of Isolation Theory

A transaction can be implemented by read, write, lock (shared and exclusive) and unlock operations, without commit and abort. A transaction is called **well-formed** if each read, write and unlock action is under control of a lock, and if every lock is released by the end of the transaction. A transaction is called **two-phase** if it acquires all of its locks before it releases any of them.

A history of a set of transactions is a way in which they could possibly have been run together. A history is serial if it is possible to run the transactions sequentially, and legal if it obeys the locking rules (that is, does not grant conflicting locks).

A transaction T1 is dependent on transaction T2 if T1 reads data that T2 writes. That is, T1's actions are dependent on the data it reads, and some of that data was written by T2. A history defines such a dependency relationship.

Dependency relationships determine an ordering of the transactions and pinpoint transactions which are not isolated. If T1 is dependent on T2, then T1 must run after T2 in any serialized ordering of T1 and T2. In order to keep transactions isolated, we should consider combining T1 and T2 into one overall transaction.

Degrees of Isolation

Isolation is sometimes compromised for performance reasons. For instance, there is a tension between queries and updates in a database system. Queries run for a relatively long time and touch many rows. They therefore set many locks, and this can cause performance to deteriorate.

Therefore, some systems employ strategies that do not have fully guaranteed isolation. A taxonomy of degrees of isolation has been developed. For each degree of isolation, a corresponding lock protocol has been developed, with a guarantee that following the protocol will result in the required degree of isolation.

We can define four degrees of isolation:

▶ Degree 3 isolation is true isolation — no lost updates, no dirty reads, no unrepeatable reads. The lock protocol is two-phase and well formed as previously described.

▶ Degree 2 isolation, known in databases as cursor stability, has no lost updates and no dirty reads, but may have unrepeatable reads. The locking protocol is two-phase for exclusive locks and well formed.

> Degree 1 isolation, known as browse mode, has no lost updates.

> Degree 0 isolation is only limited to not overwriting the data of any other transaction that is of degree 1 isolation or greater. The locking protocol is well formed for writes.

Lower degrees of isolation reduce the time for which locks are held and therefore increase concurrency. The locks are of short duration, as opposed to locks that are held to the end of the transaction, which are called long duration. Usually, write locks are long duration and read locks are short duration.

Durable

Once a transaction commits, the effect it has on the database is permanent. It does not matter if the hardware or software fails — the effects are permanent. This can be accomplished through redundancy, backups and so forth. No failure of memory, disk storage or system software should be able to undo the effects of a transaction. The transaction is **durable**.

It is possible to create this durability by ensuring that the transaction can be replicated. That is, if you know the starting state before corruption and you know the details of the transaction, you may be able to restore the transaction by re-enacting it. In any case, when restoration is complete, the transaction's effects have been sustained.

Nested Transactions

Flat transactions are all-or-nothing affairs. There are situations, however, where an application can make progress on a business function even without being able to complete it. The option of backing out of all of the work may be too expensive. There may be some work that is meaningful, even if other parts of the request need to be aborted.

For example, if a customer requests that you book his flight and debit his account to pay for it, the customer service representative may need to gather a great deal of information about the flight before debiting the payment account. He may gather the customer's name, preferred airline and departure time, for example. If, after all this information has been gathered, the customer decides to wait on payment until his supervisor approves the flight, it would be better if the system could preserve the information, even if it can't complete the transaction.

One solution is to define a hierarchy of transactions, parallel to the hierarchy of business actions. A set of rules could be defined to allow sub-transactions to commit or abort and have the desired affect on the parent transaction and sibling sub-transactions. For example, the data being manipulated by a sub-transaction is not available to its siblings until it commits. A parent transaction cannot commit until all of its children have committed.

This can be implemented using **savepoints**. A savepoint is a point in a program where the state of the program itself and all of the application's objects are saved to persistent store. This is similar to a checkpoint in a database; in a checkpoint, the state of the database is stored, but in a savepoint the state of the running system is stored. Savepoints, are expensive to implement, but can be used to back out of part of a transaction.

This can be useful if some error path should be taken, for example, to issue an alarm instead of completing the normal business function. Queue-based systems will normally rerun a transaction that fails. In this case, we want to commit the transaction after running the error-handling code. This can be done by declaring a savepoint near the beginning of the transaction, but after the request is obtained. The exception-handling code can then return to the savepoint, raise the alarm and commit the transaction.

Savepoints can also be used to implement nested transactions if sub-transactions cannot run in parallel. Then, when a sub-transaction is run, the first time it uses any **resource manager** it issues a savepoint for that **resource**. If that sub-transaction aborts, you ask each resource it used to return to the savepoint. This effectively aborts just the effects of the one sub-transaction.

> *In transactions, permanent stores are known as* **resources,** *and the software that manages a resource is called a* **resource manager.**

Transaction Styles

When you bracket a transaction you tell the system, "I'm starting a transaction here," (**Start**), you then put in the entire set of operations that must be atomic, and then tell the system that you're ending the transaction (**Commit**).

Transaction processing systems (discussed below) provide either **explicit transaction bracketing** or **implicit transaction bracketing**. In implicit systems, the application does not have to issue **start** or **commit** operations, because this is done automatically. In explicit transaction bracketing, the developer must include both the **start** and the **commit** operations explicitly.

There are two ways that applications can bracket transactions. One is for the program to be divided into a set of alternating regions, like black and white boxes. The white boxes would represent work done inside a transaction and the black boxes would represent work done outside of any transaction. This is known as the **unchained model**. In this model, the programmer would issue all **start**, **commit**, and **abort** operations, and thus the transaction bracketing is explicit.

In the alternative model, all work is done inside a transaction. When one transaction ends, another is automatically started. Thus, committing or aborting a transaction starts another transaction. This is known as the **chained model**, and the transaction bracketing is implicit.

The only advantage to the unchained model is that there may be some time saved if operations can be issued outside of a transaction. The chained model provides a safer environment, as all operations are transaction controlled. The overhead the chained model incurs as a result of the added cost of processing all requests from within a transaction is small in most cases.

Transaction Processing Systems

Getting transaction processing right is not a trivial exercise. While you can certainly write your own transaction processing software, it is often a better design decision to purchase this technology from a vendor who specializes in these issues. Creating a robust transaction processing system which operates in a multi-tasking environment is not for the faint hearted.

Most commercial TP systems consist of:

- ▶ A client that interacts with the user and issues transaction requests
- ▶ A collection of transaction programs that process the request. These are the equivalent of the resource managers we mentioned earlier.
- ▶ A switch in the middle is that sends the request to the correct transaction program

Requirements for a TP system

Transaction processing systems are often called Transaction Management systems, and commercial systems that integrate all of the transaction management mechanisms are called **TP Monitors**.

Requirements for a good TP system are stringent:

- ▶ Processing the transaction must leave the database in a consistent state. This means that, if the results of processing the transaction would leave the database in an inconsistent state, then the whole transaction must be aborted. That is, the database must be returned to the state that it was in before the transaction began. From the viewpoint of the contents of the database tables, it is as if the transaction never happened. This is the idea that a transaction must be atomic.
- ▶ Once a transaction is processed successfully, future events should not be able to undo the effects of the transaction on the database. That is, once a transaction is "committed", it cannot be undone.
- ▶ Transaction processing systems typically are used in mission-critical applications. They should work for a long time without failing. This is measured by the "Mean Time Between Failures" (MTBF). They should also start working again quickly after a failure. This is measured by the "Mean Time To Repair" (MTTR).
- ▶ Typically, many users will be using the system; submitting transactions without considering what their fellow users are doing. The results of running a transaction in a crowd must be the same as running a transaction all by itself, in an isolated environment.
- ▶ To be affordable, transaction processing systems must be robust enough to support heavy use. They are expected to respond to each request quickly, even in the face of large volumes of users.

Transactions are the "unit of work" in a TP system. The application programs bracket their work with transactions. More formally, a transaction is the execution of a program that performs a function for a user in an atomic, consistent, isolated and durable fashion. A transaction typically updates a permanent store or resource, such as a database.

TP Services

TP systems support the style of client/server processing that On-Line Transaction Processing (OLTP) requires. It provides services to users, programmers and administrators.

> *On-Line Transaction Processing is defined as a soft real time system that processes transactions*

The API for a transaction monitor must support the following capabilities:

- Provide access to shared data through its resource managers
- Present a uniform abstraction for all access to resources through the verbs of **start**, **commit** and **abort**
- Integrate the actions of the resource managers to provide the ACID properties for transactions that access several resources, such as databases and persistent queues
- Provide a resource manager, used to establish communications to remote resources
- Control the presentation of information to the user
- Manage UI messages as part of the transactional environment
- Manage the presentation environment itself, treating the presentation manager as a resource manager that subscribes to the same protocols as the other resource managers
- Control the restart of all components after a failure — with the aid of the resource managers, the TP system is responsible for bringing all resources back to a consistent state

The application programmer is also given tools to develop applications for this environment. These include compilers, debuggers, transaction trace displays, database browsers and object browsers.

System administrators have their own display interfaces and applications. TP-systems often provide service to users in distributed geographic locations using a variety of equipment. Modern TP systems provide an open environment for system administration, often using standard protocols such as SNMP (Simple Network Management Protocol) to administer their devices.

The Three-tier TP Monitor

Commercial TP Monitors come in two flavors. There is a two-tier TP monitor, consisting of a presentation layer and a database server, but the most popular is a three-tier solution.

A three-tier TP monitor consists of:

- Presentation Server — responsible for the UI
- Workflow Controller — provides load balancing and request serialization
- Transaction server — provides the interface to the resource managers such as the database or file system.

The back-end programs are known as the **transaction servers**. The transaction server will interact with one or more resource managers. In addition, the transaction servers contain the business objects and implement the business logic as directed by the **workflow controller**.

The workflow controller routes requests to the transaction servers. It also provides standard services, such as lock management and log management. The application programmer supplies the logic that maps a request to a series of transactions processed by specific transaction servers.

A diagram illustrating the architecture of a 3-tier TP monitor is shown here:

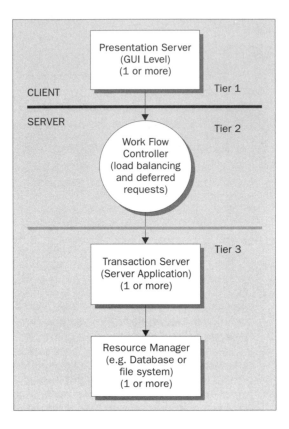

TP monitors are nothing new, and were originally implemented using procedural programming techniques. There are a few views emerging on how this functionality can be mapped to the constructs used in the object world. The views vary in whether they put the business rules in the workflow controller or in the transaction servers. A workflow-centric view is expressed by an architecture in which the workflow controller supplies the business logic and the transaction servers supply the business objects. Business objects, like **Customer** and **Account**, are reusable in many circumstances. So the workflow controller contains the logic required to exercise the business object's capabilities in support of the user's specific requirements.

The Presentation Manager

The client of the TP Monitor is known as the **presentation manager**. Classic TP systems included the presentation manager as part of a bundled solution, but modern TP systems are open systems, that is, they are designed to work with various databases and on a variety of operating systems, in which the programmer designs the UI.

The presentation manager is typically divided into two components — the front-end UI and the infrastructure needed to package the request into a standard form, and to manage the communications with the workflow controller.

Authentication, Authorization, Data Privacy and Data Security

Presentation managers require many of the capabilities of vanilla client/server support:

▶ User authentication

▶ System management interfaces

▶ Data privacy

▶ Data security

In addition, presentation managers require geographic entitlement. Geographic entitlement is authentication which maps the user's actual network location (the specific computer in use) in addition to identification and password.

Validating the User's Input

Usually you try to validate the user's data entry in the presentation manager, as opposed to letting the server software catch any errors. Users want their errors to be caught as soon as possible, so that they don't waste time filling in fields that might have to be erased when their error is caught. This means that either we have to validate on the client, or we have to send each field (or each "significant" field) back to the server to be validated. The network traffic this implies may cause the system to miss its performance goals.

Validation can be strictly syntax-based, context-free or context-based:

▶ Syntax-based validation is used to check the type of data returned. For example, a field may be restricted to be a date, or a positive number.

▶ Context-free checking does not use knowledge of the business model. An example of this type of validation would be restricting a field to be a date after January 1, 1970.

▶ Context-based validation uses information from the business model. These data are only available in (business) objects in memory or in the persistent store. An example is "the user must be over 21 on the date entered in this field".

Syntax-based validation and context-free validation can typically be done directly in the presentation manager. However, it may be too expensive in network traffic for context-based validation to be done on the client machine. This depends on the degree to which the business model is exposed in the presentation manager. If DCOM or CORBA style architecture is used, then every relevant business object will have a proxy on the client. In this case, the data is "available" to do the context-based validation directly on the server. Depending on the scheme used to cache business object data members in the proxy, running the validation may or may not add a significant amount of network traffic.

The alternative is to do some or all of the validation on the server. This means either that the user has to wait until the form is submitted to see his errors, or that network bandwidth will be allocated to validating user input as it is entered. One way to do this is to use a set of rules to determine when to send data to the server application. This can be done with a rule interpreter in the client. A simpler solution is to mark display fields with a send-immediate flag: the presentation manager would format and send a validation request to the server whenever one of these flagged fields is entered.

185

Managing the Request

The back end of the presentation manager takes the input from the form and formats the request. It then submits the request to the server using the vendor-supplied communications mechanism. Responses from the server are forwarded to the presentation component for display to the user.

The back end of the presentation manager is responsible for formatting the request. The request usually includes an identifier for the user and for the presentation manager (perhaps the network address), the request type and the request parameters. As we saw in the previous chapter, this is the type of information that is needed for any IPC request. The **begin**, **commit** and **abort** commands are typically issued by the workflow controller or the transaction servers, not the presentation manager.

The Workflow Controller

Workflow is nothing more than a sequence of steps required to accomplish a complicated task. The workflow controller is responsible for balancing the load on the transaction server; it encapsulates knowledge of which steps must be accomplished in what order.

The workflow controller is a "store and forward" object — it exists to limit the number of communications sessions required. Without the workflow controller, communication between n clients and m servers would require $n*m$ connections. With 5000 clients and 40 servers, that would require 200000 direct connections.

By using a workflow controller, you can reduce that to $n+m$. The n clients each link to the workflow controller, and the workflow controller then links to the m servers. Thus we can reduce the 200000 connections to 5040.

This is a classic hub architecture, in which all the clients and servers are on spokes, and the workflow controller sits at the hub as a central point of communication and switching. You see this architecture implemented in the phone system (where each central office is a hub), in the FedEx delivery system (all packages go into one site from which they are all dispatched) and in the mail system (where each post office is a hub).

The workflow controller also provides a façade to the back end of the TP system. This includes the transaction servers as well as four other components:

▶ Queue manager

▶ Log manager

▶ Lock manager

▶ Transaction manager

Workflow Programming

There are three approaches to writing workflow programs.

▶ With the first approach, there are no programs — each request is forwarded to a transaction server by the workflow controller infrastructure. This only works for very simple mapping

▶ Write the workflow programs in a workflow-specific language, for example, STDL (structured transaction description language)

▶ Write the workflow programs in the native programming language, such as C++

One issue that is of significance is exception handling. A transaction server or even the whole computer system may crash. This will cause the transaction to abort. Some systems allow the application programmer to supply an exception handler that runs after the system has restarted. The exception handler is passed a description of what caused the transaction to abort. If the chained model is used, a transaction is automatically started for the exception handling. If the unchained model is used, the exception handler usually brackets its work with transaction boundaries. STDL, for example, supports automatic exception handling in its own transaction.

One idiom that has evolved for workflow programming deals with lost requests. The problem is that, if the transaction aborts, the user may never receive any information on what happened. The user would have to manually resubmit the request. This can be finessed by ensuring that the TP monitor receives the request message within the transaction boundary. Then, if the transaction aborts, the request is replayed.

This wasn't a problem in classic TP systems, because they polled their clients. The client/server paradigm has the client submit the request to the server instead. Modern TP monitors support **message queues** (discussed later in this chapter) as a solution to this problem. The manager of the queue is a resource manager that supports the commit or abort of transactions like any other resource. If the transaction includes an explicit fetch of the request from the message queue, then the request will be restored to the queue by the queue manager following an aborted transaction.

Lock Manager

The lock manager is the system component used by the resource managers for managing locks. It stores all of the locks in a memory-resident lock table and has exclusive access to this table. The lock manager API typically includes functions to lock an item in a given mode (for a given transaction), to unlock a lock on an item for a transaction and to unlock all items for a transaction.

The lock manager grants a request if there are no conflicting locks. Otherwise, the request for the lock is added to the list of transactions waiting for a lock on that data item, and the transaction is suspended. When locks are changed or dismissed on the data item, the list of waiting transactions is examined. Any locks that are now compatible with the (revised) set of locks for the data item are now granted.

Transaction Management and Recovery

When a transaction is committed, all of its effects on the resources are made permanent and all of its locks are released. This has to be done in the correct order to be effective and safe. When a transaction is aborted, all of its effects are rolled back and all of its locks are released. This also has to be done in a well-defined order. Additionally, after the system recovers from a system crash, the effects of all committed transactions should be durable, and all uncommitted and aborted transactions should have no lasting effects.

The most popular way to provide these capabilities is to use a log file to record the effects of each transaction. Protocols are defined that regulate the interaction of resource writing, log writing and lock operations. The log file is also involved in the procedures that are used to recover from a disk crash.

187

Classic TP systems provided a **log manager** to manage the log file, and a **transaction manager** to coordinate the actions of the resource managers for commit, abort, system restart and media recovery activities. Modern TP systems bundle all of this under the rubric of the recovery manager, with one exception: transactions that update more than one resource require the services of a transaction manager.

Consider a transaction that updates two databases. The protocols that are used to commit the updates must ensure that both resource managers are able to commit the changes that either resource manager is asked to commit. Otherwise, it is possible that one resource manager may be able to commit the updates, while the other is not able to do so. In this case, the transaction would not be atomic — it will have been durably updated one database and not the other.

TP systems define a transaction manager that is responsible for coordinating the resource managers using a protocol that respects this requirement. The protocol is called **two-phase commit**, because it first asks each resource manager if it is able to commit and only then, in a second phase, does it ask each resource manager to commit the changes. The two-phase commit protocol is discussed in more detail later in this chapter.

Replication

Transaction servers can be replicated to improve system availability and system performance (response time and throughput). The replication architecture determines the type of improvements. For example, many servers are intimately tied to a resource, such as a database. If we replicate the server, but do not replicate the resource manager and the resource (the database), the result is that we improve availability, but do not improve performance. Most systems therefore replicate the resource and its manager, as well as the transaction server.

Replication can be synchronous (all replicas are updated at the same time), or asynchronous. Synchronous replication adds a significant load to the transaction environment and so is not used very often. If the transactions are posted asynchronously to different servers, however, the effects of the ordering of the transactions must be preserved.

This ordering requirement contributes to the complexity of replication algorithms. This is exacerbated by the requirement that when replicas fail, they should provide a recovery mechanism guaranteed to process any missed transactions, again, in the right order.

As if that wasn't bad enough, servers may mistakenly think other replicas have failed due to a communications failure. This can partition the network into two or more sets of servers, each of which think they are the only ones servicing the transactions. These sets of servers may each update a shared resource, such as a database. Eventually, the network will be reconnected and the various resulting inconsistencies must be resolved.

Replication can be done by designating one copy of the transaction server as the primary server, directing all processing to the primary server, and then updating the secondary servers. This is called **single-master replication**.

Another technique is to allow all of the transaction servers (that is, the *replicas*) to update in parallel. This is called **multiple-master replication** and is used when nodes may be disconnected from the system. For example, an insurance salesman may disconnect his laptop computer when visiting clients. The salesman will update his local database when he sells a policy. At some point, these updates must be resolved with the master database. One variant of multiple-master replication designates one server as the primary. Another variant, called distributed multiple-master replication, implements replication without a primary.

Two-phase Commit

The idea behind the two-phase commit protocol is that during the first phase, each resource manager only agrees that it can proceed with the commit. The resource manager can only do that if it has stored the transaction's updates to the log. If it says it can commit, and then fails, it uses the log to finish the commit processing when it recovers.

In the case of a single transaction manager, the two-phase commit protocol is straightforward:

▶ Phase 1: The transaction manager asks each resource manager to prepare to commit ("Request to Prepare")

Each resource manager writes its updates to the log and responds that it is ready to commit ("Prepared") — end of phase 1

▶ Phase 2: If any resource manager answers "unable to commit", then the transaction manager asks each resource manager to abort the transaction ("Abort")

Otherwise, the transaction manager asks the resource managers to commit the transaction ("Commit")

The resource managers respond to the transaction managers when they have carried out the commit or abort ("Done") — end of phase 2

The two-phase commit protocol is defined in terms of a **coordinator** and **participants**. In the case where there are resource managers on more than one node, one of the transaction managers (the coordinator) is held responsible for directing the overall two-phase commit. If a given transaction includes resource managers from other nodes, the transaction managers from those nodes become participants in the two-phase commit. The prime transaction manager sees the secondary transaction managers as resources. They, in turn, ask their resource managers (and any transaction managers that are subordinate to them for this transaction) to prepare and to commit.

The transaction managers and resource managers thus form a tree. This is called the tree-of-processes model. The "Request to Prepare", "Commit" and "Abort" messages move down this tree and the "Prepared" and "Done" messages move up. Each transaction manager at an interior node of this tree is responsible for managing the sub-tree below it.

Message Queues

A message queue is nothing more than a sequenced list of messages. Store-and-forward message switches receive messages from a variety of communication lines over a variety of protocols, convert them to a standard format, and save them in message queues until they are requested by the destination nodes in the network. Their queues are prioritized and persistent. Queue management is usually under operator control from a console.

TP systems require that a message is queued in order to serialize requests. They also require that the request message will be restored to the queue if the transaction aborts or the system fails.

Queued Transactions

There are a number of mechanisms by which the client may pass messages to the workflow controller. The first way is to use the transactional RPC mechanism. This makes the request look like a local procedure call. The second uses peer-to-peer communication. This puts a greater burden on the programmer, but provides more complex patterns of communication. As an alternative, you may want to build a transactional message queue as an interface between the client and the workflow controller.

Queues are one of the fundamental data structures in C++ programming. The Standard Template Library (STL) offers a variety of queue-like structures. A container accepts component items (in this case, request messages), stores them, and returns them upon demand. A queue is a container that returns items in the order in which they were received (first in, first out, or FIFO). A priority queue is a container that allows messages to define a sort-order, and returns items based on their order in the queue. A persistent message queue is a message queue that can survive a program or system crash. A transactional queue understands transactional semantics (commit, roll-back, etc.).

Queued transaction processing requires a transactional, ordered, persistent message queue. This includes participating in the protocols that define how transactions are started, committed and aborted. It also means participating in the protocols that define how the system is restarted after a failure and how permanent media such as disk are restored after a failure.

There are several advantages to using a queue for message requests to a TP system:

- Without a queue, if the server is down the request would be rejected. With the queue, the request can be stored until the server is available.

- Without a queue, if the client crashes after it issues the request, the response from the server is lost. With the queue, the response can be stored until the client is available.

- Without a queue, it is difficult to implement a scheme for request prioritization.

- When transactions abort, the request is put back on the queue. The request is not lost and will be eventually processed.

- Using a queue makes it possible to use a variety of load-balancing algorithms across a server process class. It would be difficult to transfer the data needed for these algorithms to the client's workstation. The queue provides a central location to cache the request for the load-balancing process.

The architecture typically includes a queue manager that functions as a TP resource manager, a request queue and a response queue. The response queue may be logically or physically segregated by the client workstation or cluster in which it is located.

The server requires one transaction to process a queue element. After the transaction starts, the message queue provides the server with the highest priority request, which is processed by that server, based on the message type. The server processes the message and puts the result on the response queue. The server then ends the transaction. If the transaction rolls back, then the response is removed from the response queue, and the request is added back to the request queue, where it will be processed the next time.

The client runs one transaction to submit the request to the server. After the server transaction puts the result on the response queue, the client runs a third transaction to obtain the result. Committing this third transaction releases the queue element from the response queue. The net effect is that the request is processed under correct conditions or error conditions, and always results in either a response to the caller or an exception being generated.

Standardization Efforts

Two standards have been proposed for TP systems. The first is from the Open Group: X/Open has developed a standard for transaction processing, which defines the interfaces between the TP system components. The second is from the International Standards Organization (ISO). They have defined a standard for communications between heterogeneous TP monitors, known as the ISO TP protocol.

TP standards are important to users as they guarantee the interoperability of TP components from multiple vendors.

X/Open's DTP Model

The X/Open Distributed Transaction Processing (DTP) model is shown in the diagram below:

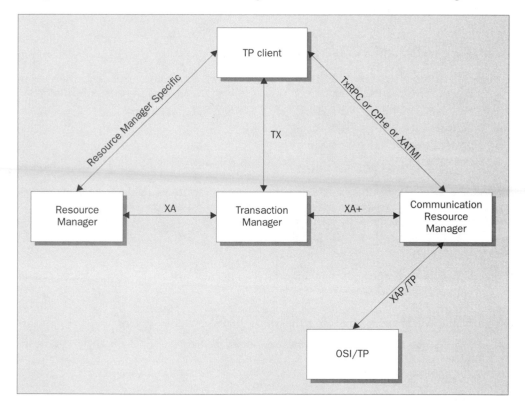

The point of the X/Open DTP model is to define the interfaces between these components, so that different products from different vendors can interoperate.

Six interfaces are shown in the above diagram. Five of them are defined by the DTP model. The communication between the application and the resource manager is not defined. DTP assumes that standard database languages, such as ISAM (Indexed Sequential Access Method) or SQL (Structured Query Language), will be used here.

> The most well known part of this standard is the interface between the resource managers and the transaction manager, known as XA. Most resource managers, such as RDB (relational database) systems, are "XA compliant". This means that they can participate in transactions, including being a participant in two-phase commit. Transaction managers use **xa_start**, **xa_commit** and **xa_rollback** calls to manage a transaction. Resource managers use **xa_reg** calls to register with the transaction manager. XA also allows one-phase commit for transactions that access a single resource manager.

> The XA+ standard is a superset of the XA standard. The extension is used by the communication resource manager to tell the transaction manager that a node (i.e. another transaction manager) has joined the transaction.

> The TX standard is used to communicate between application programs and the transaction manager. Applications issue **tx_begin**, **tx_commit**, and **tx_rollback** calls to manage transactions.

Microsoft Transaction Server

The Microsoft Transaction Server (MTS) for Windows NT is an object-oriented transaction server for COM-based components. It includes a transaction manager, the Distributed Transaction Coordinator (DTC), and currently supports two protocols:

> OLE Transactions
> XA protocol

It also includes some ORB-like capabilities — MTS provides tools to deploy clients and servers, and a snap-in to the Microsoft Management Console, a GUI-based system management framework, which it shares with Internet Information Server (IIS) and other Microsoft servers.

MTS Architecture

MTS defines system components that map nicely into our overall TP architecture. Besides the DTC, the components include:

> Clients, which correspond directly with our presentation servers
> MTS objects, which contain application logic and correspond to both workflow controller and transaction servers
> Resource managers
> Resource dispensers.

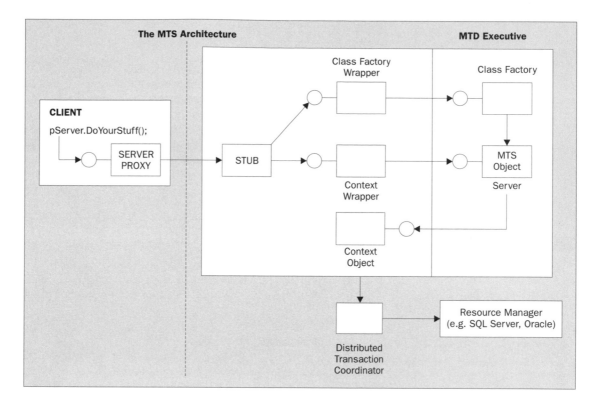

The MTS executive manages the MTS object threads in a server process, and is responsible for starting and committing transactions for applications written using implicit transaction bracketing, as explained below. Thus, the usual problems associated with managing multiple users using the same business objects are handled for you behind the scenes. MTS objects shouldn't be multi-threaded themselves — instead, their classes should support multiple instancing, and leave the details to MTS.

MTS objects are used to build both workflow controllers and transaction servers. MTS does not enforce any architectural distinction between these components. It is up to the system architect to configure the components accordingly.

Resource dispensers are like resource managers, but the objects they control are not persistent. An example would be a shared memory heap that is used to construct objects for several processes. Resource dispensers do not participate in two-phase commits, as they have no persistent data, but they are shared resources, and applications access them using synchronization primitives.

MTS Objects

Programming an MTS object requires you to adhere to three simple rules:

- The MTS objects must be compiled into an in-proc (DLL) server, as they will need to run within the MTS server process

- A standard COM class factory is required for each object, so that MTS can create them automatically

> ◗ The MTS object must support standard COM marshaling mechanisms, so that it can be invoked by clients both local and remote

MTS objects are grouped together by function into **packages**, the creation of which couldn't be easier. Dragging the DLL into the package folder on the management window, exposes all the public COM objects. Security is organized at the package level, using the concept of **roles**.

> *A **role** is a list of NT users or groups allowed to access that package, defined according to how they will need to use it. Thus clerks have one role, managers another, sys-admins yet another. Different components and component interfaces within the package can support differing access, depending on what role the client is playing. Thus a clerk would have access to the data entry objects, while a manager might also have access to report-creation objects.*

Transaction Bracketing

MTS applications may be designed using implicit transaction bracketing. This is done by marking all DCOM components with respect to the relationship of their transactional boundary and that of their parent. Specifically, all DCOM components follow one of the following four types of semantics:

> ◗ Not Supported: The object must not run within a transaction.

> ◗ Required: The object must run within a transaction.

> ◗ Requires New: The object must run within its own transaction.

> ◗ Supported: The object may run within the parent's transaction.

Context Object

An important part of the architecture is the **context object**. It contains the information about any transactions in which the MTS object is engaged, and which role the client has assumed.

The MTS executive creates one every time an MTS object is created. The MTS object can get a reference to an **ObjectContext** object, available from the MTS type library, using the **GetObjectContext()** call. **IObjectContext**'s methods include:

> ◗ **SetComplete()** — specifies that this object's transaction may complete and the object be deactivated, other things being equal.

> ◗ **SetAbort()** — abort the transaction, when the transaction manager asks and deactivate the MTS object.

> ◗ **DisableCommit()** — your MTS object may maintain state while it's working; for instance, if it calls another object and waits for that to return, or if the client makes several calls during a transaction. If this is the case, the transaction mustn't commit in the meantime.
>
> However, MTS may reuse an MTS object for a different client — by default, it assumes that the object carries no state between method calls. **DisableCommit()** guarantees that the client will get the same MTS object during a transaction.

> ◗ **EnableCommit()** — this re-enables the MTS object's ability to commit or abort if asked.

▶ **CreateInstance()** — if your MTS object creates another MTS object as part of its work within a transaction, you don't want to lose that transaction's context information. If the second object fails, the calling object must know, so that it can rollback its changes. **CreateInstance()** allows an MTS object to create a child object, such that it shares its context information.

▶ **IsCallerInRole()** — this allows your MTS objects to check that their client has the right security clearance to continue.

Calling **DisableCommit()** and **EnableCommit()** needs to be done when an MTS object is first activated and when it is ready to be deactivated, respectively — and this is handled by the **IObjectControl** interface, and its **Activate()** and **Deactivate()** methods.

MTS Clients

MTS clients are normal DCOM components. This includes standalone programs written in Visual C++ as well as COM objects that live inside a web page. DCOM provides the communications infrastructure that allows clients to use the normal object-invocation mechanism in their programs. Of course, if the method is for a remote object, the invocation will be on a proxy object. To help you with deployment, MTS can create an installation program that can be used to provide the correct proxy on each client machine.

TP Benchmarks

Just to get an idea of the ballpark capabilities associated with transaction processing, let's look at the benchmark TPC-C, which has been designed by the Transaction Processing Performance Council to compare TP systems. It defines a (scalable) database and a workload designed to exercise the TP system. The results of running the benchmark are measured in "transactions per minute" (tpm). They also measure the cost of TP systems: they divide the five year purchase price plus maintenance by the tpm rating to give a dollar per transaction per second.

TPC-C is an order entry application and combines interactive and batch transactions, queued transactions, and aborted transactions. The sample TPC-C database is centered on the warehouse. The size of the database is proportional to the number of warehouses: each warehouse contributes the same rows. These include a warehouse record, 10 District records (geographic information), 30000 customer, history, and order records, 9000 new order records, 100000 stock and order items and 300000 order line items. These rows vary from eight bytes for each new order entry to 655 bytes for the customer entries. The transactions processed include new order, order status, delivery, payments, and stock level. These transactions use a combination of queries and updates.

For example, the stock level transaction determines the stocking for a district. The input to the query is a threshold, the output is all items that have been ordered recently whose stock level is below the threshold. It is processed as a query that:

▶ Retrieves the appropriate district record

▶ Retrieves the order line records for the last twenty orders in that district

▶ Examines each of the order lines for the twenty orders

▶ Determines, for each order item, whether the amount in stock is less than the threshold

195

Object Pooling

One last problem we should mention when discussing multiple clients accessing the same server was the issue of **scalability**. A scalable server application is simply one where an increase in the number of clients accessing the server can be offset by a linear increase in hardware capacity.

In a traditional DCOM application, the client object obtains and holds a reference to the server so long as both are alive. In practical terms, that means that the server object has spun off another thread for that client. The expense of obtaining the initial link to the server object means that client objects should be reluctant to release their reference.

However, thread creation versus resources consumed does not follow a linear relationship, so adding more clients to a server will have a progressively greater impact.

Now add to this the fact that many client-server applications do not require constant client communication with the server, just a connection on demand. Just think of email clients and servers.

So we see that clients often require a reference to a server application as long as they remain in use, but that they really only need the server occasionally. The answer is to pool the objects the server uses to work with clients.

There are three ways to improve a server application's scalability.

Thread Pooling

The simplest implementation of this is where the server application limits the number of threads it supports. This is common in web servers, where the simultaneous HTTP connections the server supports is set to match the hardware.

Just-In-Time Activation

But this doesn't answer the need to keep a client-server session open while the client is alive. To illustrate how to solve this problem, we'll use Microsoft Transaction Server (MTS). MTS intercepts client calls to the server objects running within. It gives the client a reference to itself and then deals with client requests — so the client has a long-lived reference as desired.

MTS creates a server object on demand, along with its associated context object, and the server does its work. When the server object is finished, it calls the 'transaction' methods **SetComplete()** or **SetAbort()** (even if the object isn't supporting transactions), which tells MTS that the object can be deactivated and memory reclaimed.

> *Note that there are times when the server object must maintain state, that is, session information. In this situation there are a few solutions. Either we can use a direct client-server connection as we discussed above, we can use the context object or we can save the object's state to some datastore between each client call.*

In designing such systems, the client gets a reference and hangs onto it, just as before. However, the server design needs some consideration. The server objects must implement the **IObjectContext** interface to tell MTS when they are finished, with the two methods above. Ideally, for good scalability, they should do this as quickly as possible — even to the point of the objects acting as 'function fulfillers' with little or no state.

Object Recycling

When a server object requires a lengthy initialization period, just-in-time activation won't be an adequate solution. It's possible to recycle an object, preserving its initial state (for instance, with an ODBC connection to some datastore) and provide a pool of such objects to clients.

> *Object recycling has been tabled for inclusion in MTS for some time, using the* **CanBePooled()** *method of the* **IObjectControl** *interface. However, it transpires that recycling an object instance, rather than creating a new object, may only be more efficient in a certain limited number of cases.*

> *This has to do with MTS' use of resource dispensers. For example, MTS can hold a number of ODBC connections open for MTS objects, which turns the programming model on its head, as the MTS objects should return the ODBC connection to the pool as quickly as possible.*

Summary

In this chapter, we've looked at what issues will affect the process view of the architecture document.

When we use a client-server design, with its centralized data source and business objects to act on the data stored there, we quickly need to find a happy medium between the problem of data corruption by server threads, and unacceptably slow and unscalable server performance.

Specifically we've seen:

▶ How multi-tasking operating systems introduce multiple processes, and threads within a process, but can also interrupt program execution at any time. The application developer is responsible for making programs thread-safe.

▶ The need for atomic operations and synchronization to protect shared resources

▶ General locking strategies, and those used in the MFC

▶ How to avoid deadlock

▶ What it takes to be a transaction — ensuring reliability of operations, especially when execution is distributed across multiple objects, machines and datastores

▶ The ACID test

▶ What help TP systems provide

▶ The use of two-phase commit to control diverse resource managers

▶ Message queuing and queued transactions

▶ Object pooling for scalability

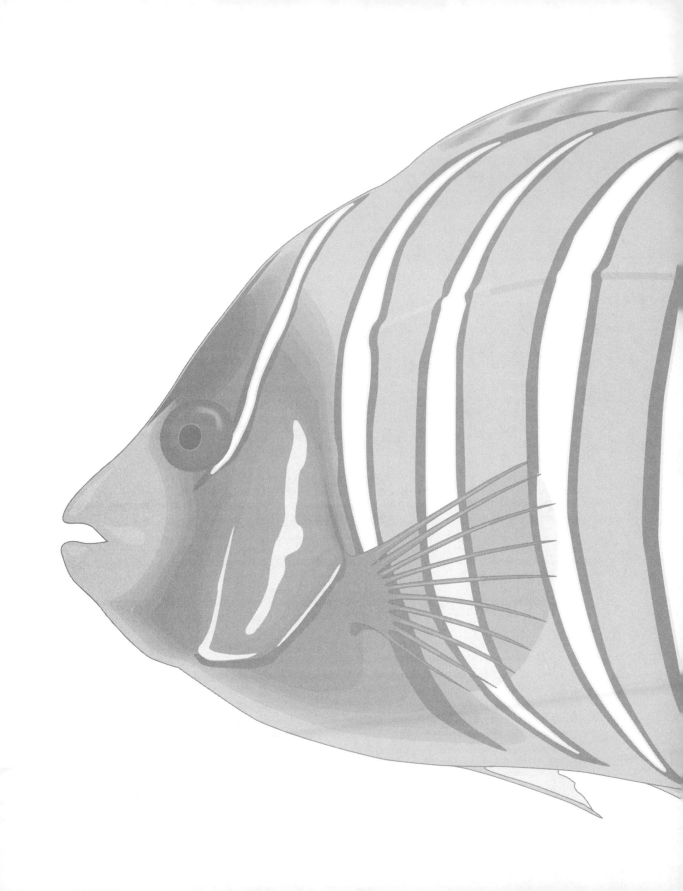

Persistence Mechanisms

In the analysis phase, we detail the information that needs to be persistent, and in the design phase, it is time to decide on a persistence mechanism. We can make objects persistent by using flash ROM, by writing to a simple file system, by creating our own B-tree or by utilizing a commercial database management system.

If we decide to use a DBMS, we must decide whether to use a **relational database management system** (RDBMS) or an **object database management system** (ODBMS). The ODBMS has the advantage that we will not need to transform our objects into tables and back again, but with the cost that ODBMS systems are not as mature, and therefore not as robust as RDMS systems.

These are important early architectural decisions that we'll have to revisit in greater detail as we work further on the design of the system. In many ways, the decision about which type of database system to use will be dictated both by our emerging understanding of the relative complexity (or simplicity) of the system, and also by the number of classes we design and the complexity of their interactions.

The decisions about the persistence mechanism we should use and the details of how we'll implement persistence will be captured in the logical view. This will include the details of transaction management, record locking, database synchronization and data integrity.

What is Persistence?

> **Persistence** *is the ability to restore an object to its previous state after shutting off the system or exiting the program.*

Normally, any objects created by a C++ program cease to exist when the program exits. Persistence is the ability to keep the object available after the program exits and to be able to access that object in other programs. Specifically, we want to preserve the object's state, so that we can recreate it later, either in another program or when we rerun the current program.

In Star Trek, Captain Kirk was forever stepping into the transporter and twinkling his way to the planet surface. You can imagine that the transporter was storing his state so that he could be restored elsewhere. If his state were restored perfectly, neither he nor anyone else would doubt he was the same person.

Imagine, further, that instead of restoring him immediately, the computer wrote his state to hard disk (or titanium holographic memory, if you prefer). This would be a persistence mechanism, which would allow the computer to restore Kirk to his former vainglorious self at a later date.

A real-world example of this is the ever-popular ATM example, in which a bank account must be updated for a user's transaction. Assume the user deposits $500 into an account that had a previous balance of $1000. Now, the new state of the account must be preserved so that the next time the account is accessed (perhaps through the customer's home banking program), the balance is shown as $1500, not as the original $1000. Even if the ATM goes off line, the bank balance must be maintained. The bank accomplishes this by writing the balance to an account in a database.

Without persistence, the moment the bank's computers shut down, every record of every transaction would be wiped out. The next month you'd get your statement. "Greetings. Due to a power failure, we reset our memory. Your new balance is $100."

Even if the computer were never turned off and never crashed, without persistence every item of information would have to be maintained in RAM. There is only so much RAM in most computers as cost is a major factor. To buy an additional Gigabyte of RAM costs about a thousand dollars, the cost of disk storage is one tenth that or less. In short, modern database systems would be impossible without some form of persistence.

What do we Persist?

Despite the Oxford English Dictionary's pedantic insistence that persist is an intransitive verb, programmers like to talk about *persisting* an object. When we persist an object, we store it away so that we can get at it later. You'll find us talking about persisting our money for a rainy day.

Typically, we persist an object or a "web" of connected objects. A web of objects consists of a starting object (called the **focus**) and all the objects connected to that focus. The web also includes all the objects connected to these other objects, and so on. After a change is made to the state of the object, it may be persisted again.

The operations that need to be available to persist an object or a web of objects are similar to those that are classically used in relational database management systems:

- **Create** — store an object in the database (a new object from the database's viewpoint)
- **Read** — query the database to obtain an object or objects that meet a set of criteria
- **Update** — update the state of an object in the database
- **Delete** — delete an object in the database

> *These form the acrostic CRUD: Create, Read, Update, Delete*

The way these operations are implemented depends on the type of persistence storage used. A number of different persistence mechanisms will be considered in the following pages, but the essential issues are the same across all techniques.

Issues in Persistence

The application programmer is typically concerned with the business logic that must be developed to implement the processing involved in a use case. Adding persistence to the objects that implement this logic (business objects) engenders a number of issues:

▶ Each element of an object's structure (attribute, association, hierarchy) must be mapped to an element of the persistent storage.

▶ The application source code must include saving, updating and retrieving business objects to and from the persistent store. This code must be written and tested for a specific persistence mechanism.

▶ The format of the persistent store must be kept in "synch" with the definitions of the objects that are kept in that store. During the development process, the definition of an object will change (its attributes, relationships etc.), and the definition of the persistent store must be changed accordingly.

Adding persistence to an application design complicates the run-time flow. If an RDB (relational database) or OODB (object-oriented database) is being used as the persistence store, it is typically implemented as a set of processes running on the application host or another machine. Debugging the run-time flow becomes more complicated, since:

▶ References to objects may vary, depending on whether the object is in memory or only available in the persistent store.

▶ The notion of object "identity" becomes important. As objects are retrieved from the persistent store, it becomes very important to know if two objects represent the same object in the persistent store (and in the real world).

Performance may be dramatically diminished by using a database. Anyone who has ever written embedded SQL in a traditional C or C++ based RDB implementation knows that after all of the code is written and tested, the real work begins. Tweaking the SQL to optimize the performance of the application is a difficult and time-consuming task.

Categories of Persistence Frameworks

Persistence may be explicit, meaning the programmer asks for an object to be saved or loaded. Alternatively, persistence may be implicit, in which case the system determines when and how to save and load objects. RDBMS systems are typically explicit, while ODBMS systems are typically implicit.

Although most persistence schemes built to date use **explicit persistence**, there are two great advantages to **implicit persistence**:

▶ The application programmer does not have to worry about loading and saving his objects. This is done transparently by the persistence framework.

▶ The application programmer does not have to worry about when his objects are in memory and when they are only in the persistent store. He therefore addresses them with normal C++ references all of the time, as if they were always memory resident. This is a very natural way for C++ programmers to work.

Do You Care If It Is In Memory?

When I worked on the Interchange Online Network for Ziff Davis (and later for AT&T), we wanted to offer implicit persistence. On the other hand, for some objects, we did not want to take the chance that the object would be swapped out to the database since we needed lightening fast access to the object. We needed to be able, on demand, to overrule the implicit persistence.

The database team decided to retain objects in memory with two types of pointers: a locker or a holder. A locker *locked* the object in memory and the programmer was required to unlock the object when he was done with it. This was not used often, but it did solve the problem of instant access. Unlocking the object caused it to be written back to the database. Lockers implemented explicit persistence.

A holder, on the other hand, was a proxy for the object, which was taken out of persistence and returned to the object store at the instigation of the object store itself. The goal was to have the object in memory when it was needed, but to be able to clear it out of memory when memory was scarce. This form of implicit persistence was a powerful mechanism of encapsulation, as the programmer could use the holder as if it were the object, without regard as to whether or not the object actually was in memory. If he needed to ensure the object would have optimal performance, he could *lock* the holder (changing it into a locker) and when he was done, he could *unlock* the locker, turning it back into a holder.

As an aside, we had to override the pointer operator (->) to refer to the held (or locked) object, and the dot operator (.) to refer to the holder or locker itself. Thus the holder (or locker) acted as a smart pointer. We added reference counting, so that if multiple holders (or lockers) referred to the same object, only one instance had to be kept in memory. In an object-oriented database that supports true implicit persistence, the programmer would not be aware of these issues. He would not differentiate between the proxy (holder or locker) and the object itself; as far as the programmer is concerned, the object is in memory when used, and in the database when not in use.

Accessing the Object

Whether you use implicit or explicit persistence, an object database or a relational one, each object in your system will have one or more of the following levels of access permission:

> ▶ Write semantics — objects have write semantics if they may be saved to the persistent store (Create)

> ▶ Read semantics — objects have read semantics if they may be recreated from the persistent store (Read)

> ▶ Modify semantics — objects have modify semantics if their image in the persistent store may be changed (Update)

> ▶ Delete semantics — objects have delete semantics if their image in the persistent store may be deleted (Delete)

When you persist an object, you put it somewhere other than in memory — to a byte stream (**serialization**), to a file or to a database. Streaming the object allows you to send it between processes on your computer, across a network, through a modem or over the Internet. Writing it to a file or a database allows you to store it for retrieval at a later time.

Serialization

> **Serialization** *is the process of taking objects and converting their state information into a form that can be stored or transported.*

The process of serialization involves turning pointers into object references or IDs, and converting binary data into a representation as a stream of bytes. How the receiving object interprets this stream of data is entirely up to an agreed-upon protocol. It may be that the receiving object just stores the stream "as is", or it may be that the object is converted into entries in a database.

> *Other uses of serialization include the marshalling process used by inter-process communication mechanisms (such as CORBA or DCE) and formatting data for communication over low-level network technologies such as TCP/IP sockets.*

In the case of persisting to a RDB, the receiving object is your persistence mechanism: an object which converts the stream of data into relational table entries. When the application retrieves objects, the persistence mechanism reads from the database and provides an object back to the application as a stream of bytes. The application then "reconstitutes" the object from the stream. With proper encapsulation, the application always produces and receives a stream, and thus is indifferent to the structure of the database.

Application classes should have no knowledge of the external representation format. As the interpretation of the stream changes, the application classes should be unaffected.

One way to enforce this separation of concerns is presented in the Serializer design pattern in PLOP 3 (*Pattern Languages of Program Design 3,* edited by Martin et al., ISBN 0-201-31011-2, Addison-Wesley). This pattern allows your application to read from and write to a variety of storage mechanisms using a uniform mechanism. The pattern makes use of a *reader* and a *writer*. The writer writes the object out to a serial stream and the reader uses the serial stream to recreate the object(s). A different reader/writer pair can be used for each persistent store that needs to be supported, but nothing else in your application need change.

To support this capability, an abstract base class called **Serializable** is defined. Any class that needs to be serialized must inherit from **Serializable**. This interface defines two methods: a **readFrom** method that takes a reader as a parameter, and a **writeTo** method that takes a writer as a parameter.

The reader and writer are implemented as classes which typically overload the operators **<<** and **>>**. These will be overloaded to take each of the primitive data types (e.g. **int**, **long**, **short** and so forth). Here is an excerpt from a typical version of such a class:

```
class Writer
    {
    public:
        virtual Writer& operator<<(int&);
        virtual Writer& operator<<(long&);
        virtual Writer& operator<<(short&);
        virtual Writer& operator<<(char*);
```

```
        //...
    };

class Reader
    {
    public:
        virtual Reader& operator>>(int&);
        virtual Reader& operator>>(long&);
        virtual Reader& operator>>(short&);
        virtual Reader& operator>>(char*&);

        //...
    };

class Serializable
    {
    public:
        Serializable readFrom(Reader&) = 0;
        virtual void writeTo(Writer&) = 0;
    };
```

This pattern shows you how to read and write all the built in primitive types such as **int** and **long**, but begs the question of how you read and write complex user-defined types. The answer is that each object delegates responsibility to read and write any non-primitive data members to the member itself! That is, user-defined types write out their primitive members and tell their user defined members to write themselves. Each one in turn recursively delegates this responsibility. Ultimately, every user-defined type is composed of primitive types, so that every object can be written and read.

Let's take a simple, if fanciful, example. Assume that you have the following classes:

```
class Employee
{
public:
//...
private:
 Address myAddress;
 int myAge;
};

class Address
{
public:
//...
private:
 Street myStreet;
 char* myCity;
 char* myState;
};
```

```
class Street
public:
//...
private:
int myNumber;
char* StreetName;
};
```

When you tell an **Employee** object to persist itself, it will write the variable **myAge** (an integer) and will tell the variable **myAddress** to write itself. The **Address** object will write out **myCity** and **myState** but will delegate to the **Street** class the responsibility to write out **myStreet**. **myStreet** has only primitive member variables (an **int** and a **char***) and so can write itself out without any further delegation.

Thus, serializing an object is done by following this algorithm:

1   Ask your parents in the inheritance hierarchy to serialize themselves

2   Serialize your primitive data members

3   Serialize your object pointers (discussed below)

4   Ask your sub-objects (those user-defined objects of which you are composed) to serialize themselves

This last act — asking your member objects to serialize themselves — allows for the implementation of serialization to be fully encapsulated and localized in that object which knows best how to do it. This means that, as you add new classes, the **Serializable** base class need not change. Classes that contain a new type do not need to change either; the responsibility for serializing that new type is encapsulated in the new type itself.

Serializing Pointers

Serializing object pointers requires a method of uniquely identifying objects. The identifier of the object that is being referenced is saved in the serialization process. This identifier is used to recreate the pointer to the object when the web of objects is recreated in memory. Typically, each saved object is given an ID, and these IDs are stored instead of the pointer. This also solves the issue of objects that are referenced by multiple pointers — only one copy of these objects should be created when the web of objects is recreated in memory.

The use of these IDs guarantees that if two objects are pointing at the same third object before they were serialized, then they will point at the same (recreated) third object when they are recreated. Using the IDs instead of pointers also allows the serialized objects to be recreated in an environment different from the one in which they were serialized, which can be very important in distributed systems. An example of this is support for load balancing — objects can be moved in a way that is transparent to the objects that point to them.

The Serializer Pattern decouples the application code from the reading and writing responsibilities. On the other hand, each time a new class is defined it must inherit from the **Serializable** class and implement the read and write methods.

The Serializer Pattern also undermines encapsulation by allowing access to the object's internal state. This can be solved with yet another design pattern, the Memento Pattern, described in the *Design Patterns* book by Gamma et al.

The Memento (or Token) Pattern is used to create an external representation of the internal state of an object, so that the state of the object can be persisted without violating encapsulation. A **memento** object is created, which stores the internal state of the original object, so that it may be restored at a later time. A **caretaker** object holds the **memento**, then provides it back to the original object so that it can restore its previous state. The **caretaker**, however, cannot access or alter the data held by the **memento**. This extra level of indirection allows the original object to keep its internal state hidden from the reader and writer, but at the cost of some extra overhead.

The **memento** itself must be **serializable** in this particular usage of the Memento Pattern. If the **memento** uses non-primitive data to capture the state of the object, this can mean a second recursive level of **memento**s and **serializable** objects, adding complexity.

Persisting to a Flat File

Instead of using an **ostream** or an **iostream** as the target of the serialization process, an **fstream** (file stream object) can be used to persist to a flat file. The state of one or more objects may be persisted to the file. The name of the file and the placement of the file in the directory structure may be used by the persistence mechanism to keep track of a set of objects across applications.

Sample classes would have these interfaces:

```
class Writer
    {
    public:
       Writer(char *fileName):fout(fileName,ios::binary){};
       ~Writer() {fout.close();}
       virtual Writer& operator<<(int&);
       virtual Writer& operator<<(long&);
       virtual Writer& operator<<(short&);
       virtual Writer& operator<<(char*);

    private:
            ofstream fout;
    };

class Reader
    {
    public:
       virtual Reader& operator>>(int&);
       virtual Reader& operator>>(long&);
       virtual Reader& operator>>(short&);
       virtual Reader& operator>>(char*&);
```

```
        Reader(char *fileName):fin(fileName,ios::binary){}
        ~Reader(){fin.close();}

    private:
        ifstream fin;
    };
```

File Contents

Saving one object to a file is easy — just serialize it and away you go. Saving a web of objects requires storing the relationships, so that the web can be recreated from the file. There are several schemes that can be used to do this:

▶ Use a serialization service that allows you to save a web of objects.

▶ Otherwise, save each object as a continuous set of bytes in the file. This file (or an associated file) must contain enough information to map from object references (created from pointers as part of the process of serializing an object) to file offsets. These offsets are used to recreate the web by creating the focus object and then following object references.

▶ Additional information may be needed for each object, such as the class name, the class's version number or the object ID.

Directory Structure

The directory hierarchy may be employed to capture information about the name of the application, sub-system or module, the name of the class, its version or any other information that is used to classify the files that contain the serialized images of persisted objects.

Relational Databases

Most real-world commercial applications persist their data to a relational database — and with good reason.

▶ Most business systems are not created in a vacuum. Typically, they must interoperate with legacy systems, and they must access legacy data. This means that your customer may specify a particular existing relational database as your persistence mechanism.

▶ Relational database technology is mature. It has been tested, its performance is well understood and there are good tools to support the development and maintenance of large relational database applications.

Basic Concepts

You can build a very simple database by creating records and storing them sequentially in a large file. The problem, of course, is that it is difficult to find your records quickly. Typically, the solution to this is to build an **index**. An index is a file which is sorted by whatever value you are indexing. In theory an index could duplicate all the values in a file, sorting them in the particular way desired (e.g. by name or by date). This would be tremendously wasteful, as you wouldn't want all that data duplicated for every index. Thus, an index is typically implemented as a file containing a single table with two fields, the first field is the sorted value (for example, the name), and the second field is an offset into the data file, pointing at the complete record.

For example, suppose you are building a database of video tapes for the VideoMagix system. You might have a data file with one record for each video tape, and you might have an index file which lists the titles alphabetically. Note, the index file does *not* duplicate the entire data record, it contains only the sorted field (title) and the location of the corresponding record in the data file. Thus, from the title, you can find the entire data record in the data file.

Your data file would consist of a set of fixed-length records. Each video tape record might include entries for the title, the actors, the release date and whether or not it is available. Each record would begin at an offset, which is a multiple of the size of the record. Thus, if the record were 100 bytes, the fifth record would begin at offset 400. The *nth* record would begin at an offset of *(n-1)*100*. Your index file might consist of much smaller data structures, holding nothing more than the title and the offset into the data file. You might have another index file that listed the release dates, the title and the offset, so that you could quickly find all new movies or all vintage flicks.

		Offset				
		0				
2001	100		Gone with the Wind	1939	Gone Wind	000
Amadeus	400	100		1942	Casablanca	700
Casablanca	700		2001: A Space Odyssey	1952	Singing	300
English Pt.	200	200		1968	2001	100
Ghandi	600		The English Patient	1982	Ghandi	600
Gone Wind	000	300		1984	Amadeus	400
Singing	300		Singin' in the Rain	1996	English Pt.	200
		400				
			Amadeus			
		500				
			The Music Lovers			
		600				
			Ghandi			
		700				
			Casablanca			

The index file allows you to sort your main data on many different fields, without having to duplicate all the information. For example, by using these indexes, it is as if you had sorted the entire data set both by title and by release date. When the customer chooses a title (e.g. "Ghandi"), the system can quickly locate it in the index and find the offset into the data file (600). It can then jump to that offset and find the data record.

This is fast because of two underlying technologies: **binary searches** and **seeking**.

Binary Searches

In a binary search, you look halfway into the file and decide if your target data is before or after your current record. For example, if your target is "Ghandi" and you search the index sorted by names, half way in will bring you to "English Pt". You know that "Ghandi" is after this record, so you search half way through the remaining records, which brings you to "Gone Wind". "Ghandi" is before this, so you then search half way through the remaining records. The advantage of a binary search is that when your files grow, the number of searches you need to conduct grows far more slowly. For a file containing n records, you need, on average, to search only $log_2(n)$ records. If, on the other hand, you were to look at every record in the original database you'd have to examine an average of $n/2$ records.

With a database of 65536 records, brute force searching would average 32768 searches, but a binary search would average 16 searches — a significant performance enhancement! In addition, the 32 thousand searches must each read in the entire data block while the 16 searches may read in the much smaller index records. There is simply no comparison in performance.

Seeking

Once you know the offset of the record you require, you can seek directly to the record and read it into memory as a block. This is a very fast operation.

Data Structures

Rather than storing your records in a simple list, you may decide to optimize performance of your index (and perhaps retrieval of your data records) by building somewhat more complex data structures. Most languages offer you very simple data structures, such as an array. Arrays allow you to keep simple collections of objects, but each object is fixed in size and the array itself is fixed in size at compile time. If you know you may keep 50-75 records, then an array is a good choice; you just need to allocate room for the larger amount, that is, declare an array of 75 records. How many records should you allocate for a phone list? Some of your customers might want to keep a dozen numbers. Others might keep a hundred. A politician might keep a thousand. A large organization might keep ten thousand.

It would be very wasteful to allocate room for 10 000 records, if you only need to keep a few dozen. Each record might be 1K of data, so 10 000 records would take up ten megabytes, quite a lot for your customers who have only a few phone numbers to track. What you need is a **collection** that grows as you use it.

The Standard Template Library (STL) offers a variety of collection classes to C++ programmers. These come in two flavors: sequence and associative. Sequence collections are used to hold (you guessed it!) sequences of objects, while associative collections help you match up objects with "keys".

Sequence Containers

The first of the STL sequence collections is a **vector**. A vector is like an array that grows as you use it. The second sequence collection is the **deque**. Deque is short for "double-ended queue". In America we talk about lining up for the bus or for a movie, but in Britain they talk about "queuing up". A queue is like a line at the ticket window. The first person on line is served first, all the others queue behind and wait their turn. You can build a data structure that behaves like a queue; objects added to the queue are removed in the order they arrive. This can be very handy when you have a limited resource (such as a printer) to which you must regulate access. Jobs are added to the queue and taken off the queue as the resource becomes available. They are removed on a first in, first out (FIFO) order.

The third and last of the sequence STL collections is the **list**. A list implements a **doubly-linked list** collection. To understand this, you must start by understanding a linked list, and to understand this, we should think first about arrays. An array is like an egg carton — there is a space for each object (egg) you want to store, but each carton holds a predetermined number of eggs. If you have a carton for six eggs, you allocate space in your refrigerator for six eggs, whether you have one or six. If you have seven eggs, then you're in trouble, you need another carton or you have to hold the extra egg in your hand all day.

Imagine instead a new kind of egg container. It has space for one egg, but it also has a hook on one side and an eye on the other. If you want to store four eggs, you snap four of these containers together. This results in a little train of cartons, each holding one egg. A linked list is just like such a train. We build a structure called a "node", which holds our object and also points to the next node in the list. The diagram below shows a linked list that we might want to use to store the names of our video tapes:

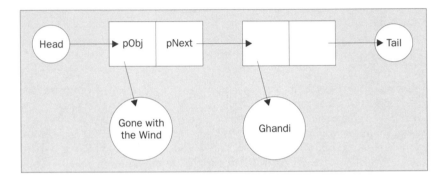

Head marks the beginning of the list and it points to the first node. That node keeps a pointer, **pObj**, to the first video tape and a second pointer, **pNext**, which points to the next node in the list. That second node in turn points to a video tape and the next node in the list. It turns out that this is the last node in the list, so it points to tail.

The above example illustrates is a singly-linked list. In a doubly-linked list, nodes not only point to the *next* node in the list, but also point back to the *previous* node in the list. This is shown in the diagram below:

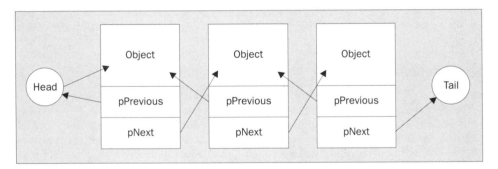

Linked lists are the foundation of a number of other, more complex, data structures. These include B+ trees, Red/Black trees and other intriguing denizens of books and classes on data structures (for example, *Algorithms in C++*, by Robert Sedgewick, Addison-Wesley ISBN 0-201-51059-6). The essence of each of these structures, however, is to provide enhanced performance. Some data structures are optimized for the ability to add records to the list quickly. Others are optimized for fast searching and/or fast retrieval.

While learning about advanced data structures can be fascinating, the truth is that most often you'll just buy a ready made solution. The most common solution for these problems is a commercial **relational database management system** or **RDBMS**.

Architecture of an RDB

Databases can be understood at three conceptual levels:

▶ External level

▶ Conceptual level

▶ Physical or internal level

The external level represents the application view of the data, including application-specific semantics and constraints. For the VideoMagix application, for example, you might decide that the customer can only belong to a single club, or that a video tape can only be borrowed by one customer at a time.

The next level is the conceptual level. This is the level of entity-relationship modeling. From this perspective, we consider tables, rows, columns and indexes. A table is a structure which looks like this:

Tape ID	Title Name	Release Date	Cost	Period	Available?
001	Gone with the Wind	1939	$4.00	2 day	Y
002	Ghandi	1982	$3.00	2 day	N
003	2001	1968	$4.50	1 day	Y
.	.	.	.	.	.
.	.	.	.	.	.
.	.	.	.	.	.

Each row represents a single record. Each column represents a field in the record. At this level, we are concerned with understanding the relationships among the various objects in the domain and how these translate to tables and their interrelationships.

The most basic level is the physical level, which corresponds directly to the contents of the disk files used to capture these data and indexes. Here, you consider questions about the size of the records in the file, data access blocks, disk access methods and so forth.

The architecture of relational databases assumes three types of users:

▶ The end user, who is not aware of the internal database structures at the physical or logical level. End users are not responsible for programming, but rather they use the applications prepared by the programmer and the query tools provided by the database product. They operate at the conceptual and external level.

▶ The programmer, who is responsible for developing the applications used by the end users. He is responsible for the creating the external level of the architecture.

211

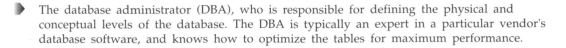 The database administrator (DBA), who is responsible for defining the physical and conceptual levels of the database. The DBA is typically an expert in a particular vendor's database software, and knows how to optimize the tables for maximum performance.

Each row in a table has a unique identifier. This identifier consists of one or more fields in the row. The same fields are used as the identifier for all rows in a table. This is called the **primary key** for the table.

Relational databases are all about relations among tables. One way for two tables to be related to one another is for Table A to contain the primary key of Table B. This is called a **foreign key** in Table A, and it serves as a reference to a row in Table B.

Tape Name (primary key)	Release Date	Cost	Days	Who rented (foreign key)
Gone With The Wind	1939	$3.00	2	10010
Ghandi	1982	$4	2	10021
.	.	.	.	.
.	.	.	.	.
.	.	.	.	.

Table A

ID (primary key)	Name	Address	City/ State	Phone	Club?
10021	John Doe	1 Main St.	Anytown	999-123-4567	N
10010	Jesse Liberty	1 Till Dr.	Acton, MA	617-747-7301	Y
.	.	.	.	.	.
.	.	.	.	.	.
.	.	.	.	.	.

Table B

In this example the **ID** in Table B is the key on which Table B will be indexed. It is also a foreign key into Table A. If you want to find out who rented a tape listed in Table A, you look up the **ID** in Table B and get the customer's record.

A table is always indexed on its primary key. It is also possible to index on any other field to speed up searching for a record on that field. For example, you might index **Name** in Table B. Or, for that matter, you might index the combination of **Address** and **City/State** as a single key. These additional indexed fields are called **secondary keys**.

There are restrictions on the contents of the rows. For example, duplicate rows are not allowed and all primary keys must be unique within the table. The order of the rows is not important to the conceptual model, although it can be important to the physical model. The value of each field is atomic — each field represents a single, indivisible bit of information, thus, lists are not allowed within a single field.

There are three types of table:

- **Entity table** — contains user-meaningful data
- **Relationship table** — represents relationships between tables, using foreign keys to reference the underlying rows in the entity tables
- **Virtual table** — used to present a "view" of the database to an application; it is usually not possible to update a database through a view

Normalization

Normalization is the process of eliminating duplication of data from within your database. Duplicate data can cause your database to grow too large. More important, having the same data in two places can create significant problems when the data get out of synch with one another. This is known as database corruption, and is not only difficult to prevent, but is even more difficult to correct.

If the customer table lists customer John Doe as living at 1 Main Street and this information is duplicated in the club membership table, your database will be larger than it could be. Furthermore, if you update his address in the customer table, but fail to update his record in the club membership table, then you have two different addresses for the same customer.

Normalization aims to reduce this duplication. Database theorists have defined several **normal forms** for relational databases. These are a series of increasingly restrictive constraints on the layout of the database tables.

For example, the first normal form, which is the least restrictive, requires that each attribute only store one value (as opposed to a list of values). The second normal form builds on first normal form and adds the constraint that each row in the database be uniquely identifiable. This is typically accomplished by using an *identity* column — a unique ID for each row. If you have no other value on which to index you may make the identity the primary key, but these two concepts are quite different. The identity ensures that each field is unique; the primary key is the principal sorting mechanism.

The third normal form, called 3NF, is the most popular compromise between too little normalization and too much. In 3NF, you essentially remove all redundant information in your tables.

Denormalization

There are normal forms beyond the third one, but they put such difficult constraints on the database that few developers go beyond this point. In fact, even the third normal form can cause significant performance penalties. For example, your customer's name should not appear both in the customer table and in the club table. This is duplication of non-key data and a violation of third normal form. What you are supposed to do is to get the customer's record from the club table, look up his ID, and then look him up in the customer table. This is a lot of overhead, however, and you almost always need the customer's name when you are looking up his record. Many developers will intentionally violate this rule — they will deliberately denormalize their tables to recover the performance penalty exacted by rigorous normalization.

DBAs typically start by designing their tables to a given normal form (say, the third normal form) and then they will begin a denormalization process in order to improve the performance of the system. It is not unusual to start with a completely normalized database and then to denormalize extensively when the system runs too slowly. The database that eventually emerges is denormalized where necessary for performance reasons. This has proven to be a better methodology than starting with a denormalized database and adding normalization, or, worse, ignoring the whole issue altogether.

SQL — Defining and Querying the Database

SQL, the Structured Query Language, is an industry standard language for querying relational databases. It provides a data manipulation language (DML) used to query the data.

However, SQL is not just a query language it is also a data definition language (DDL). DDL statements are used to create the tables, views, keys and constraints that define the database.

Data definition includes the name of the table and each of the fields, the contents and restrictions on the fields (field type, field length, restrictions on whether the field can be **NULL**, etc.). DDL can be used to define primary and secondary keys and to establish **referential integrity** through database constraints.

> **Referential integrity** *is the requirement that the various tables in a database are consistent in their representation of objects. A failure in referential integrity might allow a customer record to show that a given rental is outstanding, while the tape shows itself as returned.*

Queries are structured to return an answer set or a view. An answer set is a set of rows in a table, and a view is a "virtual database", which looks to the user like a standalone database, but which represents a subset of the real database based on the results of the query. The answer set may be arbitrarily large. A placeholder, called a cursor, is used to iterate through the answer set, marking which rows have been examined already.

SQL is, as its name implies, structured. You can, for example, search the database using a **SELECT** statement. You might write:

```
SELECT CustomerID, CustomerName, CustomerAddress FROM Customer WHERE
MemberDate > 'January 1 1997'
```

This statement will select every row from **Customer** that meets the search criteria and report the results in rows, consisting of the three columns that you requested (**CustomerID**, **CustomerName** and **CustomerAddress**). The **SELECT** statement includes a simple **WHERE** clause, which restricts the answer set. You can build much more complicated **WHERE** statements, which can even include sub-queries. The **SELECT** statement also allows you to sort the results arbitrarily (though it will run faster if you sort on an indexed field), and you can eliminate duplicate rows from your answer.

The real power in queries to a relational database, however, comes from **joins**.

Joins

The very act of normalizing the database limits the utility of your queries, unless you can *join* two or more tables together. Joining the tables allows you to treat the tables as if their data were shared in a single table. There are various ways to join tables. The first and most common is an **equi-join** or **natural join**. You perform an equi-join on two tables which share a column in common. In the example shown earlier, both Table A and Table B share the customer's ID (in Table A's **WhoRented** column and in Table B's **ID** column). You join these columns in the query statement itself, using the **WHERE** clause. Thus you might write:

```
SELECT TableA.TapeName, TableB.Name FROM TableA, TableB WHERE
TableA.WhoRented = TableB.ID
```

It is the **WHERE** clause that creates the equi-join. Note that the **FROM** clause lists two tables. If you leave out the equi-join and just join the tables by listing two or more in the **FROM** clause, that is called a **cross-join**.

A variant on an equi-join is a **theta-join**. A theta-join is just like an equi-join, except that rather than equating the two columns, you use another relational operator.

You can generalize these statements into **inner-join** statements by explicitly naming the table columns to match. Note that with an inner join, you do not have to compare the same columns in the two tables. Thus you can write:

```
SELECT TableA.TapeName
FROM TableA inner join TableB ON TableA.WhoRented = TableB.ID
AND TableA.ReleaseDate > January 1 1997 AND TableB.Club = y
```

This will produce a set of records with the **TapeName** for every tape that has a release date during or after 1997 and was rented by someone who is a member of a club. In effect, you've joined these tables together and are searching against criteria in each.

If there is an inner-join, you can guess that there is an **outer-join**. An outer join examines two tables and returns the records of one table when there is a matching record in the second table. This is a way to say, "Show me all the records in Table A and also all the records in Table B which have matches in A."

Outer joins are handed — either left or right handed. A left handed outer join looks like this:

```
SELECT * FROM TableA left outer join TableB ON TableA.WhoRented =
TableB.ID
```

This will return every record from Table A (the left table) and all the records in Table B which match the criteria.

> *For more detailed information on SQL, check out Instant SQL Programming (Joe Celko, Wrox Press, 1-874416-50-8).*

Persisting to an RDB

If you choose to make an RDBMS your persistence mechanism, you must begin by deciding how an object's state will be mapped to a set of rows in one or more tables in your RDB. The decisions that are made here will affect the system's performance.

We begin by mapping from C++ objects to database tables. This includes deciding how to represent an object's primitive data (mapping from C++ data types to database data types) and how to represent hierarchies, associations, etc. This is done once. Typically, a tool is defined that uses these definitions to map from a given object model to the corresponding DDL. In essence, this tool bridges the conceptual gulf between the relational database world (which thinks in terms of data definitions) and the object world (which thinks in terms of objects and their interactions).

We then define the methods that create the database image of the objects, update them and delete them. These methods need to be defined for every persistent class. In general, there are three ways of writing this code, as well as the other class-specific code that is required:

> Write it all by hand — time consuming and error-prone

> Generate it from the header files

> Generate it from the object model

We then define the queries that are used to obtain these data. If the database has a C-level API and no object interface, we write the component that talks to the database API. The API will communicate with the class's member functions (e.g. **save**, **delete**) through a C structure or equivalent. We define these structures, again either by hand, from the header files or from the model.

These days, most of these features are provided by the application framework (e.g. MFC). The framework should provide an object which manages the connection to the database, typically via ODBC (Open Database Connectivity), as well as an iterator (or recordset), whose member variables correspond to the fields in the database.

Mapping from Objects to Tables

Each data member must be preserved during the process of transformation from objects to tables. This includes all "simple" attributes (native types, such as **int** or **char**), attributes aggregated in sub-objects, and pointers to associated objects. Note that this also includes data members from all of your ancestors in the static object model.

One-to-One Mapping vs Use of Blobs

Mapping each attribute to a database table column can dramatically slow the performance of the system. In this one-to-one mapping model, each record is built by setting the value of the column corresponding to a particular attribute to the value of that attribute. For many attributes, the value must be transformed to match the requirements of the database. For example, a date may be stored differently in the database than it is in your object.

An alternative method is to store the entire object as a binary stream of bytes, known as a **blob**. Key values are stored as attributes in columns, but the bulk of the data is undifferentiated. The database cannot manipulate or sort on that data, but by using the keys, it can retrieve the blob, which can then be reconstituted in the application.

The decision of which fields to put in the blob is critical. This decision changes as the physical design of the database is modified during the development and maintenance cycles. Indexes can only be put on columns, not on a part of a blob — because the blob is just binary bits to the database. This forces us to decide once and for all time which fields to key on. The decision to add new keys requires a change to the definition of the table as well as a redefinition of the blob — an expensive maintenance decision.

This makes the design more viscous— it is harder to change as requirements shift. For this reason, many developers don't use a blob; they just make columns for their data and accept the trade off in performance. You can "throw money" at performance issues by buying bigger and faster machines, but it is more difficult (and often more expensive) to try to solve maintenance issues with cash.

Object Identifiers

In C++, we use pointers to name one object in the description of another object. This is done, for example, to capture associations. In mapping to database tables, this naming function is provided by **object identifiers** (OIDs). An OID is typically generated by the persistence framework as each object is saved for the first time to the database.

An OID is typically implemented using a database type, such as a **long** or a **char[N]**, where **N** is between 6 and 12. OIDs should be unique, but how unique? Arguably, they should be unique across the system, but ought they be unique across time? That is, can deleted OIDs be reused? Further, should they be unique across instances of the program (can two processes use the same OID to refer to different objects?) Should they be unique across all machines on the network? What if the network is the Internet?

An OID that is absolutely unique is very hard to create. In theory, it would be unique across the world and across time. Microsoft offers such OIDs, called Globally Unique Identifiers (GUIDs). These are used to create unique identification for classes, interfaces and any other object. Microsoft GUIDs are 128-bit unique numbers generated by a complex algorithm, which is statistically unlikely to create duplicated numbers any time soon.

*This algorithm, however, could end up creating the year 3400 problem. While I'm told you can use Microsoft's **GuidGen.exe** to create enough unique identifiers to name every atom in the universe, there is a known problem in their design. Each GUID includes 60 bits for the timestamp, representing the count of 100-nanosecond intervals since 00:00:00.00 on October 15, 1582. This clock will rollover in the year 3400. Watch for books on the Y3.4K problem, appearing in your bookstores early in the fourth millenium.*

For more information on the GUID design take a look at:
`ftp://ftp.isi.edu/internet-drafts/draft-leach-uuids-guids-00.txt`
`ftp://ftp.isi.edu/internet-drafts/draft-kindel-uuid-uri-00.txt`

Mapping C++ Data Elements to the RDB

Each data member that is mapped to a column in a database table is represented in C++ as a primitive data type, a user-defined type or a pointer or reference to an object. Each of these must be mapped to a type that is native to the database.

Typically, the RDB will support various integer and floating formats, but they may not be the same as the ones supported by the C++ compiler you are using. The database type may be best implemented using a user-defined class in C++. Database vendor-specific code needs to be written to support these translations. Translators can be implemented by following the Strategy Pattern.

The Strategy (or Policy) Pattern (*Design Patterns*, Gamma et al.) is used when you may have a number of implementations to accomplish a single goal. In this case, a number of vendor-specific implementations must support the goal of translating between the C++ objects and the database itself.

The Strategy Pattern separates the translation work from the object that is doing the translation. The class responsible for translation has a **Translator** object. **Translator** is an abstract base class from which you can derive concrete classes to encapsulate the specific translation algorithms for the different databases you might use. You can then plug in the appropriate derived translator object into any class that needs to interface with the database.

Fixed Length vs Variable Length Strings

Character strings typically come in fixed-length and variable-length formats in databases, and you may find yourself using both types. Fixed length strings are fast, but they can waste space. Variable length strings don't waste space, but they bring some overhead that can slow performance. The usual heuristic is to use fixed length strings for strings which are within narrow size limits, and then to use variable length strings for memos, notes and other fields of unpredictable length.

NULL Fields

Databases typically support the notion of a **NULL** field. This is a field whose value is unknown. Note that there is a difference between an empty string and a **NULL** character string — one says that we have a value and it is of zero length, the other says we have no value at all.

Representing Inheritance

The diagram below defines class **A** and two subclasses **B** and **C**:

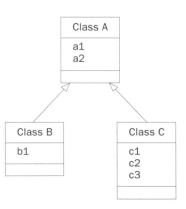

The next diagram shows the memory layout for these classes:

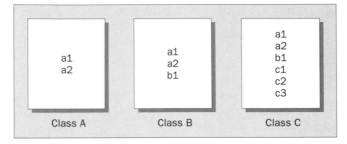

Note that the attributes defined for class **A**, in this case **A.a1** and **A.a2**, are part of any object of class **B** or **C**. Thus, the question is this — how do we define our tables for the objects of our base class and our derived classes? It turns out that there are three schemes that tradeoff disk space and database performance. These options are:

▶ Put the attributes defined in class **A** into one table, those defined directly in class **B** in another table and those defined directly in class **C** in a third table

▶ Put those attributes defined directly in class **B** in one table, those defined directly in class **C** in a second table, and fold the attributes defined in class **A** into both tables

▶ Put all the attributes defined in class **A**, class **B** and class **C** into one big table, and leave **NULL** the attributes that are not meaningful for this type of subclass — this is known as the flat table approach

The first approach corresponds to one class mapping into one or more tables. The diagram below shows the layout of the tables for classes **A**, **B** and **C** under this approach. Note that the OID of the base class is captured as a column (or foreign key) in each of the tables that represent the derived classes. A join must then be done to recreate the object from the tables. This approach uses less space than the flat table approach because there are no extraneous **NULL** fields — the fields of each table map to each attribute of the corresponding object. The approach, however, runs slower than the other two due to the joins.

Table A
a1
a2
OID
Date of Creation
// other attributes

Table B
b1
A.OID
OID
Date of Creation
// other attributes

Table C
c1
c2
c3
A.OID
OID
Date of creation
// other attributes

The layout of the tables for the classes **A**, **B** and **C** under the second approach is shown below. In this case, one class maps into one table. Note that the attributes defined directly in the base class are captured as columns in each of the tables that represent the derived classes. No join is required to recreate the object from the tables. This approach uses less space than the flat table approach, and runs faster than the earlier approach, because there isn't a join.

Table A
a1
a2
OID
Date of Creation
// other attributes

Table B
a1
a2
b1
OID
Date of Creation
// other attributes

Table C
a1
a2
c1
c2
c3
OID
Date of Creation
// other attributes

The final diagram shows the layout of the table for classes **A**, **B**, and **C** under the flat table approach — that is, more than one object maps into just one table. Note that all of the attributes defined for all of the classes are represented in the table definition for the derived classes. No join is required to recreate the object from the tables. This approach uses more space than the other two approaches but may run faster because they are always loaded. On the other hand, it may run slower, as the tables are larger in this case, and may require more disk I/O. There will be many extraneous **NULL** fields. For example, an object **A** stored in this table would have to leave **NULL** all the fields for the attributes **b1**, **c1**, **c2** and **c3**.

Flat Table
a1
a2
b1
c1
c2
c3
OID
Date of Creation
// other attributes

Representing Relationships

How we represent the relationship between two objects depends on the **multiplicity** of the relationship. That is, one-to-one relationships are represented differently from one-to-many or many-to-many. You find this multiplicity in the object model and must implement it in the database.

There are two ways of mapping the relationships between the objects into the database. In the first approach, a relationship between two objects is mapped into the database by using the OID of one object as the value of a column in the table that represents the other object. In the second approach, a separate table is used to capture the relationship information. The decision on which approach to use in a specific case is based on:

> The multiplicity of the relationship

> Whether it is a unidirectional or bidirectional relationship

One-to-One Relationships

If we were representing a one-to-one bidirectional relationship, then the table definition for each object should include the OID of the other object as a "pointer" to the identity of that object. For example, suppose you have a **transaction** object and a **receipt** object. Each **transaction** has one **receipt** and each **receipt** represents a single **transaction**. If you modeled the **receipt** as one record and the **transaction** as another record, you would put the ID of the **receipt** into the **transaction** record and the ID of the **transaction** into the **receipt** record.

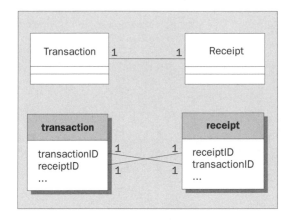

On the other hand, if it is a one-to-one unidirectional relationship then the object that is being pointed to has the OID of the object doing the pointing. This seems backwards. What is going on here is that we have to search the table defining the pointed-to objects, in order to find the one that has the OID of the pointing object in it. Thus, the rule is that the pointer goes "the other way" in the table.

Assume, for example, that the **receipt** object needs to find the **transaction**, but there is no reason for the **transaction** to find the **receipt**. In this case, you have a one-to-one, unidirectional relationship (from **receipt** to **transaction**). You might expect that the **receipt** would have the ID of the **transaction**, but in fact it goes the other way — that is, the database representation of the object being pointed to (the **transaction**) has the OID of the object doing the pointing (the **receipt**). Thus, you can ask the database to find the **transaction** with the OID of the **receipt**.

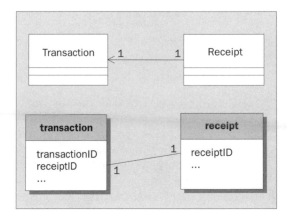

One-to-Many Relationships

This rule about unidirectional relationships makes much more sense when you are looking at a one-to-many relationship. For example, assume you have a **VideoTitle** which has many actual **VideoTape**s. The **VideoTitle** points to each of the **VideoTape** objects (and, for whatever reason, you model that as a one-way relationship — the **VideoTape**s never need point back to the **VideoTitle**). In this case, it makes sense for the object being pointed to (**VideoTape**) to have the OID of the object doing the pointing (**VideoTitle**). Now you could query the database for every tape that has this title in its target field.

Let me give you another example from VideoMagix. Imagine a club that some customers might belong to, the most frequent borrowers, perhaps. We could model this using a one-to-many unidirectional relationship between the club and the customers. To keep things simple, let's assume that a customer can belong to one and only one club. The record for each **customer** object would keep the **clubID** as an entry in its record, whereas if it were the other way around, then the record for the club would have to store many **customerID**s.

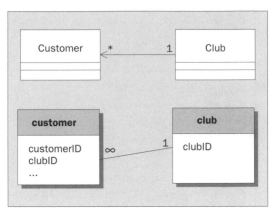

If it is a many-to-many bidirectional relationship, then putting the OID of either object as the value of a column in the other object will not work. In this case, a separate table, known as a **join table**, is used. This is demonstrated in the diagram below:

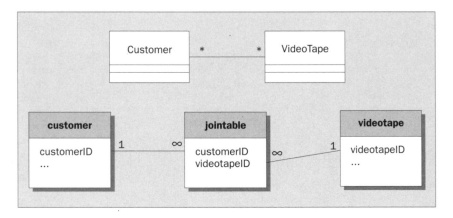

Many **customer**s will rent each **videoTape**, and each **Customer** will rent many **VideoTape**s. It wouldn't work to store every **customerID** in every **VideoTape**, nor does it work to store the ID of every **VideoTape** in every **Customer** (who knows how many values we'll need). It is therefore much more efficient to create a join table, which joins **Customers** to **VideoTapes**, where each entry corresponds to a single **customerID** and a single **VideoTape**.

Representing Collections

There are two reasons that collections are generated from the database. The first is in the representation of associations that are not one-to-one. In this case, the object on at least one end of the association needs a collection to represent the set of objects on the other end of the association.

The second way that collections are used is as a representation of the results of a query. Queries typically result in a collection of objects, or a collection of strings that describe these objects. Each of these sets of results should be represented in the return value of the query function with an instance of a collection class.

In the MFC, queries produce **RecordSet**s. The **RecordSet** is an iterator over the set of records that satisfy the query. The actual collection of the records is hidden behind the interface to the **RecordSet**; you use the **RecordSet** to iterate over each record in turn.

If you are writing your own collections to manage the results of queries, you'll want to store the results in a collection and provide an iterator for that collection. The typical implementation will use an STL collection and an STL forward iterator. Member functions will also be needed, if only to append to the collection, add by position, delete from the front or back, delete by position and get the length etc. These collections can typically be implemented as template classes, as all of the objects that satisfy a query are of the same type or are all descended from a common base type.

A C++ Persistence Interface

A number of issues arise when you translate the theory of persistence into actual C++ code. For example, you will probably choose a collection framework (e.g. the STL) to simplify your development. Rather than implementing all of the collection types yourself, you will use this library's well tested code to handle your collection requirements. While this will save months of work, it doesn't come without a price. The library itself will require you to write some code to support its collections, and this code must be integrated into your own code with sufficient encapsulation, so that if you decide to change your collection mechanism, you won't break the entire application.

Swizzling References

When you recreate an object from the information stored in the database, you need to recreate its associations with other objects as well. If the associated object is not yet in memory, you cannot initialize a pointer to it and you certainly cannot create a reference (references to null objects are illegal in C++). We use the OID to represent the object until it is loaded. An OID is unique, and it typically corresponds to a primary key in a database table, so pulling the referenced object out of the database should be fast.

> **Swizzling** *is the process of turning a pointer into an OID and writing it to persistent storage, or using an OID to retrieve an object from persistent storage*

Once an object is in memory, the OID can be **swizzled** into a pointer. Although a regular C++ pointer can be used here, there are some subtle complications. Some memory allocation schemes allow objects to be shared. That is, if two parts of an application run a query that results in the same object being retrieved, then it will be retrieved once and shared. This can easily happen, since the result of most queries is a collection class, and an object can be in more than one of these returned collections.

This raises the problem of how you know when it is safe to delete an object. Since the persistence framework is generating these references, and the application programmer is using them, neither party necessarily knows the lifetime of a given reference. The application programmer doesn't know whether or not he is the only one pointing to the object, so he can never safely delete it. The persistence framework also cannot know when the application is finished with the object, and so it cannot delete it either. This leads to memory leaks.

There are two solutions to this problem. You can either disallow sharing of memory, or you must implement reference counting. In reference counting, each time you share an object you increment its reference count. As you delete objects, the object decrements its reference count. When the reference count returns to zero, then the object is destroyed.

Queries

In a typical persistence framework, all objects are accessed from the database through queries. This is the way that the application obtains any objects that have been previously persisted.

Typically, there are two types of queries and two types of return values. In the first type of query, you provide an OID and the database then returns the object that corresponds to that OID. This turns into a simple SQL query, whose **WHERE** clause is just an **EQUALS** match on the OID. This should run very fast.

In the second type of query, you provide an SQL **WHERE** clause, and the system returns the object, collection or web of objects that satisfies the SQL query. In this case the **WHERE** clause can be as complex as the application programmer desires. Of course, a complex **WHERE** clause may require a significant amount of database processing.

Query Signatures

Each of the above types of query is codified by one static member function for the class — the **focus** of the query. The OID-based queries are of the following (approximate) format:

```
PersistentObject* Get(const OID &);
```

There is one of these **Get()** functions for each persistent class. They each take an OID as an input parameter and return a pointer to a persistent object. A pointer is used as the return value instead of a reference, so that **NULL** can be returned if the object is not found.

Physical Database Modeling

Classically, database architects build a logical model of the domain, including the entities that exist and the relationships between them. They capture much of the knowledge that we now capture in the static object model. They then map these entities and their relationships into a set of database tables.

For each table, the database designer must decide on the order of the fields in the rows. Typically, a field corresponds to a single data member in an object. One of the first decisions the database designer confronts is deciding which field (or fields) should be the primary key for the table. The primary key must be unique in a table and will be indexed for fast access. Typically, the OID will be the primary key for any given table.

Furthermore, the database designer may add additional (secondary) indexes. These additional indexes speed up retrieval, at the cost of slowing down the operations of adding and deleting records.

Once the designer has created the fields in the table, then he must decide on the appropriate data types, and must designate which fields may have **NULL** values. He may include foreign keys. Remember that a foreign key is a field that is a primary key from another table and is used for quickly joining and searching other tables.

Finally, the designer must allocate sufficient space for the tables and then add the necessary constraints to the system to ensure referential integrity.

Use of Referential Integrity

One type of referential integrity constraint in databases is a check that a foreign key that is used really exists — the value of the foreign key in this table should be the primary key of a record in another table. Referential integrity checks that a record with this key exists in the other table. This prevents the database equivalent of "dangling pointers".

We can also use referential integrity to enforce the multiplicity constraints indicated in the object model. Let's say we want to refer to a row of another table from within a given row in the current table. We can include columns in the current table that have the same definition as the columns used as the primary key in the second table. Since we use an OID as the primary key for all objects, we'll use the OID as the foreign key of the current table.

If the object model says that an object of class **A** has an association to objects of class **B** with a multiplicity of **1** on the **A** end, and **1..*** on the **B** end, then an attempt to store an **A** object that has no **B** objects associated to it will fail. An attempt to delete the last **B** object associated with an **A** object will also fail. Referential integrity will be enforced by the foreign key constraints in the database tables.

Scenario Development and Referential Integrity

Referential integrity does not have a sense of time. It is absolute. However, all of our business processes start, flow and stop. Sometimes they are interrupted in the middle. How can your system maintain referential integrity if it is interrupted in the middle of its work?

Let's look at a simple example in the form of a bank account application. Say there is a customer account which must have an association to one or more account objects. A bank employee is on the phone with a customer, who wants to open an account. The bank employee gathers all the necessary information about the customer, including his name, social security number, phone number and so forth. He is about to gather information about the type of account the customer wants to open, when the customer announces that he must run off to a meeting and will call back later.

It would be unfortunate if the bank employee had to throw away the records he has built so far, but if he saves the customer without opening at least one account, he will violate the referential integrity of the system. The system is *not* referentially correct, yet we need to save its current (temporary) state.

One solution is to change the multiplicity of the account end of the relationship from **1..*** to **0..***. Unfortunately, this sacrifices referential integrity (in this case, that each customer must have an account) to support a boundary condition. Moreover, this boundary condition is unstable; it should resolve either to a fully opened account relationship or it should, eventually, be closed.

A second possibility is to create a temporary set of tables for "work in progress" which maintains less referential integrity. This works, but creates a certain amount of duplication in the system.

A better solution, perhaps, is to factor out the referential integrity from the business logic and build a framework to enforce referential integrity among the business objects. This framework could take into consideration the work in progress, but segregate it from the rest of the processing so that it is not visible to applications that would not understand the implications of it being work in progress.

Connecting to the Database

The application should be isolated from information about the specific database. It should not know which vendor was chosen (e.g. SQL Server vs Oracle), nor should it know where the database is running on the network. Typically, a class is defined that encapsulates all access to the database for the rest of the system. This class is then a façade for the database API, and if you replace the database, you need only replace the façade.

Development-time Issues

In order to support persistence, each class must know if it is persistent and if so, it must be able to chain up to its parent class in support of persistence. Query functions will probably be implemented as static member functions. The query functions must know which attributes persist and whether or not their value can be **NULL**. In addition, the query functions must know the type and length of each member variable to be persisted. This kind of knowledge is known as meta-data — it describes how we manage the data

A decision has to be made as to where this (meta-) data will be kept. The place of choice is in the static object model. If you use a CASE tool you may be able to extend their metamodel to include the meta-data at the class and attribute level.

Generating the Code for each Class

Some of the code that will be written implements the persistence framework. The rest of the code is the class-specific code for the CRUD (**Create**, **Read**, **Update** and **Delete**) queries and other functions that allow the class to interact with the rest of the persistence framework. In a large application, there will be hundreds or thousands of persistent objects. Writing all of this code by hand is a large undertaking. Furthermore, this code will change. Keeping it all tested and coordinated is not going to be easy.

There are several advantages to basing the code generator on a CASE-tool supplied metamodel:

> If you extend the metamodel, you can include the class and attribute-specific persistence-related information that we need to capture directly in the model.

> The CASE tool probably supplies a mechanism to iterate through all of the classes, all of the attributes in a class and so on. Either there is a scripting language, in which case it includes these iteration constructs, or there is an API to get at the model information, in which case you can use the API to iterate.

> The CASE tool probably comes with a set of GUI screens that are used to enter the model information.

Validating the Object Model

The object model is the most important intellectual capital that your development efforts will generate. As requirements change and as hardware comes and goes, the object model will provide continuity to your requirements and design.

As such, it needs to be accurate and up to date. It is obvious that if you are generating code from the static object model, the model must be valid, or you will not be able to build and run your application successfully. What is more difficult is keeping your model up to date when you've gone over to coding. The inevitable outcome is that your code evolves while the model remains fixed, and they drift out of synch with one another.

The issue of documentation going out of phase with code is not new. Typically, there is a failure in the procedures that are put in place to guarantee the validity of documentation. It is not unusual for developers to be under enormous pressure to getting the code out the door on time, which results in the documentation work taking second place.

This is the most compelling reason to use round-trip CASE tools — if you always generate the code from the model, then it is impossible for the code and the model to go out of phase with one another. Unfortunately, for many small development organizations, these tools are prohibitively expensive.

To ensure that your model matches your database design and ultimately your code, you will want to create a checklist that you can use in design reviews. Here is a list of some of the things that you should check:

> For each member function, each parameter in the signature is "reachable" from the class (there is an association path from this class to the class mentioned in the parameter)

> Syntax restrictions on the names of classes, attributes etc. are followed

> All of the member functions that are queries are static

> All of the CRUD member functions are non-static

> The character values used in the names in the model are all legal to the C++ compiler

> The types of all attributes are legal

> The lengths are all non-negative

> The names of classes used in the interaction or sequence diagrams all correspond to classes in the static object model

> Canonical methods — constructor, destructor, copy constructor and assignment operator — are in place

When you've validated your model against your code, you will then want to flag certain design characteristics as possibly representing design problems. These are not necessarily problems, but they merit further investigation:

> List all classes that have no parents

> List all classes that have no children

> List all classes that have no queries

▶ List all classes that have no associations

▶ List all diamonds in the inheritance structure where the base class has data members

▶ List all uses of multiple inheritance where more than one base class has data members

▶ List all classes with more than 20 data members or more than 20 member functions

▶ List all non-virtual functions that shadow virtual functions

▶ List all virtual functions whose attributes are different than in a parent class

The Development Lifecycle

If only it were the case that we just define the static object model, generate the code and submit the bill. Instead we iterate. The requirements evolve, and this then changes the design. The design evolves as we learn more and as we write more. Changes in the static object model impact the code. Changes in the implementation of member functions feed back into the design.

The entire system churns and heaves. In a healthy system the overall movement is forward, wriggling up out of the primeval soup of design until it takes flight in working code. In an unhealthy system your project begins to feed upon itself, with diseased parts of the design infecting the implementation, until the system becomes a boiling writhing wretched mass of convoluted code.

Adding Operations

If a tool is used to generate code from the static object model, it usually has some way for you to take the files it outputs and add the implementations of the member functions that you write by hand. The goal is to allow you to work both through the tool and also manually, but at the same time to keep the code and the model in synch with one another.

Promulgating Model Changes to the Database

Synchronizing model changes with code changes is not too difficult if the code is generated from the model. Otherwise, it is a time-consuming error-prone manual process. That said, most of us do at least some of it by hand. It's not just that CASE tools which generate code are expensive, or that they never quite do it all — many of us have a deep-seated distrust of system-generated code.

This presents a problem: How do you unit test any changes to a class? You can't persist the class because the DDL has changed. If you change the DDL, then no one else can use the database. One solution is to use a hierarchical set of databases. One database is the project master. You also need a database for each development team and perhaps even one for each developer. That way, DDL can be generated and put into effect in synchronization with the changes in the model and the code, without affecting the other developers. As the code is unit tested, the changes to the DDL can percolate up through the database hierarchy, until they are available at the project master.

In a traditional development environment, the configuration management system allows another programmer to pick up a new copy of your module more or less when he chooses. There are always one or two back versions available, so he doesn't have to interrupt his development to integrate changes made by other developers. The freedom to choose when to pick up new versions of classes will be reduced by this interaction with the database layout.

You must also ensure that the data remains usable as the DDL changes. There are utilities that will copy tables, and some of these will allow you to define default values for newly created columns. Of course, if the new column corresponds to an OID, there may not be any good default value to use. This strategy works in the traditional database world, but is insufficient in the object world.

Rearranging the object hierarchy may change the nature of the relationships between the tables in the database. This happens, for example, any time more than one table is used to store all of the data attributes of an object, both those it directly defines and those it inherits from its ancestors. It would be difficult to automate these types of changes in a replication tool, even one with some scripting capabilities.

One solution is to write a database program that reads the old versions of the tables and writes the new version of the tables. Another solution is to retrieve all of the objects that are of the class that has changed, write them to their new object format, and then persist them. You would do this by defining a class that represents the old format and a class that represents the new format, give them separate names, and provide a conversion function as a member of the old class.

Optimizations

As with all development, optimizations should be deferred until the system is up and running and debugged. As you approach your ship date, you will want to profile the system and determine where the performance bottlenecks are. At that time (and not before), you should tweak your system to make it run faster.

Places to consider for potential optimization include:

- The database definitions
- Embedded SQL
- Any database utility classes you've developed

Classically, when you build a database-centric system, you build it first, and then you spend a good deal of time tweaking the database to make it run faster. The database definitions, the SQL embedded in the application code, the database utilities — they are all suspects when it comes to finding performance bottlenecks.

Lazy Evaluation

When an object is created from the database it may have member variables which are references to other objects. As we saw earlier, you normally swizzle these objects into memory by examining the OID stored with your object and retrieving the referred-to object. These objects in turn may need to swizzle their member objects into memory. Creating an object may cascade through a number of creations and can therefore be a very expensive process.

One answer to this problem is to defer swizzling the member objects until they are needed. This **lazy evaluation** of member references can dramatically improve performance at run-time.

For example, when an object is created in memory as the result of a query, the object's associated objects would not initially be retrieved from the database. The new object would, under lazy evaluation, just hold the OID, rather than creating a proper reference to its member variables.

In other words, only the object that is explicitly the result of the query would be brought into memory. The first time any of the object's associations are followed or referenced, the object represented by the OID is then recreated in memory from its disk image, and the OID is swizzled into a reference to the newly recreated object.

You can also use lazy evaluation to create only the base part of an object without creating the specific subtype. If the return type of the query is wider than the actual returned type, then only the OIDs that are in the sliced portion of the object are turned into memory references. That is, if the return type of a query is a pointer to a base object, but the actual returned object is a sub-type, you can instantiate only the base type to save time.

Let's look at an example to illustrate this. Say your code is written to call a query and assign the result to a pointer to an **Animal**. In fact, the query returns a pointer to a **Dog** (**Dog** is a subclass of **Animal**). Rather than evaluating the entire **Dog** object, you can just swizzle the **Animal** portion into memory, and keep an OID to refer to the **Dog** part. Later, if you refer to a method of **Dog**, or you need data from the **Dog** part, you can then use that OID to swizzle the **Dog** part into memory.

Since the client code may only be using the functionality provided by the base class, it might never need to swizzle any of the remaining pointers. The point, of course, is not just saving the time it takes to turn the OID into a memory reference, but the time spent recreating the object from its disk image. Of course, there is a tradeoff. If the database is on a remote machine, then more trips across the network will be required to obtain the non-base class (**Dog**-specific) information. The time to set up the necessary messaging connections might more than make up for any savings that lazy evaluation otherwise provides.

Another possible use of lazy evaluation is for queries that return collections of objects. The idea here would be to return a collection of OIDs, and only turn them into objects the first time they are accessed. This will not usually be of any value, as collections of objects that are returned from queries are usually iterated through. The iterator causes the database to be hit for each object, one at a time. That's N+1 trips across the interface, 1 for the primary object and 1 for each association, as opposed to not doing lazy evaluation and getting all of the objects in 1 trip across the interface.

Gets and Sets

It is best to write the **Get()** and **Set()** functions for attributes yourself, even if you are using a CASE tool would generate them automatically.

A **Get()** function for a data member's value needs to check to see whether or not the value of the data member is an OID. If this is the case, then it must be swizzled into a pointer (and the object loaded) before the **Get()** can return. A **Set()** of a data member should mark the object as dirty, so that the saving of objects can be optimized. That is, as we walk through the web of objects we are saving, if we come to an object that has not been modified (the "dirty bit" is not set), we do not have to write it to the database.

If you really want to optimize database access, you can have dirty bits at the data member level as well as the class level. If you segregate the data members defined in the base class from the those defined in the derived class, and put this information into different rows in the database, then you can choose which parts of the object to write to the database when you save the object. If you changed the state of the sub-class but not of the base class, you may be able to minimize the amount of information you write into the database for updates.

Secondary Indexes

The easiest way to speed up the database is to make it faster to find a particular row. It is much faster to find the row that has a given key if the keyed fields are indexed. If the fields that make up the key are indexed, then the database provides what is known as a secondary index. This is a table that maps keys to row indexes for the regular data table. This secondary index table is usually very small and very fast.

Adding a secondary index makes creating, updating and deleting rows in the table slightly slower. This is because the secondary index has to be updated. This cost is low, and the increase in speed is usually noticeable; it is almost always a good idea to build this index.

Rewriting SQL

A good starting point for optimizing your use of a database is to tweak the SQL. Examine the **WHERE** clause. There are many examples of systems where rewriting or just changing the order of the sub-clauses in the **WHERE** clause has dramatically changed the overall responsiveness of the system.

Some of the ways that you can change the **WHERE** clause do not require any changes in the underlying DDL. These are the easiest changes to make.

Look for opportunities to eliminate joins. These tend to be quite expensive. Try to structure your complicated searches, so that the first search eliminates most rows, and subsequent searches are against a very small data set. Also structure your searches so that the first, larger part of the search is against indexed columns.

Sharing Tables

One way to speed up a join is to eliminate it. If there is, for example, a one-to-one correspondence between two objects, then the OID of the second one can be the value of a column in the first one. This "join" turns into a keyed lookup for the primary key, the OID, of the second object. Following this join can slow performance. Because this is a one-to-one relationship, the two tables easily can be combined. That is, the columns that hold the second table's data can be concatenated onto the end of the table, after the columns that hold the first table's data.

Denormalizing the Database Tables

Normalization attempts to reduce duplication of information in the database. When two tables hold the same data, it is possible for them to get out of synch with one another. For example, suppose you keep your customer's social security number in both the **Customer** object and in the **Account** object. This might speed up some of the processing as you could get the customer's social security number without having to touch an **Account** object. However, if you were implementing a use case that required you to update the social security number, it would be easy to forget to update both the **Customer** object and any **Account** objects for that customer, and the data would then get out of synch.

Typically, you'll want to start with a normalized database, and only denormalize as an optimization; allowing you to speed up your performance at the risk of corrupting data.

Persisting to an OODB

While many systems routinely manage the conversion between objects and relational databases, there is something unnatural about this relationship. You can encapsulate the issues, but you can't escape them — relational databases think in terms of relations, not objects.

An obvious alternative is to build your system on top of a true object-oriented database. OODBs are a natural match when using objects in programs. From the user's viewpoint, there is no need to serialize or otherwise transform the object. The system takes care of any transformations required to transmit the object from the program to the OODB and any transformations required to store the object in the OODB.

What is an OODB?

An OODB is a database where the natural unit of storage is an object. Just as fixed length rows in tables are the natural unit of storage in a RDB, objects are the natural unit of storage in an OODB.

There are several advantages of an OODB when working in an OO language like C++:

▶ There is no need to do "data modeling" as the unit of storage is the object.

▶ There is usually no need to translate between the language's type system and the database's type system as they are the same.

▶ There is no need to translate objects into rows and rows into objects, as there is when using a RDB. For certain types of applications, this means that the runtime performance of an OODB can be superior to a RDB.

▶ OODBs use implicit persistence. This means that the user of the OODB does not have to worry about loading and saving his objects; about when they are in memory and when they are only on the OODB. This is all done transparently by the OODB.

These advantages are especially important in applications where the data consists of a small number of objects that have complex interrelationships, and you won't be making many queries. RDBs tend to perform better when you have a large numbers of objects with simpler interrelationships and where you'll be creating boatloads of queries.

Defining the Objects

OODBs for C++ typically use native C++ as the language to define and manipulate objects. Definitions are essentially just the header files normally produced as part of developing your application. Manipulation is accomplished through the normal C++ syntax of accessing data members of objects and pointers to objects.

Querying the OODB

There are two camps on the subject of query languages. One camp tries to embed SQL in C++, so that the same types of queries are available as are used in traditional RDBs. The other camp tries to stay in C++. For example, one approach is not to query a whole database, but to query a container. A query on the container is a binary expression; the query returns the subset of the elements in the container that are true for the expression.

As the OODB market matures, clients expect that these products will support the same set of multi-user features that RDBs support. This includes transactional control, journaling, security, protection etc. OODBs are beginning to penetrate the transactional processing market (banks and insurance companies), and this will require them to support thousands of simultaneous users and to store terabytes of data.

ODMG-93

The Object Database Management Group (ODMG) put together a set of standards known as ODMG-93. Their goal was to allow a programmer to write portable applications that work with different vendors' OODBs. ODMG-93 is designed to support large numbers of fine-grained objects.

The standards cover the following issues:

> **Object Models** — ODMG-93 is based on the OMG object model, adding a profile with constructs for object databases. The OMG object model was developed to work with OO programming languages, OODBs and object request brokers.

> **Object Definition Language** — The ODL is a programming-language independent specification language based on OMG's IDL. Additional constructs have been added for object databases. It is a specification language used to define interfaces only. It is defined to support portability and interoperability of applications.

> **Object Query Language** — The OQL is based on SQL, with additional constructs for object databases.

> **Language bindings** — This is the identification of the constructs in C++ that are used to write portable applications that manipulate objects stored in the OODB. The C++ bindings allow ODL and OQL statements in C++ syntax.

Summary

In this chapter we've looked at the issues we face when making the state of our objects persistent. Specifically, we've considered:

- Serializing objects
- Using flat files
- Relational database theory
- Data structures
- Normalization
- Structured Query Language

One of the key features of your design will involve mapping your objects to tables. The main issues here are your need to:

- Identify objects
- Represent inheritance
- Preserve relationships

Then we looked at how these ideas can be implemented in a C++/RDB scenario, and at possible optimizations to the design. Lastly, we quickly introduced OODBs, a maturing area.

In the next chapter, we'll look more closely at general issues surrounding design implementation in C++.

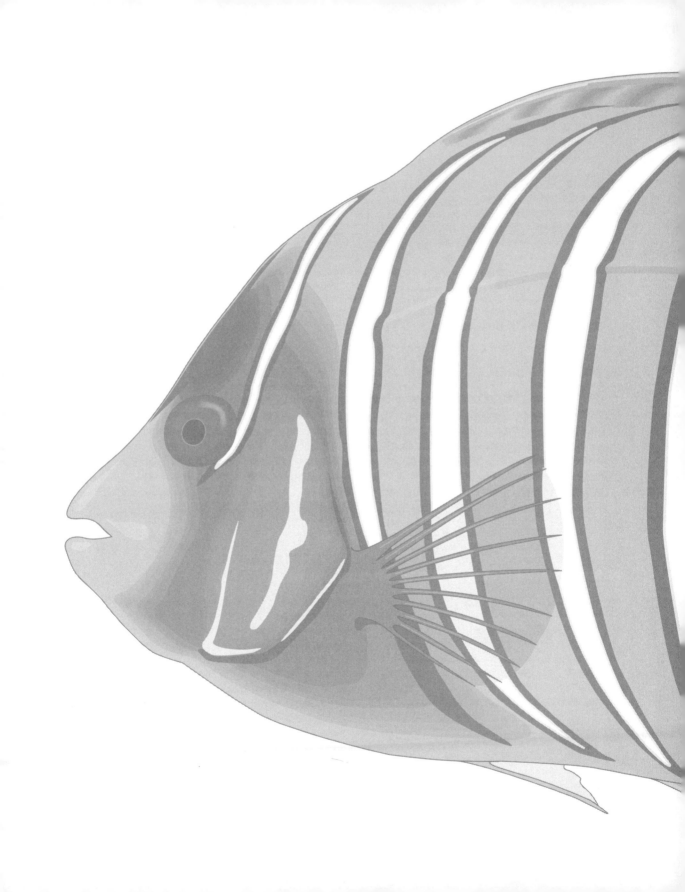

Implementation Issues

In Chapter 2 we looked at how you would find the use cases that dictate the set of requirements for your software, and in Chapter 3 we went on to discover how to create the object model that describes the objects and their implementation. We now turn to the issue of implementing these objects in code.

The interfaces of the classes you design offer a contract specifying their behavior. This behavior may be implemented most easily in an object-oriented programming language such as C++. If done correctly, the code ensures and enforces the contracts offered by the class interfaces.

Writing reliable and robust C++ is an exercise in realizing these contracts in the code itself. You will use a variety of techniques to ensure that your implementation corresponds to the commitments described in your design. These techniques include:

- Liberal use of asserts
- Exception handling
- Class invariants
- Pre- and post-condition checking

Each object you create must be testable as a stand-alone entity, and all of the interactions among the objects, described in your sequence and collaboration diagrams, must be testable and verified before the product is shipped. At each level of abstraction you must be able to describe, test and verify the interactions among the objects and components of your design.

The use cases become the foundation of your testing, providing scenarios which must be examined in detail, looking at every possible interaction between the system and the user and probing for conditions under which the product might fail.

Building a reliable and robust product requires planning and extensive testing. It is not possible to begin this work once the programming is completed; the testing must be "cooked in" to the product from the very beginning. Test planning begins with the creation of use-cases and tracks along with the implementation from the first lines of code.

Unit Testing

In a well-designed product, every object you create will have been designed and modeled. The requirements of this object should be captured in a collaboration diagram, and so it should be possible to understand and to test all of its functionality. When you code the object, you will also want to code a **test-harness**. A test-harness is a body of code designed to test the functionality of the object, but which will not ship in the final product.

A test-harness lets you test the client in the absence of the server; it lets you test each object individually and allows you to control and log the internal state of the object. This ensures that the object only moves through legal internal states, and is never left in an indeterminate condition.

Typically the test-harness will be provided as a hidden menu choice, which the developer can use to invoke specific methods on the object and get back validating information. A well-designed test-harness will include a suite of tests, which can be run individually or as a set, one time or repeatedly. A first class test suite will include the ability to kick off a set of tests to be run repeatedly and will provide a comprehensive log of its results. This facilitates *regression testing*. It is imperative to test the entire product after each change, however unrelated that change appears to be. Automated tests facilitate regression testing, as they overcome the temptation to cut corners.

The various states of each object will be modeled in state transition diagrams, and each of these transitions should also be testable. Your test harness will move the object into and out of various states, confirming that the integrity of the object is maintained through the transitions, and, equally important, that only legal transitions are possible.

Every interaction between this object and all other objects in the system should be modeled in the collaboration diagrams. These interactions will be tested in higher-level interaction tests; again, as part of a test-harness. You may build test suites which test each object individually, and then test various interactions among the objects, documenting the results of these interactions.

Building the test-harness is a big job, and one that should be designed in advance, in cooperation with whomever will be doing the quality assurance (QA) of the product. The testing software will be used by QA throughout the development cycle — you should avoid the temptation to pass your product to QA as a final step in development. The waterfall method doesn't work in quality assurance any better than it does in development; what you want is a series of small iterations, in which features are designed, developed *and tested*.

An additional benefit to building these tests as you go along is that they require you fully to understand the properties, methods and interactions of each object. Developing the test-harness forces you to think through all the methods and their potential results, and this can feed back into your design and model, creating a more complete model of each object and its interactions.

Testing is a big subject; doing it justice could fill a book of equal size. In addition to unit testing you must put your system through extensive integration testing (proving that the components work together). You must then turn to performance testing, to ensure that you've met the performance requirements you documented in your architecture document, and finally you must put the system under load — testing its ability to perform under stress and to scale to realistic conditions.

Finally, when all of this testing is complete, it is time to put the code in front of "friendly users" — alpha testers who will give you preliminary feedback on real-world use of the application. Assuming that you survive alpha-testing, it is time to go to beta-testing; that is testing with real-world users who don't know you and have no reason to be particularly kind in their review of the product. The significant difference between alpha and beta testing is that alpha testers know you and understand that they are using a fragile and nascent product. Beta testers know they are giving the final imprimatur to the product, and are apt to be harsher in their review.

If you get through beta testing without finding "show stopping" bugs; it is time to go to FCS: First Customer Ship. Shrink wrap it, send it out to tens of thousands of users and wait for the reviews. If you are lucky, the checks start rolling in. If you were sloppy, the bug reports roll in. And if you are dreadfully unlucky you will be met with a deafening silence.

ASSERT

Programmers draw a distinction between exceptions and bugs. An exception is a predictable untoward result of conditions that is beyond the control of the programmer, and your program must handle the problem gracefully. Some examples of exceptions are:

- The user runs out of memory
- The hard disk is full
- A connection is broken

A bug is a failure in the code itself. Bugs must be identified and removed before shipping the product, if at all possible. One way to identify bugs is to articulate and document your assumptions at every step of the program. If your program is only valid when a pointer is non-null — assuming it is a *bug* for that pointer to be null at this particular step — then this assumption must be validated. You validate this assumption using **ASSERT**.

Let's start by defining the macro. The **ASSERT()** macro takes a Boolean expression as a parameter. If the expression evaluates to **FALSE**, then it takes some kind of action, but does nothing if it evaluates to **TRUE**. Many compilers will abort the program on an **ASSERT()** that fails, whereas others will throw an exception.

ASSERT() macros are only used in debug mode, and must collapse into nothing when Debug is not defined. This allows you use assert macros aggressively when building your program without paying a performance penalty in the release version.

While you would normally use the **ASSERT()** macro provided by your compiler, it can be helpful to write your own, if only to understand in some detail what the macro does. Here's a simple **ASSERT()** macro I've used in debugging applications, using standard input and output (non-windows applications):

```
#define DEBUG
#ifndef DEBUG
 #define ASSERT(x)
#else
 #define ASSERT(x) \
        if (! (x)) \
        { \
```

```
            cout << "Assert " << #x << " failed\n"; \
            cout << " on line " << __LINE__  << "\n"; \
            cout << " in file " << __FILE__ << "\n";  \
    }
#endif
```

You can test this macro with the following code:

```
#include <iostream.h>

int main()
{
int x = 5;
cout << "First assert: \n";
ASSERT(x == 5);
cout << "\nSecond assert: \n";
ASSERT(x != 5);
cout << "\nDone.\n";
return 0;
}
```

If you try out this code you should see the following output:

First assert:

Second assert:
Assert x != 5 failed
 on line 24
 in file myTest.cpp

Done.

As you can see, the first time we call **ASSERT()** the result is **TRUE**, and the macro does nothing. The second time we call **ASSERT()**, however, the result is **FALSE**, and the program prints out the line number and file name where **ASSERT()** failed. Microsoft's Visual C++ 5 provides an assert macro which allows you to abort the program, ignore the **ASSERT()** or enter the debugger at the line where the assert failed. (Debugging is discussed in some detail towards the end of this chapter.) The source code is the same but the output is quite different.

```
BOOL CMyTestApp::SomeFunction()
{
int x = 5;
cout << "First assert: \n";
ASSERT(x == 5);
cout << "\nSecond assert: \n";
ASSERT(x != 5);
cout << "\nDone.\n";
return 0;
}
```

This window provides the necessary information to decide whether to continue past the **ASSERT()** or to examine the code at the point of failure to see why the assertion failed.

> *I have no idea why Microsoft thinks the right button name for debugging the application is* Retry. *This dialog would be much easier to understand if the buttons were* Abort, Debug *and* Ignore *— but perhaps they were able to save a line or two of code by reusing this trilogy of choices.*

Asserts do more than just allow you to test your assumptions — they *document* those assumptions in the body of your code. Examine these two blocks of code:

```
SomeClass* pSomePointer = SomeFunction();
if ( pSomePointer )
      pSomePointer->SomeMethod();

SomeClass* pSomePointer = SomeFunction();
ASSERT ( pSomePointer );
pSomePointer->SomeMethod();
```

There are no comments on either block, yet each speaks volumes about **SomeFunction()** and what the programmer expects. In the first case, **SomeFunction()** obviously returns a pointer to **SomeClass**, at least some of the time. The programmer is careful to test the pointer before using it, and if the pointer is **NULL**, the call to **SomeMethod()** is skipped.

Note that in the second line of this code snippet, I test **pSomePointer** as if it were a Boolean. This common C/C++ idiom relies on the fact that a non-null pointer is treated as **TRUE** by the compiler. It would be more explicit (but less macho/cool/hip) to write:

```
if ( pSomePointer != NULL )
```

In the second block, the programmer clearly expects that **SomeFunction()** *always* returns a valid pointer. He asserts that the pointer is valid, but if it is **NULL**, this is a programming bug. If **SomeFunction()** might ever legally return a null pointer, then this block of code would reflect a very poor design; but if, on the other hand, it is in fact a violation of the contract for **SomeFunction()** to return **NULL**, then this body of code is perfectly valid.

In this case, the **ASSERT()** macro is serving a double duty; it not only tests the pointer, but it also documents the programmer's assumptions about the **SomeFunction()** call. There is no need to add the comment,

```
// SomeFunction() always returns a valid pointer
SomeClass * pSomePointer = SomeFunction();
ASSERT ( pSomePointer );
pSomePointer->SomeMethod();
```

because the assert provides sufficient documentation of the assumption.

Assert is Just for Debugging

Remind yourself again and again that **ASSERT()** macros disappear in run-time mode. The **ASSERT()** macro is only for debugging and should always be read as, "If this is false, there is a bug in the code." This means that you must not use asserts to handle runtime error conditions, such as bad data, out-of-memory conditions and unable to open file — these should be handled by exceptions.

Conscientious programmers know it is imperative to check the return value from calls to **new** — it is possible to run out of memory on even the most forgiving operating system. It is a common mistake to use **ASSERT()** to test the return value:

```
Employee *pEmployee = new Employee;
ASSERT(pEmployee);    // bad use of assert
pEmployee->SomeFunction();
```

This is a classic programming error — every time the programmer runs the program, there is enough memory and the **ASSERT()** never fires. After all, the programmer is running with lots of extra RAM to speed up the compiler and debugger. The programmer then ships the executable, and the poor user, who has less memory, reaches this part of the program and the call to **new** fails and returns **NULL**. The **ASSERT()**, however, is no longer in the code, and there is nothing to indicate that the pointer points to **NULL**. As soon as the statement **pEmployee->SomeFunction();** is reached, the program crashes.

Getting **NULL** back from a memory assignment is not a programming error, although it is an exceptional situation, and thus should be managed with the C++ exception mechanism.

We should rewrite this bit of code to use exceptions, which are the correct mechanism for handling those areas of your code where exceptional, and undesirable circumstances may arise:

```
Employee *pEmployee = new Employee;
If ( ! pEmployee )
      throw new xOutOfMemory;
pEmployee->SomeFunction();
```

We'll look at exception handling in more detail a little bit later in the chapter.

Side Effects

A common but infuriating problem for programmers is the bug which only appears in the run-time code, but which runs perfectly in debug mode. If this happens to you, the first thing to suspect is the inadvertent reliance on a side-effect in your use of an **ASSERT()** macro.

For example, you might write:

```
Employee* pEmp;
ASSERT( PEmp = SomeFunction(); )
```

If you do this, you will create a particularly nasty bug. You meant to test that **SomeFunction()** has returned a valid, non-null pointer, but in fact, the assignment is occurring in the body of the **ASSERT()** itself. When you compile in non-debug mode, this macro will equate to nothing, and consequently, the call to **SomeFunction()** will not be made — the pointer will be left pointing to whatever happened to be in memory at the time it was allocated.

A similar problem arises when you attempt to test a value in **ASSERT()**, but inadvertently use the assignment operator instead:

```
ASSERT (x = 5);
```

Here, you meant to test whether **x** is equal to **5**, but you accidentally assigned the value **5** to **x** instead. The test returns **TRUE**, because **x** = **5** not only sets **x** to **5**, but returns the value **5**, and because **5** is non-zero it evaluates as **TRUE**.

Once you pass the **ASSERT()** statement, **x** is equal to **5** (you just set it!). Your program runs fine until you turn debugging off. At that point the **ASSERT()** macro disappears, and **x** is no longer set to **5**; if you had actually set **x** to another value prior to this line of code, then **x** is now left at that old value and the behavior of your program changes.

The bottom line is that **ASSERT()** macros should *only* test a value, and never assign or take any other action on which the success of your program depends.

Invariants

You will want, as part of your design, to document the invariant properties of every class in your program. The **invariants** are those aspects of your class which must be true of any object for that object to be a valid instance of the class. For example, an **Employee** object might define its invariants as follows:

▶ Every **Employee** has a name

▶ Every **Employee** has a social security number

▶ Every **Employee** has a level between 1 and 99

▶ Every **Employee** earns between $23,000 and $100,000,000

▶ Every **Employee**'s salary must be within band

243

The definition of "within band" might be defined such that level 3 employees always earn between $32,000 and $67,500, level 4 employees earn between $45,000 and $98,000 and so forth. If the issues are sufficiently complex, you might encapsulate these policies in an **EmployeeLevel** object, and this invariant of **Employee** would then become "Every **Employee** must have a valid **EmployeeLevel**."

Careful definition of the invariants is critical to designing robust objects, and these invariants should be captured in a method of the class. Each class you design should have an **Invariants()** member method, which returns **TRUE** if all of the invariants are true, for example:

```
bool Employee::Invariants()
{
return
(
            ( myName.Length() > 0 ) &&
            ( mySocialSecurityNumber.IsValid() ) &&
            ( myEmployeeLevel.IsValid())
);
}
```

This simple method can be called to test whether the **Employee**'s **myName** variable has content, whether the **Employee**'s social security number is valid (defined by the **mySocialSecurityNumber** object itself) and also whether the **EmployeeLevel** object is valid (again defined by that object itself). Tests of greater or lesser complexity can be encapsulated in this single method.

Each remaining method of **Employee** can then assert that the object is in a valid state at the beginning and end of each method call. For example:

```
bool Employee::SomeMethod()
{
        Assert(Invariants());
        // do some work here
        Assert(Invariants());
}
```

This idiom causes **SomeMethod()** to assert that the object is in a valid state, both when the method begins and after the method completes its work. It is perfectly legal for a method to move an object into an invalid state *during the course of the method*, so long as the object is valid when the method completes.

Thus, if a method might change the employee's level and then update his salary, it is possible that in the middle of this method, the object would have an invalid **EmployeeLevel** object. This is fine, so long as the object is returned to a valid state before the method returns.

Note that you are using **ASSERT()** with **Invariants()**. This indicates that you consider it to be a bug if **Invariants()** returns **FALSE**. This is a reflection of the design of the class — the invariants represent only those things that *must* be true for the object to be valid.

The premise that an object can be temporarily invalid becomes somewhat more complex in the presence of multithreading, as it may be that an object cannot tolerate being invalid when the thread loses control. In this case, you should introduce synchronization mechanisms (discussed in Chapter 5) to protect the object from being accessed by other objects, until it is returned to a valid state.

There are two methods which *cannot*, by definition, bracket their work with an assertion that the object is valid:

 The constructor

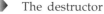 The destructor

The constructor's job is to create a valid object; until its work is done, there is little point in asserting that the object is correct. Thus, you should **ASSERT()** the invariants only at the conclusion of the constructor. Similarly, while you can (and should) **ASSERT()** that the object is valid at the start of the destructor, by definition, the object will no longer be valid when the destructor completes.

As your class evolves, it is critical that you update your **Invariants()** method to reflect the definition of a valid object. Careful use of the **Invariants()** method and religiously asserting their validity at the start and conclusion of every member method can root out and identify bugs early in the development process.

Exception Handling

A bug is a failure in the design or execution of your code. An exception, on the other hand, is a predictable event, which you must handle, but which is outside the normal flow of execution. For example, if your code is supposed to add two numbers, but instead divides them, that is a bug. If your code is supposed to write a file to disk but the disk is full, that is an exception.

Running a class member function is a process of executing the machine instructions defined by the compiled version of the member function. These steps represent an attempt to fulfill the contract that defines the member function. At times, it makes no sense to complete this processing.

Member functions are supposed to complete their work and return a value. It may be impossible to tell the caller that the function has failed and that the returned values are meaningless. Even if there is a way to return this status, it can be very cumbersome to check these return values throughout the code. Exceptions provide a mechanism to follow the thread of execution, and yet handle problems as they arise.

Before exception handling, C and C++ programmers had two choices. They could miss some errors, or they could build solid robust code that checked the return value of *every* function call and handled errors appropriately. Unfortunately, this *good* code was so encrusted in error handling routines that it became difficult to find the main line of execution. Such code is difficult to write, debug, understand and maintain.

C++ now provides native exceptions. The contract the compiler offers is this: if you call a function, you will either get back a meaningful result or the system will throw an exception.

Exceptions are classes, and as such they can have both methods and data. Because exceptions are classes, you can delegate most of the work for understanding the error to the exception itself.

The C++ Exception Handling Mechanism

The C++ exception handling mechanism was designed after the first releases of C++. The language did not include exceptions until the developers were satisfied that it could be done in an elegant and efficient manner. They succeeded, for the most part, in building an efficient mechanism — one that will not diminish the run-time efficiency of code that doesn't throw exceptions. They kept to the original **try-throw-catch** schema, and improved upon it by throwing objects as exceptions. These objects can be arranged in a C++ hierarchy and handled polymorphically.

The design of the C++ exception handling mechanism made certain assumptions as to how developers will use exceptions. Exceptions are designed to be used to handle run-time errors, rather than as an escape mechanism from deeply nested function calls. They are designed to be thrown infrequently, to protect systems from total failure.

Every exception that is thrown should be caught in your program. The default behavior for handling uncaught exceptions is not very different from a system crash. Responsibility for what to do when an exception is caught is delegated to a special section of code, within the same function, called the **catch** block. Typically, when you are about to try something that might throw an exception, you put it in a **try** block and immediately follow this with a **catch** block designed to handle any exceptions thrown.

```
try
{
        SomeFunction();
}
catch (...)
{
        // handle the problem
}
```

If the catch block cannot fully resolve the error, it is free to rethrow the exception to whatever method is higher on the stack.

Exception Handling and Resource Management

C++ exceptions present a significant challenge to memory and resource management. Normally, when you allocate memory on the heap (free store), you receive a pointer. When you are finished with that memory, you call **delete()** on the pointer and the memory is returned to the heap.

If your method throws an exception after the memory is allocated, but before the memory is restored, you will create a memory leak. The exception immediately exits the function and the pointer is never deleted. This greatly simplified example illustrates the issue:

```
#include <iostream.h>

class test
{
public:
test():myVariable(5)
{
        cout << "test constructor, allocating memory for "
                                        "myVariable.\n";
}
~test()
{
        cout << "test destructor, memory restored!\n";
}

private:
int myVariable;
};

class myException
{
};

void SomeFunction();

int main()
{
try
{
        SomeFunction();
}
catch (...)
{
        cout << "Caught exception! Not much I can do now to "
                                        "clean up the memory.\n";
        return 0;
}
cout << "Completed SomeFunction.\n";
return 0;
};

void SomeFunction()
{
for (int i = 0; i < 5; i++)
{
        test* pTest = new test; // create and initialize

        if (i == 4)
                throw new myException;

        delete pTest;
}
}
```

The output from this code is as follows:

test constructor, allocating memory for myVariable.
test destructor, memory restored!
test constructor, allocating memory for myVariable.
test destructor, memory restored!
test constructor, allocating memory for myVariable.
test destructor, memory restored!
test constructor, allocating memory for myVariable.
test destructor, memory restored!
test constructor, allocating memory for myVariable.
Caught exception! Not much I can do now to clean up the memory.

The **main()** method calls **SomeFunction()** within a **try** block. **SomeFunction()** consists of a loop in which memory is allocated and deleted. On the fifth iteration, an exception is thrown. The output reflects that this allocated memory is never restored.

In large complex systems, this can represent a significant threat to the integrity of the system. When an exception is thrown, the stack is unwound and any variables on the stack will be destroyed. Memory allocated on the heap cannot be tracked, however. Since C++ does not provide garbage collection, this memory is lost to the system until the program ends.

The reason that the objects pointed to by pointers are not destroyed by the exception mechanism is exactly the same reason that C++ does not have garbage collection — there is tremendous overhead (and thus a significant performance penalty) in tracking this memory. Languages providing these services produce programs that typically run more slowly than those produced by C++.

Smart Pointers

The solution to this dilemma is to create an **auto_ptr**. An **auto_ptr** is a stack-based object, which encapsulates a pointer and which is destroyed when the stack is unwound. This is critical: memory on the heap is managed by an **auto_ptr** on the stack. When an exception is thrown, the stack is unwound and the **auto_ptr** is destroyed. As part of its destructor, it deletes the memory on the heap. We thereby ensure that when the exception is thrown, we do not create a memory leak.

The C++ standard library provides an implementation of **auto_ptr**. The **auto_ptr** supplied by the C++ standard library supports the idiom of "resource acquisition is initialization". That is, when you create the **auto_ptr**, you allocate the memory, and when you destroy the **auto_ptr**, the memory is returned. Once the **auto_ptr** is created, you can use it like a pointer, but it will ensure that the memory will be de-allocated when it is destroyed.

It is important to note that an **auto_ptr** owns the object to which it points. Copying **auto_ptr**s has a special set of semantics: when you copy one **auto_ptr** to another, you *transfer* this ownership. This is to prevent having that object deleted more than once.

C++ Exception Hierarchies

Different types of conditions can be best processed at different levels of your program. Therefore, as the call stack is unwound, it might be appropriate to handle some exceptions, (e.g. divide by zero) and not others (e.g. database errors) in any given **catch** block. You can arrange the **catch** clauses to field the exceptions that pertain to them by defining a hierarchy for the exception classes. The first **catch** clause would handle the most specific exception and subsequent **catch** clauses can handle more general exceptions.

Your project should define a base exception class for your system's domain. This base class will have methods to get the exception type (as a **string**), and to provide or display the text describing the particular error. You will then subclass the root exception class, based on types of errors. The complexity of this hierarchy should be in direct correspondence to the complexity of your system as a whole.

Memory Management

Your decisions about memory management will be strongly influenced by your earlier decisions on language and operating system, and you should detail such decisions in you architecture guidelines document, discussed in Chapter 4. C++ provides a versatile and customizable memory environment. The three principal areas of memory of concern to the application developer are

- Global memory
- Local variables on the stack
- Local variables on the heap

You can think of global memory as being initialized before **main()** runs and being destroyed after **exit()**. Local variables are destroyed at the end of the block in which they are defined. You cannot explicitly delete a local variable, but the compiler destroys it for you when the object goes out of scope. Objects on the heap are created by a call to **new** and destroyed by a call to **delete**.

In C++, memory management is the responsibility of the application programmer. C++ has no garbage collection. If you create an object on the heap, and then lose the pointer without deleting the object, that memory is lost to the system. We call that a **memory leak**, because it is as if the memory leaked away. Over time, memory leaks will bring your system to its knees.

It is possible, though difficult, to write a system without putting objects on the heap. You can declare all your objects on the stack, and aggregate objects only by value, thus avoiding the use of pointers altogether. This can be terribly inefficient, however, as passing by value is very expensive at run time.

Several idioms have been developed for C++ to make it easier and safer to work with dynamic memory. These include:

- **auto_ptrs**
- Counted pointers

> Memory pools

> Garbage collectors

Counted Pointers

Counted pointers are used to share implementations of two or more identical objects. If an object is copied by value, then there is no reason to allocate memory for the second object (the copy), until and unless one of the objects changes its state.

Thus, if I have a string **A**, which says "Hello world!" and I copy it to string **B**, I can save memory by keeping only one copy of the string in memory. On the other hand, if I change string **B** to say "Goodbye world!" then I'd better make sure I have two different strings, or I'll inadvertently change string **A**, thus violating the semantics of copy by value.

Counted pointers also deal with the situation of two objects pointing to the same third object. It is possible in this situation for incorrectly written code to destroy the object twice (an error) or not at all (a memory leak), or even for one object to be left with a pointer to memory which is no longer valid (a stray pointer). Counted pointers eliminate these possibilities.

Several counted pointer implementations have been discussed in the literature and on the news groups. They all revolve around two ideas. The first idea is to use a counter to keep track of how many other objects are referencing the target object. The second is to define a second class, often called the handle, and to structure the code so that only handles may reference the target object.

The proposed programming idioms vary significantly. Some authors put the counter in the target class; others assume that the target class is predefined, perhaps in a library for which you do not have the source code. In this case, they wrap the target class with another class: the handle. The handle holds the counter and provides pointer-like access to the object. Some approaches implement the handle as a template. This requires the handle class to be a friend of the target class, or otherwise able to access the counter.

The C++ code below shows an implementation of these ideas. In this case, we assume that the **Handle** and the **Target** are designed together. A pointer to the **Target** class, **pTarget**, is put in the **Handle**. The **counter** is put in the **Target** class and the **Handle** made a **friend** of the **Target** class. Note that the constructor of the **Target** is made **private**. This is done so that only a **Handle** object (which is a **friend**) can instantiate a **Target** object. The constructor of the **Handle** class sets the reference counter to **1** and the pointer, **pTarget**, to refer to the **Target** object. The copy constructor and assignment operator copy the pointer and increment the counter. The de-referencing operators return the pointer to the **Target**, thereby delegating all member function calls to the **Target** object.

```
#include <iostream.h>

class Foo
{
//...
};
```

```cpp
class Handle;

class Target
{
public:
friend class Handle;
// real member functions go here
// ...
private:
int counter;
Target(Foo* foo) {}
~Target() {}
};

class Handle
{
public:
Handle(Foo* foo)
{
        pTarget = new Target(foo);
        pTarget->counter=1;
}

Handle(const Handle& rhs)
{
        pTarget = rhs.pTarget; pTarget->counter++;
}

~Handle()
{
        if ((--(pTarget->counter)) <= 0) delete pTarget;
}

Handle& operator=(const Handle& rhs)
{
        (rhs.pTarget->counter)++;
        if ((--(pTarget->counter)) <= 0 )
              delete pTarget;
        pTarget = rhs.pTarget;
        return *this;
}

Target* operator->()
{
        return pTarget;
}

private:
Target* pTarget;
};
```

Clustered Allocation

The operators **new()** and **delete()** are expensive.

When we talk about a method or an approach being expensive, we mean that this method uses a lot of resources, such as memory or CPU cycles. Using **new()** and **delete()** is expensive because they have a lot of overhead, and allocating memory does not happen quickly.

It is sometimes more efficient to grab a large area from **new()** and manage it yourself. Doing so cuts down on the number of times that **new()** and **delete()** are called. You grab a large area, and you don't call **new()** again until you use it up. If you use it up quickly you may want to grab twice as much next time.

Managing this pool of objects takes some overhead as well, however. You will have to decide if the cost of managing the pool of memory is greater than the cost of repeatedly calling **new()**. Generally, if you are creating a lot of objects, they are all of the same size and performance is critical, then this may be worth doing.

Garbage Collection

Garbage collection is a background process, which cleans up objects that are no longer in use by your program. Garbage collectors were originally designed for symbolic languages, such as LISP. Smalltalk and Java also come with built-in garbage collectors.

Garbage collection is not free (TANSTAAFL* applies here as everywhere). Garbage collection brings significant run-time overhead, and for this reason C++ does not provide garbage collection. I might argue that garbage collection should be a compiler option, but that would be beside the point. Understanding how garbage collection works can provide insight into the cost, into how other languages do implement it, and into what it would take to create your own.

One of the most common algorithms for garbage collection is **stop and copy**. In *stop and copy* you divide your memory in half. The first half is designated as working memory, where all of the "real" objects live, and the second half is designated as free memory. When working memory fills up, you begin garbage collection. This is a process of locating all of the useful objects in working memory and transferring them to free memory. You compact as you go, disposing of unneeded objects. The result is that free memory contains the useful objects and none of the garbage. You now make free memory into the new working memory, and free the old working memory to be the new free memory.

Another algorithm used for garbage collection is called **mark and sweep**. In *mark and sweep* you start at the globally available objects (e.g. static objects) and use them as the center of a pattern that fans out from them, following the pointers in these objects. Any objects reached are "marked". All objects are then reviewed. Those that are not marked are discarded as garbage. A new mark value is used for each garbage collection pass to ensure that the marking phase is done correctly.

Traditional garbage collectors ran a complete *mark and sweep* or *stop and copy* cycle. This meant that the user might be forced to wait while the system "did nothing". In some cases, this could take several seconds, or even several minutes. More modern garbage collectors employ incremental techniques, cleaning up a little bit here, a little bit there, so that there is no obvious delay in the system's processing due to the garbage collection activities.

*There Ain't No Such Thing As A Free Lunch, from Robert Heinlein's "The Moon is a Harsh Mistress".

Coding Against Bugs

There are a variety of other techniques you can employ to ensure that your code is as robust as possible. One of the most important tasks is to ensure that you are allocating and freeing memory safely. In addition, you want to enlist the compiler's help to find bugs — bugs detected at compile time are far less expensive to correct than those found at run-time. Compile-time bugs will fail reliably at every compile; run-time bugs can be far more elusive.

Pointers

Certainly you will want to set your pointers to **NULL** when deleted (or when declared if they are not initialized) and you'll want to test your pointers to ensure that they are not null before using them.

```
SomeClass * pPointer = NULL;        // initialize to NULL if not otherwise
                                    //                         initialized


pPointer = SomeMethod();            // now assign the pointer

if ( pPointer != NULL)              // test before using!
   pPointer->SomeMemberFunction();

//...continue using the pointer

delete pPointer;                    // delete the pointer
pPointer = NULL;                    // reset to NULL after deleting!
```

Setting the pointer to **NULL** (or **0**) has two advantages. First, it allows you to test your pointer before using it. If the test fails (if **pPointer** is **NULL**), then you can then take appropriate action (e.g. throw an exception, skip a block of code, etc.) More important, deleting a pointer (or more accurately, the object pointed to by the pointer) which has already been deleted is not legal in C++. Deleting a **NULL** pointer, however, is perfectly safe. By setting the pointer to **NULL** after calling delete, you protect yourself from crashing should you subsequently delete the same (already deleted) pointer.

Pointers are quite tricky, even for experienced programmers. It is quite easy to lose the pointer and to create a memory leak, or to find yourself with a stray pointer which no longer points to valid memory. Copying objects with pointers is even trickier, and it is critical to be careful about ensuring that objects are properly allocated and deleted when you are done with them.

A key element in using pointers well is to ensure that you provide the four canonical C++ methods:

▶ The constructor
▶ The destructor
▶ The copy constructor
▶ The assignment operator

Do *not* use the default methods provided by the compiler. You must write your own so that you can be certain to manage memory appropriately.

When you pass an object by value, a temporary copy of that object is made by the compiler. You pass by value when you pass a parameter that is not a pointer or a reference, or when you return an object from a method.

If the object you pass is of a user-defined class, the class's copy constructor is called by the compiler. All copy constructors take a single parameter: a reference to a constant object of the same type. For example:

```
Employee::Employee(const Employee & rhs);
```

The convention is to refer to the parameter as **rhs**, which stands for right hand side. This convention began because of the assignment operator, discussed shortly. When you write,

```
myEmployee  = yourEmployee;
```

the compiler translates this code into:

```
myEmployee.operator=(yourEmployee);
```

Thus, the parameter passed in is the variable on the *right hand side* of the assignment operator (**=**).

In any case, if you do not create a copy constructor, the compiler will provide one for you, but that compiler-provided copy constructor will perform a member-wise (or shallow) copy of the object. This means that each member variable of the first object will be copied into the member variables of the second object.

> A **shallow** *or* **member-wise** *copy copies the exact values of one object's member variables into another object.*

If these member variables are just objects, this will work fairly well, but if they are pointers, then disaster ensues. Let's look at an example to see why. Suppose you have an **Employee** class that looks like this:

```
class Employee
{
public:
Employee();
~Employee();
// note no copy constructor
// using the compiler-supplied shallow copy constructor

// other methods here...

private:
int myAge;                      // how old is the employee
EmployeeLevel* pEmpLevel;       // ptr to EmployeeLevel object
};
```

For the moment, we don't care what an **EmployeeLevel** object looks like, but we note that every **Employee** object has a pointer to one. If we then pass an **Employee** object into a method by value, like this:

```
Employee fred;
SomeMethodWhichTakesAnEmployeeByValue(fred);

Void SomeMethodWhichTakesAnEmployeeByValue(Employee theEmployee)
{
// does some work with theEmployee
}
```

Then the compiler must copy **fred** to a temporary object, named **theEmployee**, inside the method **SomeMethodWhichTakesAnEmployeeByValue()**. Because we did not provide a copy constructor, the compiler-supplied shallow copy constructor will take over. It will copy the value in **fred.myAge** into **theEmployee.myAge** and it will copy the value inside **fred.pEmpLevel** into **theEmployee.pEmpLevel**.

What is wrong with that? The value in **fred.pEmpLevel** is a memory address — the address of the **EmployeeLevel** object which was presumably created on the heap when **fred** was initialized. Unfortunately, now two objects point to that same memory:

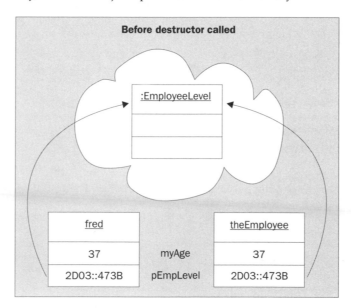

When the function returns, the temporary object (**theEmployee**) will be destroyed. The **Employee** destructor will be called, which ought to delete the pointer. Unfortunately, the pointer points to the same object in memory as that pointed to by **fred**, leaving **fred** with a pointer to what is now a destroyed **EmployeeLevel** object. The result is that when you use **fred**'s pointer again, the system will crash.

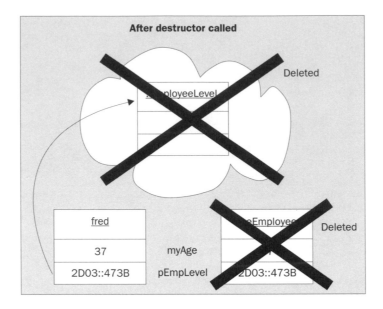

The alternative is to write your own copy constructor and to allocate memory for the new pointer. This creates a deep copy — one which copies not only the absolute value of each member variable, but which copies those objects that are pointed to as well.

> **A deep copy** *copies the values allocated on the heap to newly allocated memory.*

```
Employee::Employee(const Employee & rhs):
myAge(rhs.myAge),
pEmpLevel(new EmployeeLevel(rhs.pEmpLevel))
{
}
```

This copy constructor now initializes the member variables appropriately, allocating memory for the object pointed to by **pEmpLevel**. If you are not familiar with object initialization, take a moment to look up this technique*. It is far more efficient to initialize these objects than to assign them in the body of the constructor:

```
Employee::Employee(const Employee & rhs)
{
myAge = rhs.myAge;
pEmpLevel = new EmployeeLevel(rhs.pEmpLevel);
}
```

While this works, it creates unnecessary temporary copies, and thus is slower and uses more memory. In addition, if any of the member variables are constant or are references you *must* initialize and cannot use assignment.

*See, for example, Beginning Visual C++, by Ivor Horton, Wrox Press, ISBN 1-861000-08-1

Assignment Operator

The same concern about shallow versus deep copy also applies to the assignment operator. In this case, however, there is an additional complication. Suppose you initialized two **Employee** objects, **fred** and **wilma**:

```
Employee fred, wilma;
// other work here
fred = wilma;
```

You want to assign to **fred**'s member variables all the values in **wilma** (with a deep, not a shallow copy). However, what happens to **fred**'s existing values? They must be deleted, especially if they are pointers, or you will create a memory leak. Thus, before doing the deep copy assignments, you must first delete any pointers already in use by **fred**:

```
Employee & Employee::operator=(const Employee & rhs)
{
delete pEmpLevel;
pEmpLevel = new EmployeeLevel;
* pEmpLevel = * rhs.pEmpLevel;
myAge = rhs.myAge;
return *this;
}
```

Note that we first delete **pEmpLevel**, freeing this memory, and then we reallocate memory and reassign. There is still a problem, however. It is possible to write:

```
Employee fred, wilma;
fred = wilma;
wilma = fred;
```

The problem here is that this second statement is much the same as writing

```
fred = fred;
```

Now the object and **rhs** are the same. The first thing you do is delete **pEmpLevel**. You then reassign memory and attempt to copy ***rhs.pEmpLevel** into that newly created memory, but **pEmpLevel** has already been deleted. Whoops. To protect yourself, add these two lines to the beginning of the method:

```
if (this == &rhs)
        return *this;
```

Thus, if the two objects are the same, there is no work to be done. Here's the complete assignment operator:

```
Employee & Employee::operator=(const Employee & rhs)
{
if (this == &rhs)
        return *this;
delete pEmpLevel;
```

```
pEmpLevel = new EmployeeLevel;
* pEmpLevel = * rhs.pEmpLevel;
myAge = rhs.myAge;
return *this;
}
```

Using const

Another issue with pointers you need to consider is that they are volatile; they provide indirect access to the object itself and can be the source of inadvertent and difficult-to-track changes to the object. If you are passing a pointer for efficiency (to avoid copying large temporary objects on the stack) be sure to use the keyword **const**.

The keyword **const** can be used with pointers in a variety of ways:

```
const Employee* pOne;
Employee* const pTwo;
const Employee* const pThree;
```

It is important to understand the differences in these three declarations. **pOne** points to a constant **Employee** — you cannot use this pointer to change the values of the **Employee** object to which it points. **pTwo** is a constant pointer to an **Employee** — you cannot reassign this pointer to point to anything else. **pThree** has both restrictions.

The goal, again, is to constrain your behavior and to enlist the compiler in finding your bugs. If you are passing by reference only for efficiency, then you should declare the pointer to point to a constant object. If you then attempt to modify that object using the pointer, the compiler will flag your error and save you many hours of aggravation.

Declaring a member function constant declares that you will not use that member function to modify the object. Here's how it works. Every member function has an implicit and invisible parameter, which is the **this** pointer. The **this** pointer points to the object itself, and when you refer to a member variable or a method from within a member method, the compiler uses the invisible **this** pointer to resolve the reference. Thus, if you write:

```
void Employee::SomeFunction()
{
myAge = 7;
}
```

The compiler translates this into:

```
void Employee::SomeFunction(Employee * this)
{
this->myAge = 7;
}
```

If you declare **SomeFunction()** to be **const**, the **this** pointer is set to be constant. If you wrote:

```
void Employee::SomeFunction() const
{
myAge = 7;
}
```

This would be translated to:

```
void Employee::SomeFunction(const Employee * this)
{
this->myAge = 7; // compiler error!
}
```

Since it is not legal to use a pointer to a constant object to change that object (e.g. to set a member variable's value), this will be flagged as a compile-time error. Incidentally, this is why static member methods cannot be declared as constant. Static member methods do not have a **this** pointer — they are not tied to a particular object.

Coding Style Issues*

When you write code, you have two audiences: the compiler and other programmers. The compiler doesn't care at all about your coding style. As far as it's concerned, white space is meaningless. Your peers, however, will curse your soul if you make your code unreadable. Write every line as if someone else will maintain it. When you return to it a few months later, you'll be very glad you did.

If you are working as a team, create a document which details your style decisions; this helps reinforce the fact that, while the decisions may be arbitrary, they are worth following.

Braces

Let's start with braces. Deciding how to align braces can be the single most controversial topic between programmers. Since the choice of brace style is arbitrary and unimportant, most of us are quite ferocious and unyielding in our prejudices about it.

You have three choices. Choice one is often called K&R, after Brian Kernighan and Dennis Ritchie, whose seminal book *The C Programming Language* taught so many of us how to program. The classic K&R style is this:

```
if ( condition == true ){
    a += b;
    SomeFunction();

    if ( c == d ){
        SomeOtherFunction();
    }
}
```

The material in this section is adapted from part of Chapter 1, Clouds to Code

An alternative is to indent the braces:

```
if ( condition == true )
{
a += b;
SomeFunction();

if ( c == d )
    {
SomeOtherFunction();
    }
}
```

I honestly don't know anyone who likes this style, but you do see it used now and again.

The third variant aligns the braces with the conditional, and there is no code on the same line as the brace:

```
if ( condition == true )
{
    a += b;
    SomeFunction();

    if ( c == d )
    {
        SomeOtherFunction();
    }
}
```

I used to use K&R and believed it was the only right solution. About five years ago I switched over to the third option, and now I know that this one, of course, is the only true way to write code. The important thing to remember is that whatever style you adopt, you should use it consistently.

Indentation

switch statements get special indentation, as they can otherwise waste a lot of space:

```
switch(variable)
{
case ValueOne:
   ActionOne();
   break;

case ValueTwo:
   ActionTwo();
   break;

default:
   assert("bad Action");
   break;
}
```

Keep all lines fairly short, and break the line if it will scroll off to the right. If you do break a line, indent the following lines. Try to break the line at a reasonable place, and if there is an operator, leave it at the end of the previous line (as opposed to the beginning of the following line). This way, it is clear that the line does not stand alone and that there is more to come.

Use of White Space

Strive to make your code easy to read, because code that is easy to read is easy to maintain. Use a lot of white space where it will help to make things clear. As a rule, I treat objects and arrays as a single thing, and I don't put space before the references (e.g. `myObject.SomeMethod()`).

Unary operators are associated with their operand, so I don't put a space between them. On the other hand, I *do* put a space on the side *away* from the operand. When it comes to binary operators, I put a space both sides. Here are some other suggestions:

Don't use spaces to indicate precedence. For that matter, don't depend on operator precedence, use parentheses.

```
( 4+ 3*2 ) // don't do this
( 4 + ( 3 * 2 ) ) // much better
```

Put a space after commas and semicolons, not before.

Parentheses should have spaces on the inside, and keywords should be set off with a space:

```
if ( a == b )
```

Declaring Variables

Place the pointer or reference indicator next to the type name. Don't put it next to the variable name or place it with a space on either side. In other words, do this:

```
char* foo;
int& theInt;
```

And not this:

```
char *foo;
int &theInt;
```

Only declare a single variable on any line. Combining this rule with the last one will prevent you from writing something like this:

```
int* varOne, varTwo;
```

If you were to write this, you would have declared one pointer and one integer variable, when in fact you meant to declare two pointers.

Naming Variables

Be careful about how you name identifiers. The name should be long enough to be descriptive, and it is worth the extra effort to spell names out. Consider limited use of Hungarian notation. For example, prefix pointers with **p** (**pSomePointer**) and references with **r**. Don't get carried away, however, as Hungarian notation breaks down pretty quickly with user-defined types.

Use a consistent prefix for member variables. I've used a single letter (e.g. **dAge** is a data member, while **age** is just a local variable). I've also used *my* (**myAge**) and *its* (**itsAge**). Microsoft uses *m_* as its member variable prefix (**m_age**);

The length of a variable's name should be proportional to its scope. Within a **for** loop, it is fine to have a variable named **j**, but if the variable is going to live for any time at all it should have a more descriptive name.

> Note, the ANSI standard has changed the scoping rule for **for** loops. Variables declared in the header used to be scoped to the outer loop:

```
int SomeFunction()
{
for ( int i = 0; i < Max_Int; i ++ )
{

}

for (i = 0; i < Max_Int; i ++ )
{

}
}
```

> With the change to the standard, the variable **i** is now scoped to the **for** loop itself, thus this will no longer compile (if you are using an ANSI compatible compiler) as **i** is not declared for the second **for** loop.

Avoid having two variables whose names differ only by capitalization. While the compiler won't be confused, you certainly will be. Adopt a capitalization strategy — variables should begin with a lower case letter, and methods begin with an upper case letter.

Consider making variable names abstract nouns (**theCount**, **windSpeed**, **windowPosition**), while methods should be verb/noun phrases like **Find()**, **ShowButton()**, and **MoveWindow()**. We used to call this **kill dwarf notation**, from the old interactive computer games where you specified a verb (**move**, **lift**, **kill**) and a noun (**scroll**, **wand**, **dwarf**).

Use Comments Well

I was watching a ball game on TV, and the pitcher was really struggling. He had walked the last two batters, and the manager and catcher went out to the mound to talk with him. It was obvious that the manager wasn't ready to take the pitcher out of the game, but was going to give him some advice. The play by play reporter asked the color commentator what was going on. "You were a catcher; what does the manager say when he gets out there?" The color commentator thought a moment and said, "He says, 'Throw strikes.' And the pitcher says, 'I'm trying to throw strikes.' And the manager says, 'Yeah, but throw strikes.' "

Telling you to comment well is rather like telling the pitcher to throw strikes. It's a great idea, but how *exactly* do you do it? Well, your comments should never speak for the code. For example:

```
myCounter++;  // increment myCounter
```

This is worse than useless. The code speaks for itself, so get rid of the comment. There is always the danger that the comment will get out of date and you'll end up with:

```
myCounter += theNewValue;  // increment myCounter
```

Now instead of being just obvious, it is plain wrong. Comments should only be used to clarify obscure code. Ideally, of course, you should endeavor to make your code less obscure, not paper it over with a comment. Don't comment:

```
a = j / 60; // compute how many minutes
```

Instead, you should make the code clearer:

```
howManyMinutes = howManySeconds / SECS_IN_MINUTE;
```

Comments should be used to explain what a section of code is *for*, not what it is *doing*. Use complete English sentences; the extra effort involved is paid back in extra clarity. By the same logic, try to avoid abbreviations. What seems exceedingly clear to you as you write the comment will seem cryptic some months later. Use blank lines and white space to help the reader understand what is going on. Separate statements into logical groups.

Organizing the Source Code

Each source and header file should have a consistent layout; it makes finding and managing the code much easier. The way you access portions of your program should also be consistent.

Always use **public**, **private**, and **protected** specifiers; don't rely on the defaults. List the public members first, then protected ones and finally the private ones. List the data members in a group after the methods. This is trickier when using classes built by the Microsoft Wizards, but it is worth the time to rearrange these files and get it right.

Line up function return values, names and parameters. Consider these two listings; which do you find easier to read?

```
bool GetStartFromEnd (CTime& start, CTime end, int nSizeOfList, int
nAudioDuration);
int GetWhichList (CCaller* pCaller, CString customerID, bool onlyOne);
void GetWhenToCall (CCaller* pCaller, CString customerID, bool&
alwaysNow, CTime& start, CTime& end, bool& useTimeZones, int& whichTilt,
int& nIsCrisis);
```

```
void GetStartTime (CCaller* pCaller, CString customerID, CTime&
start,CTime& end);
void GetEndTime (CCaller* pCaller, CString customerID, CTime&
start,CTime& end);
```

```
bool   GetStartFromEnd (CTime& start, CTime end, int nSizeOfList,
                        int nAudioDuration);
int    GetWhichList    (CCaller* pCaller, CString customerID,
                        bool onlyOne);
void   GetWhenToCall   (CCaller* pCaller, CString customerID,
                        bool& alwaysNow, CTime& start,
                        CTime& end, bool& useTimeZones,
                        int& whichTilt, int& nIsCrisis);
void   GetStartTime    (CCaller* pCaller, CString customerID,
                        CTime& start, CTime& end);
void   GetEndTime      (CCaller* pCaller, CString customerID,
                        CTime& start, CTime& end);
```

Put the constructor(s) first in the appropriate section, followed by the destructor. Alphabetize the rest of the methods, both in the header file and in the implementation file. Or, rather than alphabetizing, consider grouping your methods by sets of functionality. This gives you a quick view of what your objects do, and is a good check on whether you are asking any one object to do too much.

Alphabetize the **#include** directives at the top of your implementation files (be careful about order dependencies, but to the extent that they are under your control, consider an order dependency to be a bug, and fix it). Comment each **#include** statement if it isn't obvious why you needed it. And be sure that *every* header file has inclusion guards to protect against multiple includes.

Debugging

One of the most important skills for a C++ programmer to develop is expertise with the debugger. This critical technique is often given little time in primers and introductory programming courses. It is only after a number of months or years of struggling that many programmers discover how powerful their debuggers can be, not only in finding bugs but also in the initial development of their software. Expert use of the debugger can help you expand your skills in the language as well, and can give you insight into the workings of code developed by other developers.

Many of the lessons of debugging are universal, and apply to any debugging software, whether it is the simple line debugger available on some operating systems, the integrated debugger which comes with modern compilers, or expensive after-market professional debuggers now available from many vendors. This discussion will focus on the debugger built into the Microsoft Visual Studio software, but the lessons should be universal.

Using a Debugger as Part of Development

The first and most important point is that the debugger is not a tool to be used only after the software is complete; good use of the debugger should be integrated into the development process. Typically, primers which introduce the debugger provide you with code which is broken and walk you through the steps of finding the bug. While we'll do that in a moment, let's start by using the debugger, not to find a bug, but to understand a complex bit of code.

The code we're going to look at for this example is the implementation of a linked list. This creates enormous confusion for novice programmers; until they "get" the idea of how a linked list works, it is difficult to understand what is going on (see the discussion of linked lists in the section on data structures in Chapter 6).

A simple object-oriented implementation of a singly linked list will consist of a series of nodes, each node containing a pointer to the object to be held in the list and a pointer to the next node, if any.

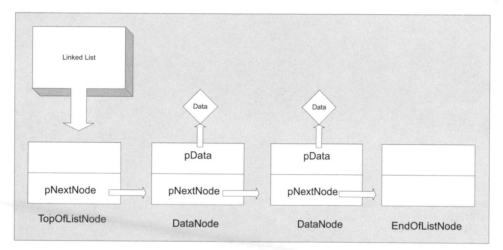

The **TopOfListNode** has a special job. It does not contain data, but it does point to the next node in the list. The **EndOfListNode** also has a special job, it is a sentry of the end of the list and also does not contain data, but it does not have another node to point to either. The job of the **EndOfListNode** becomes critical when nodes are added to the list.

The class diagram is straightforward:

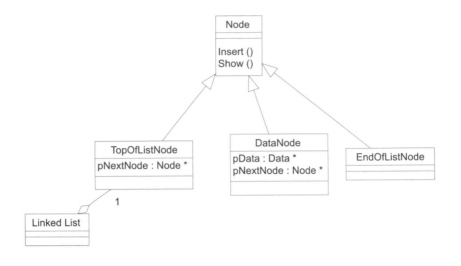

Every linked list has one **TopOfListNode**. When the list is created, that **TopOfListNode** points to the **EndOfListNode**, and the list is empty:

When it is time to insert data, the data is handed to the **TopOfListNode**. The **TopOfListNode** always does the same thing — it passes the data to whatever node is pointed to by its **pNextNode** pointer, calling **Insert()** on that node. Then it sets its own **pNextNode** pointer to point to the result of that operation.

In the case of the empty list, it will pass the new data to the **EndOfListNode**. The **EndOfListNode** always does the same thing when it is given data to insert — it creates a new **DataNode** and returns that pointer to whomever called it. In this first use of the list, this will be the **TopOfListNode**, thus the **TopOfListNode** has its **pNextNode** pointer set to point to the new **DataNode**. The parameters to the **DataNode** constructor are the pointer to the data and a pointer to the **EndOfListNode** itself.

The **DataNode** constructor initializes its **pData** pointer to the new data and its **pNextNode** pointer to the second parameter (in this case the **EndOfListNode**).

Thus, adding the first data item is easy. You pass the data to the **TopOfListNode**, which passes it to the **EndOfListNode**. This creates a new node and tells that node to point to the **EndOfListNode**. The return value to the **TopOfListNode** is the new node, and thus the new node is inserted.

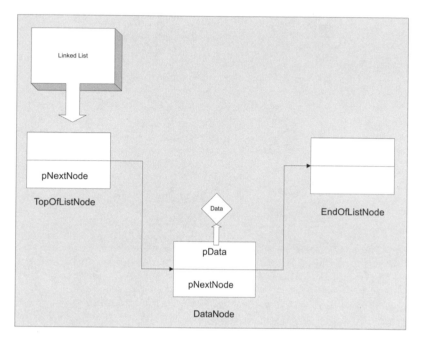

When the next item of data is inserted into the list, the **TopOfListNode**, as usual, passes it to the node that its **pNextNode** pointer points to. In this case, it passes it to the **DataNode**. The **DataNode**'s **Insert()** method tells its data to compare itself with the new data, and if the new data is less than or the same (defined by the data object itself!) then the new node must be inserted before this node. Thus, a new **DataNode** is created and told to point to the existing **DataNode** as the next node in the list. A pointer to the new node is in turn passed back to the **TopOfListNode**:

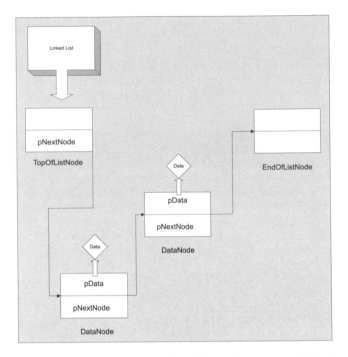

Said in words, this explanation is rather complex. The code is also difficult to grasp at first reading, but if you put the code into a debugger, then the operation becomes much easier to understand. The code is listed below:

```
#include <iostream.h>

enum { IS_SMALLER, IS_LARGER, IS_EQUAL };

    class ValueObject
    {
    public:
        ValueObject(int theVal):mValue(theVal){}
        ~ValueObject(){}

        int Compare(const ValueObject &);
        void Display() { cout << mValue << endl; }

    private:
        int mValue;
    };

    int ValueObject::Compare(const ValueObject & rhs)
    {
        if (mValue < rhs.mValue)
            return IS_SMALLER;

        if (mValue > rhs.mValue)
            return IS_LARGER;
```

```
        return IS_EQUAL;
}

// forward declarations

class Node;
class TopOfListNode;
class EndOfListNode;
class DataNode;

class Node
{
public:
    Node(){}
    virtual ~Node(){}
    virtual Node * Insert(ValueObject * theData)=0;
    virtual void Display() = 0;
private:
};

class DataNode: public Node
{
public:
    DataNode(ValueObject * theData, Node * pNext);
    ~DataNode(){ delete pNextNode; delete pData; }
    virtual Node * Insert(ValueObject * theData);
    virtual void Display() { pData->Display(); pNextNode->Display(); }
private:
        ValueObject * pData;
        Node * pNextNode;
};

DataNode::DataNode(ValueObject * theData, Node * pNext):
pData(theData),pNextNode(pNext)
{
}

Node * DataNode::Insert(ValueObject * theData)
{
    int result = pData->Compare(*theData);

    Node * pNode;

    if ( result == IS_LARGER)
    {
            pNode = new DataNode(theData, this);
    }
    else
    {
            pNextNode = pNextNode->Insert(theData);
            pNode = this;
    }
```

```
        return pNode;
}

class EndOfListNode : public Node
{
public:

    EndOfListNode(){}
    ~EndOfListNode(){}
    virtual Node * Insert(ValueObject * theData);
    virtual void Display() { }
private:
};

Node * EndOfListNode::Insert(ValueObject * theData)

{
    Node * dataNode = new DataNode(theData, this);
    return dataNode;
}

class TopOfListNode : public Node
{
public:
    TopOfListNode();
    ~TopOfListNode() { delete pNextNode; }
    virtual Node * Insert(ValueObject * theData);
    virtual void Display() { pNextNode->Display(); }

private:
    Node * pNextNode;

};

TopOfListNode::TopOfListNode():
pNextNode ( new EndOfListNode )
{
}

Node * TopOfListNode::Insert(ValueObject * theData)
{
    pNextNode = pNextNode->Insert(theData);
    return this;
}

class LinkedList
{
public:
    LinkedList();
    ~LinkedList() { delete pHeadNode; }
    void Insert(ValueObject * theData);
```

```cpp
    void DisplayList() { pHeadNode->Display(); }
private:
    TopOfListNode * pHeadNode;
};


LinkedList::LinkedList():
pHeadNode( new TopOfListNode )
{
}


void LinkedList::Insert(ValueObject * pData)
{
    pHeadNode->Insert(pData);
}


int main()
{
    ValueObject * pData;
    int testValue;
    LinkedList theLinkedList;
    for (;;)
    {
        cout << "Please enter a value to add to the list "
                                            "(0 to quit): ";
        cin >> testValue;
        if (!testValue)
            break;
        pData = new ValueObject(testValue);
        theLinkedList.Insert(pData);
    }

    theLinkedList.DisplayList();
    return 0;   // theLinkedList falls out of scope and is destroyed!
}
```

This program, **SinglyLinkedList.cpp** is shipped as a single file (with the header information in with the implementation) to simplify this example. It is designed to be run as a console application — that is, it uses standard input and output and is *not* a Windows application.

To begin, create a console application project, type in the code (or download the code from the Wrox Press website: **http://www.wrox.com**). Compile and link it. Your window should look more or less like this:

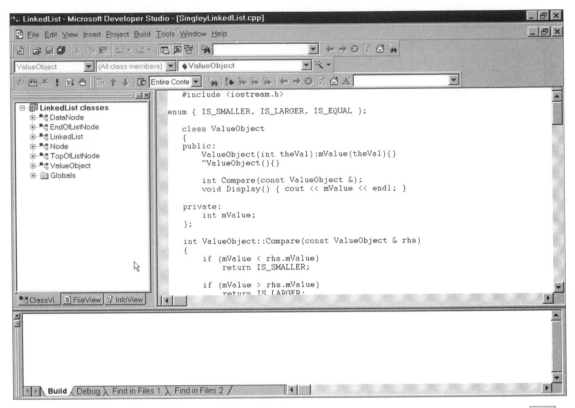

Execute the program to by pressing either *Ctrl+F5* or the Execute Program button:

This will cause the program to begin. Interact with the program a couple of times to get a sense of what it is like:

We're going to explore exactly how the linked list works using the debugger. One of the most powerful debugger options is the **breakpoint**. This simply instructs the debugger to run the program right up to the debug point, and then to stop. Once you stop, it is possible to **step into** your function calls, which causes the debugger to follow the thread of execution into and through each function call. At times you won't want to plunge into a particular function, so instead you can **step over** that call, which causes the debugger to run until the next line in your current function.

I'll be using the Microsoft debugger with Visual C++ for this example, and all of the screenshots will reflect this. Other debuggers will display things a bit differently, but the ideas will be the same. If you find yourself in code which isn't yours (or worse, if you've not installed the Microsoft libraries, if you find yourself in assembler!) then just press Step Out (Shift+F11) to get back to your code.

To get started, you'll want to see the creation of the linked list itself. The third line of **main()** is where the linked list is created, so put a breakpoint there. Place the cursor in this line and press the Insert/Remove Breakpoint button (or alternatively, press *F9*):

You should see a red dot in the margin of the line with a breakpoint, and your code window should look like this:

```
int main()
{
    ValueObject * pData;
    int testValue;
    LinkedList theLinkedList;
    for (;;)
    {
        cout << "Please enter a value to add to the list (0 to quit): ";
        cin >> testValue;
        if (!testValue)
            break;
        pData = new ValueObject(testValue);
        theLinkedList.Insert(pData);
    }

    theLinkedList.DisplayList();
    return 0;   // theLinkedList falls out of scope and is destroyed!
}
```

Press the Go (or *F5*) to start the debugger running the program:

The program should run uninterrupted until the line in which you placed the breakpoint:

```
int main()
{
    ValueObject * pData;
    int testValue;
    LinkedList theLinkedList;
    for (;;)
    {
        cout << "Please enter a value to add to the list (0 to quit): ";
        cin >> testValue;
        if (!testValue)
            break;
        pData = new ValueObject(testValue);
        theLinkedList.Insert(pData);
    }

    theLinkedList.DisplayList();
    return 0;  // theLinkedList falls out of scope and is destroyed!
}
```

The yellow arrow within the red dot now indicates that the debugger has stopped at the line you've requested. Before you step into the code, take a look around. You should find that you have a number of useful windows. If not, you can open them from the Debug toolbar.

> *If you can't see the Debug toolbar, you should go to Tools/Customize and select the Toolbars tab. Check the box against Debug and close the dialog.*

The first and most immediately useful window is the variables window:

Name	Value
testValue	530
⊞ theLinkedList	{...}
⊞ pData	0x0000013f

Context: main()

Auto \ **Locals** \ this

There are a couple things you should notice about this window. First, this is a tabbed window, with three tabs visible, Auto, Locals and this. Locals is the default and it displays the local variables. At the moment there are three local variables. **pData** is the pointer to a **ValueObject**. Like **testValue**, it is uninitialized, and thus has whatever garbage happened to be in memory. **theLinkedList** is the locally defined linked list variable. Note the + sign next to these variables. You can "open" a variable to see its internal structure. Expanding the plus sign next to **theLinkedList** at the moment won't do much good, as the list hasn't been created.

Press the Step Into button (or *F11*):

This should take you to the constructor for a linked list:

```
LinkedList::LinkedList():
pHeadNode( new TopOfListNode )
{
}
```

You can see that the constructor creates a new instance of **TopOfListNode**. If you press *F11* again, you'll end up stepping into the code for the keyword **new**, which you are probably not interested in at the moment — whenever something like this happens, just use Step Out (or *Shift+F11*) to get out of the function and continue:

The next time you press *F11*, you should step into the code for the constructor of **TopOfListNode**. Of course, since **TopOfListNode** is a **Node** object, you'll first step into the constructor for the base class.

TopOfListNode's constructor creates a new **EndOfListNode**. Keep stepping through the code until you are back into **main()** again, and by this time, you should have created both the **TopOfListNode** and **EndOfListNode**.

The new object, **theLinkedList** has now been initialized. If you press the + symbol next to **theLinkedList** in the variables window, its structure will be revealed. You see that **theLinkedList** has a **TopOfListNode**, which is comprised of two components, **Node** and **pNextNode**. **Node** is its base class. **pNextNode** has, in turn, a member variable, which is of type **EndOfListNode**, which is just what we'd expect:

Name	Value
testValue	530
⊟ theLinkedList	{...}
⊟ pHeadNode	0x007807e0
⊞ Node	{...}
⊟ pNextNode	0x00780810
⊞ [EndOfListNode]	{...}
⊞ __vfptr	0x00418088
⊞ pData	0x0000013f

Context: main()

Auto \ **Locals** \ this

Continue stepping along and you will pass the line which calls **cin**. This will force you to enter a value in a console window. Enter the value 18. If you look in the variables window now, you will see that the variable **testValue** has been set to this value. After you've typed in this number, you will return to the debugger and can continue stepping. Step to the line which says:

```
pData = new ValueObject(testValue);
```

A **ValueObject** will be created with this integer, and the next line will insert it into **theLinkedList**:

```
theLinkedList.Insert(pData);
```

275

Step into this call to
Insert():

```
void LinkedList::Insert(ValueObject * pData)
{
    pHeadNode->Insert(pData);
}
```

The debugger immediately jumps to the **LinkedList**'s **Insert()** method, where we see that the effect of this call is only to call **Insert()** on the **LinkedList**'s **pHeadNode** pointer. Step into the code again, and you will end up in the **TopOfListNode**'s **Insert()** method, which does nothing but call **Insert()** on *its* **pNextNode** member. Press Step Into again and we step into the **EndOfListNode**'s **Insert()** method (which makes sense, if you think about it, because the **TopOfListNode** is pointing to the **EndOfListNode**):

```
Node * EndOfListNode::Insert(ValueObject * theData)

{
    Node * dataNode = new DataNode(theData, this);
    return dataNode;
}
```

This creates a **DataNode** to hold the **ValueObject**, and passes the **EndOfListNode** node as a parameter. Step into the constructor:

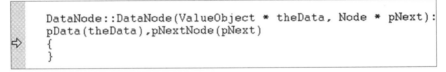

```
DataNode::DataNode(ValueObject * theData, Node * pNext):
pData(theData),pNextNode(pNext)
{
}
```

We see that the new node is created, holding the data and pointing to the tail of the list. This puts us in the following position:

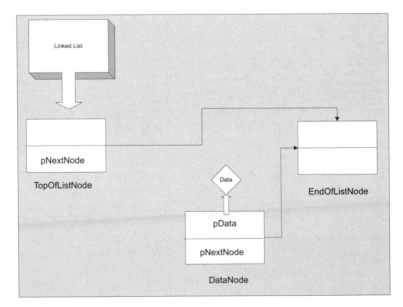

The new node is pointing to the **EndOfListNode**, and the head node is pointing to this node as well. Press Step Out or *Shift+F11*.

```
Node * EndOfListNode::Insert(ValueObject * theData)

{
    Node * dataNode = new DataNode(theData, this);
    return dataNode;
}
```

We see that a pointer to the new node will be returned from the **EndOfListNode::Insert()** method. Clicking Step Out once more reveals that the pointer returned is assigned to **TopOfListNode**'s **pNextNode**.

```
Node * TopOfListNode::Insert(ValueObject * theData)
{
    pNextNode = pNextNode->Insert(theData);
    return this;
}
```

This breaks the connection from **TopOfListNode** to **EndOfListNode** and replaces it with a connection from **TopOfListNode** to **dataNode**:

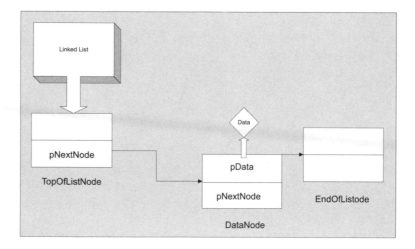

The insertion is now complete. Continue stepping through the code and you will return to **LinkedList::Insert()** and then back to **main()**. You will then be prompted to enter another value, and you can watch as the new node is added into the list.

Using the Debugger to Find a Bug

Let's make a small change to the program. Rewrite the **DataNode::Insert()** method to look
like the code below. It is the highlighted line that has changed:

```
Node * DataNode::Insert(ValueObject * theData)
{
int result = pData->Compare(*theData);

Node * pNode;

if ( result == IS_LARGER )
{
        pNode = new DataNode(theData, this);
}
else
{
        pNextNode = Insert(theData);
        pNode = this;
}

return pNode;
}
```

In a large body of code, this looks fairly reasonable, and it will compile and link. Don't examine
it too closely, after all, in a real debugging situation you would *not* know that this is the area of
code with a problem. Run the program and enter the following values: 18, 9, 3, 0. It should run
to completion without a problem. Now try it again with 18, 3, 9, 0. Oops! An exception from
the operating system:

Apparently the program has a bug, and this bug depends on the order in which values are
added. Let's use the debugger to find out what is going on. This is a nasty bug to find, because
the exception it throws may stop the debugger altogether. If that happens, the best way to get
started is a binary search of the code. How far into the code can we go before we see the bug?

Let's start by putting a breakpoint half way through **main()**:

```
int main()
{
    ValueObject * pData;
    int testValue;
    LinkedList theLinkedList;
    for (;;)
    {
        cout << "Please enter a value to add to the list (0 to quit): ";
        cin >> testValue;
        if (!testValue)
            break;
        pData = new ValueObject(testValue);
        theLinkedList.Insert(pData);
    }

    theLinkedList.DisplayList();
    return 0;  // theLinkedList falls out of scope and is destroyed!
}
```

If we can get to this breakpoint without crashing, then we know that we can, at least, create an empty linked list. This should work, because it would seem that the bug has to do with processing the values. It is safer, however, to leave nothing to chance.

Try running the code to this point. Sure enough, we get to this line of code without a problem. Time to stop and think. If the two sets of values you entered were 18, 9, 3, 0 and 18, 3, 9, 0, the earliest problem *may* be with entering 3.

Let's try putting a breakpoint in the line in **main()** where we attempt to enter the input value into the linked list:

theLinkedList.Insert(pData)

Clear all the breakpoints and set a breakpoint on this line. Now run the program. You will be prompted to enter the first value, 18. Enter 18, hit return and you are back in the code. Hit Run again and it runs just fine, prompting for the second value, 3. Enter it, hit Run and, once again, that works. Now enter the third value, 9 and run it. Aha! This time it crashes:

```
int main()
{
    ValueObject * pData;
    int testValue;
    LinkedList theLinkedList;
    for (;;)
    {
        cout << "Please enter a value to add to the list (0 to quit): ";
        cin >> testValue;
        if (!testValue)
            break;
        pData = new ValueObject(testValue);
        theLinkedList.Insert(pData);
    }

    theLinkedList.DisplayList();
```

Microsoft Developer Studio

(i) Unhandled exception in LinkedList.exe: 0xC00000FD: Stack Overflow.

OK

Context: main()	
Name	Value
⊞ pData	0x00780900
testValue	9
⊞ theLinkedList	{...}

Auto / Locals \ this /   Watch1 / Watch2 \ Watch3 \ Watch4 /

Okay, now we know that running this line of code with the value 9 will crash the program. It is time we tried to close in on the problem. Let's do this carefully, one step at a time. Remember — we know that trying to insert the value 9 into the list is causing the program to crash — what we need to do now is find out exactly where the problem is.

Stop debugging and restart with the breakpoint on the same line. Start the program running and enter 18 when prompted, as before. Repeat this for the 3 value, but when you have entered 9, then hit return to get back to the breakpoint, but do not start the program running again. Rather, you should press the Step Into button — you should reach this line in the **LinkedList::Insert()** method:

```
pHeadNode->Insert(pData);
```

Stop debugging, clear all the breakpoints and set a new one at this line. Run the program as before, entering each value as prompted until you reach the breakpoint again with the value 9. No problems so far, so try stepping in again. This time you should reach the line,

```
pNextNode = pNextNode->Insert(pData);
```

in the **TopOfListNode::Insert()** method. Again, stop debugging, reset the breakpoint to this line and repeat the whole process, until you return to this breakpoint with the value 9. Step into the code once more. This brings you to the **DataNode::Insert()** method.

Note, this is an interesting piece of code, because it has a conditional. We are looking for a conditional, because we know this crash only happens with some values and not with others. At this point, let's clear all the breakpoints and set two new ones, as shown below:

```
Node * DataNode::Insert(ValueObject * theData)
{
    int result = pData->Compare(*theData);

    Node * pNode;

    if ( result == IS_LARGER)
    {
        pNode = new DataNode(theData, this);
    }
    else
    {
        pNextNode = Insert(theData);
        pNode = this;
    }

    return pNode;
}
```

Now, let's start over. Run the code again with the new breakpoints. The very first thing to notice is that we don't hit either breakpoint when we enter 18. Entering 3 brings us to the **if** statement, and running that works fine (no crash). Entering 9 brings us to the **else** clause. That makes sense from the logic of the program. Run it to see if it crashes.

It does not crash, but brings us back into the **else**. We appear to be in the next node. Run it again. Again we're back in the **else** clause the next node. Keep running it and notice that you are never exiting from this list. That is odd because there are only three values in the list, so where are we?

Take a look at the value of **pNextNode**, shown in the variables window:

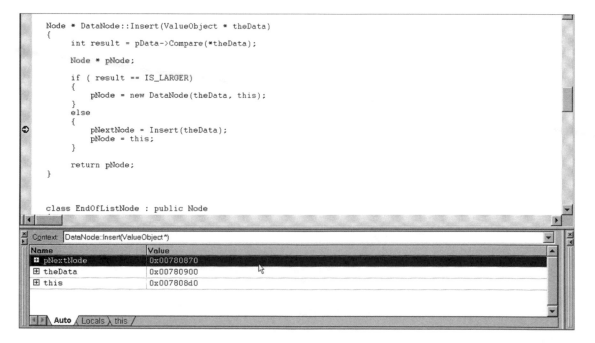

The value of this pointer isn't **NULL**, so we can step into the **Insert()** call. Stepping in seems to work — we're back at the top of the method — we must be in the next node. Continue stepping though the code — something appears to be wrong. We're stepping through node after node, but the list isn't that long. Take a look at the call stack (you can open this from the Debug toolbar). This window shows the recent set of function calls:

```
Call Stack                                                 ×
⇨ DataNode::Insert(ValueObject * 0x00780900)
  DataNode::Insert(ValueObject * 0x00780900)
  DataNode::Insert(ValueObject * 0x00780900)
  DataNode::Insert(ValueObject * 0x00780900)
  DataNode::Insert(ValueObject * 0x00780900)
  DataNode::Insert(ValueObject * 0x00780900)
  TopOfListNode::Insert(ValueObject * 0x00780
  LinkedList::Insert(ValueObject * 0x00780900
  main() line 171
  mainCRTStartup() line 257 + 25 bytes
  KERNEL32! bff88e93()
  KERNEL32! bff88d41()
  KERNEL32! bff87759()
```

This shows that from **TopOfListNode::Insert()**, we called into **DataNode::Insert()**, and from there into another instance of **DataNode::Insert()** and so on and so on. This list of recursive calls has begun to build up. Go back and take another look at that error message box that pops up when the program fails: "Unhandled Exception in SinglyLinkedList.exe:0xC00000FD:Stack Overflow." A stack overflow seems consistent with what we're seeing here.

You should begin to smell a rat. Look at the address of **pNextNode** — each time you call **Insert()** on the *next* node, it's own **pNextNode** has the *same* address:

```
×   Context: DataNode::Insert(ValueObject *)                ▼
───────────────────────────────────────────────────────────
Name                    │ Value                          ▲
⊞ pNextNode             │ 0x00780870
⊞ theData               │ 0x00780900
⊟ this                  │ 0x007808d0
 ⊞ Node                 │ {...}
 ⊞ pData                │ 0x007808a0
 ⊞ pNextNode            │ 0x00780870
                                                         ▼
◄ ► \ Auto / Locals \ this /
```

You appear to be calling **Insert()** on yourself! You shouldn't be calling **Insert()** on yourself, you should be calling it on the node pointed to by your **pNextNode** member variable.

Finding this bug without a debugger would have been a Herculean task. With the debugger, it was fairly straightforward. There are a number of other windows worthy of exploration, including:

▶ watch window — lets you keep track of specific variables
▶ memory window — lets you examine the contents of specific areas of memory
▶ threads window — lets you identify which specific thread is currently executing

I strongly recommend spending a good bit of time exploring your debugger and coming to understand how it works *before* you need it.

Roll Out

The process of writing software starts with the initial idea, is nurtured through requirements analysis, given form in the design phase, and realized in the implementation. All of that will be worthless, however, if the product is not thoroughly tested. The rule which must never be violated is that *schedule yields to quality, and features yield to schedule*. Shipping a product which does not work will kill you in the market.

That said, let's be honest. The biggest danger to software is not a bug here or there, and certainly not a missing feature. It is that you will hold up the schedule for so long that you miss the market opportunity. We know of many wildly successful products (and even operating systems) which were not 100% bug-free before release, but which established their market niche even while the development team worked feverishly to get a second, fixed release out the door.

There are simple market realities that may force you to go out with a product with a few minor known bugs. If your core functionality works, if your product has something to offer which outweighs its limitations, then you may be better off fixing the minor problems in a second release. It isn't pretty, and few will say it out loud, but that is the reality of the market place.

Summary

This chapter has covered may of the tricks and techniques you should employ, if you want to write reliable, efficient, robust and maintainable code. We have covered many new concepts throughout this book, and examined the process of developing an application from the initial seed of an idea, through to testing and debugging the final product.

In the final chapter, Phish, we will tie together many of these ideas, by discussing them in the context of the development of an example program.

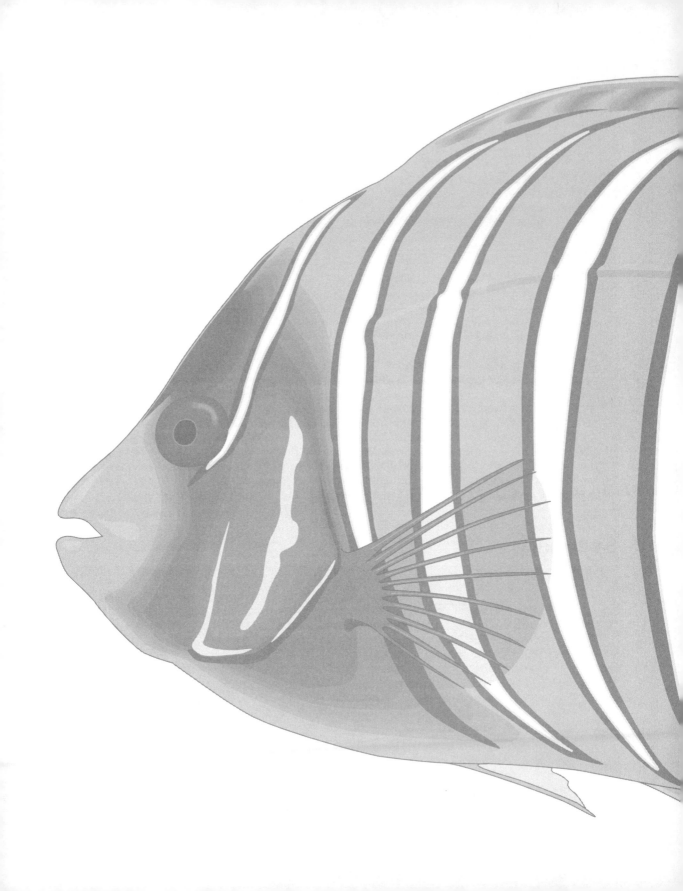

Phish

In this chapter I will work though a complete example from inception through to delivery. While the application itself is fairly simple, it does touch on many of the principal issues encountered at each stage of an iteration of a larger program.

The Vision

Phish is loosely based on Wator, which was invented by A. K. Dewdney, in his *Computer Recreations* article in the December, 1984 issue of Scientific American, and on John Conway's famous simulation game, *Life*. The original vision statement set the tone for the project, but doesn't supply a lot of detail:

> In Phish, the world starts out populated by a variety of fish of many different species. Each species has rules about reproduction, movement, food supply, life span and size. These rules can change through spontaneous mutations, producing new animals with different characteristics. This game has no 'point', but it is interesting and it makes pretty patterns. The game will be given away as a promotional device.

Phish will allow us to focus on a number of important issues, including the transition between different states in an object, interactions among objects and the separation of the user interface from the underlying Phish mechanism.

Requirements Analysis

You can believe the visionary has something pretty clear in his own mind, but you certainly don't have enough to start writing code. We should start by asking the visionary to expand on his vision of the product. We'll just let him talk about what he has in mind. This will tell us a lot about what he wants and will structure the rest of the discussion.

> This is a game, or more accurately, a toy. It starts off by asking you to set up your species, and how many fish of each species you want. When you start the game the fish are born and begin to interact; eating and reproducing with one another.

> Each has rules about how to reproduce. For example, if two fish are within a certain distance of each other, and they are not starved, then they can reproduce. Every so many reproductions, there is a mutation; the children are just like the parents, but the rules have changed a bit.
>
> Each fish moves a certain distance each turn, depending on how recently it has eaten and how old it is. For example, a young fish which hasn't recently eaten will move further than either an older fish or one that has just finished eating.
>
> If fish don't eat they die. Some fish die of old age.
>
> Each instance of a species will have the basic characteristics of that species, but the individual fish within a species may vary in their particulars.

This extended description lays the foundation for further analysis. He has told you more, but much of it is done in a hand-waving fashion, that is, it is very imprecise, for example, "...if two fish are within a certain distance..." and "...every so many reproductions...".

At this point you can engage in a structured interview. Ask questions that probe at those areas that are well understood and those which need further clarification. Be sure to ask about platform considerations, performance and so forth. These questions will span the use cases, the systems analysis and the application analysis.

How does the user interact with the system?
Actually, there isn't much interaction. The user can create the species and vary their characteristics. In an advanced version, perhaps the customer can drag and drop the fish and sharks directly onto the game board. Then they set it going, and stand back.

What does it look like?
I think that depends on the platform. On Windows, I'd expect there to be a square that represents the world. In it the fish would appear as tiny dots or perhaps as small icons of a fish. Below the field would be a score report, showing information about the number of fish of each species there are right now, and the most and least there have been etc.

How does it end?
I'm not sure it ever ends. Maybe there is a button marked "End", or "Restart". At some point all the fish die out; I guess that's a pretty good end.

These questions tease out various aspects of the system and allow you to begin to formulate an idea of the overall architecture of the system. In a large project, this will quickly become overwhelming, as it is almost impossible to do an interview like this systematically. Use cases can help you structure your thinking. The use cases will make you think through the interactions with the system and they will begin to systematize your understanding of the requirements.

Use Cases

The initial use cases for Phish are:

1   The user can initialize the fish and establish their rules
2   The user can start a new game. He can determine how many fish there will be
3   The user can watch the game, observing the patterns of fish
4   The user can inject new animals into the mix

The problem with an exercise like this, is that for a problem to be small enough to explore in every detail, and to code in depth, it must be so simple that there isn't much to analyze.

Nonetheless, an interesting thing has happened even with these few use cases. The visionary seems to be implying that there can be more animals than just fish. This is a subtle hidden feature which wasn't clear from the original vision statement, and which makes the project significantly more complex.

It is time to explore the difference between a new animal and a mutation of an existing animal. Furthermore, are we going to allow the user to create an arbitrary number of animals at the beginning of the game?

As we talk this through, it becomes obvious this is a powerful mechanism. We agree that each animal will have a name (e.g. blowfish, tuna or shark). Every animal will have certain characteristics and values for those characteristics. For example, there might be a characteristic "eats other fish", which can be true or false. We will need to have a strength characteristic, measured as a number. Stronger fish can kill and eat weaker ones. We may even want more complicated rules, so we can take into account strength changing over time, depending on how recently the animal has eaten, reproduced or fought.

The initial use case of setting up the animals and establishing their rules now becomes more interesting, more complicated and more challenging. In essence, we're deciding that the user can create an arbitrary set of fish to start with, and then the system will generate mutations as it goes.

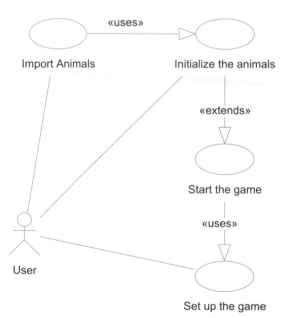

The player initializes the animals. Initializing the animals may involve setting various characteristics and behavioral patterns for the various species. Whatever is involved, initializing the animal is an extension of starting the game. You can start the game without initializing the animals. When you start the game, you also set it up, deciding how many of each animal type you want to place on the board. You always set up the game when you start the game. Thus, initializing the animals sets their characteristics; setting up the game determines how many of each species to use, and starting the game launches play.

All of this is part of the *Playing The Game* package of use cases. Thinking about this package immediately makes us realize that there is a second package, *Comparing Games*. If Phish will let us keep a record of how different fish do and which combinations are strongest and most likely to survive, then each game can influence the next. Comparing games might include:

1   The user can print a report of the game
2   The user can export information about a game to a spread sheet
3   The user can save an animal for use in future games

This third use case generates the next:

4   The user can import existing animals into their game

This clarifies what happens in setup. At setup time the game asks you to designate how many of your existing set of animals you want, and where you want to put them. Let's assemble the use cases and begin to break out their details while we name them and establish their priority:

1   The user can initialize the animals and establish their rules
2   The user can start a new game, determining how many fish and how many sharks there will be
3   The user can watch the game, observing the patterns of fish and sharks
4   The user can print a report of the game
5   The user can export information about a game to a spreadsheet
6   The user can save an animal for use in future games
7   The user can import existing animals into his game

The first and most noticeable thing is that the only actor continues to be the user. This is pretty rare, but not unheard of, especially in such a simple example.

Animal Initialization

The user can establish the rules for the set of animals at the start of the game. For each animal he can specify:

▶   The name of the animal (for example, blow fish)

▶   How many units the animal moves on a normal turn

▶   By how many units movement is increased when the animal is hungry

- By how many units movement is decreased when the animal has just eaten
- How many units of food the animal needs in five turns to survive
- How strong the animal is
- How fast the animal is
- How much the animal's strength is reduced when hungry
- How much the animal's flight speed is reduced when hungry
- How many turns between reproduction cycles
- Whether the animal is carnivorous

Preconditions: The game is not yet running.
Postconditions: The set of available animals is complete.

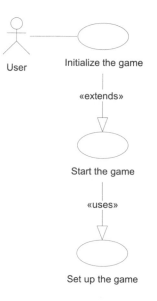

Save Animals

The user can save animals they create to a file.

Preconditions for saving: The user has created at least one type of animal.
Postconditions for saving: A file is created with the necessary information about the animal.

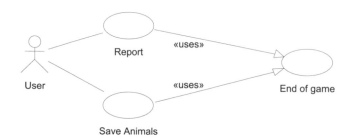

Import Animals

The user can import animals from previous games.

Preconditions for importing: There is a file in the correct format with information about the fish that you wish to import. You are in game initialization.

Postconditions for importing: The current set of fish has grown to include the imported fish.

Start a Game

The user can start a new game, choosing among the animals already recorded, and establish the starting numbers of each, as well as their starting positions on the board.

Preconditions: The game is not currently running.

Postconditions: The game is ready to run.

Run the Game

The user can watch the progress of the game.

Preconditions: Starting the game has completed.

Postconditions: The game is running.

Interact with the Game

While the game is running, the user can introduce *events*. In the first game, these include solar flares (increase mutations) and lightening strikes (kills some animals at random). Other events will be added to future versions.

Preconditions: The game is running.

Postconditions: The number of fish and/or the number of types of fish has changed.

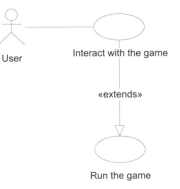

Stop the game

The user can tell the game to stop running.

Preconditions: The game is running.

Postconditions: The game is not running.

Report the Game

The user can save a report of the game, so that they can compare the performance of various animals. These reports can be printed and the information exported in comma delimited form for import into other packages, such as spreadsheets. We break out *Report the Game* from *Stop the Game*, because we may well want to develop the game with the ability to start and stop before we bother implementing the ability to report on the results.

Preconditions: The game is not running.
Postconditions: A report is generated.

Note that some of the use cases were consolidated as we broke out the detail, and one or two were split apart. This is a natural outcome of better understanding of the use cases and their relationship to one another.

Even these few use cases fit cleanly into a couple of packages, which helps us think about their organization. Our first organization is functional, set up, run, post-game:

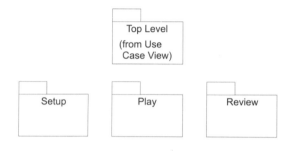

An alternative organization is to group together the most important use cases, and hold the less important use cases in a second folder. Whether or not we organize the folders, we do need to prioritize the use cases so that we know what to build first.

The most important use cases are *Game Initialization*, *Start A Game*, *Run the Game* and *Stop the Game*. Of secondary importance are the ability to *Interact With The Game*, *Report On the Game* and *Import Animals*. This tells us, right away, that we'll probably want our first iteration to provide the four primary use cases, and only subsequent iterations will take on the latter use cases.

The use case *Run the Game* is where all the action is, but we've said very little about it. What happens when the game is running? The different fish are moving, reproducing, eating and dying, but this raises several questions, for example:

▶ What causes this activity?

▶ Is each fish living independently?

▶ What is causing the fish to move?

▶ How does a fish know it is time to eat?

Clearly, each fish must be responding both to internal and external stimuli. There may be an optimization, which implements all or some of these stimuli by using a timer or a central activity manager (poking each object into action in turn), but that would be an artifact of the implementation. The domain perspective says that each animal is alive and responding to the stimulation of its environment (for example, run away, you're being chased) and its own internal stimulation (eat, you're hungry).

When we get to the design phase, we'll need to return to these very important questions about the *state* of each of the fish. For now, let's take a step back and put this game into a business perspective.

The Architecture Document

The architectural understanding of Phish is fairly straightforward. The principal use cases have been identified and the visionary has described enough of his assumptions to begin the domain analysis.

Platform Assumptions

Phish was originally conceived to be platform independent. It was our intention to release it first for our primary market, Windows 95 & Windows NT. Our second platform would probably be Unix (using the X Window System) and then finally, the Mac and OS/2.

Portability does not come without price, however, and this is a good time in the process to challenge these assumptions. Building this as a Windows-only product will be quicker, cheaper and easier. Whether or not this meets our business plan will depend on what we want to do with this product. If it is an advertisement of skills and abilities, then producing a Windows-only solution may be too narrow; if it is intended as a quick demonstration program for a book or a class on object-oriented programming, or a class on C++, then Windows may be sufficient.

The first version, therefore, will be a C++ application to run on 32-bit Windows. We will design for portability, but code for a single platform and then see how our business requirements evolve.

Extensibility and Maintainability

As a demonstration program, we expect to add features continually. The program must be designed so new requirements can be met without breaking the underlying architecture. As a learning tool, we'll probably release the source code, so we can count on developers who are not familiar with its intricacies being called upon to tinker with it. We will want to be very careful about documentation, making this project easy to maintain and upgrade as time goes on.

Reliability and Robustness

Since this project will be used as a demonstration, it is imperative that it be reliable and robust. It would be very bad to give away this program as an advertisement of our skills and then have it crash when the customer tries to run it. It should be possible to let Phish run day and night on your computer without it ever crashing and without it interfering with your other system resources. It should be light on its feet, nimble and small.

Cost and Planning

Because we'll be giving this product away, we'd like to hold costs to a minimum. Given the information currently available, I'm estimating that this job will take a few weeks of development time, spread out over the elapsed time of the development of this book (about four months).

Visualization

The visionary of Phish has a very specific user interface in mind. He sketches out some pictures for us to get us started thinking about what this product will look like:

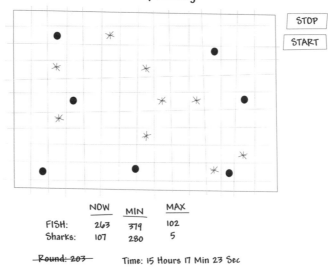

Phish - Preliminary Drawing

	NOW	MIN	MAX
FISH:	263	379	102
Sharks:	107	280	5

~~Round: 203~~   Time: 15 Hours 17 Min 23 Sec

The quality of the user interface specification will range from the very crude (as you see here) to a polished and detailed specification provided by graphic artists. Even the most crude UI visualizaiton, however, can provide useful information at this stage of the analysis.

We can see that we need to keep track of elapsed time, the maximum and minimum numbers of each species of fish in the entire game etc. This diagram doesn't act as a specification, so much as a starting point for discussion. A more complete visualization will provide details on where the information is displayed, in what size font, how large the playing board is and so forth.

Domain Analysis of Phish

From the user's perspective, the objects in the problem domain are fairly straightforward: there are algae, fish of various types and the environment (the game board). There is also a scoreboard — a display which provides feedback telling the user the state of the game, including:

▶ How much time has passed

▶ How many fish there are of each type

▶ The highest and lowest number of each type of fish so far

At this stage, we have done the initial analysis for Phish, and can map some of the relationships between the objects we have uncovered:

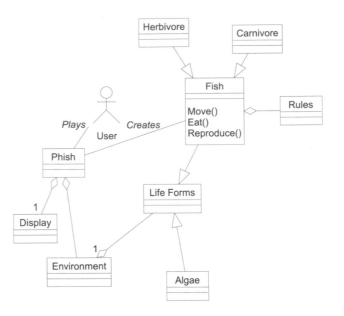

Even this simple example yields a relatively interesting diagram of the initial requirements analysis. We see the user *plays* the game. The game consists of a display, an environment and various life forms. The algae and fish are types of life forms and the user, by way of the game, can create fish. Each fish type has a set of rules.

> *This diagram is only intended to capture some of the principal relationships already understood during the requirements analysis. It is not the intention for this diagram to represent the objects in the design — those will be determined later in the process. Right now, we just want to make sure that we've understood the requirements in sufficient detail, before we begin the design in earnest.*

Class Design

Many of the issues discussed in this book will play themselves out in the design and implementation of this little game. For this project, I will serve in the role of "visionary" and customer. Advanced Technology Consulting Inc. will subcontract the implementation.

We begin with a discussion of the design guidelines. This application will initially be implemented as an MFC application to run on Windows 95 and Windows NT. Over time, we may want to move the application to a number of platforms, and so we must consider a platform-independent design.

Concurrency

We need to decide whether or not Phish will be multithreaded. Designing a multithreaded application presents certain advantages. We could make each individual fish a thread, so that the various different fish are independent of one another, thus closely mimicking the real world. Each fish would move about and interact with its environment on its own schedule.

The alternative is to have a central managing object that provides a clock "tick". At each tick, a new round of Phish commences. At each round, every fish must move, resolve any conflicts and draw itself in the new location. This is much less realistic, but it is much easier to implement.

A second advantage of this latter, centralized approach is that we avoid taxing the operating system with hundreds of threads. Each thread brings some overhead, and the game might slow considerably if we were to implement each fish in its own thread.

In addition to the raw performance consideration, in a highly multi-threaded design there will be significant contention for shared resources, all of which would need to be under synchronization control. Each thread would need to lock these resources, use them and unlock them, and the risk of deadlock would be much greater.

We therefore decide, early in the design process, that we will implement the game using the central managing object, tentatively titled the **Simulator** class. Once the application is built and debugged, we'll revisit this decision and consider re-implementing the fish themselves as worker threads.

Cross-platform

The cross-platform requirements are the most difficult. If Phish were to be a cross-platform application, we would need to be very careful about how images are rendered, and how much we relied on any specific application framework. We would want to generalize our approach to threads and take advantage of cross-platform collection classes such as the STL. The requirement that the product be cross platform will slow our time to market, but in exchange, we'll have a more flexible product.

I propose we design for cross-platform, but implement the first version within the MFC framework. This will significantly simplify the work and will shorten the time to market. We'll note those areas of the design which are most dependent on the MFC and which we'll want to break out with a layer of abstraction, so that migrating to another application framework, or to another platform, will be easier.

Persistence

Phish will need to have the ability to save its state, so that a user can shut down the game and resume it at a later time. Once this is working, we'll also want to have the user preferences persist, though we may use a different method for this data. For example, on Windows, we may save the user preferences in the registry, rather than in a data file on disk.

As a first approximation, we will implement saving the species. This information is complex and the user will find it inconvenient to create multiple species each time he starts the game. Once this is working and tested, we'll explore implementing saving and restoring the game itself, though this may not make it into the first commercial release.

Strategies and Powertypes

The requirements analysis dictates that Phish should be able to generate new "species" while the game runs (through mutation, etc.). This is particularly tricky in a language such as C++ as it is not possible to create new classes "on the fly".

We will create a powertype (discussed in Chapter 3) **PSpecies**, which will act as the discriminator for the **PAnimal** class. Note that each concrete Phish class will begin with the prefix *P*.

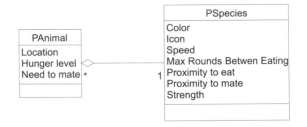

Each instance of **PAnimal** will have a reference to a single instance of **PSpecies**, but many animal instances can refer to the same instance of **PSpecies**. That instance of **PSpecies** will describe a single species of fish. Thus, if we have **Shark**, **Tuna** and **Minnow**, there will be three instances of **PSpecies**. The first instance will have its attributes set appropriate for shark, the second for tuna and the third for minnow.

Each **Shark** object (an instance of **PAnimal**) will have a pointer to the shark species instance. Each **Shark** object will know its own location, but the rules for its behavior will be dictated by the **PSpecies** object to which it points.

PAnimals will not be allowed to change their species, so the pointer must be constant throughout the game. The **PSpecies** instances will in turn delegate responsibility for determining their mating, feeding and movement behavior to a series of strategy objects, as shown in the diagram below:

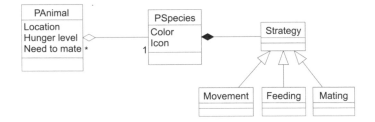

The Classes

Let's review the current class diagram. **PADisplay** is a development of the **Display** class identified earlier, **Phish** is now **PPhishTank**, and the environment is now managed by a **PSimulator** class. The big change is in the representation of the different sorts of fish:

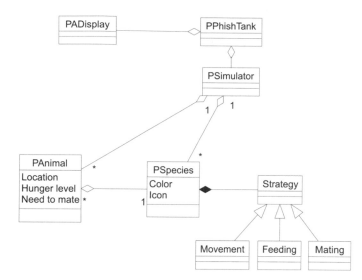

The **PAnimal** and **PSpecies** classes are aggregated by the **PSimulator** class, which is responsible for generating the clock tick that we discussed earlier. The **PSimulator** class is aggregated in turn by the **PPhishTank** which also aggregates the **PADisplay**.

The goal is to separate out responsibilities and to position the design for portability across platforms. Responsibility for displaying the Phish is delegated to the **PADisplay** class. The prefix **PA** indicates that this is an abstract type. The concrete classes derived from **PADisplay** will manage the platform-specific display details.

The **PPhishTank** thus becomes an agent, linking the display to the simulator. The simulator is responsible for the logic of the game, the display is responsible for the user interface, and together they compose a Phish tank which represents the totality of the game.

This design may be mapped to the MFC document/view design in various ways, depending on how we want to balance ease-of-programming with portability. If we make the **PPhishTank** class derive from **CApplication**, the **PADisplay** class derive from, for example, **CDialog** and the **PSimulator** class derive from **CDocument**, then we fit cleanly into the MFC architecture. Alternatively, we can derive a concrete display class (**CDisplay**) class from **PADisplay** and have **CDisplay** aggregate and delegate to the MFC view class (or a Windows window directly). Similarly, we can set aside the **CDocument** class, or we can have the **PPhishTank** object wrap the document class. The question is about the level of isolation required to allow for future portability.

Sequence Diagrams

The next step in fleshing out the design is to consider how the various objects might interact. To begin with, we'll sketch out a number of interactions. The core interaction involves the **PAnimal** instances receiving a **Tick** message from **PPhishTank**.

Each tick of the game clock represents a *time slice* in the game. Within each time slice, each animal may move and if it encounters another fish it may either eat (or be eaten by) that fish, if it is of a different species, or mate if it are of the same species.

This is demonstrated by the following sequence diagram:

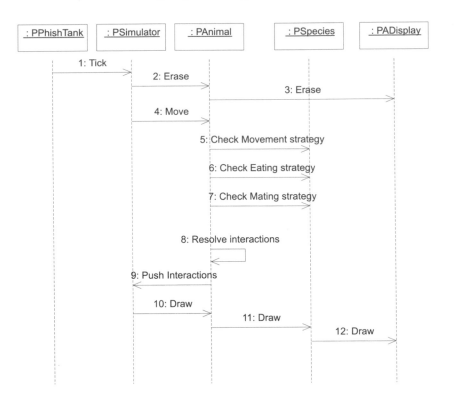

The **PPhishTank** sends the **Tick** message to the simulator. The **PSimulator** object understands a simple algorithm:

1   Tell everyone to erase

2   Tell everyone to move

3   Each animal then resolves its interactions

4   Tell everyone to redraw themselves

Note that this algorithm can easily be migrated down into the **PAnimal** class if **PAnimal** becomes a thread in its own right. For now, the **PAnimal** is told to erase itself. It collaborates with the display to erase itself. It is then told to move. It gets the **MovementStrategy** from the **PSpecies** so that it knows how far to move. It then asks **PSpecies** for the various interaction strategies (eating and mating) so that it can resolve its interactions with other **PAnimal**s. Once this is accomplished, it must feed this information back to **PSimulator**, so that other affected **PAnimal**s can be updated (e.g. any **PAnimal** object that this one eats should be removed from the simulation). Finally, the simulator tells the **PAnimal** to draw itself. The **PAnimal** delegates this to its **PSpecies** (passing in its location), because it is the **PSpecies** that knows what color and icon to use.

Creating an Animal or Species

When two fish mate, a new fish is created. The work of creating the **PAnimal** is delegated by the **PSimulator** to the **PSpecies**. It is the species which knows the range of possible values for each characteristic of the new animal. The specific value within that range is 'assigned by God' — that is to say, here it is stochastic.

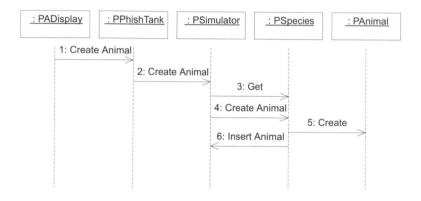

> **PPhishTank::CreateAnimal (string Name, PLocation location)**

The **CreateAnimal()** method takes two parameters: the **Name** of the species and a **location** object. The **location** object represents the site of the mating of the parent fish. There is no privacy in this game!

Animal creation is delegated to the **PSimulator**, which obtains the **PSpecies** object for the species it needs. This **PSpecies** is a singleton, which knows in turn how to create the right kind of **PAnimal**. The **PSpecies** creates the **PAnimal**, and inserts it in the **PSimulator** with which the **PSpecies** is associated. The Factory Pattern will be used to allow creation of a derived animal by a derived species.

Singleton Pattern

It is not uncommon that your design calls for a class which will never have more than a single instance. For example, in a given system there may be only a single database. An application may want to ensure that only one instance of itself is instantiated at any one time, or that there is only one open document on which there will be various views.

The Singleton Pattern (see the Design Patterns book by the Gang of Four) is typically implemented by providing a public static method (often named **Instance()**), which returns a pointer to a static instance of itself, thus:

```
Class myClassWithASingleton
{
public:
        // all creation is through this method
    static myClassWithASingleton* Instance()
protected:
    myClassWithASingleton(); // constructor
```

```
private:
   static myClassWithASingleton* theInstance
};
```

The **Instance()** method checks to see if **theInstance** is **NULL**, and if so, it creates a new instance and returns the pointer, otherwise it just returns the pointer.

```
// allocate the pointer and initialize to null
myClassWithASingleton* myClassWithASingleton::theInstance = 0;

myClassWithASingleton* myClassWithASingleton::Instance()
{
    if ( ! theInstance )
       theInstance = new myClassWithASingleton;

    return theInstance;
}
```

Prototyping

These preliminary design decisions are enough to begin prototyping the application. We decide to implement Phish in five iterations, each of which should take approximately one week of development time. We will work incrementally, so that each iteration builds on the work of the previous one:

▶ The first iteration (0) is the proof of concept, and will create a single fish and show that it can move.

▶ Iteration 1 will add a second species, and the species will be differentiated by color. We'll also add logic so that two fish cannot occupy the same space at the same time. Phish will monitor their hunger level, and when enough time passes they will starve to death.

▶ Iteration 2 will add the ability to create an unlimited set of species and will add mating and eating strategies.

▶ Iteration 3 will add object persistence and the ability to save and load the game.

▶ The final iteration (the first release) will add the configuration GUI to allow the user to set various parameters.

The goal of the prototype is to create working code early and then to improve and expand on this code as we iterate over the design and the implementation.

The entire first release will take approximately 5 weeks of development.

Implementation

Sooner or later, it is time to turn from analyzing and designing to implementing and testing. While fully analyzing the problem and designing the solution is *necessary*, it is not *sufficient* — your customer will not be happy if you deliver a specification and a well-documented design but neglect to deliver working code.

The process of implementing a program from a well-crafted design is quite different from the kind of midnight hacking we all love and miss. When you first learn to program, you typically build smaller, less-complex programs with short shelf lives, which few other programmers will need to maintain and extend. On the other hand, in today's commercial software application environment, the initial cost of development may be dwarfed by the cost of maintenance and product enhancement. It is incumbent on us to design well and, when we do, implementation becomes an exercise in realizing that design in code.

The excerpts of code shown in the rest of this chapter are taken from the source code for the example program, Phish. The full code for Phish is available for download from the Wrox website: **http://www.wrox.com**.

Implementing the Design

While Phish is a somewhat simple program, and thus has a somewhat simplified design, we have detailed along the way a number of classes and their interactions. The task now is to turn that design into C++. Along the way, there are a number of language-specific questions that must be answered, and we must constantly trade off generalized extensible solutions against quick-to-market corner-cutting "hacks".

Get Something Working, Keep it Working

My personal approach to software development is to create a small working core of functionality, and then to extend that functionality, testing each enhancement as I progress. It is important that at virtually every stage of implementation the product continues to work, though some aspects may be "stubbed out" as interim steps along the way to full functionality.

Implementation View

The best way to approach reviewing the implementation details provided by another programmer is to focus first on the physical layout of the files. Phish divides its files into different categories of class.

Categorizing the Classes

The classes are organized both functionally and also by whether or not they are platform-specific. Functionally, there are four principal sets of classes:

- Application classes (the dialogs and the application itself)
- Utility Classes (for debugging and for memory management)
- Framework Classes (specific to the MFC idioms and requirements)
- Business Objects

The term *business object* does not strictly apply here as this isn't quite a business application. Nonetheless, the broader interpretation of business objects as those objects which encapsulate the rules and protocols of the application does fit nicely. Note that most developers don't use the term *business class* but rather *business object*. I think the strongest reason for this is that business class sounds like an airline reservation.

Platform Independence

One of the design goals of Phish was to make it platform independent. While we decided that the first iteration would run on 32-bit Windows, we wanted to ensure that porting it to other platforms, including Unix and the Web, would be a fairly straightforward exercise.

Our first design decision was that we would assume we had access to a bit-mapped display and that the operating system would provide some form of image abstraction. Other than that, we were not willing to assume any other services from the OS or from whatever application framework we might use.

A Word about Naming Conventions

We've adopted the following naming conventions in the code:

▶ All class names in this implementation will begin with **P** if they are Phish specific and with **C** if they are MFC specific. Thus, all classes beginning with **C** will be replaced when we port the application to another application framework.

▶ All resource classes are prefaced with **RC**

▶ All template classes begin with **T**

▶ All member variables begin with **d**, except collections, which begin with **c**, and pointers, which begin with **p**

Application Framework Classes

The application framework classes provide the system-specific structure for the application. In an MFC application these classes include the application (**CPhishApp**) as well as the document/view architecture classes.

The job of the framework classes is to encapsulate the framework-specific requirements and also to provide an interface to the services provided by the application framework. When the application is ported to a different environment, these will be the only classes that change.

In the case of Phish, we implemented a dialog-based window for the primary view (**CPhishDlg**). There are additional dialogs, including a property page for managing the various species (**CSpeciesManagerPage**). In addition, there are classes to represent the device context, the display window, as well as icons and images.

To provide for cross-platform portability, many of the platform-specific classes are concrete implementations of platform-independent abstract base classes. For example, **CDevice**, **CDisplay**, **CImage** are derived from **PADevice**, **PADisplay** and **PAImage**.

Utility Classes

The principal utility classes provide logging and debugging assistance. These include **Function**, **FunctionTimer** and **DebugStream**. There are also utility classes for memory management, including **RCBody** and **RCHandle**.

Model Classes

The remaining classes are the business objects, also known as model classes. These include **PAnimal**, **PLocation** and **PSpecies**, as well as those classes representing the Phish tank (**PPhishTank**) and the simulator (**PSimulator**). Also included in this category are the classes that encapsulate policy and rules, such as **PResolver**.

The User Interface (UI)

The principal UI is the game board. This consists of a tank, in which the fish live, eat, breed and die, and a control area. The control area contains a status display, which provides feedback about the health and well being of the fish, as well as a set of buttons for controlling the game. The UI is shown below:

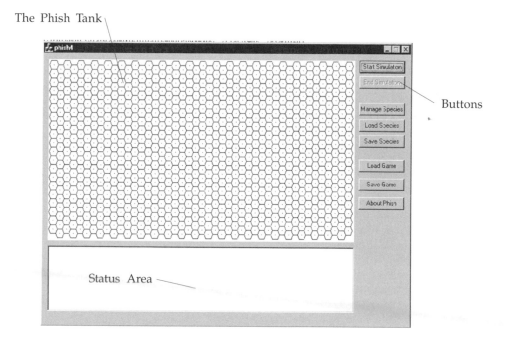

This entire window is supported as a **CDialog** in **CPhishDlg**:

```
class CPhishDlg : public CDialog
{
// Construction
public:
CPhishDlg( CWnd* pParent = NULL );       // standard constructor
~CPhishDlg();
void Update();
void ResetControls();
// Dialog Data
//{{AFX_DATA(CPhishDlg)
enum { IDD = IDD_PHISH_DIALOG };
CListBox      dStatus;
```

```
CButton       dSave;
CButton       dLoad;
CButton       dStartSim;
CButton       dManageSpecies;
CButton       dEndSim;
CPhishWnd              dPhishWnd;
//}}AFX_DATA

// ClassWizard generated virtual function overrides
//{{AFX_VIRTUAL(CPhishDlg)
protected:
virtual void DoDataExchange(CDataExchange* pDX); // DDX/DDV support
//}}AFX_VIRTUAL

// Implementation
protected:
void ResetSpecies();
HICON m_hIcon;

// Generated message map functions
//{{AFX_MSG(CPhishDlg)
virtual BOOL OnInitDialog();
afx_msg void OnSysCommand( UINT nID, LPARAM lParam );
afx_msg void OnPaint();
afx_msg void OnLoadClick();
afx_msg void OnSaveClick();
afx_msg void OnManageSpeciesClick();
afx_msg void OnStartSimClick();
afx_msg void OnEndSimClick();
afx_msg void OnTimer(UINT nIDEvent);
afx_msg void OnAboutPhish();
//}}AFX_MSG
DECLARE_MESSAGE_MAP()
private:
CFileDialog dFileOpen;
CFileDialog dFileSave;
};
```

Note that this is a wizard-generated class with handlers for the various events, such as **OnManageSpeciesClick**.

When the Manage Species button is pressed, the **OnManageSpeciesClick()** method will be called which will, in turn, bring up the Manage Species Dialog:

This dialog is designed to allow the player to create and manage the various species of Phish. In the first version of this game, new species are *not* spontaneously generated by the game itself. That feature will not be difficult to add, but for now all species are created by the user prior to beginning the game.

Each species is represented by a tab in the property sheet shown above. The various attributes of a species are captured by values, although the actual value assigned to any individual fish is not necessarily the exact number for that species — it is within a specified range for that species. Thus, if the species has a strength of 20, individual fish might range from 15 - 25.

Examine the constructor for the **PAnimal** class:

```
int PAnimal::dNextSerialNumber = 0;

PAnimal::PAnimal( const TSpeciesPtr &Species, int XPos, int YPos )
: dCurrent(XPos, YPos), pSpecies(Species), dDead (false),
dStarveTime( Species->FoodCap() ), dAge( rand()%10)
{
Function f ( "PAnimal::PAnimal" );
dLastMate = dAge;
dSerialNumber = dNextSerialNumber++;
dStrength = pSpecies->Strength() + rand() % 11 - 5;   // +-5
LogValue (dSerialNumber);
}
```

The actual strength of the individual fish is determined by starting with the overall strength of the species and then setting it to a value plus or minus five points from that starting value. This is done with the line:

```
dStrength = pSpecies->Strength() + rand() % 11-5;      // +-5
```

In a later iteration of this program, the range itself will be captured in the species — that is, some species will vary from the average more than others.

Strategy Pattern

When two fish are in the same location, the outcome of their chance encounter is determined by a strategy object, in this case a *resolver*. The **PResolver** class encapsulates the strategy of how conflicts are resolved.

Thus, one resolver might determine that when two fish encounter one another, the stronger eats the weaker. A more sophisticated resolver might implement a stochastic outcome: the stronger fish will usually win the battle, but not always. In one such implementation, the values of the two fish would establish a ratio of likely victory. Thus, if one fish had strength 20 and another 30, the first fish would win 40% of the battles and the latter fish would win 60%. A still more sophisticated resolver might take into account the length of time that had passed since each fish has eaten, mated or battled.

When we first considered the design for a strategy object, we thought we would implement it as a part of **PSpecies**, so that every object might have its own strategy for resolving conflict. For our first release, however, we need to simplify the design. As a first approximation, we decided to create the **PResolver** directly in **PSimulator**, allowing all species to share a common strategy:

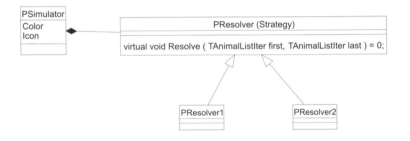

The **PResolver** class is an abstract base class, which is implemented by various concrete classes. Each of these classes implements a particular set of policies, such as, "if fish1 is stronger than fish2, fish1 eats fish2."

```
class PResolver : public RCBody
{
TSimulatorPtr pOwner;
public:
PResolver( TSimulatorPtr Owner );
virtual ~PResolver();
virtual void Resolve ( TAnimalListIter first, TAnimalListIter last ) = 0;
};
```

Note that **PResolver** derives from **RCBody**. **RCBody** is a utility class that implements smart pointers. **RCBody** will be discussed later in this chapter. The thing to notice about this class is that there is only one significant method, **Resolve()**, which is a pure virtual function. **Resolve()** takes two iterators, each of which iterates over a collection of **PAnimals**. The collection classes and their iterators will be discussed later, in the description of the utility classes and the STL.

For this example, I've implemented two resolver classes: **PResolver1** and **PResolver2**. **PResolver1** is a very simple strategy — only when two fish are in the same place must their conflict be resolved. **PResolver1** does this by saying that if they are of the same species they mate, otherwise the first one eats the second. Here is an excerpt from its **Resolve()** method:

```
if ( CurrentVal.first == hfirst->first )
{
        PAnimal &First  = *CurrentVal.second;
        PAnimal &Second = *hfirst->second;
        if ( First.SameSpecies(Second) )
        {
                First.Mate(Second);
        }
        else
        {
                First.Eat(Second);
        };
        hfirst++;
};
```

The more sophisticated strategy from **PResolver2** takes into account their relative strength:

```
if ( CurrentVal.first == hfirst->first )
{
        PAnimal &First  = *CurrentVal.second;
        PAnimal &Second = *hfirst->second;
        if ( First.SameSpecies (Second) )
        {
                First.Mate(Second);
        }
        else
        {
                int TotalStrength = First.Strength() +
                                        Second.Strength();
                if ( ( (rand() % TotalStrength ) + 1) +
                                        First.Strength() )
                {
                        First.Eat(Second);
                }
                else
                {
                        Second.Eat(First);
                };
        };
        hfirst++;
};
```

In the first release version of Phish, it is this more sophisticated strategy that is chosen every time. This is a feature that could be made an option for the user to chose at the set up stage of the game.

Once again, if two fish are in the same location and if they are of the same species, then they mate. On the other hand, if they are not of the same species this time, then their strengths are compared to decide which fish eats which. **TotalStrength** is set to the combined strength of the two fish. A random number is generated and set to the range of **1** to **TotalStrength** (by use of the modulus operator). If this new value is less than the strength of the first fish, it eats the second, otherwise the second fish eats the first.

Let's look at an example to make this a little clearer. Assume that the first fish has a strength of 60 and the second has a strength of 40. Their combined value is 100. A random number is generated and computed modulus 100, and then 1 is added. This will generate a number between 1 and 100. This is then compared with the value for the first fish (60). Any value between 1 and 60 will cause the first fish to eat the second, while any value between 61 and 100 will cause the second fish to eat the first. Thus, the odds of the first fish winning the battle are 60:40.

In a commercial program, the algorithm can be made more sophisticated. More important, you can implement the resolver as a DLL (or COM object), which can be "dropped in" at runtime. This will allow users to write their own, more sophisticated **PResolver** classes.

Other Species Values

Returning to the property sheet, we find a number of other values of interest:

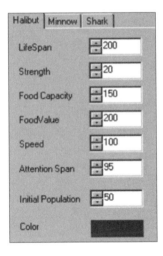

The Life Span of a species dictates that after a certain amount of time (so many rounds) the individual animals will die. Again, the particular life span of an individual fish is influenced, but not absolutely determined, by the life span of the species. You could think of this value as a life expectancy.

The Food Capacity dictates how often the fish will be hungry and the Food Value indicates how much nutrition an individual fish will supply to any other fish which eats it. Speed dictates how quickly the individual fish will move over time, and the Attention Span indicates how likely it is that the fish will change its direction of travel.

Attention span works much like strength, in that the value indicates a probability, not a deterministic number of turns. Thus, when it is time to move, if the attention span is 95, there is a 95% chance the animal will move in the same direction it moved in the previous turn. Speed works in the same way, a speed of 95 indicates there is a 95% likelihood the fish will move in a given round.

```
void PAnimal::Move () {
dAge++;
if ( dAge > pSpecies->LifeSpan() )
{
        dLast = dCurrent;
        Die();
        return;
}
if ( -- dStarveTime < 1 )
{
        dLast = dCurrent;
        Die();
        return;
}
if ( ( ( rand() % 100 ) + 1 ) > pSpecies->Speed() )
{
        return;
}
dLast = dCurrent;
if ( ( ( rand() % 100 ) + 1 ) >= pSpecies->AttentionSpan() )
{
        dCurrent.RandomDir();
}
dCurrent.Move();
}
```

When a fish is told to move it first looks to see if it has died of old age. If not, it looks to see if it has died of starvation. These are implemented as separate **if** statements. This allows us, at a later time, to write debugging code which logs the cause of death. Once we have determined that the fish is alive, the question is whether it should move in this turn, and if so, then how fast. A random number between 1 and 100 is generated and compared to the speed (which is always a value between 1 and 100). Thus if the speed is 70, 70% of the time the random number will be smaller and the fish will move.

> *You might choose to implement speed as a set of discrete values (rather than a range of 1 - 100). You might use a drop down list box with choices such as: slothful, slow, moderate, quick, speedy. Each would be assigned a value (for example, 5, 20, 40, 60, 80). The internal resolution need not change, but the UI might be more intuitive.*

Finally, another random number between 1 and 100 is generated to decide if the direction will change. If so, a random direction is chosen, otherwise the fish will move in the same direction it has been moving. When a fish hits the wall of the tank, it bounces off in the opposite direction; that is, the angle of incidence is equal to the angle of reflection.

dCurrent is a member variable of **PAnimal** which holds a **PLocation** object. The **PLocation** object encapsulates all information about the physical location of a fish and its current direction (expressed as a primary compass direction of North, East, South or West). The code for the

PLocation class is shown below:

```cpp
class PLocation {
private:
union
{
        struct
        {
                uint16 dXPos;
                uint16 dYPos;
        };
        uint32          dPos;
};
uint16                  dDir;
const static string Names[];
public:
typedef pair<uint16, uint16> TPoint;
void Move();
const string &DirName() const;
bool Correct ( const PLocation &, const PLocation &);
void SetDirName ( const string &Name );
TPoint CtrPixels () const;
TPoint NorthWestPixels() const;
TPoint SouthEastPixels() const;
void  FromPixels( const TPoint &Extent );
void  FromPixels( int x, int y );

static int Sides();
int DirCount() const { return Sides(); };

//inlines
PLocation ( int XPos = -1, int YPos = -1)
        : dXPos(XPos), dYPos(YPos)
{
        RandomDir();
};
void RandomDir ()
{
        dDir = rand()%Sides ();
};
int        Width() const                {return 11;};
int        Height() const                   {return 11;};
uint16 Dir  ()     const        {return dDir;};
uint16 XPos() const             {return dXPos;};
uint16 YPos() const             {return dYPos;};
uint32 Pos  ()     const                {return dPos;};
void   XPos(uint16 XPos)        {dXPos = XPos;};
void   YPos(uint16 YPos)        {dYPos = YPos;};
void   Dir  (uint16 Dir )               {dDir=Dir;};
bool Equals         ( const PLocation &rhs ) const
{
```

```
        return (dDir==rhs.dDir) && (dPos==rhs.dPos);
};
PLocation &IncX ()
{
        ++dXPos;
        return *this;
};
PLocation &IncY ()
{
        ++dYPos;
        return *this;
};
PLocation &DecX ()
{
        --dXPos;
        return *this;
};
PLocation &DecY ()
{
        --dYPos;
        return *this;
};
static PLocation Random ( const PLocation &MaxLoc )
{
        return PLocation (rand()%MaxLoc.dXPos, rand()%MaxLoc.dYPos);
};
};
```

The final values in the species management property sheet are Initial Population and Color. The initial population dictates how many of each species will be created when you push Start Simulation button. The color indicates how the Phish will be rendered on the screen, and can be adjusted by clicking on the color swatch, which brings up the standard color dialog.

Kill Your Own Children

I once worked for Larry Weiss, who was at the time Executive Vice President of Citibank and Director of the Development Division. Larry told me that all developers fall in love with their own ideas and innovations, and that the really great developers are not afraid to "kill their own children" — to set aside their pet ideas or innovations when they no longer make sense.

When we first considered Phish, we wanted to create a way to allow the user to set the starting number of fish for each species. The device we created was a combination combo box and slider:

The idea was that you would drop down the combo box to reveal the various species, and as you chose them, the slider would reflect how many fish would be created for each. As you changed your selection, the slider would show the current selection for each species.

To support this, we created the **CSynchroComboBox** class:

```
class CSynchroComboBox : public CComboBox
{
auto_ptr<TIntSource> pSource;
// Construction
public:
CSynchroComboBox( TIntSource *Source );

// Attributes
public:
void SyncValue();
// Operations
public:

// Overrides
// ClassWizard generated virtual function overrides
//{{AFX_VIRTUAL(CSynchroComboBox)
//}}AFX_VIRTUAL

// Implementation
public:
virtual ~CSynchroComboBox();
// Generated message map functions
protected:
//{{AFX_MSG(CSynchroComboBox)
afx_msg void OnCloseup();
afx_msg void OnDblclk();
afx_msg void OnDropdown();
afx_msg void OnEditchange();
afx_msg void OnEditupdate();
afx_msg void OnErrspace();
afx_msg void OnKillfocus();
afx_msg void OnSelchange();
afx_msg void OnSelendcancel();
afx_msg void OnSelendok();
afx_msg void OnSetfocus();
afx_msg HBRUSH CtlColor(CDC* pDC, UINT nCtlColor);
afx_msg void ParentNotify(UINT message, LPARAM lParam);
//}}AFX_MSG

DECLARE_MESSAGE_MAP()
};
```

This class is derived from **CComboBox** and keeps a smart pointer to an integer source. An integer source is any control which evaluates to an integer. **TIntSource** is an abstract base type providing an interface for any control which could set and return an integer value. A **CSlider** is such an integer source.

```
class TIntSource
{
public:
TIntSource(){};
virtual ~TIntSource(){};
virtual int value() const = 0;
virtual void value (int) = 0;
};
```

To make the code as flexible as possible, we designed a derived and parameterized type, **TIntSourceAdapter**:

```
template<class T>
class TIntSourceAdaptor : public TIntSource
{
public:
typedef int (T::*TGetFn)()const;
typedef void (T::*TSetFn)(int);
private:
T &              dSource;
TGetFn         dGetter;
TSetFn         dSetter;

public:
TIntSourceAdaptor( T &Source, TGetFn Getter, TSetFn Setter )
      : dSource(Source), dGetter(Getter), dSetter(Setter)
{
}
int value() const
{
      return (dSource.*dGetter)();
}
void value ( int rhs )
{
      (dSource.*dSetter)(rhs);
}
};
```

This class implements **TIntSource**, and adds a reference to the source object, as well as two pointers to member functions. The first pointer-to-member function is **TGetFn**, which returns **int**, takes no parameters and is constant — the typical signature for an accessor get function. The second, **TSetFn** returns void but takes an **int** as its parameter — the typical set function.

The constructor takes as parameters the source object and the two pointer-to-member functions and initializes the member variables. Calling the function **value()**, which overrides the pure virtual function in the base class, calls the appropriate accessor function.

With this design, we can make the **CSlider** control a **TIntSourceAdaptor**, and thus a **TIntSource**, which can thereby be attached to the **CSynchroComboBox**. Each entry in the **CSynchroComboBox** is a string to display, together with the value extracted from the **CSlider**. As one changes, the other is updated.

313

This design was elegant, object-oriented and quite appealing. In the end, we changed our minds. It just didn't work psychologically; we felt that the customer wouldn't make the connection between the combo box and the slider. It was tempting to keep it just because it was "cool", but we opted to toss the entire design and move the control of the number of fish of each species off the main interface and back to the property sheets.

The UI — Abstract and Platform Specific

While we have decided that out first version of Phish will run on 32-bit Windows, we want our design to maintain a level of abstraction, so that the task of moving Phish to another platform is as straightforward as possible. To this end, we abstract the display from the specific platform-dependent implementation and create **PADisplay** as an abstract base class. The **PADisplay** class provides an abstract representation of the display, and will be overridden by the framework-specific display class. The **PADisplay** class is shown below:

```
class PADisplay : public RCBody
{
public:
 int Height() const {return dHeight;};
 int Width()  const {return dWidth;};
 PADisplay();
 virtual ~PADisplay();
 virtual PADisplay *NewInstance() const = 0;
 virtual void DrawTo ( const PADevice &Device ) = 0;
 virtual void Draw
                   (const PLocation &Loc, const TImagePtr &Icon )=0;
 virtual void Draw (int x, int y, const TImagePtr &Bitmap ) = 0;
 virtual void Erase (const PLocation &Loc )=0;
 virtual void Resize (int width, int height )=0;
 virtual TImagePtr CreateBitmap
                           (const string &Name, RGBColor Color )=0;
protected:
 RGBColor dBackColor;
 int dHeight;
 int dWidth;
 typedef RCHandle<PAImage> TImagePtr;
};
```

In the MFC application, this class is made concrete by **CDisplay**. The concrete implementation of **CreateBitmap()** in **CDisplay** is framework- and operating-system dependent, as you would expect:

```
TImagePtr CDisplay::CreateBitmap (const string &Name, RGBColor ForeColor
)
{
if (!dMemDC) return TImagePtr();
HWND hDesktop = GetDesktopWindow();
CWnd Desktop;
Desktop.Attach (hDesktop);
```

```
CWindowDC DummyDC (&Desktop);
Desktop.Detach();
static int LastPos = 0;

CBitmap bwBitmap;
bwBitmap.LoadBitmap (Name.c_str());
CDC bwMemDC;
bwMemDC.CreateCompatibleDC (&dMemDC);
bwMemDC.SelectObject (&bwBitmap);
BITMAP TemporarySolution;
bwBitmap.GetObject
            (sizeof(TemporarySolution), &TemporarySolution);
const int SrcHeight = TemporarySolution.bmHeight;
const int SrcWidth  = TemporarySolution.bmWidth;
DummyDC.BitBlt (LastPos, 0, 11, 11, &bwMemDC, 0, 0, SRCCOPY);
LastPos+=10;


CDC colMemDC;
colMemDC.CreateCompatibleDC(&dMemDC);
CBitmap *pcolBitmap = new CBitmap;
CBitmap &colBitmap = *pcolBitmap;

colBitmap.CreateCompatibleBitmap(&DummyDC, SrcHeight, SrcWidth);
colBitmap.GetObject
            (sizeof(TemporarySolution),&TemporarySolution);

bwBitmap.GetObject
            (sizeof(TemporarySolution),&TemporarySolution);
colMemDC.SelectObject (&colBitmap);
colMemDC.SetBkColor (ConvertColor(dBackColor));
colMemDC.SetTextColor (ConvertColor(ForeColor));
colMemDC.BitBlt
            (0, 0, SrcWidth, SrcHeight, &bwMemDC, 0, 0, SRCCOPY);
DummyDC.BitBlt(LastPos,0,10,10,&colMemDC, 0,0,SRCCOPY);
LastPos+=10;


colMemDC.SelectObject ((CBitmap*)0);
return TImagePtr (new CImage(pcolBitmap));
};
```

All these ugly details are encapsulated by the platform-specific classes and hidden to clients of **PADisplay**, as they should be. The abstract display class knows that it has a height, width and background color, but not how these are manipulated. The concrete display class manages device contexts, bit maps, pixels and so forth.

The **PADisplay** works hand in glove with the abstract base class **PADevice** and the concrete **CDevice**. Again, the specifics of the operating system devices are hidden behind the abstraction layer.

Using the PADisplay

The **CPhishDlg** dialog class has a member variable, **dPhishWnd**, which is an instance of the class **CPhishWnd**. This represents the window in which we'll display the Phish tank. **CPhishWnd** is a **CStatic** window and is MFC specific, as is **CPhishDlg**.

CPhishWnd in turn contains a data member, **dTank** — an instance of the **PPhishTank** class. A **PPhishTank** object contains a **TDisplayPtr**, which is a pointer to a **PADisplay**:

```
typedef RCHandle<PADisplay> TDisplayPtr;
```

This allows us to polymorphically create concrete display objects (such as **CDisplay**), which can be platform-specific.

```
class PPhishTank : public RCBody
{
protected:
 TDisplayPtr          pDisplay;
```

The constructor of the **CPhishWnd** creates the **PPhishTank** passing in a new **CDisplay** (derived from **PADisplay**):

```
CPhishWnd::CPhishWnd() : dTank(new CDisplay)
{
}
```

When the **PPhishTank** or the **PSimulator** object need to be drawn, the work is delegated to **PPhishTank**'s **pDisplay** member, thus creating platform-specific implementations of all the drawing methods.

The Utility Classes

Phish, like any substantial program, requires a certain amount of infrastructure support. In a large commercial application, this support will often be provided by a dedicated team of "tool builders". Many other utility classes can be purchased as part of a library of classes sold by third party vendors. The principal utility classes in Phish provide counted pointers and debugging support.

Counted Pointers

Counted pointers were described in the last chapter. They provide a more efficient use of memory and reduce the likelihood of memory leaks. Phish implements counted pointers with two classes:

- RCBody
- RCHandle

The handle/target idiom was described in detail in the counted pointer section in the last chapter. In this implementation, the **RCHandle** class is parameterized. This allows you to create a handle to any class derived from the target, **RCBody**, and allows you to treat these objects polymorphically through the handle.

You cannot use the handle to delete the object it holds, but you can dereference the handle as you might dereference a pointer, or you can call member functions through the handle. It is nearly impossible to inadvertently delete the object itself — you would have to write,

```
delete &(*ptr)
```

or:

```
delete ptr.operator->();
```

Neither is a likely mistake. The implementation of the handle/target algorithm is fairly straightforward. The hard part is in managing the count of objects and writing the wrapper code so that clients can use the handle as if it were the object itself.

```
template<class T>
class RCHandle
{
public:
int compare ( const RCHandle &rhs ) const
{
        return compare(rhs.dBody);
}

int compare ( const RCBody *rhs ) const
{
        return ( rhs == dBody ? 0 : ( dBody > rhs ? 1 : -1 ) );
}

    RCHandle ( RCBody *Body = 0)
       : dBody(Body)
    {
if ( dBody )
       {
             dBody->inc();
       }
    }

    RCHandle          ( const RCHandle &rhs )
       : dBody(rhs.dBody)
    {
if ( dBody )
       {
             dBody->inc();
       }
    }

    RCHandle &operator = ( const RCHandle &rhs )
    {
       if ( rhs.dBody )
       {
             rhs.dBody->inc();
```

```
        }

        if ( dBody )
        {
                dBody->dec()
        }

        dBody = rhs.dBody;
        return *this;
    }
    virtual ~RCHandle              ()
    {
        if ( dBody )
        {
                dynamic_cast<RCBody&>(*dBody).dec();
        }
    }

    T*          operator->()          { return      asT(); }
    T&          operator* ()          { return     *asT(); }
    const T*    operator->()  const   { return      asT(); }
    const T&    operator* ()  const   { return     *asT(); }

    operator          bool()  const   { return dBody?true:false; }

    static void Swap ( RCHandle &lhs, RCHandle &rhs )
    {
        RCBody *Temp = lhs.dBody;
        lhs.dBody = rhs.dBody;
        rhs.dBody = Temp;
    }

    void Release ( void )
    {
        if ( dBody )
        {
                dBody->dec();
                dBody = 0;
        }
    }

private:
    RCBody *dBody;

    T* asT ()
    {
        assert(dBody);
        return (T*)dBody;
    }
    const T* asT()  const
    {
```

```
        assert(dBody);
        return (T*)dBody;
    }
};
```

Note that the **RCHandle** contains a pointer to an **RCBody**. The **asT** private helper functions manage the casting and the accessor operators (that is, **operator->** and **operator***) return either a pointer or a reference to the held object. These accessors are overloaded for **const** and non-**const**, which allows the handle to be used as either a constant or non-constant pointer or reference. It is for such casting that the **RCHandle** is made a template.

The corresponding **RCBody** class is an abstract base class from which you will inherit any classes for which you want to be able to create handles. The code for this class is shown below:

```
class RCBody {
public:
    void inc()
    {
        assert(dRefCount>=0);
        dRefCount++;
    }
    bool dec()
    {
        assert(dRefCount>0);
        --dRefCount;
        if ( !dRefCount )
        {
            delete this;
            return true;
        }
        return false;
    }
protected:
    RCBody()
        :dRefCount(0)
    {
    }
    virtual ~RCBody() = 0
    {
        assert(!dRefCount);
    }
private:
    int dRefCount;

};
```

Standard Template Library (STL)

Phish is awash in collections, all of which are implemented using the STL. The two collections which are used most extensively in Phish are the **vector** and **map**. We'll also look at the *pair* which holds two related values. Vectors are sequence collections and are described in the persistence chapter (Chapter 6). Maps are associative collections: a map associates a key with a value. These matched keys and values are implemented as *pairs*. You can manipulate pairs either within maps or simply as objects in their own right.

The **PSimulator** class uses all three of these collections, along with iterators for the vector and the map. To understand how they are used, we start by exploring the simulator. Look at this diagram:

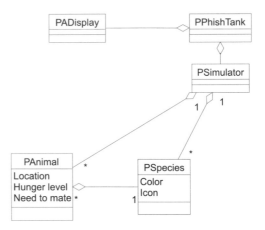

The **PPhishTank** is essentially the application itself. It has a display and a simulator. The display is responsible for the user interface, and the simulator is responsible for the state of the game.

The **PSimulator** is where all the action is, and this class is worth examining in some detail. It keeps a collection of every **PSpecies** object known to the game. Each **PSpecies** object will be held in an **RCHandle**:

```
typedef RCHandle<PSpecies>                TSpeciesPtr;
```

This declaration allows us to use the type **TSpeciesPtr** to refer to any object that acts as a pointer to a **PSpecies** object. Thus, you can declare a **TSpeciesPtr**, or you can declare a collection of them.

```
typedef map<string,TSpeciesPtr>           TSpeciesMap;
```

This line creates the type **TSpeciesMap** as a map of a string to a **TSpeciesPtr**. That is, it maps a character string to an **RCHandle** on a **PSpecies** object.

PSimulator keeps an instance of such a collection as a private member variable:

```
mutable TSpeciesMap cSpecies;
```

cSpecies is the collection of species known to a given simulator. (Remember, we are using a notation whereby all collections are prefixed with the letter **c**.) At the beginning of the game, this map will be initialized from the default species file, and the user can add to the map by creating new species, deleting species or editing existing species.

Loading The Defaults

When the game begins the **CPhishDlg**'s **initDialog()** method is called by the application framework. Here's what it does in pseudo code:

```
BOOL CPhishDlg::OnInitDialog()
{
        CDialog::OnInitDialog(); // chain up to the base class

        //... ( set up the menus )

        //... ( set the icons )

        //... ( size the tank )

        ResetSpecies(); // load the default species
        ResetControls(); // enable and disable controls appropriately
}
```

The method **ResetSpecies()** is responsible for reading **Default.phi** — the default file which loads the species:

```
void CPhishDlg::ResetSpecies()
{
PPhishTank &Tank = dPhishWnd.Tank();
        //...
        try
        {
                Tank.LoadFile("Default.phi");
        }
        //...
TStringList Species =       Tank.SpeciesNames();
TStringListIter first =     Species.begin();
TStringListIter last  =     Species.end();
}
```

Tank's **LoadFile()** method opens the file into an **ifstream** and calls the **PSimulator**'s **ReadFrom()** method passing in that stream. The **ReadFrom()** method is a bit complex, and the code for it is shown below:

```
const static string ClassName = typeid(PSimulator).name();

TSimulatorPtr PSimulator::ReadFrom ( istream &stream )
{
TSimulatorPtr pSimulator(new PSimulator());
int Count;
string CName;
char ch;
stream >> ch;
getline(stream,CName,',');
if ( CName != ClassName )
{
```

```
        throw exception ( "Corrupt input stream" );
};
stream >> Count >> ch;
for (;Count;--Count)
{
        PSpecies::ReadFrom(stream)->SetSimulator(pSimulator);
        stream >> ch;
};
return pSimulator;
};
```

First, **ClassName** is declared and initialized with the string returned by calling the **name()** method on the object returned by the **typeid()** operator, which is passed **PSimulator**. The net effect of this is that **ClassName** contains the string **PSimulator**.

Next, a new **PSimulator** is created and its address is returned as a pointer, stored in **pSimulator**. One character is read from the file and stored in the **char** variable, **ch**, and then a line is read up to the first comma, and stored in **CName**. **CName** is compared with **ClassName** to ensure we are reading what we expect. Here's the file that is being read:

```
(class PSimulator,3,(class
PSpecies,Halibut,100,150,200,95,200,20,50,16711680),(class
PSpecies,Minnow,96,98,97,95,100,99,94,8388863),(class
PSpecies,Shark,100,150,200,95,500,200,50,4194368))
```

The first character, read into **ch**, is the parentheses. Thus, the string, **CName**, contains **"class PSimulator"**. This will match the return value stored in **ClassName**, so the exception won't be thrown and we can proceed to create the various species objects.

The value, **3**, is streamed into the variable **Count**, and the **for** loop will iterate three times to pick up each of the species. For each one, the **PSpecies** method, **ReadFrom()**, is called. This will return a **PSpecies** object, on which we call **SetSimulator()**, passing in the just created **PSimulator**. The net effect is that the species are created and inserted into the collection in the new **PSimulator**, which is then returned.

The **PSpecies**'s **ReadFrom()** method is quite similar:

```
TSpeciesPtr PSpecies::ReadFrom ( istream &stream )
{
string CName;
string Name;
int        Speed;
int        FoodCap;
int        FoodValue;
int        AttentionSpan;
int        LifeSpan;
int        Strength;
int        Population;
RGBColor Color;
char ch;
```

```
    stream >> ch;
    getline(stream,CName,',');
    getline(stream,Name,',');
    stream >> Speed;
    ch = 0;
    stream >> ch;
    stream >> FoodCap;
    ch = 0;
    stream >> ch;
    stream >> FoodValue;
    ch = 0;
    stream >> ch;
    stream >> AttentionSpan;
    ch = 0;
    stream >> ch;
    stream >> LifeSpan;
    ch = 0;
    stream >> ch;
    stream >> Strength;
    ch = 0;
    stream >> ch;
    stream >> Population;
    ch = 0;
    stream >> ch;
    stream >> Color;
    stream >> ch;
    return TSpeciesPtr ( new PSpecies (Name, Speed, FoodCap, FoodValue,
                                        AttentionSpan, LifeSpan,
Strength,
                                        Population, Color) );
    };
```

Each value is read out of the file and stashed in a local variable. These are then used as parameters to the constructor of a species, which is returned. Once the species is returned, the method **SetSimulator()** of the **PSpecies** object is called:

```
void PSpecies::SetSimulator ( RCHandle<PSimulator> &Simulator )
{
assert(!pSimulator);
pSimulator = Simulator;
Simulator->AddSpecies(RCHandle<PSpecies>(this));
};
```

The species is set to point to the **PSimulator** object, to which it will now add itself. It then calls the **PSimulator**'s **AddSpecies()** method:

```
void PSimulator::AddSpecies ( const TSpeciesPtr &Species )
{
cSpecies.insert(TSpeciesMapVal(Species->Name(), Species));
};
```

323

cSpecies is, you may remember, the member variable of **PSimulator** which holds a map of **PSpecies** objects. We call **insert()** on this collection, passing in the name of the species and the **PSpecies** object itself. **TSpeciesMapVal** is a **typedef** of **TSpeciesMap::value_type**. A **value_type** is a **typedef** supplied by the standard library:

```
typedef pair<const Key, T> value_type
```

The net effect is that the species is read from the file, created and inserted into the collection in the **PSimulator**.

Starting the Simulation

When the user clicks the Start Simulation button on the dialog, it calls the **CPhishWnd**'s **StartSimulation()** method. This in turn calls the **PPhishTank**'s **StartSimulation()** method — an in-line method that resizes the display and then calls the **PSimulator**'s **StartSimulation()** method. This is shown below:

```
void PSimulator::StartSimulation ()
{
bool Invalid = false;
int Count = 0;
dRound = 0;

TSpeciesMapIter first,last;
first = cSpecies.begin();
last  = cSpecies.end();

int count = 0;

for ( ;first != last; ++first )
{
        count += first->second->Population();
        first->second->CreateInitial( dBottomRight );
}
dStatus.Reset(count);
dRunning = true;
};
```

Two iterators, **first** and **last**, are created against the collection of **PSpecies**. The **TSpeciesMapIter** type is a **typedef**:

```
typedef RCHandle<PSpecies>                TSpeciesPtr;
typedef map<string,TSpeciesPtr>           TSpeciesMap;
typedef TSpeciesMap::iterator             TSpeciesMapIter;
```

Thus, the iterator is against a map, which matches strings to **PSpecies** smart pointers. **cSpecies** is the collection of **PSpecies** objects held by the **PSimulator** itself. The iterators **first** and **last** are initialized with the first and last objects in the collection.

The **for** loop iterates through the collection. Here's how this works. The iterator is against a map, and thus returns a pair. The pair consists of **first** (the string name of the species) and **second** (the **PSpecies** object itself). We ask **first** (the first iterator) for **second** (the **PSpecies** object itself) and call **Population()** and then **CreateInitial()** on that object.

The actual work of populating the tank is delegated to the species itself, in the call to **CreateInitial()** (passing in the location of the bottom-right pixel of the display):

```
void PSpecies::CreateInitial ( const PLocation &MaxLoc )
{
for ( int i = 0; i < dPopulation; i++ )
{
        pSimulator->AddPhish(TAnimalPtr
                      (new PAnimal (this, PLocation::Random( MaxLoc ))));
}

}
```

This creates a new **PAnimal** object, passing in the **PSpecies** (as the **this** pointer) and the results of calling **Random()**, a static method on **PLocation**. The **Random()** method looks like this:

```
static PLocation Random ( const PLocation &MaxLoc )
{
    return PLocation ( rand() % MaxLoc.dXPos, rand() % MaxLoc.dYPos);
};
```

This returns a location whose **x** and **y** values are within the bounds set by **MaxLoc** (maximum location). The net result is that a new animal is created at a random location, and the pointer is passed to the **PSimulator**'s **AddPhish()** method, which adds the newly created **PAnimal** object to the **PSimulator**'s **cSpecies** collection.

Playing the Game

For the first version, the entire game is played in "rounds", and each round is set off by a timer tick. The **CPhishWnd** class establishes a timer, and responds to that timer in its **OnTimer()** method:

```
void CPhishWnd::OnTimer(UINT nIDEvent)
{
bool Done = !dTank.Tick();
Invalidate();
CStatic::OnTimer(nIDEvent);
if ( Done )
{
        KillTimer(0);
};
}
```

This simple logic calls the **PPhishTank**'s **Tick()** method. If it gets back **false**, it will kill the timer. The **Tick()** method delegates responsibility to the **PSimulator**, passing along a pointer to the display. The **PSimulator**'s **Tick()** method manages each round of the game, as illustrated by code below. I will show small excerpts of the code from **Tick()**, one at a time, and then discuss each section as I go through. The first excerpt is shown below:

```
bool PSimulator::Tick( PADisplay &Display )
{
//...
dRound++;
static RCHandle<PResolver> pResolver = new PResolver2(this);
```

The method begins by creating a **PResolver1** (strategy) object to resolve conflicts when two fish are in the same location.

```
TAnimalListIter first, last;
first = cAnimals.begin();
last  = cAnimals.end();
if ( first == last )
{
        EndSimulation();
        return false;
}
while ( first != last )
{
        (*first)->Move();
        (*first)->CorrectPos(dTopLeft,dBottomRight);
        first++;
}
```

An iterator is created for the collection of animals, **cAnimals**, held by **PSimulator**. If the **first** and **last** animals in the iterator are identical, then all of the animals must have died and the simulation is over. Assuming that is not true, then each fish is told to move. After it moves, its position is corrected to ensure that it stays in the tank (bouncing off the glass walls of the Phish tank).

```
if ( cAnimals.size() > 1 )
{
        pResolver->Resolve(cAnimals.begin(), cAnimals.end());
}
```

Once all the fish have moved, the entire set is resolved. Note that in this version the resolver is hard-wired; as mentioned earlier, but this will be more flexible in future versions. A simple first improvement would be to set the resolver based on a value in a dialog box or in a **.ini** file. Eventually the system should register a resolver object using the standard COM interface protocols.

```
first = cAnimals.begin();
last  = cAnimals.end();
while ( first != last )
{
        PAnimal & Current = **first;        // Cache this for later
```

```
            bool Moved = Current.Moved();      // This too
            bool Dead  = Current.Dead();       // This too.
            if ( Moved || Dead )
            {
                    Current.Erase(Display);
                    if ( Dead )
                    {
                            // Pre-Decrement last, since it points to the
                            // imaginary animal past the end of the array,
                            // or to the first dead animal

                            --last;
                            TAnimalPtr::Swap( *first, *last );

                            // *first is now a differant animal, try again.

                            continue;
                    }

                    else

                    {
                    first++;
                            // We now know we don't have to revisit *first
                            // And we know it has moved.
                            Current.Draw(Display);
                    }
            }
            else
            {
                    first++;
            }
    }
```

This code is fairly straightforward. The outer **while** loop iterates through the collection of **PAnimal**s. If the **PAnimal** object has moved or is dead, we must erase it so that it can be redrawn. If it is dead, we swap it with the last **PAnimal**, thus bubbling all the dead animals to the end of the array where they can be chopped off all at one fell swoop.

```
first = last; // This is the first dead animal
last  = cAnimals.end();
if ( first != last ) {
       cAnimals.erase(first,last);
};
return true;
};
```

Each of the animals has now been moved and resolved, and all the corpses have been removed. It is time to redraw. The call to **Invalidate()** in the **CPhishWnd** causes the **PSimulator** to redraw. The **PSimulator** tells all the **PAnimal**s to draw themselves, and they in turn delegate the responsibility to the **PSpecies**, passing in their current location and the display device in which to draw themselves.

```
void PSpecies::Draw(PADisplay & Display, const PLocation &Location)
{
TImagePtr &Image = dImageMap[Location.DirName()];
if ( !Image ) {
        Image = Display.CreateBitmap(Location.DirName(),dColor);
};
Display.Draw(Location,Image);
}
```

The **PSpecies** keeps a map of the images of the species pointing in various directions; the location's **DirName** returns the direction which is used as an offset into that map. The location and **Image** are then given to the **CDisplay**.

```
void CDisplay::Draw(const PLocation &Loc, const TImagePtr &Icon)
{
TPoint Point = Loc.NorthWestPixels();
Draw(Point.first, Point.second, Icon);
}
```

This method converts the **PLocation** object into a pair **TPoint** object, and then calls its own **Draw()** method, passing in the starting and ending points and the **Icon** to draw. This **Draw()** method gets the bitmap and calls **BitBlt()** to render the image in the correct location.

Summary

Creating the code from the design can be a fairly straightforward process if your design is reasonably complete. The sequence diagrams dictate the class interface and the state and activity diagrams guide the behavior of the member methods.

In a larger project you typically spend more time fleshing out the design before beginning implementation. In a smaller project, such as Phish you may find that you are eager to get to the code and that you make lighter demands on the design; keeping more in your head and less on paper.

In Conclusion

The development of software can be the most fun you can have alone in an office. It is a fascinating mixture of business and marketing insight, technological skill, planning, creative spark and dogged determination.

When I started with microcomputers, it was realistic for one person to teach himself everything he needed to know in 9-12 months. Today, no one can learn it all. Keeping up with new languages, component technology, methodologies, operating systems and multimedia development platforms is simply overwhelming. Software has become more complex, customer expectations have risen and the pace of change continues to increase.

Object-oriented analysis and design methodology is not a universal panacea. It won't provide you with a market, it won't manage your project delivery, it won't shield you from incompetent management or marketing, it won't even teach you to write clever code. It will, however, help you manage the complexity of your design and communicate your plan to other developers. I'm convinced that the fundamentals of design and modeling described in this book will stand up to the test of time.

I'm thrilled that you were willing to stick with me as we explored this technology, and I look forward to hearing from you about how things work out for you as you apply these techniques. Please feel free to contact me at **jliberty@libertyassociates.com**. You can also find supplementary material for this book at the Wrox website: **http//:www.wrox.com**, or at my web site: **http://www.libertyassociates.com** — just click on **Books & Resources**.

Thank you again.

Jesse Liberty
February, 1998

Appendix A - UML Notation

Classes and Objects

A class is represented in the UML like this:

Class
attribute1 attribute2
MethodA() MethodB()

The rectangle representing the class is divided into three compartments, the top one showing the class name, the second showing the attributes and the third showing the methods.

An object looks very similar to a class, except that its name is underlined:

<u>AnObject</u>
attribute1 attribute2
MethodA() MethodB()

Relationships

Relationships between classes are generally represented in class diagrams by a line or an arrow joining the two classes. UML can represent the following, different sorts of object relationships.

Dependency

If **A** depends on **B**, then this is shown by a dashed arrow between **A** and **B**, with the arrowhead pointing at **B**:

Association

An association between **A** and **B** is shown by a line joining the two classes:

If there is no arrow on the line, the association is taken to be bidirectional. A unidirectional association is indicated like this:

Aggregation

An aggregation relationship is indicated by placing a white diamond at the end of the association next to the aggregate class. If **B** aggregates **A**, then **A** is a part of **B**, but their lifetimes are independent:

Composition

Composition, on the other hand, is shown by a black diamond on the end of association next to the composite class. If **B** is composed of **A**, then **B** controls the lifetime of **A**.

Multiplicity

The multiplicity of a relationship is indicated by a number (or *) placed at the end of an association.

The following diagram indicates a one-to-one relationship between **A** and **B**:

This next diagram indicates a one-to-many relationship:

A multiplicity can also be a range of values. Some examples are shown below:

1	One and only one
*	Any number from 0 to infinity
0..1	Either 0 or 1
n..m	Any number in the range n to m inclusive
1..*	Any positive integer

Naming an Association

To improve the clarity of a class diagram, the association between two objects may be named:

Inheritance

An inheritance (generalization/specialization) relationship is indicated in the UML by an arrow with a triangular arrowhead pointing towards the generalized class.

If **A** is a base class, and **B** and **C** are classes derived from **A**, then this would be represented by the following class diagram:

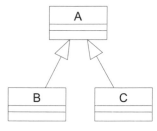

Multiple Inheritance

The next diagram represents the case where class **C** is derived from classes **A** and **B**:

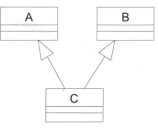

States

States of objects are represented as rectangles with rounded corners. The *transition* between different states is represented as an arrow between states, and a *condition* of that transition occurring may be added between square braces. This condition is called a guard.

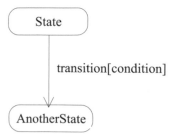

333

Object Interactions

Interactions between objects are represented by interaction diagrams — both sequence and collaboration diagrams. An example of a collaboration diagram is shown below. Objects are drawn as rectangles and the lines between them indicate links — a link is an instance of an association. The order of the messages along the links between the objects is indicated by the number at the head of the message:

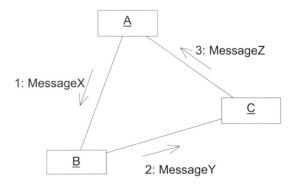

Sequence diagrams show essentially the same information, but concentrate on the time-ordered communication between objects, rather than their relationships. An example of a sequence diagram is shown below. The dashed vertical lines represent the lifeline of the object:

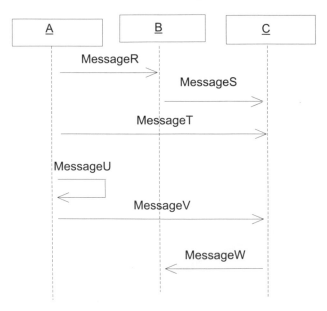

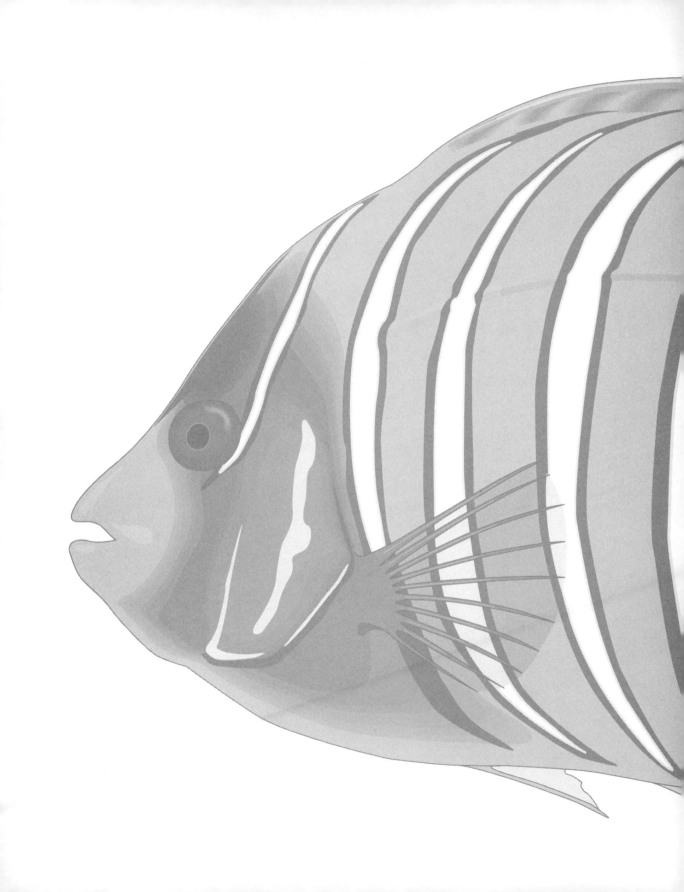

B

Bibliography

UML

UML Distilled,
Martin Fowler, Addison-Wesley, 1997, ISBN 0-201-32563-2

Instant UML,
Pierre-Alain Muller, Wrox Press, 1997, ISBN 1-861000-87-1

OOA&D

Object-oriented Design Heuristics,
Arthur J Riel, Addison-Wesley, 1997, ISBN 0-201-63385-X

Clouds to Code,
Jesse Liberty, Wrox Press, 1997, ISBN 1-861000-95-2

Using CRC Cards,
Nancy M Wilkinson, Sigs, 1995, ISBN 1-884842-07-0

The 4+1 View Model of Architecture,
Philippe Krutchens, IEEE and available at:
http://www.rational.com/support/techpapers/ieee/index.html

Patterns

Design Patterns — Elements of Reusable Object-Oriented Software,
Erich Gamma, Richard Helm, Ralph Johnson, John Vlissides, Addison-Wesley, 1995,
ISBN 0-201-63361-2

Analysis Patterns: Reusable Object Models,
Martin Fowler, Addison-Wesley, 1997, ISBN 0-201-89542-0

Pattern Languages of Program Design 3 (PLOP 3),
edited by Robert C Martin, Dirk Riehle, Frank Buschmann, Addison-Wesley, 1998,
ISBN 0-201-31011-2

Distributed Frameworks

Instant CORBA,
Robert Orfali, Dan Harkey and Jeri Edwards, John Wiley, 1997, ISBN 0-471-18333-4

Professional DCOM Programming,
Richard Grimes, Wrox Press, 1997, ISBN 1-861000-60-X

Essential COM,
Don Box, Addison-Wesley, 1998, ISBN 0-201-63446-5

Transactions

Principles of Transaction Processing,
Philip A Bernstein & Eric Newcomer, Morgan Kaufmann Publishers, 1997, ISBN 1-55860-415-4

Database Concepts

Instant SQL Programming,
Joe Celko, Wrox Press, 1995, ISBN 1-874416-50-8

C++

Professional MFC with Visual C++ 5,
Mike Blaszczak, Wrox Press Ltd, 1997, ISBN 1-861000-14-6

Algorithms in C++,
Robert Sedgewick, Addison-Wesley, 1992, ISBN 0-201-51059-6

STL for C++ Programmers,
Leen Ammeraal, John Wiley, 1997, ISBN 0-471-97181-2

The C Programming Language (2nd ed.),
Brian Kernighan and Dennis Ritchie, Addison-Wesley, 1998, ISBN 0-13-110362-8

Java vs C++ — A Critical Comparison,
Robert Martin, first published in C++ Report in January 1997, and available on his web site at
http://www.oma.com/Publications/publications.html

Miscellaneous

Mythical Man Month,
Fred Brooks, Addison-Wesley, 1975, ISBN 0-201-00650-2

The Random House Compact Unabridged Dictionary (2nd ed.),
ISBN 0-679-4499-8

The Moon is a Harsh Mistress,
Robert Heinlein, Tor Books, 1996, ISBN 0-312-86176-1

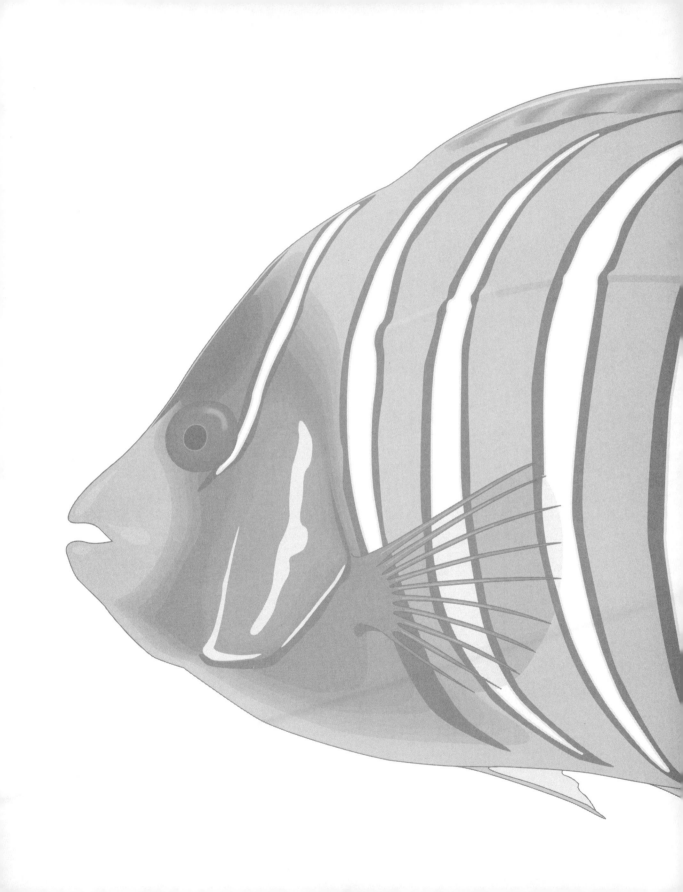

Instant UML

Authors: Pierre-Alain Muller
ISBN: 1861000871
Price: $34.95 C$48.95 £32.49

UML is the Unified Modeling Language. Modeling languages have come into vogue with the rise of object-oriented development, as they provide a means of communicating and recording every stage of the project. The results of the analysis and design phases are captured using the formal syntax of the modeling language, producing a clear model of the system to be implemented.

Instant UML offers not only a complete description of the notation and proper use of UML, but also an introduction to the theory of object-oriented programming, and the way to approach object-oriented application development. This is UML in context, not a list of the syntax without rhyme or reason.

This book is relevant to programmers of C++, VB, Java and other OO-capable languages, users of Visual Modeler (which comes with the Enterprise Edition of Microsoft's Visual Studio) and novice users of Rational Rose and similar UML-compliant tools.

Beginning ATL COM Programming

Authors: Various   ISBN: 1861001339
Price: $39.95 C$55.95 £36.99

This book is for fairly experienced C++ developers who want to get to grips with COM programming using the Active Template Library. The Beginning in the title of this book refers to COM and it refers to ATL. It does not refer to Programming.

We don't expect you to know anything about COM. The book explains the essentials of COM, how to use it, and how to get the most out of it. If you do already know something about COM, that's a bonus. You'll still learn a lot about the way that ATL works, and you'll be one step ahead of the COM neophytes.

Neither do we expect you to know anything about ATL. ATL is the focus of the book. If you've never touched ATL, or if you've been using it for a short while, but still have many unanswered questions, this is the book for you.

Beginning Java

Author: Ivor Horton
ISBN: 1861000278
Price: $36.00 C$50.40 £32.99

If you've enjoyed this book, you'll get a lot from Ivor's new book, Beginning Java.

Beginning Java teaches Java 1.1 from scratch, taking in all the fundamental features of the Java language, along with practical applications of Java's extensive class libraries. While it assumes some little familiarity with general programming concepts, Ivor takes time to cover the basics of the language in depth. He assumes no knowledge of object-oriented programming.

Ivor first introduces the essential bits of Java without which no program will run. Then he covers how Java handles data, and the syntax it uses to make decisions and control program flow. The essentials of object-oriented programming with Java are covered, and these concepts are reinforced throughout the book. Chapters on exceptions, threads and I/O follow, before Ivor turns to Java's graphics support and applet ability. Finally the book looks at JDBC and RMI, two additions to the Java 1.1 language which allow Java programs to communicate with databases and other Java programs.

Beginning Visual C++ 5

Author: Ivor Horton ISBN: 1861000081
Price: $39.95 C$55.95 £36.99

Visual Basic is a great tool for generating applications quickly and easily, but if you really want to create fast, tight programs using the latest technologies, Visual C++ is the only way to go.

Ivor Horton's Beginning Visual C++ 5 is for anyone who wants to learn C++ and Windows programming with Visual C++ 5 and MFC, and the combination of the programming discipline you've learned from this book and Ivor's relaxed and informal teaching style will make it even easier for you to succeed in taming structured programming and writing real Windows applications.

The book begins with a fast-paced but comprehensive tutorial to the C++ language. You'll then go on to learn about object orientation with C++ and how this relates to Windows programming, culminating with the design and implementation of a sizable class-based C++ application. The next part of the book walks you through creating Windows applications using MFC, including sections on output to the screen and printer, how to program menus, toolbars and dialogs, and how to respond to a user's actions. The final few chapters comprise an introduction COM and examples of how to create ActiveX controls using both MFC and the Active Template Library (ATL).

Professional MFC with Visual C++ 5

Author: Mike Blaszczak
ISBN: 1861000146
Price: $59.95 C$83.95 £56.49

Written by one of Microsoft's leading MFC developers, this is the book for professionals who want to get under the covers of the library. This is the 3rd revision of the best selling title formerly known as 'Revolutionary Guide to MFC 4' and covers the new Visual C++ 5.0 development environment.

This book will give a detailed discussion of the majority of classes present in Microsoft's application framework library. While it will point out what parameters are required for the member functions of those classes, it will concentrate more on describing what utility the classes really provide. You will learn how to write a few utilities, some DLLs, an ActiveX control and even an OLE document server, as well as examining Microsoft's Open Database Connectivity (ODBC) and Data Access Objects (DAO) strategies. At the very end of the book, you'll take a look at what the Microsoft Foundation Classes provide to make programming for the Internet easier.

There's a CD_ROM included which has the complete book in HTML format - now you can use any browser to read your book on the road.

Clouds to Code

Author: Jesse Liberty ISBN: 1861000952
Price: $40.00 C$55.95 £36.99

Clouds to Code is about the design and implementation of a real project, from start to finish, hiding nothing. Books on theory are all well and good, but there is nothing like living through the process. You'll watch as we struggle to understand the requirements, as we conceive a design, implement that design in C++, then ready it for testing and rollout. You'll see the complete iterative development process as it happens. This is not an example or a thought experiment, it's a real life case study written in real time.

Along the way you'll learn about object- oriented analysis and design with UML, as well as C++, design patterns, computer telephony, and COM. You'll also learn about professional software development and what it takes to ship a product on time and on budget. This is programming in the trenches.

'Ever thought about writing a book'?

Have you ever thought to yourself "I could do better than that"? Well, here's your chance to prove it! Wrox Press are continually looking for new authors and contributors and it doesn't matter if you've never been published before.

Interested?

contact John Franklin at Wrox Press, 30 Lincoln Road, Birmingham, B27 6PA, UK.

e-mail johnf@wrox.com

WROX

Register Beginning OO Analysis and Design and sign up for a free subscription to The Developer's Journal.

A bi-monthly magazine for software developers, The Wrox Press Developer's Journal features in-depth articles, news and help for everyone in the software development industry. Each issue includes extracts from our latest titles and is crammed full of practical insights into coding techniques, tricks, and research.

Fill in and return the card below to receive a free subscription to the Wrox Press Developer's Journal.

Beginning OO Analysis and Design Registration Card

Name _____

Address _____

_____

_____

_____

City _____ State/Region _____

Country _____ Postcode/Zip _____

E-mail _____

Occupation _____

How did you hear about this book? _____

☐ Book review (name) _____

☐ Advertisement (name) _____

☐ Recommendation _____

☐ Catalog _____

☐ Other _____

Where did you buy this book? _____

☐ Bookstore (name) _____ City _____

☐ Computer Store (name) _____

☐ Mail Order _____

☐ Other _____

What influenced you in the purchase of this book?

☐ Cover Design

☐ Contents

☐ Other (please specify) _____

How did you rate the overall contents of this book?

☐ Excellent   ☐ Good

☐ Average   ☐ Poor

What did you find most useful about this book? _____

What did you find least useful about this book? _____

Please add any additional comments. _____

What other subjects will you buy a computer book on soon? _____

What is the best computer book you have used this year? _____

Note: This information will only be used to keep you updated about new Wrox Press titles and will not be used for any other purpose or passed to any other third party.

WROX

WROX PRESS INC.

Wrox writes books for you. Any suggestions, or
ideas about how you want information given in
your ideal book will be studied by our team.
Your comments are always valued at Wrox.

Free phone in USA 800-USE-WROX
Fax (312) 397 8990

UK Tel. (0121) 706 6826   Fax   (0121) 706 2967

Computer Book Publishers

NB. If you post the bounce back card below in the UK, please send it to:
Wrox Press Ltd. 30 Lincoln Road, Birmingham, B27 6PA